I0104320

ATTP 5-0.1

Commander and Staff Officer Guide

September 2011

Headquarters, Department of the Army

Published by Books Express Publishing
Books Express Publishing, 2011
ISBN 978-1-78039-983-6

Books Express publications are available from all good retail and online booksellers. For
publishing proposals and direct ordering please contact us at: info@books-express.com

Army Tactics, Techniques, and Procedures
No. 5-0.1

Headquarters
Department of the Army
Washington, DC, 14 September 2011

Commander and Staff Officer Guide

Contents

		Page
	PREFACE	vi
Chapter 1	**MISSION COMMAND OVERVIEW**	**1-1**
	Mission Command	1-1
	Mission Command System	1-2
	The Operations Process	1-2
Chapter 2	**THE STAFF**	**2-1**
	Staff Responsibilities	2-1
	Staff Characteristics	2-2
	Staff Relationships	2-2
	Staff Organization	2-3
	Common Staff Duties and Responsiblities	2-5
	Coordinating Staff Officers	2-5
	Special Staff Officers	2-16
	Personal Staff Officers	2-25
Chapter 3	**COMMAND POST ORGANIZATION AND OPERATIONS**	**3-1**
	Command Post Organization	3-1
	Command Post Organization Considerations	3-3
	Command Post Cells and Staff Sections	3-4
	Command Post Operations	3-8
Chapter 4	**THE MILITARY DECISIONMAKING PROCESS**	**4-1**
	Characteristics of the Military Decisionmaking Process	4-1
	Steps of the Military Decisionmaking Process	4-4
	Plans in a Time-Constrained Environment	4-38
Chapter 5	**TROOP LEADING PROCEDURES**	**5-1**
	Background and Comparison to the MDMP	5-1
	Steps of Troop Leading Procedures	5-3

*This manual supersedes selected Appendices A through J of FM 5-0, dated 26 March 2010, and Appendices C through F of FM 6-0, dated 11 August 2003.

Chapter 6	**RUNNING ESTIMATES**	**6-1**
	Types of Running Estimates	6-1
	Essential Qualities of Running Estimates	6-1
	Running Estimates in the Operations Process	6-2
Chapter 7	**FORMAL ASSESSMENT PLANS**	**7-1**
	Assessment Plan Development	7-1
	Assessment Steps	7-1
Chapter 8	**REHEARSALS**	**8-1**
	Rehearsal Basics	8-1
	Rehearsal Types	8-1
	Rehearsal Techniques	8-2
	Rehearsal Responsibilities	8-6
	Rehearsal Details	8-9
Chapter 9	**LIAISON**	**9-1**
	Liaison Fundamentals	9-1
	Liaison Responsibilities	9-2
	Liaison During Unified Action	9-6
Chapter 10	**MILITARY BRIEFINGS**	**10-1**
	Types of Military Briefings	10-1
	Steps of Military Briefings	10-3
Chapter 11	**PROBLEM SOLVING, STAFF STUDIES, AND DECISION PAPERS**	**11-1**
	Problem Solving	11-1
	Staff Studies	11-6
	Decision Papers	11-12
	Staff Study Assembly	11-13
Chapter 12	**PLANS AND ORDERS**	**12-1**
	Guidance for Plans	12-1
	Types of Plans and Orders	12-2
	Characteristics of Plans and Orders	12-4
	Preparation of the Plan or Order	12-5
	Administrative Instructions	12-6
	Examples and Procedures for Creating Plans, Orders, and Annexes	12-10
Annex A	**TASK ORGANIZATION FORMAT AND INSTRUCTIONS**	**A-1**
Annex B	**INTELLIGENCE ANNEX FORMAT AND INSTRUCTIONS**	**B-1**
Annex C	**OPERATIONS ANNEX FORMAT AND INSTRUCTIONS**	**C-1**
Annex D	**FIRES ANNEX FORMAT AND INSTRUCTIONS**	**D-1**
Annex E	**PROTECTION ANNEX FORMAT AND INSTRUCTIONS**	**E-1**
Annex F	**SUSTAINMENT ANNEX FORMAT AND INSTRUCTIONS**	**F-1**
Annex G	**ENGINEER ANNEX FORMAT AND INSTRUCTIONS**	**G-1**
Annex H	**SIGNAL ANNEX FORMAT AND INSTRUCTIONS**	**H-1**
Annex I	**NOT USED**	**I-1**
Annex J	**INFORM AND INFLUENCE ACTIVITIES ANNEX FORMAT AND INSTRUCTIONS**	**J-1**

Annex K   CIVIL AFFAIRS OPERATIONS ANNEX FORMAT AND INSTRUCTIONS......K-1
Annex L   RECONNAISSANCE AND SURVEILLANCE FORMAT AND
              INSTRUCTIONS... L-1
Annex M   ASSESSMENT ANNEX FORMAT AND INSTRUCTIONS............................ M-1
Annex N   SPACE OPERATIONS FORMAT AND INSTRUCTIONS.............................N-1
Annex O   NOT USED O-1
Annex P   HOST-NATION SUPPORT ANNEX FORMAT AND INSTRUCTIONS.............P-1
Annex Q   SPARE Q-1
Annex R   REPORTS ANNEX FORMAT AND INSTRUCTIONS R-1
Annex S   SPECIAL TECHNICAL OPERATIONS ANNEX FORMAT AND
              INSTRUCTIONS... S-1
Annex T   SPARE T-1
Annex U   INSPECTOR GENERAL ANNEX FORMAT AND INSTRUCTIONS................U-1
Annex V   INTERAGENCY COORDINATION ANNEX FORMAT AND
              INSTRUCTIONS... V-1
Annex W   SPARE W-1
Annex X   SPARE X-1
Annex Y   SPARE Y-1
Annex Z   DISTRIBUTION ANNEX FORMAT AND INSTRUCTIONS.............................Z-1
              GLOSSARY Glossary-1
              REFERENCES References-1
              INDEX..Index-1

Figures

Figure 2-1. Staff structure..2-4
Figure 3-1. Functional and integrating cells 3-5
Figure 3-2. Integration of plans, future operations, and current operations 3-7
Figure 3-3. Sample shift-change briefing 3-10
Figure 3-4. Sample SOP for a division civil-military operations working group.......3-13
Figure 4-1. The steps of the military decisionmaking process 4-3
Figure 4-2. Mission analysis..4-7
Figure 4-3. COA development..4-16
Figure 4-4. Sample brigade COA sketch...4-21
Figure 4-5. COA analysis and war-gaming 4-23
Figure 4-6. Sample belt method 4-28
Figure 4-7. Sample modified belt method using lines of effort...............................4-28
Figure 4-8. Sample avenue-in-depth method..4-29
Figure 4-9. Sample modified avenue-in-depth method using lines of effort.............4-29

Figure 4-10. Sample box method... 4-30
Figure 4-11. Sample modified box method using lines of effort.. 4-30
Figure 4-12. Sample synchronization matrix technique.. 4-31
Figure 4-13. Sample sketch note technique 4-32
Figure 4-14. COA comparison 4-35
Figure 4-15. Sample advantages and disadvantages 4-36
Figure 4-16. Sample decision matrix 4-36
Figure 5-1. Parallel planning 5-2
Figure 5-2. Planning at company and below 5-3
Figure 5-3. Sample schedule 5-4
Figure 5-4. Sample mission and COA statements.. 5-9
Figure 6-1. Generic base running estimate format 6-2
Figure 7-1. Sample of end state conditions for defensive operations............................... 7-3
Figure 7-2. Sample of end state conditions for stability operations 7-4
Figure 7-3. Sample assessment framework 7-6
Figure 8-1. Rehearsal techniques.. 8-3
Figure 10-1. Information briefing format... 10-1
Figure 10-2. Decision briefing format.. 10-2
Figure 10-3. Considerations during planning 10-4
Figure 10-4. Considerations during preparation 10-5
Figure 11-1. Sample evaluation criterion 11-4
Figure 11-2. Format for a staff study... 11-8
Figure 11-3. Format for a decision paper.. 11-12
Figure 11-4. Assembling and tabbing staff action.. 11-14
Figure 12-1. Paragraph layout for plans and orders 12-6
Figure 12-2. Annotated Army OPLAN/OPORD format... 12-11
Figure 12-3. Annotated attachment format (general)... 12-22
Figure 12-4. Annotated WARNO format 12-24
Figure 12-5. Annotated sample FRAGO.. 12-25
Figure 12-6. Example of overlay order graphic... 12-26
Figure A-1. Sample task organization... A-8
Figure A-2. Sample acronym list... A-9

Tables

Table 4-1. Commander's planning guidance by warfighting function 4-15
Table 4-2. Historical minimum planning ratios... 4-18
Table 8-1. Example sustainment and protection actions for rehearsals............................. 8-11
Table 9-1. Senior liaison officer rank by echelon... 9-1
Table 9-2. Example outline of a liaison officer handbook 9-3
Table 9-3. Liaison checklist—before departing the sending unit....................................... 9-4

Table 9-4. Liaison duties—during the liaison tour 9-6
Table 9-5. Liaison duties—after the liaison tour 9-6
Table 12-1. Designated letters for dates and times 12-8
Table 12-2. List of attachments and responsible staff officers 12-18
Table A-1. Army command relationships A-3
Table A-2. Army support relationships A-4
Table A-3. Army unit listing convention A-5

Preface

This Army tactics, techniques, and procedures (ATTP) reinforces the fundamentals of mission command established in field manual (FM) 3-0, *Operations*; FM 5-0, *The Operations Process*; and FM 6-0, *Mission Command*. Whereas the above manuals focus on the fundamentals of mission command, this manual provides commanders and staff officers with tactics, techniques, and procedures (TTP) essential for the exercise of mission command.

This is a new Army publication. It includes many of the appendices currently found in FM 5-0 and FM 6-0 that addressed the "how to" of mission command. By consolidating this material into a single publication, Army leaders now have a single reference to assist them with TTP associated with planning, preparing for, executing, and continually assessing operations. This ATTP also enables the Army to better focus the material in future editions of FMs 5-0 and 6-0 on the fundamentals of the operations process and mission command, respectively.

This ATTP consist of 12 chapters and 26 annexes. It incorporates the new mission command taxonomy established in FM 3-0.

- Chapter 1 provides an overview of mission command. It summarizes the new mission command taxonomy established in change 1 to FM 3-0 (2011).
- Chapter 2 addresses the staff to include staff organization and the duties and responsibilities of individual staff officers. It updates FM 6-0.
- Chapter 3 describes how commanders cross-functionally organize their staff into command posts and offers TTP for command post operations. It updates FM 5-0.
- Chapter 4 describes the military decisionmaking process. It updates FM 5-0.
- Chapter 5 addresses troop leading procedures—a framework for planning and preparing for operations used by small unit leaders. It updates FM 5-0.
- Chapter 6 addresses how the commander and staff build and maintain running estimates throughout the operations process. This updates FM 5-0.
- Chapter 7 provides guidelines to assist commanders and staffs to develop formal assessment plans. This updates FM 5-0.
- Chapter 8 discusses rehearsal types and techniques. This updates FM 5-0.
- Chapter 9 discusses liaison principles and the responsibilities of liaison officers and teams. This updates FM 6-0.
- Chapter 10 provides guidance and formats for military briefings. This updates FM 5-0.
- Chapter 11 discusses how to prepare staff studies and decision papers, and provides formats for both. This updates FM 5-0.
- Chapter 12 offers guidelines and provides formats and instruction for building effective plans and orders. This updates FM 5-0.
- The annexes provide formats and instructions for developing attachments to the base plan or order. The sequence of these annexes corresponds to the Army operation order attachment structure. These formats and instructions are new to Army doctrine.

This ATTP applies to the Active Army, the Army National Guard/Army National Guard of the United States, and the United States Army Reserve unless otherwise stated. While this ATTP applies to all Army leaders, the primary audience is the commander and the staff.

Headquarters, U.S. Army Training and Doctrine Command, is the proponent for this publication. The preparing agency is the Combined Arms Doctrine Directorate, U.S. Army Combined Arms Center. Send written comments and recommendations on DA Form 2028 (Recommended Changes to Publications and Blank Forms) to Commander, U.S. Army Combined Arms Center and Fort Leavenworth, ATTN: ATZL-MCK-D (ATTP 5-0.1), 300 McPherson Avenue, Fort Leavenworth, KS 66027-2337; by e-mail to: leav-cadd-web-cadd@conus.army.mil; or submit an electronic DA Form 2028.

This publication is available at Army Knowledge Online (www.us.army.mil).

Chapter 1
Mission Command Overview

This chapter provides an overview of mission command. The fundamentals of mission command provide the basis for the tactics, techniques, and procedures (TTP) addressed in the proceeding chapters. In addition, this chapter describes the mission command system with an emphasis on the human dimension. The chapter concludes with a discussion of how commanders, supported by their staff, put the mission command system into action through the operations process.

MISSION COMMAND

1-1.   *Mission command* is the exercise of authority and direction by the commander using mission orders to enable disciplined initiative within the commander's intent to empower agile and adaptive leaders in the conduct of full spectrum operations. It is commander-led and blends the art of command and the science of control to integrate the warfighting functions to accomplish the mission (FM 6-0). Commanders exercise mission command throughout the conduct (plan, prepare, execute, and assessment) of operations.

1-2.   Predictability in operations is rare, making centralized decisionmaking and creating an orderly process ineffective. During operations, leaders make decisions, develop plans, and direct actions under varying degrees of complexity and uncertainty. Commanders contend with thinking, adaptive enemies in areas of operations where many events occur simultaneously. Often commanders have difficulty accurately predicting how enemies will act and react, how populations will perceive or react to friendly or enemy actions, or how events will develop.

1-3.   Effective mission command requires an environment of mutual trust and understanding among commanders, subordinates, and partners. In this command climate, commanders encourage subordinates to exercise disciplined initiative to seize opportunities and counter threats within the commander's intent. Mission command helps counter the uncertainty of operations by empowering subordinates at the scene to make decisions and act quickly without constantly referring to higher headquarters.

1-4.   The commander is the central figure in mission command. Through mission command, commanders combine the art of command and the science of control to accomplish missions. They take prudent risks, exercise initiative, and act decisively, even when the outcome is uncertain. All missions contain risk. Risk taking must focus on winning rather than preventing defeat, even if preventing defeat appears safer.

1-5.   Commanders use mission orders to focus their orders on the purpose of the operation rather than on the details of how to perform assigned tasks. Doing this minimizes detailed control and allows subordinates the greatest possible freedom of action within the commander's intent.

1-6.   Lastly, when delegating authority to subordinates, commanders do everything in their power to set the necessary conditions for success. They allocate enough resources for subordinates to accomplish assigned tasks. These resources include information, personnel, forces, materiel, and time.

ART OF COMMAND

1-7.   *Command* is the authority that a commander in the armed forces lawfully exercises over subordinates by virtue of rank or assignment. Command includes the authority and responsibility for effectively using available resources and for planning the employment of, organizing, directing, coordinating, and controlling military forces for the accomplishment of assigned missions. It also includes responsibility for health, welfare, morale, and discipline of assigned personnel (JP 1). Command is personal. An individual— not an institution or group—commands. Command provides the basis for control.

1-8. The art of command is the creative and skillful exercise of authority through decisionmaking and leadership. Authority refers to the right and power to judge, act, or command. It includes responsibility, accountability, and delegation. Commanders rely on their education, experience, knowledge, and judgment in applying authority as they decide (plan how to achieve the end state) and lead (direct their forces during preparation and execution). Decisionmaking refers to selecting a course of action as the one most favorable to accomplish the mission. Commanders apply knowledge to the situation thus translating their visualization into action. Decisionmaking includes knowing whether to decide and understanding the consequences. Leadership refers to the process of influencing people by providing purpose, direction, and motivation, while operating to accomplish the mission and improve the organization. Commanders lead through a combination of personal example, persuasion, and compulsion. (FM 6-22 discusses leadership.)

1-9. The commander's presence and personal leadership drive successful mission command. The commander focuses on three tasks necessary to ensure mission accomplishment in full spectrum operations:
- Drives the operations process.
- Understand, visualize, describe, direct, lead, and assess operations.
- Develop teams among modular formations and joint, interagency, intergovernmental, and multinational partners.
- Lead inform and influence activities.

See FM 3-0 for a detailed discussion of the commander tasks in mission command.

SCIENCE OF CONTROL

1-10. While command is a personal function, control involves the entire force. *Control* is the regulation of forces and warfighting functions to accomplish the mission in accordance with the commander's intent (FM 6-0). It is fundamental to directing operations. Staffs coordinate, synchronize, and integrate actions, keep the commander informed, and exercise control for the commander.

1-11. Commanders and staffs use the science of control to overcome the physical and procedural constraints under which units operate. Control relies on objectivity, facts, empirical methods, and analysis. Hence, the control aspect of mission command is more science than art. The science of control includes the detailed systems and procedures to improve the commander's understanding. Control demands understanding those aspects of operations that can be analyzed and measured. These include the physical capabilities and limitations of friendly and enemy organizations and systems. Control also requires a realistic appreciation for time-distance factors and the time required to initiate certain actions.

MISSION COMMAND SYSTEM

1-12. Commanders cannot exercise mission command alone except in the smallest organizations, company or troop and below. Thus, commanders perform these functions through a *mission command system*—the arrangement of personnel; networks; information systems; processes and procedures; and facilities and equipment that enable commanders to conduct operations (FM 6-0). The remainder of this Army tactics, techniques, and procedures (ATTP) focuses on personnel, networks, and procedures.

THE OPERATIONS PROCESS

1-13. Commanders, assisted by their staffs, integrate numerous processes and activities within the headquarters and across the force as they exercise mission command. The Army's overarching framework to do this is the operations process. The *operations process* consists of the major mission command activities performed during operations: planning, preparing, executing, and continuously assessing the operation. The commander drives the operations process through leadership (FM 3-0).

1-14. The activities of the operations process (plan, prepare, execute, and assess) may sequentially occur at the start of an operation. Once operations begin, a headquarters often conducts parts of each activity simultaneously. Planning, to include design, is continuous. Preparing begins when a unit receives a mission. It always overlaps with planning and continues through execution for some subordinate units. Execution puts a plan into action. Assessing is continuous and influences the other three activities.

Subordinate units of the same command may be in different stages of the operations process. At any time during the operations process, commanders may reframe based on a shift in their understanding or significant changes in the operational environment. This may lead to a new perspective on the problem resulting in an entirely new plan. (FM 3-0 discusses the operations process.)

1-15. Design permeates the operations process (see FM 5-0). *Design* is not a process or a checklist—it is a methodology for applying critical and creative thinking to understand, visualize, and describe complex, ill-structured problems and develop approaches to solve them. Design assists commanders and staffs with the conceptual aspects of planning to include developing an operational approach that guides the force during preparation and execution. A key aspect of design is reframing the problem as the force learns through action. While continuously assessing changes in the operational environment and the progress of operations, design assists commanders and staffs in determining if reframing is required, leading to a new operational approach.

1-16. At the center of the operations process is the commander. The commander's activities of understanding, visualizing, describing, directing, leading, and assessing guide the staff and subordinates throughout the conduct of operations. The commander's role in the operations process takes on different emphasis during planning, preparing, executing, and assessing. For example, during planning commanders focus their activities on understanding, visualizing, and describing while directing, leading, and assessing. During execution, commanders often focus on directing, leading, and assessing while improving their understanding and modifying their visualization.

1-17. Where commanders focus on the major aspects of operations, staffs assist commanders in the exercise of mission command throughout the operations process by—

- Providing relevant information and analysis.
- Maintaining running estimates and making recommendations.
- Preparing plans and orders.
- Monitoring operations.
- Controlling operations.
- Assessing the progress of operations.

See FM 5-0 for a detailed discussion of how commanders drive the operations process.

This page intentionally left blank.

Chapter 2

The Staff

This chapter describes the staff, their responsibilities, characteristics, and relationships as well as the importance of building staff teams. The chapter also outlines the basic staff structure common to all headquarters followed by a discussion of the common duties and responsibilities of all staff sections. The chapter concludes by describing the duties and responsibilities of specific coordinating, special, and personal staff officers by area of expertise.

STAFF RESPONSIBILITIES

2-1.   Staffs support commanders, assist subordinate units, and inform units and organizations outside the headquarters. The staff operates the commander's mission command system by supporting the commander, assisting subordinate units, and informing units and organizations outside the headquarters.

- Support the commander.
- Assist subordinate units.
- Inform units and organizations outside the headquarters.

SUPPORT THE COMMANDER

2-2.   Staffs support the commander in understanding situations, making and implementing decisions, controlling operations, and assessing progress. They make recommendations and prepare plans and orders for the commander. Staff products consist of timely and relevant information and analysis. Staffs use knowledge management to extract that information from the vast amount of available information (see FM 6-01.1). They synthesize this information and provide it to commanders in the form of running estimates (see Chapter 6) to help commanders build and maintain their situational understanding.

2-3.   Staffs communicate information to subordinates for execution. Commanders often personally disseminate their commander's intent and planning guidance. They rely on their staffs to communicate the majority of it in the form of plans and orders (see Chapter 12). Staffs communicate the commander's decisions—and the intent behind them—throughout the force.

2-4.   Finally, each staff section provides control over its area of expertise within the commander's intent. While commanders make key decisions, they are not the only decisionmakers. Trained, trusted staff members, given decisionmaking authority based on the commander's intent, free commanders from routine decisions, enabling commanders to focus on key aspects of the operations. These staff members support and advise the commander by assisting the commander within their area of expertise.

ASSIST SUBORDINATE UNITS

2-5.   Effective staffs establish and maintain a high degree of coordination and cooperation with staffs of higher, lower, supporting, supported, and adjacent units. They do this by actively collaborating and dialoging with commanders and staffs of other units to solve problems.

INFORM UNITS AND ORGANIZATIONS OUTSIDE THE HEADQUARTERS

2-6.   The staff keeps civilian organizations informed with relevant information according to their security classification as well as their need to know. As soon as a staff receives information and determines its relevancy, the staff passes that information to the appropriate headquarters. The key is relevance, not volume. Masses of data are worse than meaningless data; they inhibit mission command by distracting staffs from relevant information. Effective knowledge management helps staffs identify the information the commander and each staff section need, and its relative importance.

2-7. Information should reach recipients based on their need for it. Sending incomplete information sooner is better than sending complete information too late. When forwarding information, senders highlight key information for each recipient and clarify the commander's intent. Senders may pass information directly, include their own analysis, or add context to it. Common, distributed databases can accelerate this function; however, they cannot replace the personal contact that adds perspective.

STAFF CHARACTERISTICS

2-8. In addition to the leader attributes and core competencies addressed in FM 6-22, a good staff officer is competent, exercises initiative, applies critical and creative thinking, is adaptable, is flexible, has self-confidence, is cooperative, and communicates effectively.

2-9. Effective staff officers are *competent* in all aspects of their area of expertise. Not only experts in doctrine and the processes and procedures associated with the operations process, they understand the duties of other staff members enough to accomplish coordination both vertically and horizontally.

2-10. Staff officers exercise individual *initiative*. They anticipate requirements rather than waiting for instructions. They anticipate what the commander needs to accomplish the mission and prepare answers to those questions before they are asked.

2-11. Staffs apply *critical and creative thinking* throughout the operations process to assist commanders in understanding and decisionmaking. As critical thinkers, staffs discern truth in situations where direct observation is insufficient, impossible, or impractical. They determine whether adequate justification exists to accept conclusions as true based on a given inference or argument. As creative thinkers, staffs look at different options to solve problems. They use adaptive approaches (drawing from previous similar circumstances) or innovative approaches (coming up with completely new ideas). In both instances, the staff uses creative thinking to apply imagination and depart from the old way of doing things.

2-12. Effective staff officers are *adaptive*. They recognize and adjust to changing conditions in the operational environment with appropriate, flexible, and timely actions. They rapidly adjust and continuously assess plans, tactics, techniques, and procedures.

2-13. Staff officers are *flexible*. They avoid becoming overwhelmed or frustrated by changing requirements and priorities. Commanders often change their minds or redirect the command after receiving additional information or a new mission. They may not share with the staff the reason for such a change. Staff officers remain flexible and adjust to any changes. They set priorities when there are more tasks to accomplish than time allows. They learn to manage multiple commitments simultaneously.

2-14. Staff officers possess discipline and *self-confidence*. They understand that all staff work serves the commander, even if the commander rejects the resulting recommendation. Staff officers do not give a "half effort" even if they think the commander will disagree with their recommendations. Alternative and possibly unpopular ideas or points of view assist commanders in making the best possible decisions.

2-15. Staff officers are team players. They *cooperate* with other staff members within and outside the headquarters. This practice contributes to effective collaboration and coordination.

2-16. Staff officers *communicate* clearly and present information orally, in writing, and visually (with charts, graphs, and figures). Staff officers routinely brief individuals and groups. They know and understand briefing techniques that convey complex information in easily understood formats. They can write clear and concise orders and plans, staff studies, staff summaries, and reports.

STAFF RELATIONSHIPS

2-17. Staff effectiveness depends in part on relationships of the staff with commanders and other staff. A staff acts on behalf of and derives its authority from the commander. Although commanders are the principal decisionmakers, individual staff officers make decisions within their authority based on broad guidance and commander-approved standard operating procedures (SOPs). Commanders must insist on frank dialogue between themselves and their staff leaders. A staff gives honest, independent thoughts and recommendations so commanders can make the best possible decisions. Once the commander has decided, staff leaders implement decisions energetically, even if those decisions differ from their recommendations.

2-18. Teamwork within a staff and between staffs produces the staff integration essential to synchronized operations. A staff cannot work efficiently without complete cooperation among all staff sections. A force cannot operate effectively without cooperation among all headquarters. Commanders, chiefs of staff (COSs), and executive officers (XOs) contribute to foster this climate during training and sustain it during operations. However, frequent personnel changes and augmentation to the headquarters adds challenges to building and maintaining the team.

2-19. Often, Army headquarters are augmented to assist with mission command. Commanders integrate these teams and detachments into their command posts. For example, divisions commonly receive a civil affairs battalion when deployed. Within that battalion is a civil affairs planning team that augments the civil affairs staff section and plans cell in the headquarters. In other instances, commanders may request staff augmentation. Augmentation teams include but are not limited to—

- Army space support team.
- Civil affairs planning team.
- Combat camera team.
- Human terrain analysis team.
- Legal support teams.
- Mobile public affairs team.
- Military history team.
- Military information support element.
- Individual augmentation by specialty (for example, assessment, economic development).

2-20. While all staff sections have clearly defined functional responsibilities, none can operate effectively in isolation. Coordination among them is important. Commanders identify required interaction among staff sections early in the process of organizing the headquarters. They equip and staff each section to work not only with the rest of the headquarters but also with their counterparts in other headquarters. Developing the unit's battle rhythm to include synchronizing the various meeting, working groups and boards within the headquarters enables staff integration (see paragraphs 3-62 through 3-64).

STAFF ORGANIZATION

2-21. Staff organization is based on the mission, each staff's broad areas of expertise, and regulations and laws. While staffs at every echelon and type of unit are structured differently, all staffs are similar.

CONSIDERATIONS

2-22. The mission determines which activities to accomplish. These activities determine how commanders organize, tailor, or adapt their individual staffs to accomplish the mission. The mission also determines the size and composition of a staff to include staff augmentation.

2-23. Regardless of mission, every Army staff has common broad areas of expertise that determine how the commander divides duties and responsibilities. The duties and responsibilities inherent in an area of expertise are called functional responsibilities. Grouping related activities allows an effective span of control and unity of effort. Areas of expertise may vary slightly, depending on the echelon of command and mission. For example, at battalion level there is no resource manager, while certain sustainment units combine the intelligence and operations functions.

2-24. Army regulations and laws establish special relationships between certain staff officers and the commander. For example, AR 20-1, AR 27-1, and AR 165-1 require the inspector general, Staff Judge Advocate, and chaplain to be members of the commander's personal staff.

2-25. Every organization requires an authorization document that states a headquarters' approved structure and resources. It is the basis and authority for personnel assignments and equipment requisitions. This document is a table of organization and equipment (TOE), a modified TOE, or a table of distribution and allowances (TDA). Commanders establish authorizations by developing a modified TOE from the TOE for their individual units. Commanders prescribe in more detail the organization, personnel, and equipment to be authorized to accomplish missions in specific operational environments. Commanders can change their individual modified TOEs with Department of the Army approval.

STRUCTURE

2-26. The basic staff structure includes a COS or executive officer and various staff sections. A *staff section* **is a grouping of staff members by area of expertise under a coordinating, special, or personal staff officer**. A principal staff officer—who may be a coordinating, special, or personal staff officer for the commander—leads each staff section. The number of coordinating, special, and personal principal staff officers and their corresponding staff sections varies with different command levels. See appropriate echelon manual, such as FM 71-100, for specifics on particular types of headquarters. Figure 2-1 illustrates the basic staff structure and their relationships.

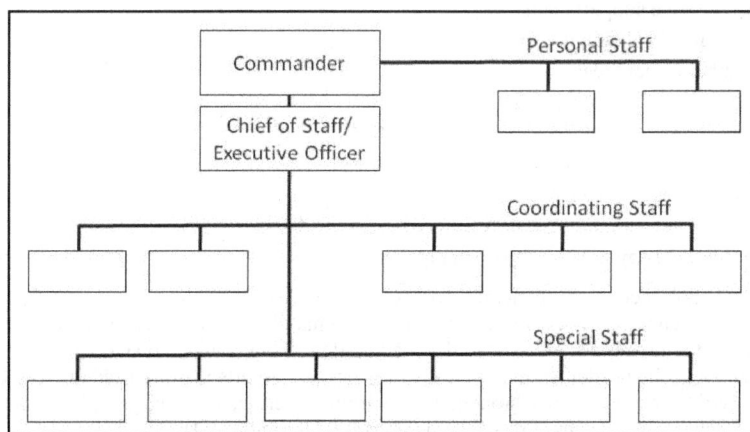

Figure 2-1. Staff structure

Commander

2-27. Commanders are responsible for all their staffs do or fail to do. A commander cannot delegate this responsibility. The final decision, as well as the final responsibility, remains with the commander. When commanders assign a staff member a task, they delegate the authority necessary to accomplish it. Commanders provide guidance, resources, and support. They foster a climate of mutual trust, cooperation, and teamwork.

Chief of Staff (Executive Officer)

2-28. The COS or XO is the commander's principal assistant. Commanders normally delegate executive management authority to the COS or XO. As the key staff integrator, the COS or XO frees the commander from routine details of staff operations and the management of the headquarters. Division and higher units are assigned a COS. Brigade and battalions are assigned an XO. The COS or XO ensures efficient and prompt staff actions. The COS or XO duties include (but are not limited to) the following:

- Coordinate and direct the work of the staff.
- Establish and monitor the headquarters battle rhythm for effective planning support, decisionmaking, and other critical functions.
- Represent the commander when authorized.
- Formulate and disseminate staff policies.

- Ensure effective liaison exchanges with higher, lower, and adjacent units and other organizations as required.
- Supervise the sustainment of the headquarters and activities of the headquarters and headquarters battalion or company.
- Supervise staff training and integration programs.
- In division through Army Service component command headquarters, the COS personally supervises the knowledge management, operations research and system analysis, red team, and special staff sections.

Principal Staff Officers

2-29. The principal staff officers consist of officers from the coordinating, special, or personal staff sections. Paragraphs 2-31 through 2-75 discuss coordinating staff officers. Paragraphs 2-76 through 2-104 discuss special staff officers. Paragraphs 2-105 through 2-114 discuss personal staff officers.

COMMON STAFF DUTIES AND RESPONSIBLITIES

2-30. Each staff section has specific duties and responsibilities by area of expertise. However, all staff sections share a set of common duties and responsibilities:
- Advising and informing the commander.
- Building and maintaining running estimates.
- Providing recommendations.
- Preparing plans, orders, and other staff writing.
- Assessing operations.
- Managing information within area of expertise.
- Identifying and analyzing problems.
- Coordinating staff.
- Conducting staff assistance visits.
- Performing composite risk management.
- Performing intelligence preparation of the battlefield.
- Conducting staff inspections.
- Completing staff research.
- Performing staff administrative procedures.
- Exercising staff supervision over their area of expertise.

COORDINATING STAFF OFFICERS

2-31. Coordinating staff officers are the commander's principal assistants who advise, plan, and coordinate actions within their area of expertise or a warfighting function. Collectively, through the COS or XO, coordinating staff officers answer to the commander. Commanders may designate coordinating staff officers as assistant chiefs of staff, deputy chiefs of staff, chiefs of a warfighting function, or staff officers. Coordinating staff officers also exercise planning and supervisory authority over designated special staff officers as designated.

2-32. The coordinating staff consists of the following positions:
- Assistant chief of staff (ACOS), G-1 (S-1)—personnel.
- ACOS, G-2 (S-2)—intelligence.
- ACOS, G-3 (S-3)—operations.
- ACOS, G-4 (S-4)—logistics.
- ACOS, G-5—plans.
- ACOS, G-6 (S-6)—signal.
- ACOS, G-7 (S-7)—inform and influence activities.

- ACOS, G-8—resource management.
- ACOS, G-9 (S-9)—civil affairs operations.
- Chief of fires.
- Chief of protection.
- Chief of sustainment.

2-33. A chief of fires, a chief of protection, and a chief of sustainment are authorized at division through theater army. They coordinate their respective warfighting function for the commander through functional cells within the main command post (see Chapter 3).

2-34. The commander's rank determines whether the staff is a G staff or an S staff. Organizations commanded by a general officer have G staffs. Other organizations have S staffs. Most battalions and brigades do not have plans or resource management staff sections. In battalions and brigades, the operations staff section is responsible for planning and the logistics staff section is responsible for resource management.

ASSISTANT CHIEF OF STAFF, G-1 (S-1), PERSONNEL

2-35. The ACOS, G-1 (S-1) is the principal staff officer for all matters concerning human resources support (military and civilian). The G-1 (S-1) also serves as the senior adjutant general officer in the command. Specific responsibilities of the G-1 (S-1) include manning, personnel services, personnel support, and headquarters management. The G-1 (S-1) prepares a portion of Annex F (Sustainment) to the operation order or operation plan. The G-1 (S-1) has coordinating staff responsibility for the civilian personnel officer and the equal opportunity advisor. (Refer to FM 1-0 and FM 7-15 for more detailed information on the duties and responsibilities of the G-1 [S-1].)

Man the Force

2-36. Manning the force impacts the effectiveness of all Army organizations, regardless of size, and affects the ability to successfully accomplish all other human resource core competencies and key functions. Manning includes five functional tasks: personnel readiness management, personnel accountability, personnel strength reporting, retention operations, and personnel information management. Corps and division G-1s (adjutant generals [AGs]) maintain overall responsibility for personnel readiness management of subordinate elements. Corps and division G-1 (AGs) maintain the responsibility to assist brigade S-1s and the national provider in shaping the force to meet mission requirements. Personnel accountability is the by-name management of the location and duty status of every person assigned or attached to a unit. Personnel strength reporting is a numerical product of the accountability process. The Army Retention Program is the long-term answer for maintaining end strength. Personnel information management is a process to collect, process, store, display, and disseminate information about Soldiers, Army civilians, units, and other personnel as required.

Provide Human Resources Services (Essential Personnel Services)

2-37. Essential personnel services are initiated by the Soldier, unit commanders, unit leaders, G-1 (AGs) and S-1s, or from the top of the human resource command (HRC). Typical actions initiated by the Soldier are personnel action requests, requests for leaves or passes, changes to record of emergency data or life insurance elections, changes to dependent information, allotments, saving bonds, and direct deposit information. Typical actions initiated by commanders include request for awards or decorations, promotions, reductions, and bars to reenlistment. Normally, the supervisor at all levels initiates evaluation reports (such as change of rater and complete the record reports). The military postal system operates as an extension of the United States Postal Service. Casualty operations record, report, verify, and process casualty information from the unit level to the casualty and mortuary affairs operations center, notify appropriate individuals, and provide casualty assistance to the next-of-kin.

Coordinate Personnel Support

2-38. Personnel support activities encompass those functions and activities that contribute to unit readiness by promoting fitness, building morale and cohesion, enhancing quality of life, and providing recreational, social, and other support services for Soldiers, Army civilians, and other personnel who deploy with the force. Personnel support encompasses the following functions: morale, welfare, and recreation (MWR), command interest programs, and Army band operations. Commanders at all levels are responsible for the MWR support provided to their Soldiers and civilians. Command interest programs include family readiness, Army substance abuse program, suicide prevention program, and other programs as directed. Army bands provide music for ceremonial and morale support in all operations to sustain Soldiers and to inspire leaders.

Headquarters Management

2-39. Headquarters management includes, but is not limited to—
- Managing the organization and administration of the headquarters.
- Providing administrative support for military and civilian personnel, including leaves, passes, counseling, transfers, awards, and personal affairs.
- Providing information services, including publications, printing, distribution, and material for the Freedom of Information Act.
- Providing administrative support for non-U.S. forces, foreign nationals, and civilian internees.
- Administering discipline, law, and order (with the provost marshal), including desertion, court-martial offenses, punishments, and straggler dispositions.

ASSISTANT CHIEF OF STAFF, G-2 (S-2), INTELLIGENCE

2-40. The ACOS, G-2 (S-2) is the chief of the intelligence warfighting function and the principal staff officer responsible for providing intelligence to support current and future operations and plans. This officer gathers and analyzes knowledge on enemy, terrain, weather, and civil considerations for the commander. The G-2 (S-2) leads the staff in the intelligence preparation of the battlefield process and assists the G-3 (S-3) with developing and executing the reconnaissance and surveillance plan. The G-2 (S-2) provides intelligence support to lethal and nonlethal targeting operations, ensuring units base targeting priorities on intelligence threat assessments and include the priorities in the reconnaissance and surveillance plan. The G-2 (S-2) prepares Annex B (Intelligence) to the operation order or operation plan. (See FM 2-0 and FM 7-15 for more information on the duties and responsibilities of the G-2 [S-2].)

2-41. The intelligence warfighting function includes the following tasks that facilitate the commander's visualization and situational understanding of the operational environment:
- Supporting force generation.
- Supporting situational understanding.
- Performing reconnaissance and surveillance.
- Supporting targeting and information superiority.

2-42. The G-2 (S-2) is also responsible for intelligence readiness, intelligence tasks, intelligence synchronization, other intelligence support, counterintelligence, and support to security programs. The G-2 (S-2) has coordinating staff responsibility for the staff weather officer and the foreign disclosure officer.

2-43. The G-2 (S-2) facilitates reconnaissance and surveillance integration by giving the commander and G-3 (S-3) the initial intelligence synchronization plan and helping the G-3 (S-3) develop the initial reconnaissance and surveillance plan.

2-44. Other intelligence support includes—
- Supporting the conduct of collection operations:
  - Providing intelligence updates, other products, and additional support reconnaissance and surveillance integration, the concept of operations, and mission accomplishment.

- Advising the commander so that all collection, production, and dissemination adhere to special security, legal, and regulatory restrictions.
- Facilitating the military intelligence-unique deconfliction of collection among assigned, attached, and supporting intelligence collection assets and other collection assets in the area of operations (AO).
- Preparing the intelligence estimate and intelligence annex to plans and orders.
- Coordinating technical control and technical support for military intelligence assets and units.
- Debriefing friendly personnel when necessary.
- Performing language-related functions:
  - Identifying linguist requirements pertaining to intelligence support and coordinating contracted linguist support.
  - Determining all foreign languages (spoken and written) and dialects in which proficiency is needed for mission accomplishment.
  - Coordinating for security investigations of local-hire linguists.

2-45. Counterintelligence includes—
- Coordinating counterintelligence activities.
- Identifying enemy intelligence collection capabilities, such as efforts targeted against the unit.
- Evaluating enemy intelligence capabilities as they affect operations security, signals security, countersurveillance, security operations, military deception planning, military information support operations, and protection.
- Vetting all contractors and their employees to deter the subversive nature of insurgent activities.

2-46. Support to security programs includes—
- Supervising the command and personnel security programs.
- Evaluating physical security vulnerabilities to support the G-3 (S-3) and G-6 (S-6).
- Performing staff planning and supervising the special security office.

ASSISTANT CHIEF OF STAFF, G-3 (S-3), OPERATIONS

2-47. The G-3 (S-3) operations officer's responsibilities are unique within the coordinating staff. In addition to coordinating the activities of the movement and maneuver warfighting function, the operations officer is the primary staff officer for integrating and synchronizing the operation as a whole for the commander. While the COS or XO directs the efforts of the entire staff, the operations officer ensures warfighting function integration and synchronization across the planning horizons in current operations integration, future operations, and plans integrating cells (see paragraphs 3-37 through 3-46). Additionally, the operations officer authenticates all plans and orders for the commander to ensure the warfighting functions are synchronized in time, space, and purpose in accordance with the commander's intent and planning guidance. In conjunction with the G-5 (S-5), the G-3 (S-3) prepares Annex A (Task Organization), Annex C (Operations), and Annex M (Assessment) to the operation order or operation plan. The G-3 (S-3) prepares Annex L (Reconnaissance and Surveillance), Annex R (Reports), Annex V (Interagency Coordination), and Annex Z (Distribution). (See FM 3-0, FM 5-0, FM 6-0, and FM 7-15 for more information on the duties and responsibilities of the G-3 [S-3].)

2-48. The ACOS, G-3 (S-3) is the chief of the movement and maneuver warfighting function and the principal staff officer responsible for all matters concerning training, operations and plans, and force development and modernization. The G-3 (S-3) has coordinating staff responsibility for the G-5 (S-5), chief of fires, aviation officer, engineer officer, force management officer, and space operations officer.

Training

2-49. G-3 (S-3) training responsibilities include—
- Conducting training within the command.
- Preparing training guidance for the commander's approval.
- Helping the commander develop the unit's mission-essential task list (METL).

- Identifying training requirements, based on the unit METL and training status.
- Determining requirements for and allocation of training resources.
- Organizing and conducting internal schools, and obtaining and allocating quotas for external schools.
- Conducting training inspections, tests, and evaluations.
- Maintaining the unit readiness status of each unit in the command.
- Compiling training records and reports.

Plans and Operations

2-50. The G-3 (S-3) has responsibilities for plans and operations. Overall, this officer prepares, coordinates, authenticates, publishes, reviews, and distributes written operation orders and plans. This includes the command SOP, plans, orders (including fragmentary orders and warning orders), exercises, terrain requirements, and products involving contributions from other staff sections. The G-3 (S-3) provides coordination, integrates reconnaissance and surveillance, and allocates resources.

2-51. The G-3 (S-3) coordinates with other staff officers during plans and operations. This list is not all-inclusive. This officer coordinates with the G-1/AG (S-1) for civilian personnel involvement in tactical operations and with the G-9 (S-9) on using Army forces to establish or reestablish civil government. By coordinating with the commander, the COS (XO), G-6 (S-6), and the G-3 (S-3) can establish, oversee, and supervise staff activities of the command post. Coordinating with the engineer officer, G-2 (S-2), chief of protection, G-9 (S-9), and surgeon, the G-3 (S-3) establishes environmental vulnerability protection levels. Coordinating with the chief of protection and operations security officer, the G-3 (S-3) establishes operations security priorities, plans, and guidance.

2-52. The G-3 (S-3) integrates reconnaissance and surveillance during plans and operations. This officer integrates reconnaissance and surveillance into the concept of operations and manages the reconnaissance and surveillance effort through integrated staff processes and procedures. The G-3 (S-3) also synchronizes reconnaissance and surveillance with the overall operation throughout the operations process (with the rest of the staff). By developing the reconnaissance and surveillance plan (with rest of the staff) to support the commander's visualization, the reconnaissance and surveillance plan produces an initial reconnaissance and surveillance order.

2-53. The G-3 (S-3) allocates resources during plans and operations. This officer ensures units provide necessary support requirements when and where required. The G-3 (S-3) retasks and refocuses collection assets during execution (considering recommendations from the rest of the staff). This officer recommends use of resources, including resources required for military deception, and sustainment requirements (with the G-1/AG [S-1] and G-4 [S-4]).

2-54. During plans and operations, the G-3 (S-3) also—

- Develops the reconnaissance and surveillance annex to plans and orders (with the rest of the staff).
- Allocates reconnaissance and surveillance tasks (considering recommendations from the rest of the staff).
- Integrates fire support into operations.
- Plans tactical troop movements, including route selection, priority of movement, timing, security, bivouacking, quartering, staging, and preparing movement orders.
- Develops the ammunition required supply rate (with the G-2, chief of fires, and G-4).
- Requisitions replacement units (through operations channels).
- Participates in course of action and decision support template development (with the G-2 [S-2] and the chief of fires).
- Recommends general command post locations.
- Recommends task organizations and assigns missions to subordinate elements.
- Supports linguist requirements, to include consolidating linguist requirements and establishing priorities for using linguists.

ASSISTANT CHIEF OF STAFF, G-4 (S-4), LOGISTICS

2-55. The ACOS, G-4 (S-4) is the principal staff officer for sustainment plans and operations (general), supply, maintenance, transportation, services, and operational contract support. The G-4 (S-4) helps the support unit commander maintain logistics visibility with the commander and the rest of the staff. The G-4 (S-4) has staff coordinating responsibility of the transportation officer and the air mobility officer. The G-4 (S-4) prepares Annex F (Sustainment) and Annex P (Host-Nation Support) to the operation order or operation plan. (Refer to FM 4-0 and FM 7-15 for more detailed information on the duties and responsibilities of the G-4 [S-4].)

Sustainment Plans and Operations (General)

2-56. The G-4 (S-4) responsibilities for sustainment plans and operations (general) include, but are not limited to—

- Developing the logistic plan to support operations (with the G-3 [S-3]).
- Coordinating with the G-3 (S-3), G-2 (S-2), and engineer officer to requisition cataloged topographic foundation data and existing mission-specific data sets from the Defense Logistics Agency.
- Coordinating with the G-3 (S-3) and G-1/AG (S-1) on equipping replacement personnel and units.
- Coordinating with the support unit commander on the current and future support capability of that unit.
- Coordinating the selection of—and recommending to the G-3 (S-3)—main supply routes, and logistic support areas (with the engineer officer).
- Performing logistic preparation of the battlefield (with the support command).
- Recommending command policy for collecting and disposing of excess property and salvage.

Supply

2-57. The G-4 (S-4) responsibilities for supply include, but are not limited to—

- Determining supply requirements, except medical (with the support unit commander and the G-3 [S-3]).
- Coordinating all classes of supply except Class VIII (which is coordinated through medical supply channels).
- Coordinating the requisition, acquisition, and storage of supplies and equipment, and the maintenance of materiel records.
- Recommending sustainment priorities and controlled supply rates.
- Ensuring that accountability and security of supplies and equipment are adequate (with the provost marshal).
- Calculating and recommending to the G-3 (S-3) basic and prescribed loads, and helping the G-3 (S-3) determine required supply rates.

Maintenance

2-58. The G-4 (S-4) responsibilities for maintenance include, but are not limited to—

- Monitoring and analyzing the equipment readiness status.
- Determining maintenance workload requirements, less medical (with the support command).
- Coordinating equipment recovery and evacuation operations (with the support command).
- Determining maintenance time lines.

Transportation

2-59. The G-4 (S-4) responsibilities for transportation include, but are not limited to—

- Conducting operational and tactical planning to support mode and terminal operations, and movement control.
- Planning administrative troop movements (with the G-3 [S-3]).
- Coordinating transportation assets for other Services.
- Coordinating with the G-9 (S-9) for host-nation support.
- Coordinating special transport requirements to move the command post.
- Coordinating with the G-1 (S-1) and the provost marshal to transporting replacement personnel and enemy prisoners of war.
- Coordinating with the G-3 (S-3) for sustainment of tactical troop movements.

Services

2-60. The G-4 (S-4) responsibilities for services include, but are not limited to—

- Coordinating the construction of facilities and installations, except for fortifications and signal systems.
- Coordinating field sanitation.
- Coordinating organizational clothing and individual equipment exchange and replacement.
- Coordinating unit spill-prevention plans.
- Coordinating or providing food preparation, water purification, mortuary affairs, aerial delivery, laundry, shower, and clothing/light textile repair.
- Coordinating the transportation, storage, handling, and disposal of hazardous material or hazardous waste.

Staff Planning and Supervision

2-61. The G-4 (S-4) has the following staff planning and supervisory responsibilities:

- Identifying requirements the unit can meet through contracting.
- Identifying requirements and restrictions, in conjunction with the Staff Judge Advocate, for using local civilians, enemy prisoners of war, civilian internees, and detainees in sustainment operations.
- Coordinating with the Staff Judge Advocate on legal aspects of contracting.
- Coordinating with financial managers on the financial resources availability.
- Coordinating real property control and fire protection for facilities.

2-62. A support operations officer or materiel officer is authorized in support commands and battalions. As the principal staff officer for coordinating logistics, the support operations officer or materiel officer provides technical supervision for the sustainment mission of the support command and is the key interface between the supported unit and support command. The responsibilities of the support operations officer or materiel officer include, but are not limited to—

- Advising the commander on support requirements versus support assets available.
- Coordinating external support requirements for supported units.
- Synchronizing support requirements to ensure they remain consistent with current and future operations.
- Planning and monitoring support operations and making adjustments to meet support requirements.
- Coordinating with other staff.
- Preparing and distributing the external service support SOP that provides guidance and procedures to supported units.

ASSISTANT CHIEF OF STAFF, G-5 (S-5), PLANS

2-63. The ACOS, G-5 (S-5) is the principal staff officer for planning operations for the mid- to long-range planning horizons. In conjunction with the G-3 (S-3), the G-5 (S-5) prepares Annex A (Task Organization),

Annex C (Operations), and Annex M (Assessment) to the operation order or operation plan. The G-5 (S-5) has staff coordination responsibility for the military deception officer. (See FM 3-0, FM 5-0, FM 6-0, and FM 7-15 for detailed information on duties and responsibilities for the G-5 [S-5].)

2-64. Plans and orders consist of—

- Preparing, coordinating, authenticating, publishing, and distributing operation plans, concept plans, and operation orders.
- Conducting mission analysis of higher headquarters plans and orders.
- Reviewing subordinate supporting plans and orders.
- Coordinating and synchronizing warfighting functions in all plans and orders.

2-65. The G-5 has staff planning and supervisory responsibility for—

- Overseeing operations beyond the scope of the current order (such as the next operation or the next phase of the current operation).
- Developing plans, orders, branches, and sequels.
- Conducting military deception planning.
- Developing policies, and other coordinating or directive products, such as memorandums of agreement.

ASSISTANT CHIEF OF STAFF G-6 (S-6), SIGNAL

2-66. The ACOS G-6 (S-6) is the principal staff officer for all matters concerning communications, electromagnetic spectrum operations, and networks within the unit's area of operations. The G-6 (S-6) prepares Annex H (Signal) to the operation order or operation plan. (See FM 6-02.43 and FM 7-15 for more detailed information on the duties and responsibilities of the G-6 [S-6].) G-6 (S-6) responsibilities include, but are not limited to—

- Managing and controlling all network capabilities and services.
- Preparing and maintaining network operations estimates, plans, and orders.
- Monitoring and making recommendations on all technical network operations activities.
- Coordinating and managing electromagnetic spectrum operations and communications security within the AO.
- Establishing and overseeing procedures to disseminate intelligence throughout the AO.
- Establishing automation systems administration procedures for all information systems.
- Assessing network operations vulnerability and risk management—with the G-2 (S-2), G-3, and G-7.
- Recommending command post (CP) locations, based on operational requirements and the information environment.
- Recommending communications- and network-related essential elements of friendly information.
- Coordinating contractor support for all cyber/electromagnetic systems.
- Managing and distributing official military mail.

Network Operations

2-67. The network operations officer integrates mission intelligence applications with information systems and communications and computer operations of the warfighting information network. Network operations include network management, information dissemination management, and information assurance. G-6 (S-6) responsibilities related to network operations include, but are not limited to—

- Coordinating, planning, and directing all signal support interfaces with joint and multinational forces, including host-nation support interfaces.
- Coordinating the availability of commercial information systems and information services for military use.
- Coordinating unit commercial and military satellite communications requirements with the space operations officer.

- Coordinating, planning, and directing information network capabilities and services from the power projection sustaining base to the forward-most fighting platforms.
- Coordinating, planning, and directing communications protocols and user interfaces as part of the LandWarNet and Global Information Grid for all warfighting functions.
- Following higher headquarters network operations policies and procedures for network interfaces.
- Configuring wide-area networks.
- Providing operational and technical support to all assigned or attached units.
- Managing radio frequency allocations and assignments and providing electromagnetic spectrum management within the AO.
- Ensuring that information dissemination management meets the command's information management requirements.
- Coordinating, planning, and directing all command information assurance activities.
- Providing information assurance.

Information Management

2-68. The G-6 (S-6) is responsible for information management in coordination with the staff. Information management uses procedures and information systems to collect, process, store, display, and disseminate information. The G-6 (S-6) coordinates with the knowledge management officer on matters relating to knowledge management.

ASSISTANT CHIEF OF STAFF, G-7 (S-7), INFORM AND INFLUENCE ACTIVITIES

2-69. The ACOS, G-7 (S-7) is the principal staff officer responsible for planning, coordinating, and integrating inform and influence activities of the command. The G-7 (S-7) assists the commander to establish, synchronize, and integrate actions with information themes and messages. This coordination provides consistent messages to diverse audiences, including foreign friendly, neutrals, adversaries, and enemies. The G-7 (S-7) has staff coordination responsibility for synchronizing, deconflicting, and integrating public affairs, military information support operations, Soldier and leader engagement, military deception, and commander-designated enablers. The G-7 (S-7) prepares Annex J (Inform and Influence Activities) to the operation order or operation plan. (Refer to FM 3-13 and FM 7-15 for more detailed information on the duties and responsibilities of the G-7 [S-7].) Responsibilities related to inform and influence activities include, but are not limited to—

- Coordinating across unified action partners to nest inform and influence activities efforts.
- Integrating enablers of inform and influence activities across operational activities and lines of effort and lines of operations.
- Developing and integrating themes and messages that support the concept of operations.
- Performing staff planning and coordination of inform and influence activities.
- Advising the commander on the information environment and its possible effects on military operations.
- Establishing inform and influence activities measures of performance and effectiveness.
- Synchronizing inform and influence activities with higher commands and major subordinate commands.
- Writing the inform and influence activities annex to plans and orders and updating as necessary.
- Conducting and leading inform and influence activities working groups.
- Participating in the targeting meeting by nominating lethal and nonlethal inform and influence activities targets.
- Allocating organic and requesting external resources to support inform and influence activities efforts as part of the tasking and request process.

- Coordinating input and making recommendations to the commander on the assets to be included in the critical and defended asset lists.
- Monitoring and assessing the protection effort.
- Conducting staff coordination with other headquarters cells, nodes, and functional groupings.
- Managing protection support for major operations.
- Synchronizing protection operations between CPs.
- Managing training and materiel enhancements.
- Providing guidance on the execution of protection tasks and systems.

CHIEF OF SUSTAINMENT

2-75. The chief of sustainment is the principal staff officer responsible for coordinating all matters concerning the sustainment warfighting function at division and above headquarters. Brigade and below headquarters are not authorized a chief of sustainment. The S-4 serves as the principal coordinator of sustainment for brigade and below. The chief of sustainment has coordinating staff responsibility for the G-1, G-4, and G-8. At division level and higher, the chief of sustainment prepares Annex F (Sustainment) to the operation order or operation plan. (Refer to FM 4-0 and FM 7-15 for more detailed information on the duties and responsibilities of the chief of sustainment.)

SPECIAL STAFF OFFICERS

2-76. Every staff has special staff officers. This section addresses the specific duties of each special staff officer. The number of special staff officers and their responsibilities vary with authorizations, the desires of the commander, and the size of the command. If a special staff officer is not assigned, the officer with coordinating staff responsibility for the area of expertise assumes those functional responsibilities. During operations, special staff officers work in parts of the CP designated by the commander, COS, or their supervising coordinating staff officer. The COS (XO) exercises coordinating staff responsibility over special staff officers.

AIR AND MISSILE DEFENSE OFFICER

2-77. The air and missile defense officer is responsible for coordinating air and missile defense activities and plans with the area air and missile defense commander, joint force air component commander (JFACC), and airspace control authority. The air and missile defense officer coordinates the planning and use of all joint air and missile defense systems, assets, and operations. Army forces air and missile defense plans are synchronized with the area air defense commander's area air defense plan, the JFACC's joint air operations plan and daily air tasking order (ATO), and the airspace control authority's airspace control plan, and daily airspace control order (ACO). The air and missile defense officer prepares a portion of Annex E (Protection) to the operation order or operation plan. (Refer to FM 3-01, FM 3-27, FM 3-52, and FM 7-15 for more information on the duties and responsibilities of the air and missile defense officer.)

2-78. The air and missile defense officer is the senior air defense artillery officer in the command and the commander of an air defense artillery unit supporting it. An air and missile defense officer is authorized at the division, corps, and theater army levels. Examples of air and missile defense officer responsibilities include, but are not limited to—

- Disseminating ATO and ACO intelligence to air defense artillery units. Normally, units receive ATO and ACO intelligence electronically through the mission command system, which receives it from the Theater Battle Management Core System.
- Coordinating airspace control measures to support air and missile defense operations.
- Recommending active and passive air defense measures.
- Determining requirements and recommending assets to support air and missile defense.
- Planning and coordinating airspace use with other staff.
- Providing information on the status of air and missile defense systems, air and missile attack early warning radars, and air defense artillery ammunition.

- Estimating the adequacy of the air defense artillery ammunition controlled supply rate.
- Coordinating and synchronizing Army forces air and missile defense with joint force air and missile defense.

AIR LIAISON OFFICER

2-79. The air liaison officer is responsible for coordinating aerospace assets and operations, such as close air support, air interdiction, air reconnaissance, airlift, and joint suppression of enemy air defenses. The air liaison officer is the senior Air Force officer with each tactical air control party. (Refer to unit SOPs.) Air liaison officer responsibilities include, but are not limited to—

- Advising the commander and staff on employing aerospace assets.
- Operating and maintaining the Air Force tactical air direction radio network and Air Force air request network.
- Transmitting requests for immediate close air support and reconnaissance support.
- Transmitting advance notification of impending immediate airlift requirements.
- Acting as liaison between air and missile defense units and air control units.
- Planning the simultaneous employment of air and surface fires.
- Coordinating tactical air support missions with the chief of fires or fire support officer, and the appropriate airspace command and control element.
- Supervising forward air controllers and the tactical air control party.
- Integrating air support sorties with the Army concept of operations.
- Participating in targeting team meetings.
- Directing close air support missions.
- Providing Air Force input into airspace command and control.

AVIATION OFFICER

2-80. The aviation officer is responsible for coordinating Army aviation assets and operations. (Refer to FM 3-52 and FM 7-15 for duties and responsibilities for the aviation officer.) The aviation officer responsibilities include, but are not limited to—

- Exercising staff supervision and training over Army aviation operations.
- Monitoring aviation flying-hour, standardization, and safety programs.
- Planning and supervising Army aviation operations.
- Providing technical advice and assistance on using Army aviation for evacuation (medical or other).
- Participating in targeting meetings.

CHEMICAL, BIOLOGICAL, RADIOLOGICAL, AND NUCLEAR OFFICER

2-81. The chemical, biological, radiological, and nuclear (CBRN) officer is responsible for CBRN operations, obscuration operations, and CBRN asset use. The CBRN officer prepares a portion of Annex E (Protection) and a portion of Annex C (Operations) to the operation order or operation plan. (See ATTP 3-11.36 and FM 7-15 for details.) The CBRN officer's responsibilities include, but are not limited to—

- Recommending courses of action to minimize friendly and civilian vulnerability, and assessing the probability and effect of CBRN-related casualties.
- Assessing the probability and effect of CBRN-related casualties.
- Coordinating across the entire staff while assessing the effect of enemy CBRN-related attacks and hazards on current and future operations.
- Coordinating Army health system (AHS) support requirements for CBRN operations with the surgeon.
- Coordinating with other staff for CBRN-related operations.

- Planning, supervising, and coordinating CBRN decontamination (except patient decontamination) operations.
- Assessing weather and terrain data to determine environmental effects on potential CBRN hazards and threats.
- Overseeing construction of CBRN shelters.
- Planning and recommending integration of obscuration into tactical operations.
- Advising the commander on CBRN hazards and passive defense measures.

CIVILIAN PERSONNEL OFFICER

2-82. The civilian personnel officer manages and administers the civilian employee personnel management program. This civilian employee has a permanent position on the staff at divisions and corps. The AR 690 series discusses civilian personnel officer functions. Specific duties include, but are not limited to—

- Advising the commander and staff concerning, and supervising the management and administration of, the civilian employee personnel management program within the command.
- Administering civilian personnel management laws and regulations.
- Participating, when appropriate, in negotiations with host nations on labor agreements.
- Developing plans and standby directives for procuring, using, and administering the civilian labor force and using local labor in foreign areas during emergencies (with other staff members).

COMMAND LIAISON OFFICER

2-83. The command liaison officers are the commander's representative at the headquarters or agency to which they are sent. They promote coordination, synchronization, and cooperation between their parent unit and higher headquarters, interagency, coalition, host-nation, adjacent, and subordinate organizations as required. As subject matter experts from their assigned headquarters, command liaison officers are usually embedded in another organization to provide face-to-face coordination. (See also Chapter 9 and unit SOPs.)

DENTAL SURGEON

2-84. The dental surgeon coordinates dental activities within the command. All dental activities are planned at the medical brigade, medical command deployment support, or Army Service component command. (Refer to FM 4-02.19 for details on the duties and responsibilities of the dental surgeon). Dental surgeon responsibilities include, but are not limited to—

- Coordinating dental activities with the command surgeon.
- Exercising staff supervision over and providing technical assistance to dental activities.
- Planning and supervising the dental functions.
- Developing a program for dental support of humanitarian and civil action operations.
- Providing advice and technical assistance in constructing, rehabilitating, and using dental facilities.

ELECTRONIC WARFARE OFFICER

2-85. The electronic warfare officer is a specially trained officer who performs electronic warfare duties. The electronic warfare officer prepares a portion of Annex D (Fires) to the operation order or operation plan. Electronic warfare officer responsibilities include, but are not limited to—

- Leading the electronic warfare element in the fires cell.
- Integrating and synchronizing the cyber/electromagnetic activities.
- Coordinating, preparing, and maintaining the electronic warfare target list, electronic attack taskings, electronic attack requests, and the electronic warfare portion of the sensor/attack matrix.
- Coordinating with other staff when conducting electronic warfare.
- Assessing opponent vulnerabilities, friendly capabilities, and friendly missions in electronic warfare terms.

- Developing a prioritized adversary target list based on high-value targets and high-payoff targets (with the chief of fires and fire support officer).
- Coordinating the electronic attack target list with organic military intelligence units and with adjacent and higher commands, including joint and multinational commands when appropriate.
- Coordinating with the higher headquarters electronic warfare officer to deconflict inform and influence activities on the communications spectrum.

ENGINEER OFFICER

2-86. The engineer officer in the protection cell is responsible for planning and assessing survivability operations. The engineer officer prepares Annex G (Engineer) to the operation order or operation plan. (Refer to FM 3-34 and FM 7-15 for more detailed information on the duties and responsibilities of the engineer officer.) Specific duties include, but are not limited to—

- Advising the chief of protection on survivability operations.
- Coordinating and synchronizing survivability operations.
- Coordinating with the engineer officer for engineering capabilities.
- Synchronizing and integrating engineer operations (combat and construction) between multiple command posts and organizations.
- Writing engineer fragmentary orders, warning orders, and related products.
- Providing real-time reachback linkage to United States Army Corps of Engineers knowledge centers and supporting national assets.
- Updating the running estimate.

EXPLOSIVE ORDNANCE DISPOSAL OFFICER

2-87. The explosive ordnance disposal officer is responsible for coordinating the detection, identification, recovery, evaluation, rendering ordnance safe, and final disposal of explosive ordnance. An explosive ordnance disposal officer is authorized at corps and divisions and normally serves as the explosive ordnance disposal group, battalion, and company commander. The explosive ordnance disposal officer prepares a portion to Annex E (Protection) to the operation order or operation plan. (Refer to AR 75-15 and FM 7-15 for detailed duties and responsibilities of the explosive ordnance disposal officer.) Explosive ordnance disposal officer responsibilities include, but are not limited to—

- Establishing and operating an explosive ordnance disposal incident reporting system.
- Establishing, operating, and supervising technical intelligence reporting procedures.
- Coordinating requirements for explosive ordnance disposal support with requesting units, other Army commands, other Services, federal agencies, and multinational partners. Coordination may include arranging for administrative and logistic support for subordinate explosive ordnance disposal units.
- Monitoring the supply status of and expediting requests for special explosive ordnance disposal tools, equipment, and demolition materials.

EQUAL OPPORTUNITY ADVISOR

2-88. The equality opportunity advisor coordinates matters concerning equal opportunity for Soldiers and their families. Commanders at every echelon are authorized to appoint an equality opportunity advisor. AR 600-20 discusses the responsibilities and duties of the equality opportunity advisor:

- Advising and assisting the commander and staff on all equal opportunity matters, including sexual harassment, discrimination, and affirmative action.
- Recognizing and assessing indicators of institutional and individual discrimination and sexual harassment.
- Recommending, developing, and monitoring affirmative action and equal opportunity plans and policies to reduce or prevent discrimination and sexual harassment.
- Collecting and processing demographic data concerning all aspects of equal opportunity climate assessment.

- Managing or conducting all equal opportunity education and training programs within the command, to include conducting ethnic observances.
- Receiving and helping process complaints.

FORCE MANAGEMENT OFFICER

2-89. The force management officer is responsible for accounting for the force and its resources. This officer evaluates the organizational structure, functions, and workload of military and civilian personnel to ensure their proper use and requirements (manpower utilization and requirements). By conducting formal, on-site manpower and equipment surveys, this officer ensures documents for the modified table of organization and equipment and the table of distribution and allowances reflect the minimum essential and most economical equipment needed for the mission.

FOREIGN DISCLOSURE OFFICER

2-90. The foreign disclosure officer is responsible for the oversight and coordination of specific disclosure of or access to classified military information or controlled unclassified information to representatives of foreign governments and international organizations. (See AR 380-10 for more information.)

HISTORIAN

2-91. The historian is responsible for coordinating the documentation of the command's historical activities. The historian, normally an Army civilian, is authorized at corps and divisions. (AR 870-5 discusses the Army historical program.) Historian responsibilities include, but are not limited to—

- Preparing the command history.
- Supervising the command's historical activities.
- Injecting historical perspective and institutional memory into command activities.
- Collecting and maintaining records, such as staff journals, plans and orders, and after action reviews.
- Preparing special studies and reports, based on assembled historical material.
- Maintaining a command historical research collection adequate to support the historical mission.

KNOWLEDGE MANAGEMENT OFFICER

2-92. The knowledge management officer provides the commander and staff with Battle Command Knowledge Management capabilities. (Refer to FM 6-01.1 for more information on the duties and responsibilities of the knowledge management officer.) This officer provides these capabilities by integrating and managing information systems and the Army Battle Command System. Responsibilities include, but are not limited to—

- Translating operational requirement and strategies into knowledge management strategies enabled by information systems.
- Incorporating and managing a set of integrated applications, processes, and services that enable command post operations.
- Supporting continuous operations.
- Developing the knowledge management plan in accordance with the commander's guidance.
- Tailoring the knowledge management plan to support the command post SOPs.
- Assisting with organizing, sharing, and displaying a common operational picture for the command.
- Continuously monitoring the external information environment and recommending changes to the information management plan.
- Developing file and data management procedures.
- Coordinating support from the G-6 for network, data base, storage, and technical support.

- Coordinating with external knowledge sources and integrating them into the organizational knowledge network.
- Training the organization on how to use and apply the Battle Command Knowledge System.

MILITARY DECEPTION OFFICER

2-93. The military deception officer is responsible for coordinating military deception assets and operations working within the G-5 plans section. A military deception officer is authorized at corps and theater army levels. The military deception officer prepares a portion of Annex J (Inform and Influence Activities) to the operation order or operation plan. Responsibilities include, but are not limited to—

- Exercising staff supervision over military deception activities.
- Providing expertise in military deception operations planning.
- Managing information required to conduct military deception operations and civil considerations analysis to better determine the effects of the ambiguity.
- Determining requirements or opportunities for military deception operations (with the G-2) through red teaming the adversaries' most probable courses of action.
- Coordinating with the military information support planner for support to the deception targets, deception objectives, and deception story.
- Producing, distributing, briefing, and coordinating the military deception plan on a need-to-know basis.
- Coordinating operations security measures to shield the military deception plan with the operations security officer.
- Integrating military deception assets (both conventional and unconventional).
- Assessing execution of military deception operations and their effects.

MILITARY INFORMATION SUPPORT OFFICER

2-94. The military information support officer is responsible for synchronizing military information support operations (MISO) with elements conducting other inform and influence. A military information support officer is authorized at theater army, corps, and divisions. A military information support noncommissioned officer is authorized at the brigade combat team level. If no military information support noncommissioned officer is assigned, the commander of an attached military information support element may assume the military information support staff officer's responsibilities. The military information support officer prepares a portion of Annex J (Inform and Influence Activities) to the operation order or operation plan. (See FM 3-05.301 and FM 7-15 for more details.) Responsibilities include, but are not limited to—

- Coordinating with the G-7 to ensure synchronization of MISO.
- Planning, coordinating, and synchronizing MISO to support the overall operation.
- Recommending prioritization of the efforts of attached military information support forces.
- Evaluating enemy information efforts and the effectiveness of friendly MISO on target groups (with the G-2 and G-9).
- Assessing MISO effectiveness.
- Assessing the psychological impact of military operations on the enemy and the civilian populace.
- Assessing the potential effects of adversary information and, in conjunction with the G-7 and public affairs officer, determining the best response, if any.
- Assisting military deception operations in developing deception story to meet command objectives.

OPERATIONS SECURITY OFFICER

2-95. The operations security officer is responsible for the command's operations security program. AR 530-1 contains operations security policy and procedures. The operations security officer prepares a portion of Annex E (Protection) to the operation order or operation plan. The operations security officer's responsibilities include, but are not limited to—

- Identifying and recommending the essential elements of friendly information (EEFIs).
- Conducting analysis of adversaries as part of the intelligence preparation of the battlefield (IPB) process.
- Conducting analysis of vulnerabilities as part of the IPB process.
- Assessing operations security risk.
- Developing, coordinating, and applying operations security measures across the staff.
- Writing the running estimate for operations security.
- Writing the operations security appendix to the protection annex.
- Monitoring, assessing, and adjusting operations security as required.
- Reviewing internal staff documents, information system logs, and news releases for sensitive information and potential compromise of EEFIs.
- Searching news sources, Web logs (blogs), and other Web sites for sensitive information and compromise of EEFIs.
- Attending the inform and influence activities working group as required.

PERSONNEL RECOVERY OFFICER

2-96. The personnel recovery officer is responsible for the coordination of all personnel recovery related matters. (Refer to FM 3-50.1 and FM 7-15 for details.) The personnel recovery officer prepares a portion of Annex E (Protection) to the operation order or operation plan. Personnel recovery officer duties include, but are not limited to—

- Developing and maintaining of the organization's personnel recovery program.
- Recommending recovery courses of action to the commander.
- Coordinating personnel recovery issues, both vertically and horizontally.
- Developing personnel recovery SOPs, plans, and annexes.
- Supporting joint personnel recovery or establishing a joint personnel recovery center as required.
- Assisting personnel recovery officers developing subordinate recovery programs.

PROVOST MARSHAL

2-97. The provost marshal is responsible for planning, coordinating, and employing all organic, assigned, or attached military police assets. Usually the senior military police officer in the command, the provost marshal augments the staff with a small planning cell that typically works within the G-5. A provost marshal is authorized at corps and divisions. The provost marshal prepares a portion of Annex C (Operations) and a portion of Annex E (Protection) to the operation order or operation plan. (Refer to FM 3-37, FM 3-39, and FM 7-15 for more information on the duties and responsibilities of the provost marshal.) Provost marshal responsibilities include, but are not limited to—

- Conducting maneuver and mobility support operations, including route reconnaissance, surveillance, circulation control, dislocated civilian and straggler control, and information dissemination.
- Directing components of area security operations, including activities associated with antiterrorism operations, zone and area reconnaissance, checkpoint access control, and physical security of critical assets, nodes, and sensitive materials.
- Managing, in coordination with the G-4, the internment and resettlement of enemy prisoners of war, civilian internees, dislocated civilians, and U.S. military prisoners.
- Coordinating and directing law and order operations, including liaison with local civilian law enforcement authorities.
- Conducting police intelligence operations, including activities related to the collection, assessment, development, and dissemination of police intelligence products.
- Coordinating customs and counterdrug activities.

- Providing physical security guidance for commanders.
- Assisting with area damage control and CBRN detection and reporting.
- Helping the G-1 (AG) administer discipline, law, and order.
- Preparing statistical data on absent without leave and desertion to the G-1 (AG) through the chief of protection.
- Coordinating, along with the G-4, for all logistic requirements relative to enemy prisoners of war, civilian internees, U.S. military prisoners, and dislocated civilians.

OPERATIONS RESEARCH AND SYSTEMS ANALYSIS OFFICER

2-98. The operations research and system analysis officer conducts analysis in support of operations, across staff elements and forces employed. This officer's responsibilities include, but are not limited to—

- Managing, analyzing, and visualizing data using statistical, geospatial, spreadsheets, and graphics software.
- Developing customized tools for staff elements.
- Providing quality control capability.
- Supporting course of action analyses and operations planning.
- Conducting assessments to determine effectiveness of an operation.
- Conducting analyses to support the military decisionmaking process by all the staff.

RED TEAM OFFICER

2-99. The red team officer is a special staff officer coordinated by the chief of staff. Red teaming enables commanders to fully explore alternative plans and operations in the context of the operational environment and from the perspective of partners, adversaries, and others. Red teams assist the commander and staff with critical and creative thinking and help them avoid groupthink, mirror imaging, cultural missteps, and tunnel vision throughout the conduct of operations. Red teams are part of the commander's staff at division through theater army. Brigades may be augmented with a red team as required. Commanders use red teams to provide alternatives during planning, execution, and assessment. The red team officer's duties and responsibilities include, but are not limited to—

- Broadening the understanding of the operational environment.
- Assisting the commander and staff in framing problems and defining end state conditions.
- Challenging assumptions.
- Ensuring the perspectives of the adversary and others are appropriately considered.
- Aiding in identifying friendly and enemy vulnerabilities and opportunities.
- Assisting in identifying areas for assessment.
- Anticipating cultural perceptions of partners, adversaries, and others.
- Conducting independent critical reviews and analyses of plans and concepts to identify potential weaknesses and vulnerabilities.

SECRETARY OF THE GENERAL STAFF

2-100. The secretary of the general staff (SGS) is the special staff officer who acts as XO for the COS. Corps, divisions, major support commands, and general officers with a staff are authorized a secretary of the general staff. SGS responsibilities include, but are not limited to—

- Planning and supervising conferences chaired by the commander, deputy or assistant commanders, or the COS.
- Directing preparation of itineraries for distinguished visitors to the headquarters and monitoring their execution.
- Monitoring preparation and execution of all official social events and ceremonies involving the commander, deputy or assistant commanders, or the COS.
- Acting as the informal point of contact for liaison officers.

STAFF WEATHER OFFICER

2-101. The staff weather officer coordinates operational weather support and weather service matters through the G-2 (S-2) and other staff members. The G-2 (S-2) normally assists the staff weather officer with Army staff processes and coordination as required. The staff weather officer is an Air Force officer or noncommissioned officer who serves as a member of the supported commanders' special staff. This officer typically leads a team of two or more personnel. These teams are organized as flights or detachments operating in locations under an Air Force weather squadron. The squadron commander assigns teams to provide or coordinate support to one or more Army units. Typically, the staff weather officer is assigned to support Army Service component commands, corps, divisions, combat aviation brigades, brigade combat teams, and special operations forces. This officer focuses on integrating weather into Army decisionmaking processes. Staff weather officer responsibilities include, but are not limited to—

- Providing or overseeing staff, mission and airfield weather services in direct support of the supported Army commander.
- Integrating tailored mission planning and execution forecasts in support of operational decisionmaking and mission execution.
- Identifying weather areas of interest and helping manage the Army commander's weather data collection plan.
- Advising the Air Force on Army operational weather support requirements.

Note: Army Regulation 115-10/Air Force Inter-Service Publication 15-157, *Weather Support for the U.S. Army,* and FM 34-81, *Weather Support for Army Tactical Operations,* have a more detailed analysis of weather support criteria, including mission and airfield weather services.

SPACE OPERATIONS OFFICER

2-102. The space operations officer is in charge of the space support element and is responsible for providing space-related tactical support and coordination of space-based capabilities available to the command. An Army space support team is often placed under operational control to a command if it has no space operations officer assigned. The team's officer in charge fulfills the space operations officer's responsibilities. The space operations officer prepares Annex N (Space Operations) to the operation order or operation plan. (Refer to FM 3-27 and FM 7-15 for details.) Space operations officer responsibilities include, but are not limited to—

- Advising the commander on the space architectures, capabilities, limitations, and use of theater, strategic, national, and commercial space assets.
- Calculating, analyzing, and disseminating global positioning system satellite coverage and accuracy data.
- Facilitating the dynamic retasking of space-based assets to support current and future operations.
- Assisting in acquiring Department of Defense (DOD) and commercial satellite terrain and weather imagery (classified and unclassified) to enhance mapping, mission analysis, and other actions requiring near real-time imagery from denied areas.
- Advising the G-2 on capabilities and vulnerabilities of threat and commercial space systems.
- Providing estimates on the effects of space weather activities on current and future operations and the effects of terrestrial weather on space-based capabilities.
- Nominating threat or foreign ground stations for targeting (with the G-3 and fire support coordinator).
- Coordinating the activities of the Army space support team supporting the command.
- Integrating into special technical operations to maximize all the unique and specialized space-related technical capabilities into operations.

TRANSPORTATION OFFICER

2-103. The transportation officer coordinates transportation assets and operations. (Refer to FM 7-15 and FM 55-1 for details.) Transportation officer responsibilities include, but are not limited to—

- Planning and directing administrative movements, including onward movement from ports of debarkation, sustainment movements, and other movements as directed.
- Planning movement scheduling and regulations of main supply routes.
- Planning the mode of operations (truck, rail, air, and water).
- Planning the movement of materiel and personnel.
- Monitoring movements on routes two echelons down.

VETERINARY OFFICER

2-104. The veterinary officer is responsible for coordinating assets and activities concerning veterinary services within the command. All veterinarian activities are planned at the medical brigade, medical command deployment support, or Army Service component command. (Refer to FM 4-0, FM 4-02.18, and FM 7-15 for details.) Veterinary officer responsibilities include, but are not limited to—

- Coordinating veterinary activities with the surgeon and other staff.
- Determining requirements for veterinary supplies and equipment.
- Ensuring safety of food and food sources.
- Advising on health and operational risks of animal disease, including possible biological warfare events.
- Monitoring the sanitation of food storage facilities and equipment.
- Managing veterinary equipment and facilities.
- Coordinating animal housing.
- Participating in civil-military operations.
- Coordinating the use of medical laboratory services by veterinary personnel.
- Preparing reports on command veterinary activities.

PERSONAL STAFF OFFICERS

2-105. Personal staff officers work under the immediate control of, and have direct access to, the commander. The commander establishes guidelines or gives guidance on when a personal staff officer informs or coordinates with the COS (XO) or other staff members. Some personal staff officers have responsibilities as special staff officers and work with a coordinating staff officer. They do this case-by-case, depending on the commander's guidance or the nature of the task. Personal staff officers also may work under the supervision of the COS (XO). By law or regulation, personal staff officers have a unique relationship with the commander. Although there are other members in the commander's personal staff, this section discusses only staff officers and the command sergeant major.

AIDE-DE-CAMP

2-106. The aide-de-camp serves as a personal assistant to a general officer. An aide-de-camp is authorized for general officers in designated positions. The rank of the aide-de-camp depends on the rank of the general officer. No officer exercises coordinating staff responsibility over the aide-de-camp. Aide-de-camp responsibilities include, but are not limited to—

- Providing for the general officer's personal well-being and security, and relieving the general officer of routine and time-consuming duties.
- Preparing and organizing schedules, activities, and calendars.
- Preparing and executing trip itineraries.
- Coordinating protocol activities.
- Acting as an executive assistant.
- Meeting and hosting the general officer's visitors.
- Supervising other personal staff members (secretaries, assistant aides, enlisted aides, and drivers).
- Performing varied duties, according to the general officer's desires.

CHAPLAIN

2-107. The chaplain is responsible for religious support operations. The chaplain advises the commander on matters of religion, morals, and morale as affected by religion, and on the impact of indigenous religions on military operations. No officer exercises coordinating staff responsibility over the chaplain. A unit ministry team consisting of one chaplain and one chaplain assistant is authorized at every echelon from battalion through corps. (Refer to FM 1-05 and FM 7-15 for more detailed information on the duties and responsibilities of the chaplain).The chaplain's responsibilities include, but are not limited to—

- Providing the commander with pastoral care, personal counseling, advice, and privileged communications.
- Developing and implementing the commander's religious support program.
- Coordinating religious support with unit ministry teams of higher and adjacent headquarters, other Services, and multinational forces.
- Helping the commander ensure all Soldiers have the opportunity to exercise their religion.
- Performing or providing religious rites, sacraments, ordnances, services, and pastoral care and counseling to nurture the living, care for casualties, and honor the dead.
- Providing religious support to the command and community, including confined or hospitalized personnel, enemy prisoners of war, civilian detainees, and refugees.
- Providing liaison with indigenous religious leaders (with the G-9 [S-9]).
- Training, equipping, and supporting subordinate chaplains and chaplain assistants.

COMMAND SERGEANT MAJOR

2-108. The command sergeant major is the senior noncommissioned officer of the command at battalion and higher levels. Command sergeants major carry out policies and enforce standards for the performance, training, and conduct of enlisted Soldiers. They give advice and initiate recommendations to the commander and staff in matters pertaining to enlisted Soldiers. In operations, a commander employs the command sergeant major throughout the area of operations to extend command influence, assess morale of the force, and assist during critical events.

INSPECTOR GENERAL

2-109. The inspector general is responsible for advising the commander on the command's overall welfare and state of discipline. The inspector general is a confidential advisor to the commander. An inspector general is authorized for general officers in command positions. The inspector general prepares Annex U (Inspector General) to the operation order or operation plan. (AR 20-1 discusses inspector general responsibilities and duties.) Inspector general responsibilities include, but are not limited to—

- Advising commanders and staffs on inspection policy.
- Advising commanders on the effectiveness of the organizational inspection program.
- Conducting inspections as the commander requires and monitoring corrective actions.
- Receiving allegations and conducting investigations and investigative inquiries.
- Monitoring and informing the commander of trends, both positive and negative, in all activities.
- Consulting with staff sections, as appropriate, to obtain items for the special attention of inspectors and to arrange for technical assistance.
- Providing the commander continuous, objective, and impartial assessments of the command's operational and administrative effectiveness.
- Assisting Soldiers, Army civilians, family members, retirees, and other members of the force who seek help with Army-related problems.
- Identifying and helping to resolve systemic problems.

INTERNAL REVIEW OFFICER

2-110. The internal review officer provides professional internal audit capability and delivers pertinent, timely, and reliable information and advice to the commander. This information and advice evaluates risk, assesses management controls, fosters stewardship, and improves the quality, economy, and efficiency of business practices. (AR 11-7 discusses the internal review program.) Internal review officer responsibilities include, but are not limited to—

- Completing internal audits of functions or organizational entities in the command with known or suspected problems, determining the nature and cause of problems, and suggesting resolutions.
- Providing troubleshooting—quick reaction efforts to prevent serious problems from developing.
- Providing an audit compliance function by serving as the point of contact with external audit groups. In addition, the internal review office facilitates the external audit reply and response process and performs follow-up audits.
- Coordinating with higher headquarters and other agencies to ensure units properly follow all standards and policies.
- Providing financial management support.

PUBLIC AFFAIRS OFFICER

2-111.   The public affairs officer understands and coordinates the flow of information to Soldiers, the Army community, and the public. The ACOS, G-7 exercises coordinating staff responsibility for the public affairs officer, when required. The public affairs officer prepares a portion of Annex J (Inform and Influence Activities) to the operation order or operation plan. (AR 360-1 discusses public affairs officer responsibilities and duties.) Public affairs officer responsibilities include, but are not limited to—

- Planning and supervising the command public affairs program.
- Advising and informing the commander of the public affairs impact and implications of planned or current operations.
- Serving as the command representative for all communications with external media.
- Assessing the information requirements and expectations of the Army and the public, monitoring media and public opinion, and evaluating the effectiveness of public affairs plans and operations.
- Coordinating logistic and administrative support of civilian journalists under unit administrative control.
- Conducting liaison with media representatives to provide accreditation, mess, billet, transport, and escort as authorized and appropriate.
- Developing and educating the command on policies and procedures for protecting against the release of information detrimental to the mission, national security, and personal privacy.
- Coordinating with the G-7, military information support officer, and G-9 to ensure disseminated information is not contradictory.
- Informing Soldiers, family members, and Army civilians of their rights under the Privacy Act, operations security responsibilities, and roles as implied representatives of the command when interacting with news media.
- Recommending news, entertainment, and information for Soldiers and home station audiences.

SAFETY OFFICER

2-112.   The safety officer coordinates safety activities throughout the command. Commanders at every echelon from battalion through corps appoint a safety officer. An aviation safety officer is authorized for corps staffs and all aviation units. The safety officer prepares a portion of Annex E (Protection) to the operation order or operation plan. (AR 385-10 discusses the Army safety program.) Safety officer responsibilities include, but are not limited to—

- Implementing the command safety and occupational health program.
- Implementing the accident prevention program.
- Coordinating with the inspector general and provost marshal on correcting unsafe trends identified during inspections.
- Providing input to the G-1/AG (S-1) on projected accident losses.

- Providing safety training to the local civilian labor force.
- Reviewing risk assessments and recommending risk-reduction control measures for all operations.

STAFF JUDGE ADVOCATE

2-113.   The Staff Judge Advocate serves under the supervision of the COS to provide legal services to the staff and, through other staff members, responsive legal services throughout the command. The ACOS, G-1 exercises coordinating staff responsibility over the Staff Judge Advocate, when required. A legal support element—typically composed of three judge advocates—deploys in direct support of each brigade-level task force. The staff judge advocate prepares a portion of Annex C (Operations) to the operation order or operation plan. (The Staff Judge Advocate provides complete legal support encompassing the six core legal disciplines discussed in AR 27-1 and FM 1-04.) Responsibilities include, but are not limited to—

- Providing military justice advice and performing military justice duties prescribed in the Uniform Code of Military Justice.
- Resolving legal problems regarding administrative boards, investigations, or other military tribunals.
- Providing technical supervision and training of legal personnel and subjects.
- Providing legal advice and assistance.
- Providing legal counsel to the civilian personnel office, equal opportunity advisor, family advocacy case review committee, and the command.
- Serving as the command ethics counselor.
- Providing international law and operational law assistance, including advice and assistance on implementing the DOD law of war program.
- Assisting with litigation in which the United States has an interest.

SURGEON

2-114.   The surgeon is responsible for coordinating health assets and operations within the command. This officer provides and oversees medical care to Soldiers, civilians, and enemy prisoners of war. Organizations from battalion through corps are authorized a surgeon. The surgeon prepares a portion of Annex E (Protection) and Annex F (Sustainment) to the operation order or operation plan. (FM 1-0 and the FM 4-02 series detail duties and responsibilities of surgeons.) Surgeon responsibilities include, but are not limited to—

- Providing health education and training.
- Coordinating medical evacuation, including Army dedicated medical evacuation platforms (air and ground).
- Overseeing veterinary food inspection, animal care, and veterinary preventive medicine activities of the command (with the veterinary officer).
- Overseeing medical laboratory services.
- Providing preventive medicine services.
- Supervising and preparing health-related reports and statistics.
- Advising on the effects of the medical threat on personnel, rations, and water.
- Advising how operations affect the public health of personnel and the indigenous populations.

Chapter 3

Command Post Organization and Operations

This chapter describes how commanders organize their headquarters into command posts during the conduct of operations. It discusses the effectiveness and survivability factors commanders consider, and describes how commanders further cross-functionally organize the staff within command posts into functional and integrating cells. Next, this chapter provides guidelines for command post operations to include the importance of establishing standard operating procedures and an effective battle rhythm for the headquarters. See the corresponding field manual for specific guidance on command post organization by echelon or type of unit. See JP 3-33 for more information on an Army headquarters serving as a joint task force headquarters.

COMMAND POST ORGANIZATION

3-1.   In operations, effective mission command requires continuous, close coordination, synchronization, and information sharing across staff sections. To promote this, commanders cross-functionally organize elements of staff sections in command posts (CPs) and CP cells. Additional staff integration occurs in meetings, including working groups and boards (see paragraphs 3-65 through 3-71).

3-2.   A *command post* **is a unit headquarters where the commander and staff perform their activities**. The headquarters' design of the modular force, combined with robust communications, gives commanders a flexible mission command structure consisting of a main CP, a tactical CP, and a command group for brigades, divisions, and corps. Combined arms battalions are also resourced with a combat trains CP and a field trains CP. Theater army headquarters are resourced with a main CP and a contingency CP. See appropriate echelon manuals for doctrine on specific CP and headquarters' organization.

3-3.   Each CP performs specific functions by design as well as tasks the commander assigns. Activities common in all CPs include—
  - Maintaining running estimates and the common operational picture.
  - Controlling operations.
  - Assessing operations.
  - Developing and disseminating orders.
  - Coordinating with higher, lower, and adjacent units.
  - Conducting knowledge management and information management. (See FM 6-01.1.)
  - Performing CP administration.

MAIN COMMAND POST

3-4.   **The** *main command post* **is a facility containing the majority of the staff designed to control current operations, conduct detailed analysis, and plan future operations**. The main CP is the unit's principal CP. It includes representatives of all staff sections and a full suite of information systems to plan, prepare, execute, and assess operations. It is larger in size and in staffing and less mobile than the tactical CP. The chief of staff (COS) or executive officer (XO) leads and provides staff supervision of the main CP. Functions of the main CP include, but are not limited to—
  - Controlling and synchronizing current operations.
  - Monitoring and assessing current operations (including higher and adjacent units) for their impact on future operations.
  - Planning operations, including branches and sequels.

- Assessing the overall progress of operations.
- Preparing reports required by higher headquarters and receiving reports for subordinate units.
- Providing a facility for the commander to control operations, issue orders, and conduct rehearsals.

TACTICAL COMMAND POST

3-5. **The *tactical command post* is a facility containing a tailored portion of a unit headquarters designed to control portions of an operation for a limited time.** Commanders employ the tactical CP as an extension of the main CP to help control the execution of an operation or a specific task, such as a gap crossing, a passage of lines, or an air assault operation. Commanders may employ the tactical CP to direct the operations of units close to each other, such as during a relief in place. The tactical CP may also control a special task force or a complex task, such as reception, staging, onward movement, and integration.

3-6. The tactical CP is fully mobile and includes only essential Soldiers and equipment. The tactical CP relies on the main CP for planning, detailed analysis, and coordination. A deputy commander or operations officer leads the tactical CP.

3-7. When employed, tactical CP functions include the following:

- Monitoring and controlling current operations.
- Providing information to the common operational picture.
- Assessing the progress of operations.
- Monitoring and assessing the progress of higher and adjacent units.
- Performing short-range planning.
- Providing input to targeting and future operations planning.
- Providing a facility for the commander to control operations, issue orders, and conduct rehearsals.

3-8. When the commander does not employ the tactical CP, the staff assigned to it reinforces the main CP. Unit standard operating procedures (SOPs) should address the specifics for this, including procedures to quickly detach the tactical CP from the main CP.

COMMAND GROUP

3-9. **A *command group* consists of commander and selected staff members who assist the commander in controlling operations away from a command post.** The command group is organized and equipped to suit the commander's decisionmaking and leadership requirements. It does this while enabling the commander to accomplish critical mission command tasks anywhere in the area of operations.

3-10. Command group personnel includes staff representation that can immediately affect current operations, such as maneuver, fires (including the air liaison officer), and intelligence. The mission and available staff, however, dictate the command group's makeup. For example, during a deliberate breach, the command group may include an engineer and an air defense officer. When visiting a dislocated civilians' collection point, the commander may take a translator, civil affairs operations officer, a medical officer, and a chaplain.

3-11. Divisions and corps headquarters are equipped with a mobile command group. The mobile command group serves as the commander's mobile CP. It consists of ground and air components equipped with information systems. The mobile command group's mobility allows commanders to move to critical locations to personally assess a situation, make decisions, and influence operations. The mobile command group's information systems and small staff allow commanders to do this while retaining communication with the entire force.

EARLY-ENTRY COMMAND POST

3-12. While not part of the unit's table of organization and equipment, commanders can establish an early-entry command post to assist them in controlling operations during the deployment phase of an operation.

An *early-entry command post* is a lead element of a headquarters designed to control operations until the remaining portions of the headquarters are deployed and operational. The early-entry command post normally consists of personnel and equipment from the tactical CP with additional intelligence analysts, planners, and other staff officers from the main CP based on the situation.

3-13. The early-entry command post performs the functions of the main and tactical CPs until those CPs are deployed and fully operational. A deputy commander, COS (XO), or operations officer normally leads the early-entry command post.

COMMAND POST ORGANIZATION CONSIDERATIONS

3-14. Commanders consider the effectiveness and survivability of a CP when planning CP organization. In many cases these factors work against each other; therefore, neither can be optimized. Commanders make tradeoffs to acceptably balance survivability and effectiveness.

EFFECTIVENESS FACTORS

3-15. CP staff and equipment are arranged to facilitate coordination, information exchange, and rapid decisionmaking. CPs must effectively communicate with all subordinate units. Their organization enables them to quickly deploy throughout the unit's area of operations (AO). Five factors contribute to CP effectiveness: design, standardization, continuity, deployability, and capacity and range.

Command Post Design and Fusion of Command and Staff Efforts

3-16. Many design considerations affect CP effectiveness. At a minimum, commanders position CP cells and staff elements to facilitate communication and coordination. Other design considerations include, but are not limited to—

- Efficient facilitation of information flow.
- User interface with communications systems.
- Positioning information displays for ease of use.
- Integrating complementary information on maps and displays.
- Adequate workspace for the staff and commander.
- Ease of displacement (setup, teardown, and mobility).

3-17. Well-designed CPs integrate command and staff efforts. Meeting this requirement requires matching the CP's manning, equipment, information systems, and procedures against its internal layout and utilities. Organizing the CP into functional and integrating cells promotes efficiency and coordination. (See paragraphs 3-30 through 3-46.)

Standardization

3-18. Standardization increases efficiency and eases CP personnel training. Commanders develop detailed SOPs for all aspects of CP operations during all operations. Standard CP layouts, battle drills, and reporting procedures increase efficiency. Units follow and revise SOPs throughout training. Units constantly reinforce using SOPs to make many processes routine. Staffs then effectively execute them in demanding, stressful times.

Continuity

3-19. Commanders man, equip, and organize CPs to control and support 24-hour operations without interruptions by enemies, environmental conditions, or actions. However, duplicating every staff member within a CP is unnecessary. Commanders carefully consider the primary role and functions assigned to each CP and resource it accordingly. Internal CP SOPs address shifts, rest plans, and other CP activities important to operating continuously. Leaders enforce these provisions.

3-20. Maintaining continuity during displacement or catastrophic loss requires designating alternate CPs and procedures for passing control between them. SOPs address providing continuity when units lose communications with the commander, subordinates, and or a particular CP. Commanders designate seconds in command and inform them of all critical decisions. Primary staff officers also designate alternates.

Deployability

3-21. CPs deploy efficiently and move within the AO as required. Determining the capabilities, size, and sequence of CPs in the deployment flow requires careful consideration. Commanders can configure modular CP elements as an early-entry command post if needed. They also add or subtract elements to the early-entry command post as needed. CP size directly affects deployment and employment.

Capacity and Range

3-22. Commanders organize CPs to manage needed information and operate effectively. The capacity to conduct (plan, prepare, execute, and continuously assess) operations concerns both staffing and information systems. So does the ability to manage relevant information. All CP personnel require tactical and technical proficiency. Effective CPs communicate with all higher and lower headquarters, including those outside the force's AO.

SURVIVABILITY FACTORS

3-23. CP survivability is vital to mission success. CPs often gain survivability at the price of effectiveness. CPs need to remain small and highly mobile. When concentrated, the enemy can easily acquire and target most CPs. However, when elements of a CP disperse, they often have difficulty maintaining a coordinated staff effort. When developing command post SOPs and organizing headquarters into CPs for operations, commanders use dispersion, size, redundancy, and mobility to increase survivability.

Dispersion

3-24. Dispersing CPs enhances survivability. Commanders place minimum resources forward and keep more elaborate facilities back. This makes it harder for enemies to find and attack them. It also decreases support and security requirements forward. Most of the staff resides in the main CP; the tactical CP contains only the staff and equipment essential to controlling current operations.

Size

3-25. A CP's size affects its survivability. Larger CPs ease face-to-face coordination; however, they are vulnerable to multiple acquisitions and means of attack. Units can hide and protect smaller CPs more easily but may not control all force elements. Striking the right balance provides a responsive yet agile organization. For example, commanders require information for decisions; they do not need every subject matter expert located with them.

Redundancy

3-26. Some personnel and equipment redundancy is required for continuous operations. Redundancy allows CPs to continue operating when mission command systems are lost, damaged, or fail under stress.

Mobility

3-27. CP mobility improves CP survivability, especially at lower echelons. Successful lower-echelon CPs and those employed forward in the combat zone move quickly and often. A smaller size and careful transportation planning allow CPs to displace rapidly to avoid the enemy.

COMMAND POST CELLS AND STAFF SECTIONS

3-28. Within the CP, commanders organize elements of staff sections into CP cells. **A *command post cell* is a grouping of personnel and equipment organized by warfighting function or by planning horizon to facilitate the exercise of mission command.** Staff elements—consisting of personnel and equipment from staff sections—form CP cells. For example, the current operations integration cell contains elements from nearly all staff sections of a headquarters.

3-29. While each echelon and type of unit organizes CPs differently, two types of CP cells exist: functional and integrating. (See Figure 3-1.) Functional cells group personnel and equipment by warfighting function. Integrating cells group personnel and equipment by planning horizon.

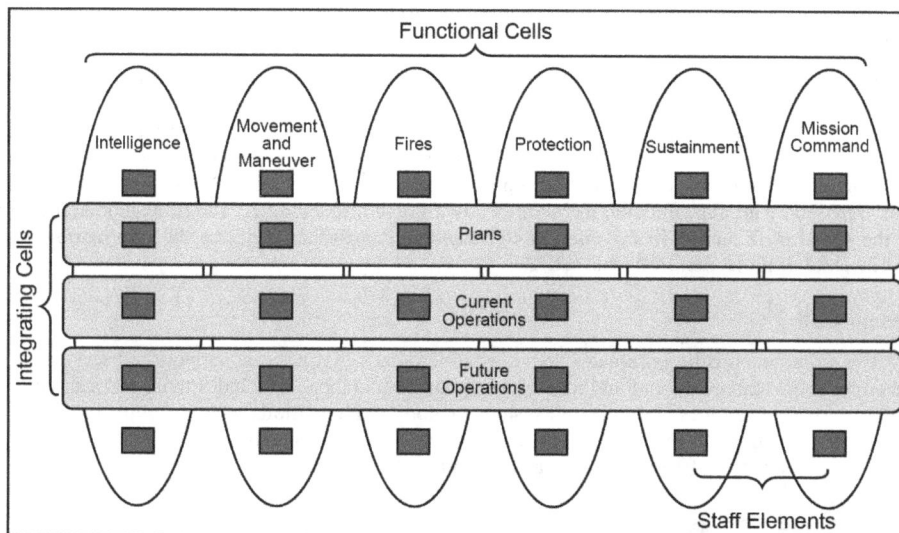

Figure 3-1. Functional and integrating cells

FUNCTIONAL CELLS

3-30. Functional cells coordinate and synchronize forces and activities by warfighting function. The functional cells within a CP are intelligence, movement and maneuver, fires, protection, sustainment, and mission command. Echelons above brigade are resourced to establish all six functional cells described in paragraphs 3-31 through 3-36. See appropriate brigade and battalion manuals for specifics on the functional cells at those levels.

Intelligence Cell

3-31. The intelligence cell coordinates activities and systems that help commanders understand the enemy, terrain and weather, and civil considerations. The intelligence cell requests, receives, and analyzes information from all sources to produce and distribute intelligence products. This includes tasks associated with intelligence preparation of the battlefield and reconnaissance and surveillance. Most of the intelligence staff section resides in this cell. The unit's intelligence officer leads this cell.

Movement and Maneuver Cell

3-32. The movement and maneuver cell coordinates activities and systems that move forces to achieve a position of advantage. This includes tasks associated with combining forces with direct fire or fire potential (maneuver) and force projection (movement) related to gaining a positional advantage. Elements of the operations, airspace integration, aviation, engineer, geospatial information and service, and space support element form this cell. The unit's operations officer leads this cell. Staff elements in the movement and maneuver cell also form the core of the current operations integration cell. (See paragraphs 3-43 through 3-45.)

Fires Cell

3-33. The fires cell coordinates activities and systems that provide collective and coordinated use of Army indirect fires, joint fires, and cyber/electromagnetic activities through the targeting process. The fires cell consists of elements of fire support, the Air Force (or air component), cyberspace operations, and the electronic warfare staff section. The unit's chief of fires (or fire support officer at brigade and below) leads this cell.

Protection Cell

3-34. The protection cell coordinates the activities and systems that preserve the force through composite risk management. This includes tasks associated with protecting personnel, physical assets, and information. Elements of the following staff sections form this cell: air and missile defense; chemical, biological, radiological, and nuclear; engineer; operations security; personnel recovery; force health protection; explosive ordnance disposal; and provost marshal. Additionally, a safety officer is assigned at theater army and with augmentation as required down to the brigade level. The protection cell coordinates with the signal staff section in the mission command cell to further facilitate the information protection task. The chief of protection leads this cell.

Sustainment Cell

3-35. The sustainment cell coordinates activities and systems that provide support and services to ensure freedom of action, extend operational reach, and prolong endurance. It includes those tasks associated with logistics, personnel services, Army health system support, and operational contract support. The following staff sections form this cell: personnel, logistics, financial management, engineer, and surgeon. The chief of sustainment (or logistics officer at brigade and below) leads this cell.

Mission Command Cell

3-36. The mission command cell is made up of the G-7 inform and influence activities section, the G-6 signal staff section, and the G-9 civil affairs operations staff section. The mission command cell is unique since it is not responsible for all the tasks associated to the mission command warfighting functions. For example, execution of the operations process primarily occurs in the plans, future operations, and current operations integration cells. The mission command cell is also unique in that the staff sections that reside in this cell report directly to the COS and not through a cell chief.

INTEGRATING CELLS

3-37. Whereas functional cells are organized by warfighting functions, integrating cells are organized by planning horizon. They coordinate and synchronize forces and warfighting functions within a specified planning horizon and include the plans, future operations, and current operations integration cells. A *planning horizon* is a point in time commanders use to focus the organization's planning efforts to shape future events (FM 5-0). The three planning horizons are long, mid, and short (generally associated with the plans cell, future operations cell, and current operations integration cell, respectively). Planning horizons are situation-dependent; they can range from hours and days to weeks and months. As a rule, the higher the echelon, the more distant the planning horizon with which it is concerned.

3-38. Not all echelons and types of units are resourced for all three integrating cells. Battalions, for example, combine their planning and operations responsibilities in one integrating cell. The brigade combat team has a small, dedicated plans cell but is not resourced for a future operations cell. Divisions and above are resourced for all three integrating cells as shown in Figure 3-2.

Plans Cell

3-39. The plans cell is responsible for planning operations for the long-range planning horizons. It prepares for operations beyond the scope of the current order by developing plans and orders, including branch plans and sequels. The plans cell also oversees military deception planning.

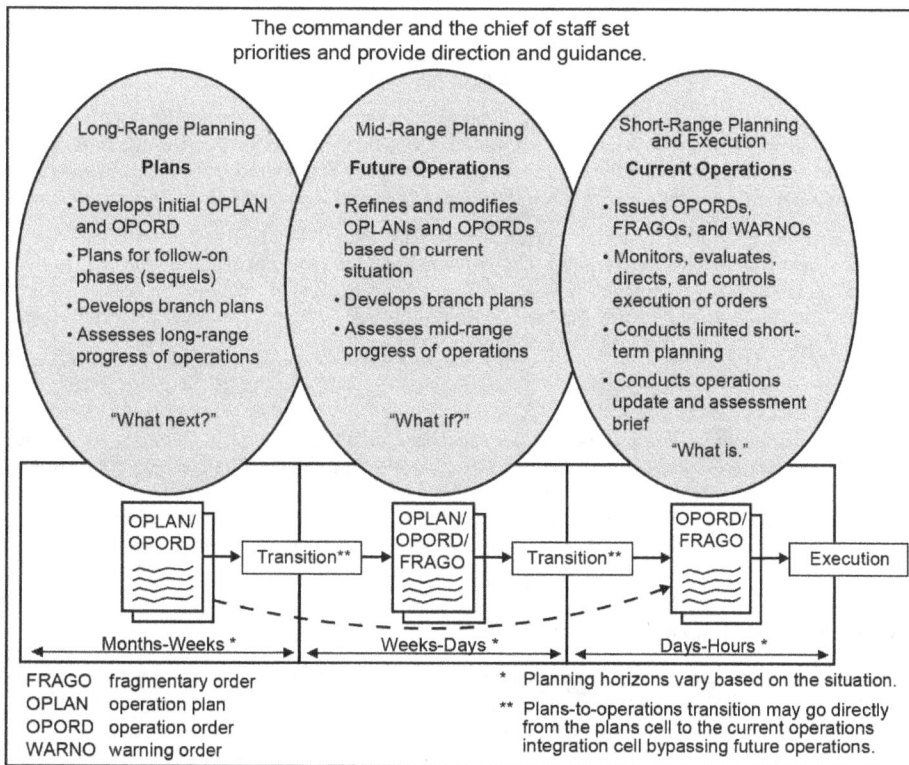

Figure 3-2. Integration of plans, future operations, and current operations

3-40. The plans cell consists of a core group of planners and analysts led by the plans officer (or the operations officer at battalion level). All staff sections assist as required. Whereas a brigade has a small, dedicated plans cell, the majority of its staff sections balance their efforts between the current operations integration and plans cells. Battalions are not resourced for a plans cell. Planning in combined arms battalions occurs in the current operations integration cell.

Future Operations Cell

3-41. The future operations cell is responsible for planning operations in the mid-range planning horizon. It focuses on adjustments to the current operation—including the positioning or maneuvering of forces in depth—that facilitates continuation of the current operation. The cell consists of a core group of planners led by an assistant operations officer (the chief of future operations). All staff sections assist as required. Divisions and above headquarters have a future operations cell. Battalion and brigade headquarters do not.

3-42. In many respects, the future operations cell serves as a fusion cell between the plans and current operations integration cells. The future operations cell monitors current operations and determines implications for operations within the mid-range planning horizon. In coordination with the current operations integration cell, the future operations cell assesses whether the ongoing operation must be modified to achieve the current phase's objectives. Normally, the commander directs adjustments to the operation, but the cell may also recommend options to the commander. Once the commander decides to adjust the operation, the cell develops the fragmentary order necessary to implement the change. The future operations cell also participates in the targeting working group since the same planning horizons normally concern them both. The future operations cell updates and adds details to the branch plans foreseen in the current operation and prepares any orders necessary to implement a sequel to the operation.

Current Operations Integration Cell

3-43. The current operations integration cell is the focal point for the execution of the operations. This involves assessing the current situation while regulating forces and warfighting functions in accordance with the mission, commander's intent, and concept of operations.

3-44. The current operations integration cell displays the common operational picture and conducts shift changes, assessments, and other briefings as required. It provides information on the status of operations to all staff members and to higher, subordinate, and adjacent units. The operations synchronization meeting is the most important event in the battle rhythm in support of the current operation.

3-45. The operations officer leads the current operations integration cell and is aided by an assistant operations officer (the chief of operations). The movement and maneuver cell forms the core of the current operations integration cell. Elements or watch officers from each staff section and liaison officers from subordinate and adjacent units form the remainder of the cell. All staff sections are represented in the current operations integration cell, either permanently or on call.

Staff Sections

3-46. Not all staff sections reside in one of the functional or integrating cells. Personal staff officers and their associated staff sections such as the inspector general and public affairs staff sections are examples. Special staff sections such as the operations research and systems analysis, red team, and knowledge management are other examples. These staff sections maintain their distinct organizations. They operate in different CP cells as required and coordinate their activities in the various meetings established in the unit's battle rhythm.

COMMAND POST OPERATIONS

3-47. Units must man, equip, and organize command posts to control operations for extended periods. Effective CP personnel, information systems, and equipment support 24-hour operations while continuously communicating with all subordinate units and higher and adjacent units. Commanders arrange CP personnel and equipment to facilitate internal coordination, information sharing, and rapid decisionmaking. They also ensure they have procedures to execute the operations process within the headquarters to enhance how they exercise mission command. Commanders use SOPs, battle rhythm, and meetings to assist them with effective CP operations.

STANDARD OPERATING PROCEDURES

3-48. SOPs that assist with effective mission command serve two purposes. Internal SOPs standardize each CP's internal operations and administration. External SOPs developed for the entire force standardize interactions among CPs and between subordinate units and CPs. Effective SOPs require all Soldiers to know their provisions and train to their standards. (Refer to FM 7-15 for more information on the tasks of command post operations.)

3-49. Each CP should have SOPs that address the following:
- Organization and setup.
- Staffing and shifts plans, including eating and sleeping plans.
- Physical security and defense.
- Priorities of work.
- Equipment and vehicle maintenance, including journals and a maintenance log.
- Load plans and equipment checklists.
- Orders production and dissemination procedures.
- Plans for handling, storing, and cleaning up hazardous materials.

3-50. In addition to these SOPS, each CP requires—
- CP battle drills.
- Shift-change briefings.

- Reports and returns.
- Operations update and assessment briefings.
- Operations synchronization meeting.
- Transferring control between CPs.

Command Post Battle Drills

3-51. Each CP requires procedures to react to a variety of situations. Specific actions taken by a CP should be defined in its SOPs and rehearsed during training and operations. Typical CP battle drills include, but are not limited to—

- React to an air, ground, or chemical attack.
- React to indirect fire.
- React to jamming or suspected communications compromise.
- Execute time-sensitive targets.
- Execute a close air support or joint fires mission.
- React to a mass casualty incident.
- React to a civil riot or incident.
- React to significant collateral damage.
- React to a misinformation incident.

Shift-Change Briefings

3-52. During continuous operations, CPs operate in shifts. To ensure uninterrupted operations, staffs execute a briefing when shifts change. Depending on the situation, it may be formal or informal and include the entire staff or selected staff members. Normally key CP leaders meet face-to-face. The COS (XO) oversees the briefing, with participants briefing their areas of expertise. The briefing's purpose is to inform the incoming shift of—

- Current unit status.
- Significant activities that occurred during the previous shift.
- Significant decisions and events anticipated during the next shift.

The commander may attend and possibly change the focus of the briefing. If the commander issues guidance or makes a decision, issuing a fragmentary order may be necessary.

3-53. The shift-change briefing format and emphasis change based on the situation. For example, the format for a force supporting civil authorities in a disaster area differs from a force conducting offensive operations abroad. To facilitate a quick but effective shift-change briefing, unit SOPs should contain tailored formats.

3-54. The shift-change briefing provides a mechanism to formally exchange information periodically among CP staff members. CP staff members coordinate activities and inform each other continuously. They give information that answers a commander's critical information requirement and exceptional information to the commander immediately. They disseminate information that potentially affects the entire force to the commander, higher headquarters, and subordinate units as the situation dictates. Situational understanding for CP staff members includes knowing who needs what relevant information and why they need it. CP staff members exercise initiative when they ensure relevant information gets to people who need it. Refer to Figure 3-3, page 3-10.

Reports and Returns

3-55. A unit's reporting system facilitates timely and effective information exchange among CPs and higher, lower, and adjacent headquarters. An established SOP for reports and returns drives effective information management. These SOPs state the writer, the frequency and time, and recipient of each report. List nonstandard reports in Annex R (Reports) of the operation plan and operation order.

Current mission and commander's intent (COS [XO])

Enemy situation (G-2 [S-2])
- Significant enemy actions during the last shift.
- Current enemy situation and changes in the most likely enemy courses of action.
- Anticipated significant threat activity in the next 12/24/48 hours.
- Changes in priority intelligence requirements (PIRs).
- Limited visibility and weather update.
- Changes to collection priorities and updates to the intelligence synchronization tools.
- Disposition and status of selected reconnaissance and surveillance units and capabilities.

Civil Situation (G-9 [S-9])
- Significant actions by the population during the last shift.
- Current civil situation.
- Disposition and status of civil affairs units and capabilities.
- Significant activities involving the population anticipated during the next shift.

Friendly situation (G-3 [S-3])
- Significant friendly actions during the last shift.
- Subordinate units' disposition and status.
- Higher and adjacent units' disposition and status.
- Major changes to the task organization and tasks to subordinate units that occurred during the last shift.
- Answers to CCIRs and changes in CCIRs.
- Changes to reconnaissance and surveillance.
- Disposition and status of selected reconnaissance and surveillance units and capabilities.
- Answers to FFIRs and changes in FFIRs.
- Significant activities and decisions scheduled for next shift (review of the decision support matrix).
- Anticipated planning requirements.

Running estimate summaries by warfighting function and staff section.

Briefers include—
- Fires.
- Air liaison officer.
- Aviation officer.
- Air and missile defense officer .
- G-7 (S-7).
- Engineer officer.
- Chemical officer.
- Provost marshal.
- G-1 (S-1).
- G-4 (S-4).
- G-6 (S-6).

Briefings include—
- Any significant activities that occurred during the last shift.
- The disposition and status of units within their area of expertise.
- Any changes that have staff wide implications (for example, "higher headquarters changed the controlled supply rate for 120 mm HE, so that means...").
- Upcoming activities and anticipated changes during the next shift.

CP operations and administration (headquarters commandant or senior operations noncommissioned officer).
- CP logistic issues.
- CP security.
- CP displacement plan and proposed new locations.
- Priority of work.

COS or XO guidance to the next shift, including staff priorities and changes to the battle rhythm.

CCIR	commander's critical information requirement	FFIR	friendly forces information requirement
COS	chief of staff	HE	high explosive
CP	command post	mm	millimeter

Figure 3-3. Sample shift-change briefing

Operation Update and Assessment Briefing

3-56. An operation update and assessment briefing may occur daily or anytime the commander calls for one. Its content is similar to the shift-change briefing but has a different audience. The staff presents it to the commander and subordinate commanders. It provides all key personnel with common situational awareness. Often commanders require this briefing shortly before an operation begins to summarize changes made during preparation, including changes resulting from reconnaissance and surveillance efforts.

3-57. During the briefing, staff sections present their running estimates. Subordinate commanders brief their current situation and planned activities. Rarely do all members conduct this briefing face-to-face. All CPs and subordinate commanders participate using available communications, including radio, conference calls, and video teleconference. The briefing follows a sequence and format specified by SOPs. That keeps transmissions short, ensures completeness, and eases note taking. This briefing normally has a format similar to a shift-change briefing. However, it omits CP administrative information and includes presentations by subordinate commanders in an established sequence.

Operations Synchronization Meeting

3-58. The operations synchronization meeting is the key event in the battle rhythm in support of the current operation. Its primary purpose is to synchronize all warfighting functions and other activities in the short-term planning horizon. It is designed to ensure that all staff members have a common understanding of current operations, including upcoming and projected actions at decision points.

3-59. The operations synchronization meeting does not replace the shift-change briefing or operation update and assessment briefing. Chaired by the G-3 (S-3), representatives of each CP cell and separate staff section attend the meeting. The operations synchronization meeting includes a fragmentary order addressing any required changes to maintain synchronization of current operations, and any updated planning guidance for upcoming working groups and boards. All warfighting functions are synchronized and appropriate fragmentary orders are issued to subordinates based on the commander's intent for current operations.

Transferring Control of Operations Between Command Posts

3-60. The employment and use of CPs are important decisions reflected in the operation order. Often, a particular CP may control part or all of the operation for a specific time. Effectively transferring control between CPs requires a well-understood SOP and clear instructions in the operation order.

3-61. While all CPs have some ability to exercise control on the move, they lose many capabilities they have when stationary. Therefore, CPs normally control operations from a static location. During moves, they transfer control responsibilities to another CP. Transfer of control requires notifying subordinates since many network operations change to route information to the new controlling CP. SOPs establish these requirements to minimize interruptions when transferring control.

BATTLE RHYTHM

3-62. A headquarters' battle rhythm consists of a series of meetings, briefings, and other activities synchronized by time and purpose. *Battle rhythm* is a deliberate daily cycle of command, staff, and unit activities intended to synchronize current and future operations (JP 3-33). The COS (XO) oversees the battle rhythm. Staffs should logically sequence each meeting, to include working groups and boards, so they have one meeting's outputs available as another meeting's inputs (to include higher headquarters meetings). The COS (XO) balances other staff duties and responsibilities with the time required to plan, prepare for, and hold meetings and conduct briefings. The COS (XO) also critically examines attendance requirements. Some staff sections and CP cells may lack the personnel to attend all events. The COS (XO) and staff members constantly look for ways to combine meetings and eliminate unproductive ones.

3-63. The battle rhythm enables—

- Establishing a routine for staff interaction and coordination.
- Facilitating interaction between the commander and staff.

- Synchronizing activities of the staff in time and purpose.
- Facilitating planning by the staff and decisionmaking by the commander.

3-64. The battle rhythm changes during execution as operations progress. For example, early in the operation a commander may require a daily plans update briefing. As the situation changes, the commander may only require a plans update every three days. Some factors that help determine a unit's battle rhythm include the staff's proficiency, higher headquarters' battle rhythm, and current mission. In developing the unit's battle rhythm, the chief COS (XO) considers—

- Higher headquarters' battle rhythm and report requirements.
- Subordinate headquarters' battle rhythm requirements.
- The duration and intensity of the operation.
- Integrating cells' planning requirements.

MEETINGS

3-65. Meetings are gatherings to present and exchange information, solve problems, coordinate action, and make decisions. They may involve the staff; the commander and staff; or the commander, subordinate commanders, staff, and other partners. Who attends depends on the issue. Commanders establish meetings to integrate the staff and enhance planning and decisionmaking within the headquarters. Commanders also identify staff members to participate in the higher commander's meeting, including working groups and boards. (JP 3-33 discusses the various working groups and boards used by joint force commanders.)

3-66. The number of meetings and subjects they address depend on the situation and echelon. While numerous informal meetings occur daily within a headquarters, meetings commonly included in a unit's battle rhythm and the cells responsible for them include—

- A shift-change briefing (current operations integration cell).
- An operation update and assessment briefing (current operations integration cell).
- An operations synchronization meeting (current operations integration cell).
- Planning meetings and briefings (plans or future operations cells).
- Working groups and boards (various functional and integrating cells).

3-67. Often, the commander establishes and maintains only those meetings required by the situation. Commanders—assisted by the COS (XO)—establish, modify, and dissolve meetings as the situation evolves. The COS (XO) manages the timings of these events through the unit's battle rhythm. (See paragraphs 3-62 through 3-64.)

3-68. For each meeting, a unit's SOPs address—

- Purpose.
- Frequency.
- Composition (chair and participants).
- Inputs and expected outputs.
- Agenda.

See Figure 3-4 for an example SOP item for a working group.

3-69. Working groups and boards are types of meetings and are included on the unit's battle rhythm. **A** *working group* **is a grouping of predetermined staff representatives who meet to provide analysis, coordinate, and provide recommendations for a particular purpose or function**. Their cross-functional design enables working groups to synchronize contributions from multiple CP cells and staff sections. For example, the targeting working group brings together representatives of all staff elements concerned with targeting. It synchronizes the contributions of all staff elements with the work of the fires cell. It also synchronizes fires with future operations and current operations integration cells.

3-70. Working groups address various subjects depending on the situation and echelon. Battalion and brigade headquarters normally have fewer working groups than higher echelons have. Working groups may convene daily, weekly, monthly, or intermittently depending on the subject, situation, and echelon. Typical working groups and the lead cell or staff section at division and corps headquarters include the—

- Assessment working group (plans or future operations cell).
- Intelligence, surveillance, and reconnaissance working group (intelligence cell).
- Targeting working group (fires cell).
- Protection working group (protection cell).
- Civil affairs operations working group (civil affairs operations staff section).
- Communications strategy working group.

Purpose/Frequency	**Purpose:** • Establish policies, procedures, priorities, and overall direction for all civil-military operations projects • Provide update on ongoing civil-military operations projects • Identify needs within the area of operations • Present suggested future projects **Frequency:** Weekly
Composition	**Chair:** G-9 **Attendees:** • Civil affairs battalion representative • G-2 planner • G-3 operations representative • G-5 planner • G-7 representative • Staff Judge Advocate representative • Military information support planner • Host-nation liaison officers • Engineer planner • Military information support element representative • Provost marshal or force protection representative • Special operations forces liaison officer • Surgeon • Chaplain • Project manager and contractor representatives • Brigade combat team and Marine Corps liaison officer
Inputs/Outputs	**Inputs:** • Project management status • Inform and influence activities working group (last week's) • Targeting board • Higher headquarters operation order **Outputs:** • Updated project status matrix • Proposed project matrix • Long-range civil-military operations plan adjustment
Agenda	• G-2 update or assessment • Operations update • Public perception update • Civil affairs project update • Engineer project update • Staff Judge Advocate concerns • Discussion or issues • Approval of information operations working group inputs

Figure 3-4. Sample SOP for a division civil-military operations working group

3-71. A *board* is a grouping of predetermined staff representatives with delegated decision authority for a particular purpose or function. Boards are similar to working groups. However, commanders appoint boards with the purpose to arrive at a decision. When the process or activity being synchronized requires command approval, a board is the appropriate forum.

This page intentionally left blank.

Chapter 4

The Military Decisionmaking Process

This chapter defines and describes the military decisionmaking process. Effectively conducting the military decisionmaking process requires leaders who understand the military decisionmaking process characteristics, steps, and plans. FM 5-0 addresses the fundamentals of planning.

CHARACTERISTICS OF THE MILITARY DECISIONMAKING PROCESS

4-1. The *military decisionmaking process* is an iterative planning methodology that integrates the activities of the commander, staff, subordinate headquarters, and other partners to understand the situation and mission; develop and compare courses of action; decide on a course of action that best accomplishes the mission; and produce an operation plan or order for execution (FM 5-0). The military decisionmaking process (MDMP) helps leaders apply thoroughness, clarity, sound judgment, logic, and professional knowledge to understand situations, develop options to solve problems, and reach decisions. This process helps commanders, staffs, and others think critically and creatively while planning.

> *Note:* An Army headquarters (battalion through Army Service component command) uses the MDMP and publishes plans and orders in accordance with the Army plans and orders format (see Chapter 12).
>
> An Army headquarters that forms the base of a joint task force uses the joint operation planning process (JOPP) and publishes plans and orders in accordance with the joint format (see JP 5-0 and CJCSM 3122.03C).
>
> An Army headquarters (such as Army Corps) that provides the base of a joint force or coalition forces land component command headquarters will participate in joint planning and receive a joint formatted plan or order. This headquarters then has the option to use the MDMP or JOPP to develop its own supporting plan or order written in the proper Army or joint format to distribute to subordinate commands.

4-2. The MDMP facilitates collaborative planning. The higher headquarters solicits input and continuously shares information concerning future operations through planning meetings, warning orders, and other means. It shares information with subordinate and adjacent units, supporting and supported units, and other military and civilian partners. Commanders encourage active collaboration among all organizations affected by the pending operations to build a shared understanding of the situation, participate in course of action development and decisionmaking, and resolve conflicts before publishing the plan or order.

4-3. During planning, assessment focuses on developing an understanding of the current situation and determining what to assess and how to assess progress using measures of effectiveness and measures of performance. Developing the unit's assessment plan occurs during the MDMP—not after developing the plan or order. (Chapter 7 discusses formal assessment plans.)

4-4. The MDMP also drives preparation. Since time is a factor in all operations, commanders and staffs conduct a time analysis early in the planning process. This analysis helps them determine what actions they need and when to begin those actions to ensure forces are ready and in position before execution. This may require the commander to direct subordinates to start necessary movements, conduct task organization changes, begin surveillance and reconnaissance operations, and execute other preparation activities before completing the plan. As the commander and staff conduct the MDMP, they direct the tasks in a series of warning orders (WARNOs).

4-5. Depending on complexity of the situation, commanders can initiate design activities before or in parallel with the MDMP. Design can assist them in understanding the operational environment, framing the problem, and considering operational approaches to solve or manage the problem. The products of design, including the design concept, would guide more detailed planning as part of the MDMP. In parallel with the MDMP, members of the staff conduct mission analysis as the commander and other staff members engage in design activities prior to course of action development. In time-constrained conditions or if the problem is relatively straight forward, commanders can conduct the MDMP without the benefit of a formal design process. During execution, the commander can conduct design to help refine the understanding and visualization, and adjust the plan as required.

THE MILITARY DECISIONMAKING PROCESS SEVEN STEPS

4-6. The MDMP consists of seven steps as shown in Figure 4-1. Each step of the MDMP has various inputs, a method (step) to conduct, and outputs. The outputs lead to an increased understanding of the situation facilitating the next step of the MDMP. Commanders and staffs generally perform these steps sequentially; however, they may revisit several steps in an iterative fashion as they learn more about the situation before producing the plan or order.

4-7. Commanders initiate the MDMP upon receipt of or in anticipation of a mission. Commanders and staffs often begin planning in the absence of a complete and approved higher headquarters' operation plan (OPLAN) or operation order (OPORD). In these instances, the headquarters begins a new planning effort based on a WARNO and other directives, such as a planning order or an alert order from their higher headquarters. This requires active collaboration with the higher headquarters and parallel planning among echelons as the plan or order is developed.

THE ROLE OF COMMANDERS AND STAFFS IN THE MILITARY DECISIONMAKING PROCESS

4-8. The commander is the most important participant in the MDMP. More than simply decisionmakers in this process, commanders use their experience, knowledge, and judgment to guide staff planning efforts. While unable to devote all their time to the MDMP, commanders follow the status of the planning effort, participate during critical periods of the process, and make decisions based on the detailed work of the staff. During the MDMP, commanders focus their activities on understanding, visualizing, and describing.

4-9. The MDMP stipulates several formal meetings and briefings between the commander and staff to discuss, assess, and approve or disapprove planning efforts as they progress. However, experience has shown that optimal planning results when the commander meets informally at frequent intervals with the staff throughout the MDMP. Such informal interaction between the commander and staff can improve the staff's understanding of the situation and ensure their planning effort adequately reflects the commander's visualization of the operation.

4-10. The chief of staff (COS) or executive officer (XO) is a key participant in the MDMP. The COS (XO) manages and coordinates the staff's work and provides quality control during the MDMP. To effectively supervise the entire process, this officer clearly understands the commander's intent and guidance. The COS (XO) provides timelines to the staff, establishes briefing times and locations, and provides any instructions necessary to complete the plan.

4-11. The staff's effort during the MDMP focuses on helping the commander understand the situation, make decisions, and synchronize those decisions into a fully developed plan or order. Staff activities during planning initially focus on mission analysis. The products the staff develops during mission analysis help commanders understand the situation and develop the commander's visualization. During course of action (COA) development and COA comparison, the staff provides recommendations to support the commander in selecting a COA. After the commander makes a decision, the staff prepares the plan or order that reflects the commander's intent, coordinating all necessary details.

Key inputs	Steps	Key outputs
• Higher headquarters' plan or order or a new mission anticipated by the commander	**Step 1:** **Receipt of Mission**	• Commander's initial guidance • Initial allocation of time
	Warning order	
• Higher headquarters' plan or order • Higher headquarters' knowledge and intelligence products • Knowledge products from other organizations • Design concept (if developed)	**Step 2:** **Mission Analysis**	• Problem statement • Mission statement • Initial commander's intent • Initial planning guidance • Initial CCIRs and EEFIs • Updated IPB and running estimates • Assumptions
	Warning order	

• Mission statement
• Initial commander's intent, planning guidance, CCIRs, and EEFIs
• Updated IPB and running estimates
• Assumptions
	Step 3:
	Course of Action (COA) Development
		• COA statements and sketches
		  - Tentative task organization
		  - Broad concept of operations
		• Revised planning guidance
		• Updated assumptions

• Updated running estimates • Revised planning guidance • COA statements and sketches • Updated assumptions	**Step 4:** **COA Analysis (War Game)**	• Refined COAs • Potential decision points • War-game results • Initial assessment measures • Updated assumptions
• Updated running estimates • Refined COAs • Evaluation criteria • War-game results • Updated assumptions	**Step 5:** **COA Comparison**	• Evaluated COAs • Recommended COAs • Updated running estimates • Updated assumptions
• Updated running estimates • Evaluated COAs • Recommended COA • Updated assumptions	**Step 6:** **COA Approval**	• Commander-selected COA and any modifications • Refined commander's intent, CCIRs, and EEFIs • Updated assumptions
	Warning order	
• Commander-selected COA with any modifications • Refined commander's intent, CCIRs, and EEFIs • Updated assumptions	**Step 7:** **Orders Production**	• Approved operation plan or order
CCIR commander's critical information requirement COA course of action		EEFI essential element of friendly information IPB intelligence preparation of the battlefield

Figure 4-1. The steps of the military decisionmaking process

MODIFYING THE MILITARY DECISIONMAKING PROCESS

4-12. The MDMP can be as detailed as time, resources, experience, and the situation permit. Conducting all steps of the MDMP is detailed, deliberate, and time-consuming. Commanders use the full MDMP when they have enough planning time and staff support to thoroughly examine two or more COAs and develop a fully synchronized plan or order. This typically occurs when planning for an entirely new mission.

4-13. Commanders may alter the steps of the MDMP to fit time-constrained circumstances and produce a satisfactory plan. In time-constrained conditions, commanders assess the situation, update the commander's visualization, and direct the staff to perform the MDMP activities that support the required decisions. (See paragraphs 4-186 through 4-189.) In extremely compressed situations, commanders rely on more intuitive decisionmaking techniques, such as the rapid decisionmaking and synchronization process.

STEPS OF THE MILITARY DECISIONMAKING PROCESS

4-14. The remainder of this chapter describes the methods and provides techniques for conducting each step of the MDMP. It describes the key inputs and expected key outputs to each step. It also describes how the staff integrates intelligence preparation of the battlefield (IPB), targeting, composite risk management (CRM), and reconnaissance and surveillance synchronization throughout the MDMP.

STEP 1 – RECEIPT OF MISSION

4-15. Commanders initiate the MDMP upon receipt or in anticipation of a mission. This step alerts all participants of the pending planning requirements, enabling them to determine the amount of time available for planning and preparation and decide on a planning approach, including guidance on design and how to abbreviate the MDMP, if required. When commanders identify a new mission, commanders and staffs perform the actions and produce the expected key outputs.

Alert the Staff and Other Key Participants

4-16. As soon as a unit receives a new mission (or when the commander directs), the current operations integration cell alerts the staff of the pending planning requirement. Unit standard operating procedures (SOPs) should identify members of the planning staff who participate in mission analysis. In addition, the current operations integration cell also notifies other military, civilian, and host-nation organizations of pending planning events as required.

Gather the Tools

4-17. Once notified of the new planning requirement, the staff prepares for mission analysis by gathering the needed tools. These tools include, but are not limited to—

- Appropriate field manuals, including FM 5-0 and FM 1-02.
- All documents related to the mission and area of operations (AO), including the higher headquarters' OPLAN and OPORD, maps and terrain products, and operational graphics.
- Higher headquarters' and other organizations' intelligence and assessment products.
- Estimates and products of other military and civilian agencies and organizations.
- Both their own and the higher headquarters' SOPs.
- Current running estimates.
- Any design products, including the design concept.

4-18. The gathering of knowledge products continues throughout the MDMP. Staff officers carefully review the reference sections (located before paragraph **1. Situation**) of the higher headquarters' OPLANs and OPORDs to identify documents (such as theater policies and memoranda) related to the upcoming operation. If the MDMP occurs while in the process of replacing another unit, the staff begins collecting relevant documents—such as the current OPORD, branch plans, current assessments, operations and intelligence summaries, and SOPs—from that unit.

Update Running Estimates

4-19. While gathering the necessary tools for planning, each staff section begins updating its running estimate—especially the status of friendly units and resources and key civil considerations that affect each functional area. Running estimates not only compile critical facts and assumptions from the perspective of each staff section, but also include information from other staff sections and other military and civilian organizations. While listed at the beginning of the MDMP, this task of developing and updating running estimates continues throughout the MDMP and the operations process.

Conduct Initial Assessment

4-20. During receipt of mission, the commander and staff conduct an initial assessment of time and resources available to plan, prepare, and begin execution of an operation. This initial assessment helps commanders determine—

- The time needed to plan and prepare for the mission for both headquarters and subordinate units.
- Guidance on design and abbreviating the MDMP, if required.
- Which outside agencies and organizations to contact and incorporate into the planning process.
- The staff's experience, cohesiveness, and level of rest or stress.

4-21. This assessment primarily identifies an initial allocation of available time. The commander and staff balance the desire for detailed planning against the need for immediate action. The commander provides guidance to subordinate units as early as possible to allow subordinates the maximum time for their own planning and preparation of operations. As a rule, commanders allocate a minimum of two-thirds of available time for subordinate units to conduct their planning and preparation. This leaves one-third of the time for commanders and their staff to do their planning. They use the other two-thirds for their own preparation. Time, more than any other factor, determines the detail to which the commander and staff can plan.

4-22. Based on the commander's initial allocation of time, the COS (XO) develops a staff planning timeline that outlines how long the headquarters can spend on each step of the MDMP. The staff planning timeline indicates what products are due, who is responsible for them, and who receives them. It includes times and locations for meetings and briefings. It serves as a benchmark for the commander and staff throughout the MDMP.

Issue the Commander's Initial Guidance

4-23. Once time is allocated, the commander determines whether to initiate design, conduct design and MDMP in parallel, or proceed directly into the MDMP without the benefits of formal design activities. In time-sensitive situations where commanders decide to proceed directly into the MDMP, they may also issue guidance on how to abbreviate the process. Having determined the time available together with the scope and scale of the planning effort, commanders issue initial planning guidance. Although brief, the initial guidance includes, but is not limited to—

- Initial time allocations.
- A decision to initiate design or go straight into the MDMP.
- How to abbreviate the MDMP, if required.
- Necessary coordination to exchange liaison officers.
- Authorized movements and initiation of any reconnaissance and surveillance.
- Collaborative planning times and locations.
- Initial information requirements.
- Additional staff tasks.

Issue the Initial Warning Order

4-24. The last task in receipt of mission is to issue a WARNO to subordinate and supporting units. This order includes at a minimum the type of operation, the general location of the operation, the initial timeline, and any movement or reconnaissance to initiate.

STEP 2 – MISSION ANALYSIS

4-25. The MDMP continues with an assessment of the situation called mission analysis. Commanders (supported by their staffs and informed by subordinate and adjacent commanders and by other partners) gather, analyze, and synthesize information to orient themselves on the current conditions of the operational environment. The commander and staff conduct mission analysis to better understand the situation and problem, and identify *what* the command must accomplish, *when* and *where* it must be done, and most importantly *why*—the purpose of the operation.

4-26. Since no amount of subsequent planning can solve an insufficiently understood problem, *mission analysis is the most important step in the MDMP*. This understanding of the situation and the problem allows commanders to visualize and describe how the operation may unfold in their initial commander's intent and planning guidance. During mission analysis, the commander and staff perform the process actions and produce the outputs shown in Figure 4-2.

Analyze the Higher Headquarters' Plan or Order

4-27. Commanders and staffs thoroughly analyze the higher headquarters' plan or order. They determine how their unit—by task and purpose—contributes to the mission, commander's intent, and concept of operations of the higher headquarters. The commander and staff seek to completely understand—

- The higher headquarters'—
  - Commander's intent.
  - Mission.
  - Concept of operations.
  - Available assets.
  - Timeline.
- The missions of adjacent, supporting, and supported units and their relationships to the higher headquarters' plan.
- The missions of interagency, intergovernmental, and nongovernmental organizations that work in the operational areas.
- Their assigned area of operations.

4-28. If the commander misinterprets the higher headquarters' plan, time is wasted. Additionally, when analyzing the higher order, the commander and staff may identify difficulties and contradictions in the higher order. Therefore, if confused by the higher headquarters' order or guidance, commanders must seek immediate clarification. Liaison officers familiar with the higher headquarters' plan can help clarify issues. Collaborative planning with the higher headquarters also facilitates this task. Staffs use requests for information to clarify or obtain additional information from the higher headquarters.

Perform Initial Intelligence Preparation of the Battlefield

4-29. IPB and the products it produces help the commander and staffs understand situations. IPB is a systematic, continuous process of analyzing the threat and operational environment in a specific geographic area. Led by the intelligence officer, the entire staff participates in IPB to develop and maintain an understanding of the enemy, terrain and weather, and key civil considerations. (See FM 2-01.3 for a more detailed discussion of IPB.)

4-30. IPB begins in mission analysis and continues throughout the operations process. Results of the initial IPB include terrain products and weather products (to include the modified combined obstacle overlay), likely enemy COAs, high-value target lists, and explanations of how key civil considerations affect the operation. Additionally, the initial IPB identifies gaps in information that the commander uses to establish initial priority intelligence requirements and requests for information.

Key inputs ➡	Process ➡	Key outputs
• Higher headquarters' plan or order • Higher headquarters' intelligence and knowledge products • Knowledge products from other organizations • Updated running estimates • Initial commander's guidance • COA evaluation criteria • Design concept (if design precedes mission analysis)	• Analyze the higher headquarters' plan or order • Perform initial IPB • Determine specified, implied, and essential tasks • Review available assets and identify resource shortfalls • Determine constraints • Identify critical facts and develop assumptions • Begin composite risk management • Develop initial CCIRs and EEFIs • Develop initial R&S synchronization tools • Develop initial R&S plan • Update plan for the use of available time • Develop initial themes and messages • Develop a proposed problem statement • Develop a proposed mission statement • Present the mission analysis briefing • Develop and issue initial commander's intent • Develop and issue initial planning guidance • Develop COA evaluation criteria • Issue a warning order	• Approved problem statement • Approved mission statement • Initial commander's intent • Initial CCIRs and EEFIs • Initial commander's planning guidance • Information themes and messages • Updated IPB products • Updated running estimates • Assumptions • Resource shortfalls • Updated operational timeline • COA evaluation criteria Warning Order

CCIR	commander's critical information requirement	IPB	intelligence preparation of the battlefield
COA	course of action	R&S	reconnaissance and surveillance
EEFI	essential element of friendly information		

Figure 4-2. Mission analysis

Determine Specified, Implied, and Essential Tasks

4-31. The staff analyzes the higher headquarters' order and the higher commander's guidance to determine their specified and implied tasks. In the context of operations, a task is a clearly defined and measurable activity accomplished by Soldiers, units, and organizations that may support or be supported by other tasks. The "what" of a mission statement is always a task. From the list of specified and implied tasks, the staff determines essential tasks for inclusion in the recommended mission statement.

4-32. A *specified task* **is a task specifically assigned to a unit by its higher headquarters**. Paragraphs 2 and 3 of the higher headquarters' order or plan state specified tasks. Some tasks may be in paragraphs 4 and 5. Specified tasks may be listed in annexes and overlays. They may also be assigned verbally during collaborative planning sessions or in directives from the higher commander.

4-33. **An *implied task* is a task that must be performed to accomplish a specified task or mission but is not stated in the higher headquarters' order.** Implied tasks are derived from a detailed analysis of the higher headquarters' order, the enemy situation, the terrain, and civil considerations. Additionally, analysis of doctrinal requirements for each specified task might disclose implied tasks.

4-34. When analyzing the higher order for specified and implied tasks, the staff also identifies any be-prepared or on-order missions. **A *be-prepared mission* is a mission assigned to a unit that might be executed.** Generally a contingency mission, commanders execute it because something planned has or has not been successful. In planning priorities, commanders plan a be-prepared mission after any on-order mission. **An *on-order mission* is a mission to be executed at an unspecified time.** A unit with an on-order mission is a committed force. Commanders envisions task execution in the concept of operations; however, they may not know the exact time or place of execution. Subordinate commanders develop plans and orders and allocate resources, task-organize, and position forces for execution.

4-35. Once staff members have identified specified and implied tasks, they ensure they understand each task's requirements and purpose. Once accomplished, the staff then looks for essential tasks. **An *essential task* is a specified or implied task that must be executed to accomplish the mission.** Essential tasks are always included in the unit's mission statement.

Review Available Assets and Identify Resource Shortfalls

4-36. The commander and staff examine additions to and deletions from the current task organization, command and support relationships, and status (current capabilities and limitations) of all units. This analysis also includes capabilities of civilian and military organizations (joint, special operations, and multinational) that operate within their unit's AO. They consider relationships among specified, implied, and essential tasks, and between them and available assets. From this analysis, staffs determine if they have the assets needed to complete all tasks. If shortages occur, they identify additional resources needed for mission success to the higher headquarters. Staffs also identify any deviations from the normal task organization and provide them to the commander to consider when developing the planning guidance. A more detailed analysis of available assets occurs during COA development.

Determine Constraints

4-37. The commander and staff identify any constraints placed on their command. **A *constraint* is a restriction placed on the command by a higher command. A constraint dictates an action or inaction, thus restricting the freedom of action of a subordinate commander.** Constraints are found in paragraph 3 of the OPLAN or OPORD. Annexes to the order may also include constraints. The operation overlay, for example, may contain a restrictive fire line or a no fire area. Constraints may also be issued verbally, in WARNOs, or in policy memoranda.

4-38. Constraints may also be based on resource limitations within the command, such as organic fuel transport capacity, or physical characteristics of the operational environment, such as the number of vehicles that can cross a bridge in a specified time.

4-39. The commander and staff should coordinate with the Staff Judge Advocate for a legal review of perceived or obvious constraints, restraints, or limitations in the OPLAN, OPORD, or related documents.

4-40. Joint doctrine's term *operational limitation* includes the terms constraints and restrictions. These latter terms differ from Army doctrine. Refer to JP 5-0 for joint definitions on operational limitations, constraints, and restraints.

Identify Critical Facts and Develop Assumptions

4-41. Plans and orders are based on facts and assumptions. Commanders and staffs gather facts and develop assumptions as they build their plan. A fact is a statement of truth or a statement thought to be true at the time. Facts concerning the operational and mission variables serve as the basis for developing situational understanding, for continued planning, and when assessing progress during preparation and execution.

4-42. In the absence of facts, the commander and staff consider assumptions from their higher headquarters and develop their own assumptions necessary for continued planning. An *assumption* is a supposition on the current situation or a presupposition on the future course of events, either or both assumed to be true in the absence of positive proof, necessary to enable the commander in the process of planning to complete an estimate of the situation and make a decision on the course of action (JP 1-02).

4-43. Having assumptions requires commanders and staff to continually attempt to replace those assumptions with facts. The commander and staff should list and review the key assumptions on which fundamental judgments rest throughout the MDMP. Rechecking assumptions is valuable at any time during the operations process prior to rendering judgments and making decisions.

Begin Composite Risk Management

4-44. The Army primarily uses CRM for identifying hazards and controlling risks during operations. *Risk management* is the process of identifying, assessing, and controlling risks arising from operational factors and of making decisions that balance risk costs with mission benefits (FM 5-19). (See FM 5-19 for a detailed discussion on CRM.)

4-45. The chief of protection (or S-3 in units without a protection cell) in coordination with the safety officer integrates CRM into the MDMP. All staff sections integrate CRM for hazards within their functional areas. Units conduct the first four steps of CRM in the MDMP. FM 5-19 addresses the details for conducting CRM, including products of each step.

Develop Initial Commander's Critical Information Requirements and Essential Elements of Friendly Information

4-46. Mission analysis identifies gaps in information required for further planning and decisionmaking during preparation and execution. During mission analysis, the staff develops information requirements (IRs). *Information requirements* are all information elements the commander and staff require to successfully conduct operations (FM 6-0). Some IRs are of such importance to the commander that staffs nominate them to the commander to become a commander's critical information requirement (CCIR). CCIRs consist of friendly force information requirements and priority intelligence requirements. (See FM 6-0.)

4-47. Commanders determine their CCIRs and consider the nominations of the staff. CCIRs are situation-dependent and specified by the commander for each operation. Commanders continuously review the CCIRs during the planning process and adjust them as situations change. The initial CCIRs developed during mission analysis normally focus on decisions the commander needs to make to focus planning. Once the commander selects a COA, the CCIRs shift to information the commander needs in order to make decisions during preparation and execution. Commanders designate CCIRs to inform the staff and subordinates what they deem essential for making decisions. The fewer the CCIRs, the better the staff can focus its efforts and allocate sufficient resources for collecting them.

4-48. In addition to nominating CCIRs to the commander, the staff also identifies and nominates essential elements of friendly information (EEFIs). Although EEFIs are not CCIRs, they have the same priority as CCIRs and require approval by the commander. An EEFI establishes an element of information to protect rather than one to collect. EEFIs identify those elements of friendly force information that, if compromised, would jeopardize mission success. Like CCIRs, EEFIs change as an operation progresses.

4-49. Depending on the situation, the commander and selected staff members meet prior to the mission analysis brief to approve the initial CCIRs and EEFIs. This is especially important if the commander intends to conduct reconnaissance and collect information early in the planning process. The approval of the initial CCIRs early in planning assist the staff in developing the initial reconnaissance and surveillance synchronization plan and the subsequent reconnaissance and surveillance plan. Approval of an EEFI allows the staff to begin planning and implementing measures to protect friendly force information, such as military deception and operations security.

Develop Initial Reconnaissance and Surveillance Synchronization Tools

4-50. Commanders use the reconnaissance and surveillance synchronization process to assess reconnaissance and surveillance asset reporting and adjust reconnaissance and surveillance activities. Reconnaissance and surveillance synchronization ensures the commander's requirements drive reconnaissance and surveillance activities and reporting in time to influence decisions and operations. Synchronizing includes all assets the commander controls, assets made available from lateral units or higher echelon units and organizations, requests for information, and intelligence reach to support intelligence production and dissemination that answer the CCIRs. During reconnaissance and surveillance synchronization, the G-2 (S-2)—

- Identifies requirements and intelligence gaps.
- Evaluates available assets (internal and external) to collect information.
- Determines gaps in the use of those assets.
- Recommends those reconnaissance and surveillance assets controlled by the organization to collect on the IRs.
- Submits requests for information for adjacent and higher collection support.
- Submits information gathered during reconnaissance and surveillance synchronization to the G-3 (S-3) for integrating and developing the reconnaissance and surveillance plan.

4-51. During mission analysis, the staff identifies IRs to support situational understanding and continued planning. Based on the commander's guidance, the staff, led by the G-2 (S-2), determines the best way of satisfying those requirements. In some instances, the G-2 (S-2) recommends the use of internal reconnaissance or surveillance assets to collect information. In other instances, the G-2 (S-2) recommends a request for information to the higher headquarters.

4-52. In many instances, a staff section within the headquarters can satisfy IRs by researching open sources. Open sources include books, magazines, encyclopedias, Web sites, and tourist maps. Academic sources, such as articles and university personnel, also provide critical information. Other open sources discuss civil considerations, such as culture, language, history, current events, and actions of governments. Teams of anthropologists and other social scientists attached to a headquarters rely heavily on open sources to satisfy IRs. The knowledge management staff section can also assist them in accessing specific data.

4-53. The results of reconnaissance and surveillance synchronization conducted during mission analysis leads to the creation of reconnaissance and surveillance synchronization tools. The intelligence staff section continues to refine these synchronization tools throughout the MDMP for inclusion in Annex L (Reconnaissance and Surveillance) of the plan or order.

Develop Initial Reconnaissance and Surveillance Plan

4-54. Reconnaissance and surveillance integration follows reconnaissance and surveillance synchronization. The G-3 (S-3) leads the staff through reconnaissance and surveillance integration to task available reconnaissance and surveillance assets to satisfy IRs identified in the initial reconnaissance and surveillance synchronization matrix. Reconnaissance and surveillance integration consists of the following tasks:

- Develop the reconnaissance and surveillance plan by developing—
  - The reconnaissance and surveillance scheme of support.
  - The reconnaissance and surveillance tasking matrix.
  - The reconnaissance and surveillance overlay.
- Issue order (warning, operation, or fragmentary order).

4-55. The initial reconnaissance and surveillance plan is crucial to begin or adjust the collection effort to help answer IRs identified during reconnaissance and surveillance synchronization. Reconnaissance and surveillance assets are tasked or dispatched as soon as possible. The initial reconnaissance and surveillance plan sets reconnaissance and surveillance in motion. Staff may issue it as part of a WARNO, a fragmentary order, or an OPORD. Upon the completion of planning, the initial reconnaissance and surveillance plan becomes Annex L (Reconnaissance and Surveillance) of the plan or order.

Update Plan for the Use of Available Time

4-56. As more information becomes available, the commander and staff refine their initial plan for the use of available time. They compare the time needed to accomplish tasks to the higher headquarters' timeline to ensure mission accomplishment is possible in the allotted time. They compare the timeline to the assumed enemy timeline or the projected timelines within the civil sector with how they anticipate conditions will unfold. From this, they determine windows of opportunity for exploitation, times when the unit will be at risk for enemy activity, or when action to arrest deterioration in the civil sector is required.

4-57. The commander and COS (XO) also refine the staff planning timeline. The refined timeline includes the—

- Subject, time, and location of briefings the commander requires.
- Times of collaborative planning sessions and the medium over which they will take place.
- Times, locations, and forms of rehearsals.

Develop Initial Themes and Messages

4-58. Gaining and maintaining the trust of key actors is an important aspect of operations. Faced with the many different actors (individuals, organizations, and the public) connected with the operation, commanders identify and engage those actors who matter to operational success. These actors' behaviors can help solve or complicate the friendly forces' challenges as commanders strive to accomplish missions.

4-59. Information themes and messages support operations and military actions. An information theme is a unifying or dominant idea or image that expresses the purpose for military action. Information themes tie to objectives, lines of effort, and end state conditions. They are overarching and apply to capabilities of public affairs, military information support operations, and leader and Soldier engagements. A message is a verbal, written, or electronic communications that supports an information theme focused on a specific actor or the public and in support of a specific action (task). Units transmit information themes and messages to those actors or the public whose perceptions, attitudes, beliefs, and behaviors matter to the success of an operation. Commanders and their units coordinate what they do, say, and portray through information themes and messages.

4-60. The G-7 (S-7) develops initial information themes and messages for the command. This officer, with support from the entire staff, reviews the higher headquarters' information themes and messages and military information support operations approval guidelines. If available, the G-7 (S-7) reviews internal design products, including the initial commander's intent, mission narrative, and planning guidance. This officer refines information themes and messages throughout the MDMP as commanders refine their commander's intent and planning guidance and staffs develop, evaluate, and decide COAs. The G-7 (S-7) coordinates inform and influence activities by chairing the communications strategy work group in the mission command cell.

Develop a Proposed Problem Statement

4-61. A problem is an issue or obstacle that makes it difficult to achieve a desired goal or objective. As such, a problem statement is the description of the primary issue or issues that may impede commanders from achieving their desired end states.

> *Note:* The commander, staff, and other partners develop the problem statement as part of design. During mission analysis, the commander and staff review the problem statement and revise it as necessary based on the increased understanding of the situation. If design activities do not precede mission analysis, then the commander and staff develop a problem statement prior to moving to COA development.

4-62. How the problem is formulated leads to particular solutions. As such, it is important that commanders dedicate the time in identifying the right problem to solve and describe it clearly in a problem statement. Ideally, the commander and members of the staff meet to share their analysis of the situation. They talk with each other, synthesize the results of the current mission analysis, and determine the problem. If the commander is not available, the staff members talk among themselves.

4-63. As part of the discussion to help identify and understand the problem, the staff—

- Compares the current situation to the desired end state.
- Brainstorms and lists issues that impede the commander from achieving the desired end state.

4-64. Based on this analysis, the staff develops a proposed problem statement—a statement of the problem to be solved—for the commander's approval.

Develop a Proposed Mission Statement

4-65. The COS (XO) or operations officer prepares a proposed mission statement for the unit based on the mission analysis. The commander receives and approves the unit's mission statement normally during the mission analysis brief. A *mission statement* is a short sentence or paragraph that describes the organization's essential task (or tasks) and purpose—a clear statement of the action to be taken and the reason for doing so. The mission statement contains the elements of who, what, when, where, and why, but seldom specifies how (JP 5-0). The five elements of a mission statement answer the questions:

- Who will execute the operation (unit or organization)?
- What is the unit's essential task (tactical mission task)?
- When will the operation begin (by time or event) or what is the duration of the operation?
- Where will the operation occur (AO, objective, grid coordinates)?
- Why will the force conduct the operations (for what purpose)?

Example 1. Not later than 220400 Aug 09 (**when**), 1st Brigade (**who**) secures ROUTE SOUTH DAKOTA (**what/task**) in AO JACKRABBIT (**where**) to enable the movement of humanitarian assistance materials (**why/purpose**).

Example 2. 1-505th Parachute Infantry Regiment (**who**) seizes (**what/task**) JACKSON INTERNATIONAL AIRPORT (**where**) not later than D-day, H+3 (**when**) to allow follow-on forces to air-land into AO SPARTAN (**why/purpose**).

4-66. The mission statement may have more than one essential task. The following example shows a mission statement for a phased operation with a different essential task for each phase.

Example. 1-509th Parachute Infantry Regiment (**who**) seizes (**what/task**) JACKSON INTERNATIONAL AIRPORT (**where**) not later than D-day, H+3 (**when**) to allow follow-on forces to air-land into AO SPARTAN (**why/purpose**). On order (**when**), secure (**what/task**) OBJECTIVE GOLD (**where**) to prevent the 2d Pandor Guards Brigade from crossing the BLUE RIVER and disrupting operations in AO SPARTAN (**why/purpose**).

4-67. The *who, where,* and *when* of a mission statement are straightforward. The *what* and *why* are more challenging to write and can confuse subordinates if not stated clearly. The *what* is a *task* and is expressed in terms of action verbs. These tasks are measurable and can be grouped as "actions by friendly forces" or "effects on enemy forces." The *why* puts the task into context by describing the reason for performing it. The *why* provides the mission's purpose—the reason the unit is to perform the task. It is extremely important to mission command and mission orders.

4-68. Commanders should use tactical mission tasks or other doctrinally approved tasks contained in combined arms field manuals or mission training plans in mission statements. These tasks have specific military definitions that differ from dictionary definitions. A *tactical mission task* is a specific activity performed by a unit while executing a form of tactical operation or form of maneuver. It may be expressed as either an action by a friendly force or effects on an enemy force (FM 7-15). FM 3-90 describes each tactical task. FM 3-07 provides a list of primary stability tasks which military forces must be prepared to execute. Commanders and planners should carefully choose the task that best describes the commander's intent and planning guidance.

Present the Mission Analysis Briefing

4-69. The mission analysis briefing informs the commander of the results of the staff's analysis of the situation. It helps the commander understand, visualize, and describe the operations. Throughout the mission analysis briefing, the commander, staff, and other partners discuss the various facts and assumptions about the situation. Staff officers present a summary of their running estimates from their specific functional area and how their findings impact or are impacted by other areas. This helps the commander and staff as a whole to focus on the interrelationships among the mission variables and to develop a deeper understanding of the situation. The commander issues guidance to the staff for continued planning based on situational understanding gained from the mission analysis briefing.

4-70. Ideally, the commander holds several informal meetings with key staff members before the mission analysis briefing, including meetings to assist the commander in developing CCIRs, the mission statement, and information themes and messages. These meetings enable commanders to issue guidance for activities (such as reconnaissance and surveillance operations) and develop their initial commander's intent and planning guidance.

4-71. A comprehensive mission analysis briefing helps the commander, staff, subordinates, and other partners develop a shared understanding of the requirements of the upcoming operation. Time permitting, the staff briefs the commander on its mission analysis using the following outline:

- Mission and commander's intent of the headquarters two levels up.
- Mission, commander's intent, and concept of operations of the headquarters one level up.
- A proposed problem statement.
- A proposed mission statement.
- Review of the commander's initial guidance.
- Initial IPB products, including civil considerations that impact the conduct of operations.
- Specified, implied, and essential tasks.
- Pertinent facts and assumptions.
- Constraints.
- Forces available and resource shortfalls.
- Initial risk assessment.
- Proposed information themes and messages.
- Proposed CCIRs and EEFIs.
- Initial reconnaissance and surveillance plan.
- Recommended timeline.
- Recommended collaborative planning sessions.

During the mission analysis briefing or shortly thereafter, commanders approve the mission statement and CCIRs. They then develop and issue their initial commander's intent and planning guidance.

Develop and Issue Initial Commander's Intent

4-72. Based on their situational understanding, commanders summarize their visualization in their initial commander's intent statement. The initial commander's intent links the operation's purpose with conditions that define the desired end state. Commanders may change their intent statement as planning progresses and more information becomes available. It must be easy to remember and clearly understood two echelons down. The shorter the commander's intent, the better it serves these purposes. Typically, the commander's intent statement is three to five sentences long.

Develop and Issue Initial Planning Guidance

4-73. Commanders provide planning guidance along with their initial commander's intent. Planning guidance conveys the essence of the commander's visualization. Guidance may be broad or detailed, depending on the situation. The initial planning guidance outlines an *operational approach*—a broad conceptualization of the general actions that will produce the conditions that define the desired end state (FM 5-0). The guidance outlines specific COAs the commander desires the staff to look at as well as rules out any COAs the commander will not accept. That clear guidance allows the staff to develop several COAs without wasting effort on things that the commander will not consider. It reflects how the commander sees the operation unfolding. It broadly describes when, where, and how the commander intends to employ combat power to accomplish the mission within the higher commander's intent.

4-74. Commanders use their experience and judgment to add depth and clarity to their planning guidance. They ensure staffs understand the broad outline of their visualization while allowing the latitude necessary to explore different options. This guidance provides the basis for a detailed concept of operations without dictating the specifics of the final plan. As with their intent, commanders may modify planning guidance based on staff and subordinate input and changing conditions.

4-75. Commanders issue planning guidance when conducting design and at specific points during the MDMP:
- Upon receipt of or in anticipation of a mission (initial planning guidance).
- Following mission analysis (planning guidance for COA development).
- Following COA development (revised planning guidance for COA improvements).
- COA approval (revised planning guidance to complete the plan).

4-76. Table 4-1 lists the commander's planning guidance by warfighting function. This list is not intended to meet the needs of all situations. Commanders tailor planning guidance to meet specific needs based on the situation rather than address each item.

Develop Course of Action Evaluation Criteria

4-77. Evaluation criteria are standards the commander and staff will later use to measure the relative effectiveness and efficiency of one COA relative to other COAs. Developing these criteria during mission analysis or as part of commander's planning guidance helps to eliminate a source of bias prior to COA analysis and comparison. Evaluation criteria address factors that affect success and those that can cause failure. Criteria change from mission to mission and must be clearly defined and understood by all staff members before starting the war game to test the proposed COAs. Normally, the COS (XO) initially determines each proposed criterion with weights based on the assessment of its relative importance and the commander's guidance. Commanders adjust criterion selection and weighting according to their own experience and vision. The staff member responsible for a functional area scores each COA using those criteria. The staff presents the proposed evaluation criteria to the commander at the mission analysis brief for approval.

Issue a Warning Order

4-78. Immediately after the commander gives the planning guidance, the staff sends subordinate and supporting units a WARNO. (See Chapter 12 for example.) It contains, at a minimum—
- The approved mission statement.
- The commander's intent.
- Changes to task organization.
- The unit AO (sketch, overlay, or some other description).
- CCIRs and EEFIs.
- Risk guidance.
- Priorities by warfighting functions.
- Military deception guidance.
- Essential stability tasks.
- Specific priorities.

STEP 3 – COURSE OF ACTION DEVELOPMENT

4-79. A COA is a broad potential solution to an identified problem. The COA development step generates options for follow-on analysis and comparison that satisfy the commander's intent and planning guidance. During COA development, planners use the problem statement, mission statement, commander's intent, planning guidance, and various knowledge products developed during mission analysis.

Table 4-1. Commander's planning guidance by warfighting function

Intelligence	Intelligence, surveillance, and reconnaissance Knowledge gaps Enemy courses of action Priority intelligence requirements High-value targets Terrain and weather factors	Local environment and civil considerations Counterintelligence Intelligence support requests Intelligence focus during phased operations Desired enemy perception of friendly forces
Protection	Protection priorities Priorities for survivability assets Air and missile defense positioning Terrain and weather factors Intelligence focus and limitations for security Acceptable risk Protected targets and areas	Vehicle and equipment safety or security constraints Environmental considerations Unexploded ordnance Operational security risk tolerance Rules of engagement Escalation of force and nonlethal weapons
Movement and Maneuver	Initial commander's intent Course of action development guidance Number of courses of action to consider or not consider Critical events Task organization Task and purpose of subordinate units Forms of maneuver Reserve composition, mission, priorities, and control measures	Security and counterreconnaissance Friendly decision points Branches and sequels Reconnaissance and surveillance integration Military deception Risk to friendly forces Collateral damage or civilian casualties Any condition that affects achievement of end state
Sustainment	Sustainment priorities—manning, fueling, fixing, arming, moving the force, and sustaining Soldiers and systems Army health system support Sustainment of internment and resettlement activities	Construction and provision of facilities and installations Detainee movement Anticipated requirements of classes III, IV, and V Controlled supply rates
Fires	Synchronization and focus of fires with maneuver Priority of fires High priority targets Special munitions Target acquisition zones Observer plan	Task and purpose of fires Suppression of enemy air defenses Fire support coordination measures Attack guidance Branches and sequels No strike list Restricted target list
Mission Command	Friendly forces information requirement Rules of engagement Command post positioning Commander's location Initial themes and messages Succession of command	Liaison officer guidance Planning and operational guidance timeline Type of order and rehearsal Communications guidance Civil affairs operations

4-80. Embedded in COA development is the application of operational and tactical art. Planners develop different COAs by varying combinations of the elements of operational design, such as phasing, lines of effort, and tempo. (See FM 3-0.) Planners convert the approved COA into the concept of operations.

4-81. The commander's direct involvement in COA development greatly aids in producing comprehensive and flexible COAs within the available time. To save time, the commander may also limit the number of COAs staffs develop or specify particular COAs not to explore. Planners examine each prospective COA for validity using the following screening criteria:

- **Feasible**. The COA can accomplish the mission within the established time, space, and resource limitations.
- **Acceptable**. The COA must balance cost and risk with the advantage gained.
- **Suitable**. The COA can accomplish the mission within the commander's intent and planning guidance.
- **Distinguishable**. Each COA must differ significantly from the others (such as scheme of maneuver, lines of effort, phasing, use of the reserve, and task organization).
- **Complete**. A COA must incorporate—
  - How the decisive operation leads to mission accomplishment.
  - How shaping operations create and preserve conditions for success of the decisive operation or effort.
  - How sustaining operations enable shaping and decisive operations or efforts.
  - How to account for offensive, defensive, and stability or civil support tasks.
  - Tasks to be performed and conditions to be achieved.

4-82. A good COA positions the force for sequels and provides flexibility to meet unforeseen events during execution. It also gives subordinates the maximum latitude for initiative. During COA development, the commander and staff continue risk assessment, focus on identifying and assessing hazards to mission accomplishment, and incorporate proposed controls to mitigate them into COAs. The staff also continues to revise IPB products, emphasizing event templates. During COA development, commanders and staffs perform the process actions and produce the outputs shown in Figure 4-3.

Note: If design precedes or is conducted in parallel with the MDMP, the updated design concept provides an overarching structure for COA development.

Key inputs ➡	Process ➡	Key outputs

• Approved problem statement
 • Approved mission statement
 • Initial commander's intent and planning guidance
 • Design concept (if developed)
 • Specified and implied tasks
 • Assumptions
 • Updated running estimates and IPB products
	• Assess relative combat power
	 • Generate options
	 • Array forces
	 • Develop a broad concept
	 • Assign headquarters
	 • Develop COA statements and sketches
	 • Conduct COA briefing
	 • Select or modify COAs for continued analysis
		• Commander's selected COAs for war-gaming with COA statements and sketches
		 • Commander's refined planning guidance to include:
		   - War-gaming guidance
		   - Evaluation criteria
		 • Updated running estimates and IPB products
		 • Updated assumptions

COA course of action	IPB intelligence preparation of the battlefield	

Figure 4-3. COA development

Assess Relative Combat Power

4-83. *Combat power* is the total means of destructive, constructive, and information capabilities that a military unit/formation can apply at a given time. Army forces generate combat power by converting potential into effective action (FM 3-0). Combat power is the effect created by combining the elements of intelligence, movement and maneuver, fires, sustainment, protection, mission command, information, and leadership. The goal is to generate overwhelming combat power to accomplish the mission at minimal cost.

4-84. To assess relative combat power, planners initially make a rough estimate of force ratios of maneuver units two levels down. For example, at division level, planners compare all types of maneuver battalions with enemy maneuver battalion equivalents. Planners then compare friendly strengths against enemy weaknesses, and vice versa, for each element of combat power. From these comparisons, they may deduce particular vulnerabilities for each force that may be exploited or may need protection. These comparisons provide planners insight into effective force employment.

4-85. In troop-to-task analysis for stability and civil support operations, staffs determine relative combat power by comparing available resources to specified or implied stability or civil support tasks. This analysis provides insight as available options and needed resources. In such operations, the elements of sustainment, movement and maneuver, nonlethal effects, and information may dominate.

4-86. By analyzing force ratios and determining and comparing each force's strengths and weaknesses as a function of combat power, planners can gain insight into—

- Friendly capabilities that pertain to the operation.
- The types of operations possible from both friendly and enemy perspectives.
- How and where the enemy may be vulnerable.
- How and where friendly forces are vulnerable.
- Additional resources needed to execute the mission.
- How to allocate existing resources.

4-87. Planners must not develop and recommend COAs based solely on mathematical analysis of force ratios. Although the process uses some numerical relationships, the estimate is largely subjective. Assessing combat power requires assessing both tangible and intangible factors, such as morale and levels of training. A relative combat power assessment identifies exploitable enemy weaknesses, identifies unprotected friendly weaknesses, and determines the combat power necessary to conduct essential stability or civil support tasks.

Generate Options

4-88. Based on the commander's guidance and the initial results of the relative combat power assessment, the staff generates options. A good COA can defeat all feasible enemy COAs while accounting for essential stability tasks. In an unconstrained environment, planners aim to develop several possible COAs. Depending on available time, commanders may limit the options in the commander's guidance. Options focus on enemy COAs arranged in order of their probable adoption or on those stability tasks that are most essential to prevent the situation from deteriorating further.

4-89. Brainstorming is the preferred technique for generating options. It requires time, imagination, and creativity, but it produces the widest range of choices. The staff (and members of organizations outside the headquarters) remains unbiased and open-minded when developing proposed options.

4-90. In developing COAs, staff members determine the doctrinal requirements for each proposed operation, including doctrinal tasks for subordinate units. For example, a deliberate breach requires a breach force, a support force, and an assault force. Essential stability tasks require the ability to provide a level of civil security, civil control, and certain essential services. In addition, the staff considers the potential capabilities of attachments and other organizations and agencies outside military channels.

4-91. When generating options, the staff starts with the decisive operation identified in the commander's planning guidance. The staff checks that the decisive operation nests within the higher headquarters' concept of operations. The staff clarifies the decisive operation's purpose and considers ways to mass the effects (lethal and nonlethal) of overwhelming combat power to achieve it.

4-92. Next, the staff considers shaping operations. The staff establishes a purpose for each shaping operation tied to creating or preserving a condition for the decisive operation's success. Shaping operations may occur before, concurrently with, or after the decisive operation. A shaping operation may be designated as the main effort if executed before or after the decisive operation.

4-93. The staff then determines sustaining operations necessary to create and maintain the combat power required for the decisive operation and shaping operation. After developing the basic operational organization for a given COA, the staff then determines the essential tasks for each decisive, shaping, and sustaining operation.

4-94. Once staff members have explored possibilities for each COA, they examine each COA to determine if it satisfies the screening criteria stated in paragraph 4-81. In doing so, they change, add, or eliminate COAs as appropriate. During this process, staffs avoid focusing on the development of one good COA among several throwaway COAs.

Array Forces

4-95. After determining the decisive and shaping operations and their related tasks and purposes, planners determine the relative combat power required to accomplish each task. Often, planners use minimum historical planning ratios shown in Table 4-2 as a starting point. For example, historically defenders have over a 50 percent probability of defeating an attacking force approximately three times their equivalent strength. Therefore, as a starting point, commanders may defend on each avenue of approach with roughly a 1:3 force ratio.

Table 4-2. Historical minimum planning ratios

Friendly Mission	Position	Friendly : Enemy
Delay		1:6
Defend	Prepared or fortified	1:3
Defend	Hasty	1:2.5
Attack	Prepared or fortified	3:1
Attack	Hasty	2.5:1
Counterattack	Flank	1:1

4-96. Planners determine whether these and other intangibles increase the relative combat power of the unit assigned the task to the point that it exceeds the historical planning ratio for that task. If it does not, planners determine how to reinforce the unit. Combat power comparisons are provisional at best. Arraying forces is tricky, inexact work, affected by factors that are difficult to gauge, such as impact of past engagements, quality of leaders, morale, maintenance of equipment, and time in position. Levels of electronic warfare support, fire support, close air support, civilian support, and many other factors also affect arraying forces.

4-97. In counterinsurgency operations, planners can develop force requirements by gauging troop density—the ratio of security forces (including host-nation military and police forces as well as foreign counterinsurgents) to inhabitants. Most density recommendations fall within a range of 20 to 25 counterinsurgents for every 1,000 residents in an AO. Twenty counterinsurgents per 1,000 residents are often considered the minimum troop density required for effective counterinsurgency operations; however, as with any fixed ratio, such calculations strongly depend on the situation. (See FM 3-24.)

4-98. Planners also determine relative combat power with regard to civilian requirements and conditions that require attention and then array forces and capabilities for stability tasks. For example, a COA may require a follow-on force to establish civil security, maintain civil control, and restore essential services in a densely populated urban area over an extended period. Planners conduct a troop-to-task analysis to determine the type of units and capabilities needed to accomplish these tasks.

4-99. Planners then proceed to initially array friendly forces starting with the decisive operation and continuing with all shaping and sustaining operations. Planners normally array ground forces two levels down. The initial array focuses on generic ground maneuver units without regard to specific type or task organization and then considers all appropriate intangible factors. For example, at corps level, planners array generic brigades. During this step, planners do not assign missions to specific units; they only consider which forces are necessary to accomplish its task. In this step, planners also array assets to accomplish essential stability tasks.

4-100. The initial array identifies the total number of units needed and identifies possible methods of dealing with the enemy and stability tasks. If the number arrayed is less than the number available, planners place additional units in a pool for use when they develop a broad concept. (See paragraph 4-101.) If the number of units arrayed exceeds the number available and the difference cannot be compensated for with intangible factors, the staff determines whether the COA is feasible. Ways to make up the shortfall include requesting additional resources, accepting risk in that portion of the AO, or executing tasks required for the COA sequentially rather than simultaneously. Commanders should also consider requirements to minimize and relieve civilian suffering. Establishing civil security and providing essential services such as medical care, food and water, and shelter are implied tasks for commanders during any combat operation. (See FM 3-07 for a full discussion on stability tasks.)

Develop a Broad Concept

4-101. The broad concept describes how arrayed forces will accomplish the mission within the commander's intent. It concisely expresses the *how* of the commander's visualization and will eventually provide the framework for the concept of operations. The broad concept summarizes the contributions of all warfighting functions. The staff develops a broad concept for each COA expressed in both narrative and graphic forms. A sound COA is more than the arraying of forces. It presents an overall combined arms idea that will accomplish the mission. The broad concept includes the following, but is not limited to—

- The purpose of the operation.
- A statement of where the commander will accept risk.
- Identification of critical friendly events and transitions between phases (if the operation is phased).
- Designation of the decisive operation, along with its task and purpose, linked to how it supports the higher headquarters' concept.
- Designation of shaping operations, along with their tasks and purposes, linked to how they support the decisive operation.
- Designation of sustaining operations, along with their tasks and purposes, linked to how they support the decisive and shaping operations.
- Designation of the reserve, including its location and composition.
- Reconnaissance and security operations.
- Essential stability tasks.
- Identification of maneuver options that may develop during an operation.
- Assignment of subordinate AOs.
- Scheme of fires.
- Information themes, messages, and means of delivery.
- Military deception operations.
- Key control measures.

4-102. Planners select control measures, including graphics, to control subordinate units during an operation. These establish responsibilities and limits that prevent subordinate units' actions from impeding one another. These measures also foster coordination and cooperation between forces without unnecessarily restricting freedom of action. Good control measures foster decisionmaking and individual initiative. (See FM 3-90 for a discussion of control measures associated with offensive and defensive operations. See FM 1-02 for doctrinal control measures and rules for drawing control measures on overlays and maps.)

4-103. Planners may use both lines of operations and lines of effort to build their broad concept. Lines of operations portray the more traditional links among objectives, decisive points, and centers of gravity. A line of effort, however, helps planners link multiple tasks with goals, objectives, and end state conditions. Combining lines of operations with lines of efforts allows planners to include nonmilitary activities in their broad concept. This combination helps commanders incorporate stability or civil support tasks that, when accomplished, help set end state conditions of the operation.

4-104. Based on the commander's planning guidance (informed by the design concept if design preceded the MDMP), planners develop lines of effort by—

- Confirming end state conditions from the initial commander's intent and planning guidance.
- Determining and describing each line of effort.
- Identifying objectives (intermediate goals) and determining tasks along each line of effort.

4-105. During COA development, lines of efforts are general and lack specifics, such as tasks to subordinate units associated to objectives along each line of effort. Units develop and refine lines of effort, to include specific tasks to subordinate units, during war-gaming. (See FM 3-0 and FM 3-07 for examples of operations depicted along lines of effort.)

4-106. As planning progresses, commanders may modify lines of effort and add details while war-gaming. Operations with other instruments of national power support a broader, comprehensive approach to stability operations. Each operation, however, differs. Commanders develop and modify lines of effort to focus operations on achieving the end state, even as the situation evolves.

Assign Headquarters

4-107. After determining the broad concept, planners create a task organization by assigning headquarters to groupings of forces. They consider the types of units to be assigned to a headquarters and the ability of that headquarters to control those units. Generally, a headquarters controls at least two subordinate maneuver units (but not more than five) for fast-paced offensive or defensive operations. The number and type of units assigned to a headquarters for stability operations vary based on factors of the mission variables (known as METT-TC). If planners need additional headquarters, they note the shortage and resolve it later. Task organization takes into account the entire operational organization. It also accounts for the special mission command requirements for operations, such as a passage of lines, gap crossing, or air assault.

Prepare Course of Action Statements and Sketches

4-108. The G-3 (S-3) prepares a COA statement and supporting sketch for each COA. The COA statement clearly portrays how the unit will accomplish the mission. The COA statement briefly expresses how the unit will conduct the combined arms concept. The sketch provides a picture of the movement and maneuver aspects of the concept, including the positioning of forces. Together, the statement and sketch cover the *who* (generic task organization), *what* (tasks), *when*, *where*, and *why* (purpose) for each subordinate unit.

4-109. The COA sketch includes the array of generic forces and control measures, such as—
- The unit and subordinate unit boundaries.
- Unit movement formations (but not subordinate unit formations).
- The line of departure or line of contact and phase lines, if used.
- Reconnaissance and security graphics.
- Ground and air axes of advance.
- Assembly areas, battle positions, strong points, engagement areas, and objectives.
- Obstacle control measures and tactical mission graphics.
- Fire support coordination and airspace coordinating measures.
- Main effort.
- Location of command posts and critical information systems nodes.
- Known or templated enemy locations.
- Population concentrations.

4-110. Planners can include identifying features (such as cities, rivers, and roads) to help orient users. The sketch may be on any medium. What it portrays is more important than its form. Figure 4-4 provides a sample COA sketch and COA statement for a brigade combat team.

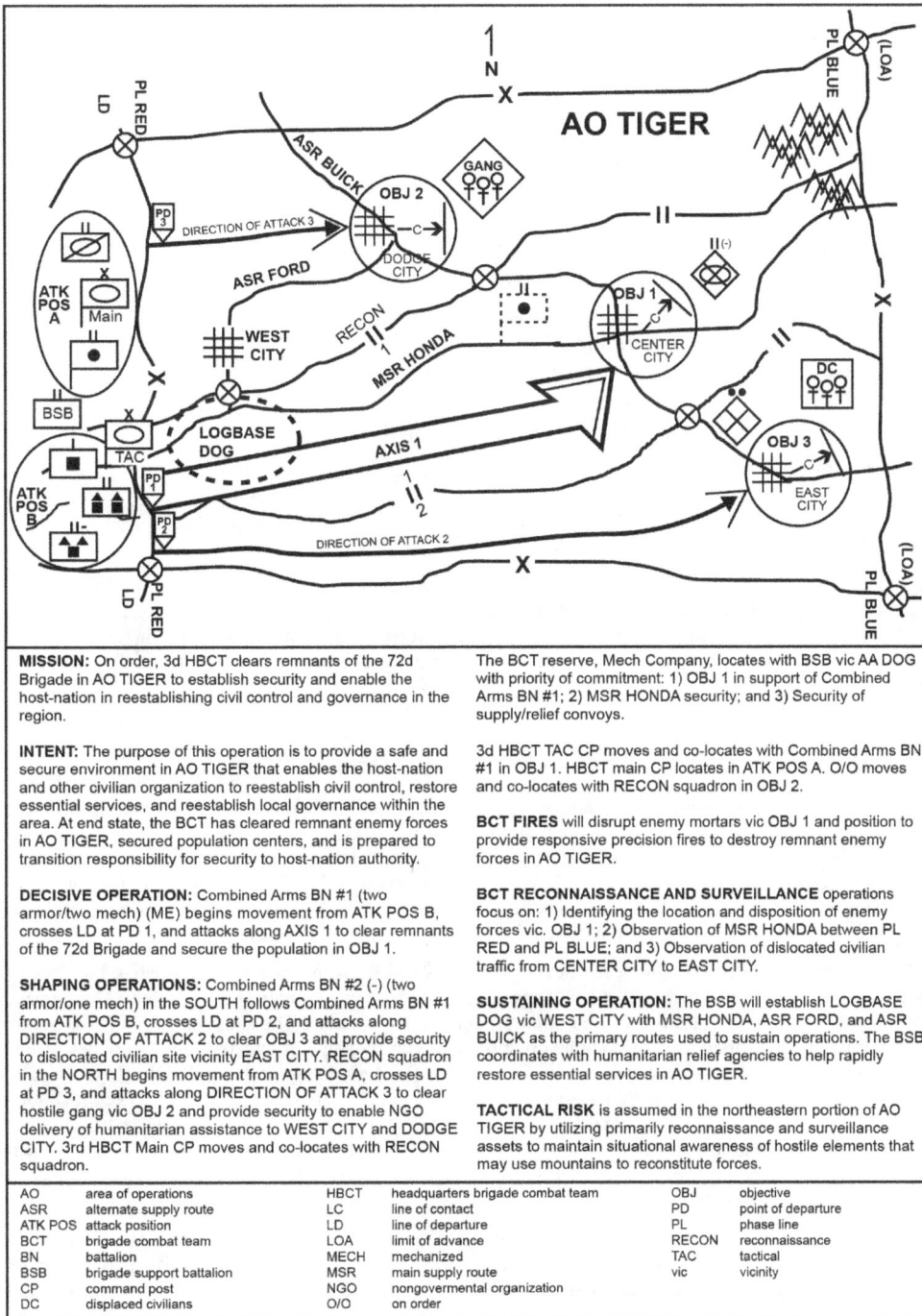

Figure 4-4. Sample brigade COA sketch

MISSION: On order, 3d HBCT clears remnants of the 72d Brigade in AO TIGER to establish security and enable the host-nation in reestablishing civil control and governance in the region.

INTENT: The purpose of this operation is to provide a safe and secure environment in AO TIGER that enables the host-nation and other civilian organization to reestablish civil control, restore essential services, and reestablish local governance within the area. At end state, the BCT has cleared remnant enemy forces in AO TIGER, secured population centers, and is prepared to transition responsibility for security to host-nation authority.

DECISIVE OPERATION: Combined Arms BN #1 (two armor/two mech) (ME) begins movement from ATK POS B, crosses LD at PD 1, and attacks along AXIS 1 to clear remnants of the 72d Brigade and secure the population in OBJ 1.

SHAPING OPERATIONS: Combined Arms BN #2 (-) (two armor/one mech) in the SOUTH follows Combined Arms BN #1 from ATK POS B, crosses LD at PD 2, and attacks along DIRECTION OF ATTACK 2 to clear OBJ 3 and provide security to dislocated civilian site vicinity EAST CITY. RECON squadron in the NORTH begins movement from ATK POS A, crosses LD at PD 3, and attacks along DIRECTION OF ATTACK 3 to clear hostile gang vic OBJ 2 and provide security to enable NGO delivery of humanitarian assistance to WEST CITY and DODGE CITY. 3rd HBCT Main CP moves and co-locates with RECON squadron.

The BCT reserve, Mech Company, locates with BSB vic AA DOG with priority of commitment: 1) OBJ 1 in support of Combined Arms BN #1; 2) MSR HONDA security; and 3) Security of supply/relief convoys.

3d HBCT TAC CP moves and co-locates with Combined Arms BN #1 in OBJ 1. HBCT main CP locates in ATK POS A. O/O moves and co-locates with RECON squadron in OBJ 2.

BCT FIRES will disrupt enemy mortars vic OBJ 1 and position to provide responsive precision fires to destroy remnant enemy forces in AO TIGER.

BCT RECONNAISSANCE AND SURVEILLANCE operations focus on: 1) Identifying the location and disposition of enemy forces vic. OBJ 1; 2) Observation of MSR HONDA between PL RED and PL BLUE; and 3) Observation of dislocated civilian traffic from CENTER CITY to EAST CITY.

SUSTAINING OPERATION: The BSB will establish LOGBASE DOG vic WEST CITY with MSR HONDA, ASR FORD, and ASR BUICK as the primary routes used to sustain operations. The BSB coordinates with humanitarian relief agencies to help rapidly restore essential services in AO TIGER.

TACTICAL RISK is assumed in the northeastern portion of AO TIGER by utilizing primarily reconnaissance and surveillance assets to maintain situational awareness of hostile elements that may use mountains to reconstitute forces.

AO	area of operations	HBCT	headquarters brigade combat team	OBJ	objective
ASR	alternate supply route	LC	line of contact	PD	point of departure
ATK POS	attack position	LD	line of departure	PL	phase line
BCT	brigade combat team	LOA	limit of advance	RECON	reconnaissance
BN	battalion	MECH	mechanized	TAC	tactical
BSB	brigade support battalion	MSR	main supply route	vic	vicinity
CP	command post	NGO	nongovernmental organization		
DC	displaced civilians	O/O	on order		

Conduct a Course of Action Briefing

4-111. After developing COAs, the staff briefs them to the commander. A collaborative session may facilitate subordinate planning. The COA briefing includes—

- An updated IPB.
- Possible enemy COAs.
- The approved problem statement and mission statement.
- The commander's and higher commander's intents.
- COA statements and sketches, including lines of effort if used.
- The rationale for each COA, including—
  - Considerations that might affect enemy COAs.
  - Critical events for each COA.
  - Deductions resulting from the relative combat power analysis.
  - The reason units are arrayed as shown on the sketch.
  - The reason the staff used the selected control measures.
  - The impact on civilians.
  - How it accounts for minimum essential stability tasks.
  - Updated facts and assumptions.
  - Refined COA evaluation criteria.

Select or Modify Courses of Action for Continued Analysis

4-112. After the COA briefing, the commander selects or modifies those COAs for continued analysis. The commander also issues planning guidance. If commanders reject all COAs, the staff begins again. If commanders accept one or more of the COAs, staff members begin COA analysis. The commander may create a new COA by incorporating elements of one or more COAs developed by the staff. The staff then prepares to war-game this new COA. The staff incorporates those modifications and ensures all staff members understand the changed COA.

STEP 4 – COURSE OF ACTION ANALYSIS AND WAR-GAMING

4-113. COA analysis enables commanders and staffs to identify difficulties or coordination problems as well as probable consequences of planned actions for each COA being considered. It helps them think through the tentative plan. COA analysis may require commanders and staffs to revisit parts of a COA as discrepancies arise. COA analysis not only appraises the quality of each COA but also uncovers potential execution problems, decisions, and contingencies. In addition, COA analysis influences how commanders and staffs understand a problem and may require the planning process to restart.

4-114. War-gaming is a disciplined process, with rules and steps that attempt to visualize the flow of the operation, given the force's strengths and dispositions, enemy's capabilities and possible COAs, impact and requirements of civilians in the AO, and other aspects of the situation. The simplest form of war-gaming is the manual method, often utilizing a tabletop approach with blowups of matrixes and templates. The most sophisticated form of war-gaming is modern, computer-aided modeling and simulation. Regardless of the form used, each critical event within a proposed COA should be war-gamed using the action, reaction, and counteraction methods of friendly and enemy forces interaction. This basic war-gaming method (modified to fit the specific mission and environment) applies to offensive, defensive, and stability or civil support operations. When conducting COA analysis, commanders and staffs perform the process actions and produce the outputs shown in Figure 4-5.

4-115. War-gaming results in refined COAs, a completed synchronization matrix, and decision support templates and matrixes for each COA. A synchronization matrix records the results of a war game. It depicts how friendly forces for a particular COA are synchronized in time, space, and purpose in relation to an enemy COA or other events in stability or civil support operations. The decision support template and matrix portray key decisions and potential actions that are likely to arise during the execution of each COA.

Key inputs	Process	Key outputs
• Updated intelligence preparation of the battlefield products • Updated running estimates • Updated commander's planning guidance • Course of action statements and sketches • Updated assumptions	• Gather the tools • List all friendly forces • List assumptions • List known critical events and decision points • Select the war-gaming method • Select a technique to record and display results • War-game the operation and assess the results • Conduct a war-game briefing (optional)	• Refined courses of action • Decision support templates and matrixes • Synchronization matrixes • Potential branches and sequels • Updated running estimates • Updated assumptions

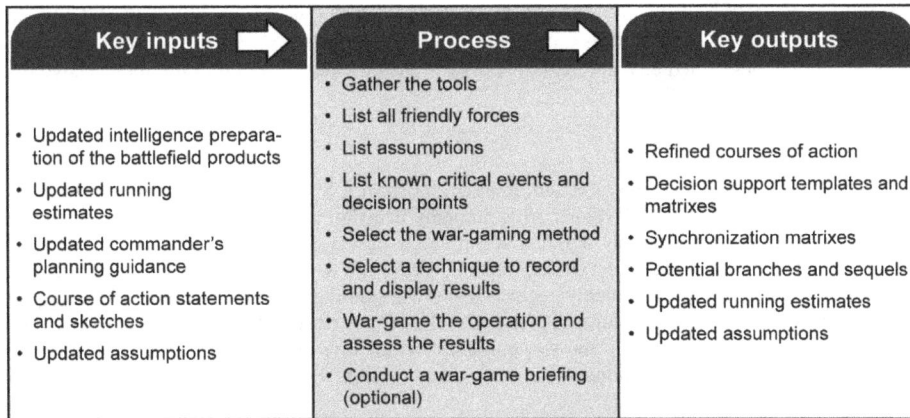

Figure 4-5. COA analysis and war-gaming

4-116.   COA analysis allows the staff to synchronize the six warfighting functions for each COA. It also helps the commander and staff to—

- Determine how to maximize the effects of combat power while protecting friendly forces and minimizing collateral damage.
- Further develop a visualization of the operation.
- Anticipate operational events.
- Determine conditions and resources required for success.
- Determine when and where to apply force capabilities.
- Identify coordination needed to produce synchronized results.
- Determine the most flexible COA.

4-117.   During the war game, the staff takes each COA and begins to develop a detailed plan while determining its strengths or weaknesses. War-gaming tests and improves COAs. The commander, staff, and other available partners (and subordinate commanders and staffs if the war game is conducted collaboratively) may change an existing COA or develop a new COA after identifying unforeseen events, tasks, requirements, or problems.

General War-Gaming Rules

4-118.   War gamers need to—

- Remain objective, not allowing personality or their sense of "what the commander wants" to influence them.
- Avoid defending a COA just because they personally developed it.
- Record advantages and disadvantages of each COA accurately as they emerge.
- Continually assess feasibility, acceptability, and suitability of each COA. If a COA fails any of these tests, reject it.
- Avoid drawing premature conclusions and gathering facts to support such conclusions.
- Avoid comparing one COA with another during the war game. This occurs during COA comparison.

War-Gaming Responsibilities

4-119.   This section describes the responsibilities of key staff members during the war game.

Chief of Staff (Executive Officer)

4-120. The COS (XO) coordinates actions of the staff during the war game. This officer is the unbiased controller of the process, ensuring the staff stays on a timeline and achieves the goals of the war-gaming session. In a time-constrained environment, this officer ensures that, at a minimum, the decisive operation is war-gamed.

Intelligence

4-121. During the war game, the assistant chief of staff (ACOS), G-2 (S-2), intelligence role-plays the enemy commander. This officer develops critical enemy decision points in relation to the friendly COAs, projects enemy reactions to friendly actions, and projects enemy losses. The intelligence officer assigns different responsibilities to available staff members within the section (such as the enemy commander, friendly intelligence officer, and enemy recorder) for war-gaming. The intelligence officer captures the results of each enemy action and counteraction as well as the corresponding friendly and enemy strengths and vulnerabilities. By trying to win the war game for the enemy, the intelligence officer ensures that the staff fully addresses friendly responses for each enemy COA. For the friendly force, the intelligence officer—

- Identifies IRs.
- Refines the situation and event templates, including named areas of interest that support decision points.
- Refines the event template with corresponding decision points, target areas of interest, and high-value targets.
- Participates in targeting to select high-payoff targets from high-value targets identified during IPB.
- Recommends priority intelligence requirements that correspond to the decision points.

Movemenent and Maneuver

4-122. During the war game, the ACOS, G-3 (S-3), operations, and ACOS, G-5 (S-5), plans, are responsible for movement and maneuver. The G-3 (S-3) normally selects the technique for the war game and role-plays the friendly maneuver commander. Various staff officers assist the G-3 (S-3), such as the aviation officer and engineer officer. The G-3 (S-3) executes friendly maneuver as outlined in the COA sketch and COA statement. The G-5 (S-5) assesses warfighting requirements, solutions, and concepts for each COA; develops plans and orders; and determines potential branches and sequels arising from various war-gamed COAs. The G-5 (S-5) also coordinates and synchronizes warfighting functions in all plans and orders. The planning staff ensures that the war game of each COA covers every operational aspect of the mission. The members of the staff record each event's strengths and weaknesses and the rationale for each action. They complete the decision support template and matrix for each COA. They annotate the rationale for actions during the war game and use it later with the commander's guidance to compare COAs.

Fires

4-123. The chief of fires (fire support officer) assesses the fire support feasibility of each war-gamed COA. The chief of fires develops the fire support execution matrix and evaluation criteria to measure the effectiveness of the fire support for each COA. This officer develops a proposed high-priority target list, target selection standards, and attack guidance matrix. The chief of fires identifies named and target areas of interest, high-value targets, high-priority targets, and additional events that may influence the positioning of fire support assets.

Protection

4-124. The chief of protection assesses protection element requirements, refines EEFIs, and develops a scheme of protection for each war-gamed COA. The chief—

- Refines the critical asset list and the defended asset list.
- Assesses threats and hazards.
- Develops risk control measures and mitigation measures of threats and hazards.

- Establishes personnel recovery coordination measures.
- Synchronizes air and missile defense.
- Implements operational area security to include security of lines of communications, antiterrorism measures, and law enforcement operations.
- Ensures survivability measures reduce vulnerabilities.
- Refines chemical, biological, radiological, and nuclear operations.

Sustainment

4-125. The following officers are responsible for sustainment during the war game:
- ACOS, G-1 (S-1), personnel.
- ACOS, G-4 (S-4), logistics.
- ACOS, G-8, financial management.
- Surgeon.

4-126. During the war game, the G-1 (S-1) assesses the personnel aspect of building and maintaining the combat power of units. This officer identifies potential shortfalls and recommends COAs to ensure units maintain adequate manning to accomplish their mission. As the primary staff officer assessing the human resources planning considerations to support sustainment operations, the G-1 (S-1) provides human resources support for the operation.

4-127. The G-4 (S-4) assesses the logistics feasibility of each war-gamed COA. This officer determines critical requirements for each logistics function (classes I through VII, IX, and X) and identifies potential problems and deficiencies. The G-4 (S-4) assesses the status of all logistics functions required to support the COA, including potential support required to provide essential services to the civilians, and compares it to available assets. This officer identifies potential shortfalls and recommends actions to eliminate or reduce their effects. While improvising can contribute to responsiveness, only accurately predicting requirements for each logistics function can ensure continuous sustainment. The logistics officer ensures that available movement times and assets support each COA.

4-128. During the war game, the G-8 assesses the commander's area of responsibility to determine the best COA for use of resources. This assessment includes both core functions of financial management: resource management and finance operations. This officer determines partner relationships (joint, interagency, intergovernmental, and multinational), requirements for special funding, and support to the procurement process.

4-129. The surgeon section coordinates, monitors, and synchronizes the execution of the Army health system (AHS) activities for the command for each war-gamed COA to ensure a fit and healthy force.

Mission Command

4-130. The following officers are responsible for aspects of mission command during the war game:
- ACOS, G-6 (S-6), signal.
- ACOS, G-7 (S-7), inform and influence activities.
- ACOS, G-9 (S-9), civil affairs operations.
- Red team officer.
- Staff Judge Advocate.
- Operations research and systems analysis officer.
- Safety officer.

4-131. The G-6 (S-6) assesses network operations, electromagnetic spectrum operations, network defense, and information protection feasibility of each war-gamed COA. The G-6 (S-6), determines communication systems requirements and compares them to available assets, identifies potential shortfalls, and recommends actions to eliminate or reduce their effects.

4-132. The G-7 (S-7) assesses how effectively the operations reflect the inform and influence activities; the effectiveness of capabilities to execute (deliver) inform and influence activities in support of each war-gamed COA; and how inform and influence activities impact various audiences of interest and populations in and outside the AO. The G-7 also integrates cyber/electromagnetic activities with inform and influence activities.

4-133.   The G-9 (S-9) ensures each war-gamed COA effectively integrates civil considerations (the "C" of METT-TC). The civil affairs operations officer considers not only tactical issues but also sustainment issues. This officer assesses how operations affect civilians and estimates the requirements for essential stability tasks commanders might have to undertake based on the ability of the unified action. Host-nation support and care of dislocated civilians are of particular concern. The civil affairs operations officer's analysis considers how operations affect public order and safety, the potential for disaster relief requirements, noncombatant evacuation operations, emergency services, and the protection of culturally significant sites. This officer provides feedback on how the culture in the AO affects each COA. If the unit lacks an assigned civil affairs operations officer, the commander assigns these responsibilities to another staff member. Under mission command, the civil affairs operations officer integrates civil-military operations that relate to inform and influence activities. This integration gains efficiencies and presents coordinated, deconflicted messages to other organizations.

4-134.   During the war game, the red team staff section provides the commander and G-2 with an independent capability to fully explore alternatives. The staff looks in plans, operations, concepts, organizations, and capabilities of the operational environment from the perspectives of adversaries, partners, and others.

4-135.   The Staff Judge Advocate advises the commander on all matters pertaining to law, policy, regulation, good order, and discipline for each war-gamed COA. This officer provides legal advice across the spectrum of conflict on law of war, rules of engagement, international agreements, Geneva Conventions, treatment and disposition of noncombatants, and the legal aspects of lethal and nonlethal targeting.

4-136.   During the war game, the operations research and systems analysis staff section provides analytic support to the commander for planning and assessment of operations. Specific responsibilities includes—

- Providing quantitative analytic support, including regression and trend analysis, to planning and assessment activities.
- Assisting other staff in developing customized analytical tools for specific requirements, providing a quality control capability, and conducting assessments to measure the effectiveness of operations.

4-137.   The safety office is integral to providing input to influence accident and incident reductions by implementing composite risk management throughout the mission planning and execution process.

Recorders

4-138.   The use of recorders is particularly important. Recorders capture coordinating instructions, subunit tasks and purposes, and information required to synchronize the operation. Recorders allow the staff to write part of the order before they complete the planning. Automated information systems enable recorders to enter information into preformatted forms that represent either briefing charts or appendixes to orders. Each staff section keeps formats available to facilitate networked orders production.

Course of Action Process Actions

4-139.   COA analysis consists of eight actions first shown in Figure 4-5 and described in paragraphs 4-140 through 4-170.

Gather the Tools

4-140.   The first task for COA analysis is to gather the necessary tools to conduct the war game. The COS (XO) directs the staff to gather tools, materials, and data for the war game. Units war-game with maps, sand tables, computer simulations, or other tools that accurately reflect the terrain. The staff posts the COA on a map displaying the AO. Tools required include, but are not limited to—

- Running estimates.
- Event templates.
- A recording method.
- Completed COAs, including graphics.
- A means to post or display enemy and friendly unit symbols and other organizations.
- A map of the AO.

List All Friendly Forces

4-141.   The commander and staff consider all units that can be committed to the operation, paying special attention to support relationships and constraints. This list includes assets from all participants operating in the AO. The friendly forces list remains constant for all COAs.

List Assumptions

4-142.   The commander and staff review previous assumptions for continued validity and necessity.

List Known Critical Events and Decision Points

4-143.   **A *critical event* is an event that directly influences mission accomplishment.** Critical events include events that trigger significant actions or decisions (such as commitment of an enemy reserve), complicated actions requiring detailed study (such as a passage of lines), and essential tasks. The list of critical events includes major events from the unit's current position through mission accomplishment. It includes reactions by civilians that potentially affect operations or require allocation of significant assets to account for essential stability tasks.

4-144.   A *decision point* is a point in space and time when the commander or staff anticipates making a key decision concerning a specific course of action (JP 5-0). Decision points may be associated with the friendly force, the status of ongoing operations, and with CCIRs that describe what information the commander needs to make the anticipated decision. A decision point requires a decision by the commander. It does not dictate what the decision is, only that the commander must make one, and when and where it should be made to maximally impact friendly or enemy COAs or the accomplishment of stability tasks.

Select the War-Gaming Method

4-145.   Three recommended war-gaming methods exist: belt, avenue-in-depth, and box. Each considers the area of interest and all enemy forces that can affect the outcome of the operation. Planners can use the methods separately or in combination and modified for long-term operations dominated by stability.

4-146.   The belt method divides the AO into belts (areas) running the width of the AO. (See Figure 4-6, page 4-28.) The shape of each belt is based on the factors of METT-TC. The belt method works best when conducting offensive and defensive operations on terrain divided into well-defined cross-compartments, during phased operations (such as gap crossings, air assaults, or airborne operations), or when the enemy is deployed in clearly defined belts or echelons. Belts can be adjacent to or overlap each other.

4-147.   This war-gaming method is based on a sequential analysis of events in each belt. Commanders prefer it because it focuses simultaneously on all forces affecting a particular event. A belt might include more than one critical event. Under time-constrained conditions, the commander can use a modified belt method. The modified belt method divides the AO into not more than three sequential belts. These belts are not necessarily adjacent or overlapping but focus on the critical actions throughout the depth of the AO.

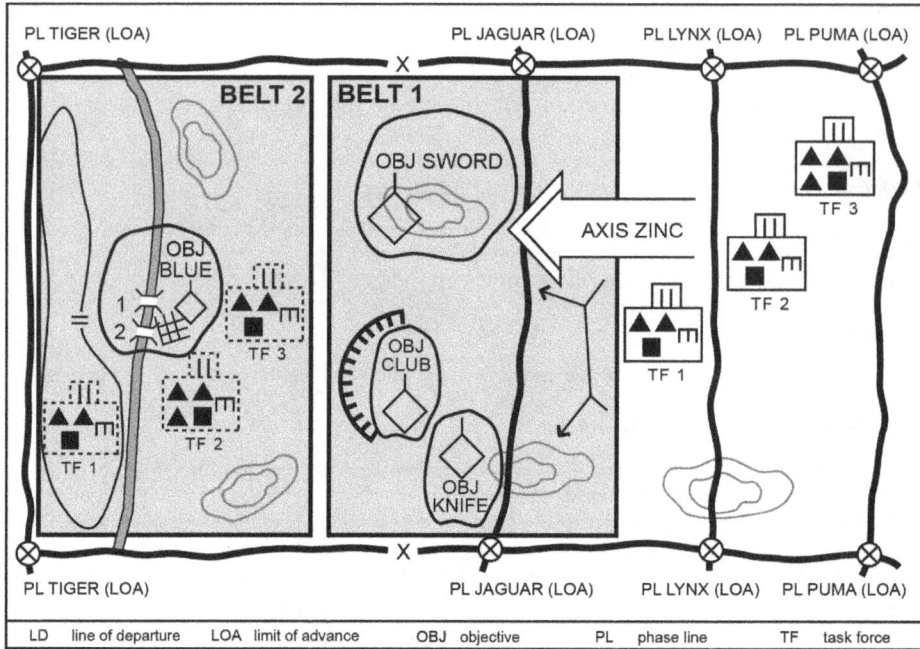

Figure 4-6. Sample belt method

4-148. In stability operations, the belt method can divide the COA by events, objectives (goals not geographic location), or events and objectives in a selected slice across all lines of effort. (See Figure 4-7.) It consists of war-gaming relationships among events or objectives on all lines of effort in the belt.

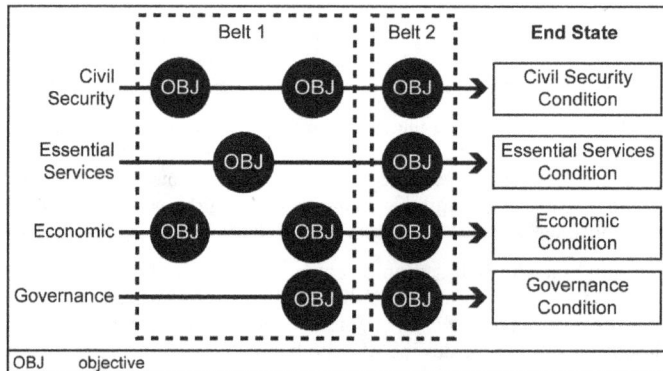

Figure 4-7. Sample modified belt method using lines of effort

4-149. The avenue-in-depth method focuses on one avenue of approach at a time, beginning with the decisive operation. (See Figure 4-8.) This method is good for offensive COAs or in the defense when canalizing terrain inhibits mutual support.

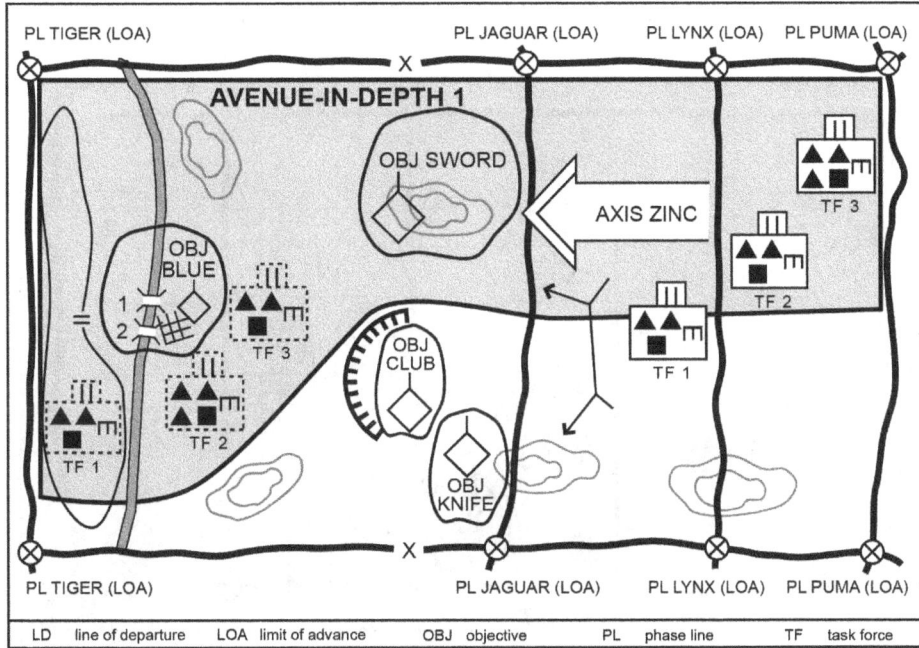

Figure 4-8. Sample avenue-in-depth method

4-150.   In stability operations, planners can modify the avenue-in-depth method. Instead of focusing on a geographic avenue, the staff war-games a line of effort. This method focuses on one line of effort at a time, beginning with the decisive line. (See Figure 4-9.) It includes not only war-gaming events, objectives, or events and objectives in the selected line, but also war-gaming relationships among events or objectives on all lines of effort with respect to events in the selected line.

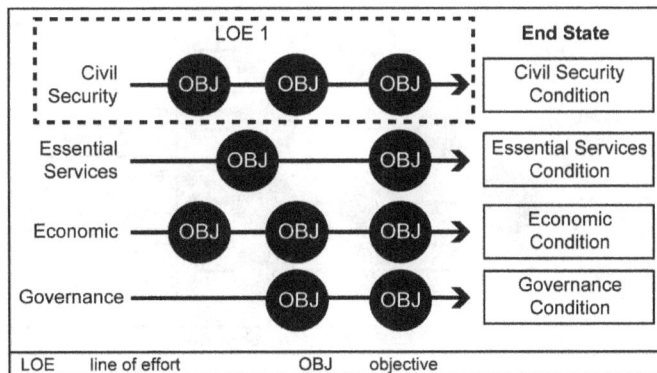

Figure 4-9. Sample modified avenue-in-depth method using lines of effort

4-151.   The box method is a detailed analysis of a critical area, such as an engagement area, a river-crossing site, or a landing zone. (See Figure 4-10, page 4-30.) It works best in a time-constrained environment, such as a hasty attack. It is particularly useful when planning operations in noncontiguous

AOs. When using this method, the staff isolates the area and focuses on critical events in it. Staff members assume that friendly units can handle most situations in the AOs and focus their attention on essential tasks.

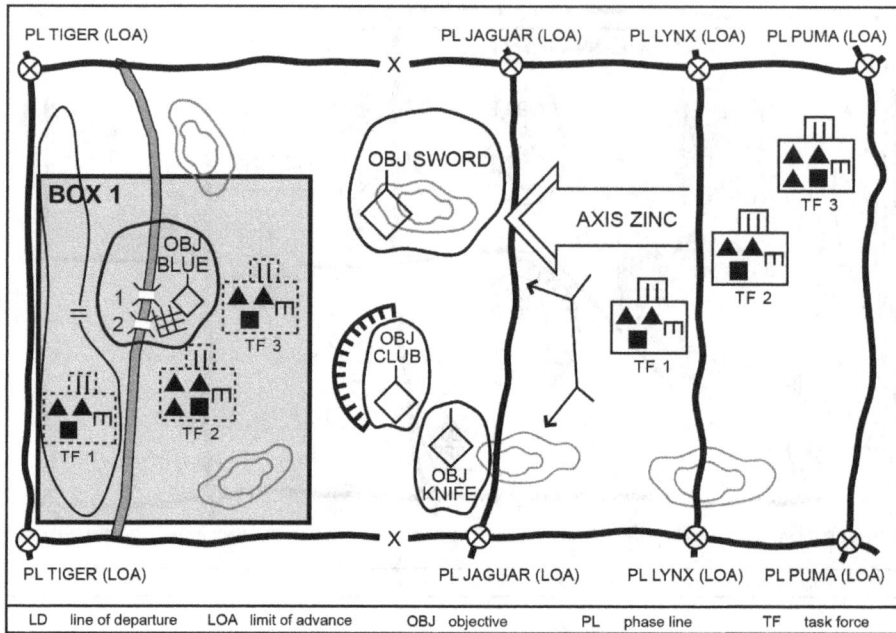

Figure 4-10. Sample box method

4-152.   In stability operations, the box method may focus analysis on a specific objective along a line of effort, such as development of local security forces as part of improving civil security. (See Figure 4-11.)

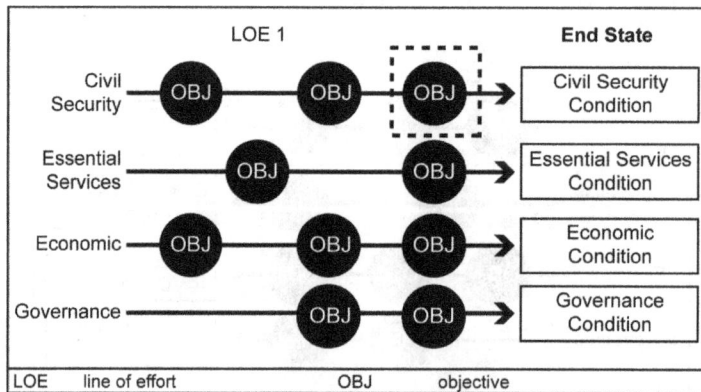

Figure 4-11. Sample modified box method using lines of effort

Select a Technique to Record and Display Results

4-153.   The war-game results provide a record from which to build task organizations, synchronize activities, develop decision support templates, confirm and refine event templates, prepare plans or orders, and compare COAs. Two techniques are commonly used to record and display results: the synchronization matrix technique and the sketch note technique. In both techniques, staff members record any remarks regarding the strengths and weaknesses they discover. The amount of detail depends on the time available. Unit SOPs address details and methods of recording and displaying war-gaming results.

4-154. **The *synchronization matrix* is a tool the staff uses to record the results of war-gaming and helps them synchronize a course of action across time, space, and purpose in relationship to potential enemy and civil actions.** (See Figure 4-12.) The first entry is the time or phase of the operation. The second entry is the most likely enemy action. The third entry is the most likely civilian action. The fourth entry is the decision points for the friendly COA. The remainder of the matrix focuses on selected warfighting functions, their subordinate tasks, and the unit's major subordinate commands.

Time/Event		H - 24 hours	H-hour	H + 24
Enemy or Adversary Action		Monitors movements	Defends from security zone	Commits reserve
Population		Orderly evacuation from area continues		
Decision Points		Conduct aviation attack of OBJ Irene		
Control Measures				
Movement and Maneuver	1st BCT	Move on Route Irish	Cross LD	Seize on OBJ Irene
	2d BCT	Move on Route Longstreet	Cross LD	Seize on OBJ Rose
	3d BCT			FPOL with 1st BCT
	Avn Bde	Attack enemy reserve on OBJ Irene		
	R&S			
Reserve				
Intelligence				
Fires		Prep fires initiated at H-5		
Protection	Engineer			
	PMO			
	AMD			
	CBRN			
Sustainment				
Mission Command			Main CP with 1st BCT	
Close Air Support				
Electronic Warfare			Enemy command and control jammed	
Nonlethal		Surrender broadcasts and leaflets		
Host Nation				
Interagency				
NGOs			Begins refugee relief	

Note: The first column is representative only and can be modified to fit formation needs.

AMD	air and missile defense	LD	line of departure
Avn Bde	aviation brigade	NGO	nongovernmental organization
BCT	brigade combat team	OBJ	objective
CBRN	chemical, biological, radiological, and nuclear	PMO	provost marshal office
CP	command post	R&S	reconnaissance and surveillance
FPOL	forward passage of lines		

Figure 4-12. Sample synchronization matrix technique

4-155.   The sketch note technique uses brief notes concerning critical locations or tasks and purposes. (See Figure 4-13.) These notes refer to specific locations or relate to general considerations covering broad areas. The commander and staff mark locations on the map and on a separate war-game work sheet. Staff members use sequential numbers to link the notes to the corresponding locations on the map or overlay. Staff members also identify actions by placing them in sequential action groups, giving each subtask a separate number. They use the war-game work sheet to identify all pertinent data for a critical event. They assign each event a number and title and use the columns on the work sheet to identify and list in sequence—

- Units and assigned tasks.
- Expected enemy actions and reactions.
- Friendly counteractions and assets.
- Total assets needed for the task.
- Estimated time to accomplish the task.
- The decision point tied to executing the task.
- CCIRs.
- Control measures.
- Remarks.

Critical Event	Seize OBJ Sword
Sequence number	1
Action	TF 3 attacks to destroy enemy company on OBJ Sword
Reaction	Enemy company on OBJ Club counterattacks
Counteraction	TF 1 suppresses enemy company on OBJ Club
Assets	TF 3, TF 1, and 1-78 FA (155-SP)
Time	H+1 to H+4
Decision point	DP 3a and 3b
Commander's critical information requirements	Location of enemy armor reserve west of PL Jaguar
Control measures	Axis Zinc and support by fire position 1
Remarks	

Figure 4-13. Sample sketch note technique

War-Game the Operation and Assess the Results

4-156.   War-gaming is a conscious attempt to visualize the flow of operations given the friendly force's strengths and disposition, enemy's capabilities and possible COAs, and civilians. During the war game, the commander and staff try to foresee the actions, reactions, and counteractions of all participants to include civilians. The staff analyzes each selected event. They identify tasks that the force must accomplish one echelon down, using assets two echelons down. Identifying strengths and weaknesses of each COA allows the staff to adjust the COAs as necessary.

4-157.   The war game focuses not so much on the tools used but on the people who participate. Staff members who participate in war-gaming should be the individuals deeply involved in developing COAs. Red team members (who can provide alternative points of view) provide insight on each COA. In stability operations, subject matter experts in areas such as economic or local governance can also help assess results of planned actions, including identifying possible unintended effects.

4-158.   The war game follows an action-reaction-counteraction cycle. Actions are those events initiated by the side with the initiative. Reactions are the opposing side's actions in response. With regard to stability operations, the war game tests the effects of actions, including intended and unintended effects, as they stimulate anticipated responses from civilians and civil institutions. Counteractions are the first side's responses to reactions. This sequence of action-reaction-counteraction continues until the critical event is completed or until the commander decides to use another COA to accomplish the mission.

4-159. The staff considers all possible forces, including templated enemy forces outside the AO, which can influence the operation. The staff also considers the actions of civilians in the AO, the diverse kinds of coverage of unfolding events, and their consequences in the global media. The staff evaluates each friendly move to determine the assets and actions required to defeat the enemy at that point or to accomplish stability tasks. The staff continually considers branches to the plan that promote success against likely enemy counteractions or unexpected civilian reactions. Lastly, the staff lists assets used in the appropriate columns of the work sheet and lists the totals in the assets column (not considering any assets lower than two command levels down).

4-160. The commander and staff examine many areas during the war game. These include, but are not limited to—

- All friendly capabilities.
- All enemy capabilities.
- Civilian reactions to all friendly actions.
- Global media responses to proposed actions.
- Movement considerations.
- Closure rates.
- Lengths of columns.
- Formation depths.
- Ranges and capabilities of weapon systems.
- Desired effects of fires.

4-161. The commander and staff consider how to create conditions for success, protect the force, and shape the operational environment. Experience, historical data, SOPs, and doctrinal literature provide much of the necessary information. During the war game, staff officers perform a risk assessment for their functional areas for each COA. They then propose appropriate controls. They continually assess the risk of adverse reactions from population and media resulting from actions taken by all sides in the operation. Staff officers develop ways to mitigate those risks.

4-162. The staff continually assesses the risk to friendly forces from catastrophic threats, seeking a balance between mass and dispersion. When assessing the risk of weapons of mass destruction to friendly forces, planners view the target that the force presents through the eyes of an enemy target analyst. They consider ways to reduce vulnerability and determine the appropriate level of mission-oriented protective posture consistent with mission accomplishment.

4-163. The staff identifies the required assets of the warfighting functions to support the concept of operations, including those needed to synchronize sustaining operations. If requirements exceed available assets, the staff recommends priorities based on the situation, commander's intent, and planning guidance. To maintain flexibility, the commander may decide to create a reserve to account for assets for unforeseen tasks or opportunities.

4-164. The commander can modify any COA based on how things develop during the war game. When doing this, the commander validates the composition and location of the decisive operation, shaping operations, and reserve forces. Control measures are adjusted as necessary. The commander may also identify situations, opportunities, or additional critical events that require more analysis. The staff performs this analysis quickly and incorporates the results into the war-gaming record.

4-165. An effective war game results in the commander and staff refining, identifying, analyzing, developing, and determining several effects. They refine—

- Or modify each COA, to include identifying branches and sequels that become on-order or be-prepared missions.
- The locations and times of decisive points.
- The enemy event template and matrix.
- The task organization, including forces retained in general support.

- Control requirements, including control measures and updated operational graphics.
- CCIRs and IRs—including the last time information of value—and incorporate them into the reconnaissance and surveillance plan and information management plan.

4-166. An effective war game results in the commander and staff identifying—

- Key or decisive terrain and determining how to use it.
- Tasks the unit retains and tasks assigned to subordinates.
- Likely times and areas for enemy use of weapons of mass destruction and friendly chemical, biological, radiological, and nuclear defense requirements.
- Potential times or locations for committing the reserve.
- The most dangerous enemy COA.
- The most likely enemy COA.
- The most dangerous civilian reaction.
- Locations for the commander and command posts.
- Critical events.
- Requirements for support of each warfighting function.
- Effects of friendly and enemy actions on civilians and infrastructure and on military operations.
- Or confirming the locations of named areas of interest, target areas of interest, decision points, and IRs needed to support them.
- Analyzing, and evaluating strengths and weaknesses of each COA.
- Hazards, assessing their risk, developing controls for them, and determining residual risk.
- The coordination required for integrating and synchronizing interagency, host-nation, and nongovernmental organization involvement.

4-167. An effective war game results in the commander and staff analyzing—

- Potential civilian reactions to operations.
- Potential media reaction to operations.
- Potential impacts on civil security, civil control, and essential services in the AO.

4-168. An effective war game results in the commander and staff developing—

- Decision points.
- A synchronization matrix.
- A decision support template and matrix.
- Solutions to achieving minimum essential stability tasks in the AO.
- The reconnaissance and surveillance plan and graphics.
- Initial information themes and messages.
- Fires, protection, and sustainment plans and graphic control measures.

4-169. Lastly, an effective war game results in the commander and staff—

- Determining requirements for military deception and surprise.
- Determining the timing for concentrating forces and starting the attack or counterattack.
- Determining movement times and tables for critical assets, including information systems nodes.
- Estimating the duration of the entire operation and each critical event.
- Projecting the percentage of enemy forces defeated in each critical event and overall.
- Projecting the percentage of minimum essential tasks that the unit can or must accomplish.
- Anticipating media coverage and impact on key audiences.
- Integrating targeting into the operation, to include identifying or confirming high-payoff targets and establishing attack guidance.
- Allocating assets to subordinate commanders to accomplish their missions.

Conduct a War-Game Briefing (Optional)

4-170. Time permitting, the staff delivers a briefing to all affected elements to ensure everyone understands the results of the war game. The staff uses the briefing for review and ensures that it captures all relevant points of the war game for presentation to the commander, COS (XO), or deputy or assistant commander. In a collaborative environment, the briefing may include selected subordinate staffs. A war-game briefing format includes the following:

- Higher headquarters' mission, commander's intent, and military deception plan.
- Updated IPB.
- Friendly and enemy COAs that were war-gamed, including—
  - Critical events.
  - Possible enemy actions and reactions.
  - Possible impact on civilians.
  - Possible media impacts.
  - Modifications to the COAs.
  - Strengths and weaknesses.
  - Results of the war game.
- Assumptions.
- War-gaming technique used.

STEP 5 – COURSE OF ACTION COMPARISON

4-171. COA comparison is an objective process to evaluate COAs independently and against set evaluation criteria approved by the commander and staff. The goal is to identify the strengths and weaknesses of COAs, enable selecting a COA with the highest probability of success, and further developing it in an OPLAN or OPORD. The commander and staff perform certain actions and processes that lead to the key outputs in Figure 4-14.

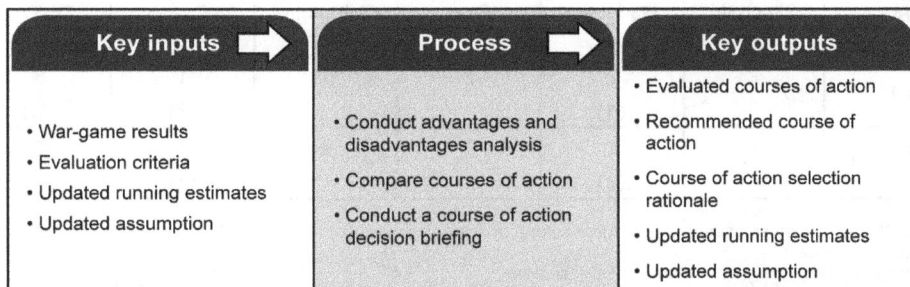

Key inputs	Process	Key outputs
• War-game results • Evaluation criteria • Updated running estimates • Updated assumption	• Conduct advantages and disadvantages analysis • Compare courses of action • Conduct a course of action decision briefing	• Evaluated courses of action • Recommended course of action • Course of action selection rationale • Updated running estimates • Updated assumption

Figure 4-14. COA comparison

Conduct Advantages and Disadvantages Analysis

4-172. The COA comparison starts with all staff members analyzing and evaluating the advantages and disadvantages of each COA from their perspectives. (See Figure 4-15, page 4-36.) Staff members each present their findings for the others' consideration. Using the evaluation criteria developed before the war game, the staff outlines each COA, highlighting its advantages and disadvantages. Comparing the strengths and weaknesses of the COAs identifies their advantages and disadvantages with respect to each other.

Course of Action	Advantages	Disadvantages
COA 1	Decisive operation avoids major terrain obstacles. Adequate maneuver space available for units conducting the decisive operation and the reserve.	Units conducting the decisive operation face stronger resistance at the start of the operation. Limited resources available to establishing civil control to Town X.
COA 2	Shaping operations provide excellent flank protection of the decisive operations. Upon completion of decisive operations, units conducting shaping operations can quickly transition to establish civil control and provide civil security to the population in Town X.	Operation may require the early employment of the division's reserve.

Figure 4-15. Sample advantages and disadvantages

Compare Courses of Action

4-173.   Comparison of COAs is critical. The staff uses any technique that helps develop those key outputs and recommendations and assists the commander to make the best decision. A common technique is the decision matrix. This matrix uses evaluation criteria developed during mission analysis and refined during COA development to help assess the effectiveness and efficiency of each COA. (See Figure 4-16.)

Weight[1]	1	2	1	1	2	
Criteria[2] **Course of Action**	Simplicity	Maneuver	Fires	Civil control	Inform and influence activities	TOTAL
COA 1[3]	2	2 (4)	2	1	1 (2)	8 (11)
COA 2[3]	1	2 (2)	1	2	2 (4)	7 (10)

Notes:
[1] The COS (XO) may emphasize one or more criteria by assigning weights to them based on a determination of their relative importance.
[2] Criteria are those assigned in step 5 of COA analysis.
[3] COAs are those selected for war-gaming with values assigned to them based on comparison between them with regard to relative advantages and disadvantages of each, such as when compared for relative simplicity COA 2 is by comparison to COA 1 simpler and therefore is rated as 1 with COA 1 rated as 2.

Figure 4-16. Sample decision matrix

4-174.   The decision matrix is a tool to compare and evaluate COAs thoroughly and logically. However, the process is based on highly subjective judgments that may change dramatically during the course of evaluation. In Figure 4-16, values reflect the relative advantages or disadvantages of each criterion for each COA as initially estimated by a COS (XO) during mission analysis. At the same time, the COS (XO) determines weights for each criterion based on a subjective determination of their relative value. The lower values signify a more favorable advantage, such as the lower the number, the more favorable the score. After comparing COAs and assigning values, the staff adds and totals the unweighted assigned scores in each column vertically under each COA. The staff multiplies the same values by the weighted score associated with each criterion and notes the product in parenthesis in each appropriate box. They add these weighted products vertically and note in parenthesis in the space for "Weighted TOTAL" below each COA column. Then the staff compare the totals to determine the "best" (lowest number) COA based on both criteria alone and then on weighted scores. Upon review and consideration, the commander—based on personal judgment—may elect to change either the value for the basic criterion or the weighted value. Although the lowest value denotes a "best" solution, the process for estimating relative values assigned to criterion and weighting is highly subjective. The "best" COA may not be supportable without additional resources. This result enables the decisionmaker to decide whether to pursue additional support, alter the COA in some way, or determine that it is not feasible.

4-175. The decision matrix is one highly structured and effective method used to compare COAs against criteria that, when met, suggest a great likelihood of producing success. Staff officers give specific broad categories of COA characteristics a basic numerical value based on evaluation criteria. They assign weights based on subjective judgment regarding their relative importance to existing circumstances. Then they multiply basic values by the weight to yield a given criterion's final score. A staff member then totals all scores to compare COAs.

4-176. Commanders and staffs cannot solely rely on the outcome of a decision matrix, as it only provides a partial basis for a solution. During the decision matrix process, planners carefully avoid reaching conclusions from mainly subjective judgments from purely quantifiable analysis. Comparing and evaluating COAs by category of criterion is probably more useful than merely comparing total scores. Often judgments change with regard to relative weighting of criterion of importance during close analysis of COAs, which would change matrix scoring.

4-177. The staff compares feasible COAs to identify the one with the highest probability of success against the most likely enemy COA, the most dangerous enemy COA, the most important stability task, or the most damaging environmental impact. The selected COA should also—

- Pose the minimum risk to the force and mission accomplishment.
- Place the force in the best posture for future operations.
- Provide maximum latitude for initiative by subordinates.
- Provide the most flexibility to meet unexpected threats and opportunities.
- Provide the most secure and stable environment for civilians in the AO.
- Best facilitate information themes and messages.

4-178. Staff officers often use their own matrix to compare COAs with respect to their functional areas. Matrixes use the evaluation criteria developed before the war game. Their greatest value is providing a method to compare COAs against criteria that, when met, produce operational success. Staff officers use these analytical tools to prepare recommendations. Commanders provide the solution by applying their judgment to staff recommendations and making a decision.

Conduct a Course of Action Decision Briefing

4-179. After completing its analysis and comparison, the staff identifies its preferred COA and makes a recommendation. If the staff cannot reach a decision, the COS (XO) decides which COA to recommend. The staff then delivers a decision briefing to the commander. The COS (XO) highlights any changes to each COA resulting from the war game. The decision briefing includes—

- The commander's intent of the higher and next higher commanders.
- The status of the force and its components.
- The current IPB.
- The COAs considered, including—
  - Assumptions used.
  - Results of running estimates.
  - A summary of the war game for each COA, including critical events, modifications to any COA, and war-game results.
  - Advantages and disadvantages (including risks) of each COA.
  - The recommended COA. If a significant disagreement exists, then the staff should inform the commander and, if necessary, discuss the disagreement.

STEP 6 – COURSE OF ACTION APPROVAL

4-180.   After the decision briefing, the commander selects the COA to best accomplish the mission. If the commander rejects all COAs, the staff starts COA development again. If the commander modifies a proposed COA or gives the staff an entirely different one, the staff war-games the new COA and presents the results to the commander with a recommendation.

4-181.   After selecting a COA, the commander issues the final planning guidance. The final planning guidance includes a refined commander's intent (if necessary) and new CCIRs to support execution. It also includes any additional guidance on priorities for the warfighting functions, orders preparation, rehearsal, and preparation. This guidance includes priorities for resources needed to preserve freedom of action and ensure continuous sustainment.

4-182.   Commanders include risk they are willing to accept in the final planning guidance. If there is time, commanders use a video teleconference (VTC) to discuss acceptable risk with adjacent, subordinate, and senior commanders. However, commanders still obtain the higher commander's approval to accept any risk that might imperil accomplishing the higher commander's mission.

4-183.   Based on the commander's decision and final planning guidance, the staff issues a WARNO to subordinate headquarters. This WARNO contains the information subordinate units need to refine their plans. It confirms guidance issued in person or by VTC and expands on details not covered by the commander personally. The WARNO issued after COA approval normally contains—

- Mission.
- Commander's intent.
- Updated CCIRs and EEFIs.
- Concept of operations.
- The AO.
- Principal tasks assigned to subordinate units.
- Preparation and rehearsal instructions not included in the SOPs.
- A final timeline for the operations.

STEP 7 – ORDERS PRODUCTION

4-184.   The staff prepares the order or plan by turning the selected COA into a clear, concise concept of operations and the required supporting information. The COA statement becomes the concept of operations for the plan. The COA sketch becomes the basis for the operation overlay. If time permits, the staff may conduct a more detailed war game of the selected COA to more fully synchronize the operation and complete the plan. The staff writes the OPORD or OPLAN using the Army's operation order format. (See Chapter 12.)

4-185.   Commanders review and approve orders before the staff reproduces and disseminates them unless commanders have delegated that authority. Subordinates immediately acknowledge receipt of the higher order. If possible, the higher commander and staff brief the order to subordinate commanders in person. The commander and staff conduct confirmation briefings with subordinates immediately afterwards. Confirmation briefings can be done collaboratively with several commanders at the same time or with single commanders. These briefings may be conducted in person or by a VTC.

PLANS IN A TIME-CONSTRAINED ENVIRONMENT

4-186.   Any planning process aims to quickly develop a flexible, sound, and fully integrated and synchronized plan. However, any operation may "outrun" the initial plan. The most detailed estimates cannot anticipate every possible branch or sequel, enemy action, unexpected opportunity, or change in mission directed from higher headquarters. Fleeting opportunities or unexpected enemy action may require a quick decision to implement a new or modified plan. When this occurs, units often find themselves pressed for time in developing a new plan.

4-187. Before a unit can effectively conduct planning in a time-constrained environment, it must master the steps in the full MDMP. A unit can only shorten the process if it fully understands the role of each and every step of the process and the requirements to produce the necessary products. Training on these steps must be thorough and result in a series of staff battle drills that can be tailored to the time available.

4-188. Quality staffs produce simple, flexible, and tactically sound plans in a time-constrained environment. Any METT-TC factor, but especially limited time, may make it difficult to complete every step of the MDMP in detail. Applying an inflexible process to all situations does not work. Anticipation, organization, and prior preparation are the keys to successful planning under time-constrained conditions.

4-189. Staff can use the time saved on any step of the MDMP to—
- Refine the plan more thoroughly.
- Conduct a more deliberate and detailed war game.
- Consider potential branches and sequels in detail.
- Focus more on rehearsing and preparing the plan.
- Allow subordinate units more planning and preparation time.

THE COMMANDER'S ROLE

4-190. The commander decides how to adjust the MDMP, giving specific guidance to the staff to focus on the process and save time. Commanders shorten the MDMP when they lack time to perform each step in detail. The most significant factor to consider is time. It is the only nonrenewable, and often the most critical, resource. Commanders (who have access to only a small portion of the staff or none at all) rely even more than normal on their own expertise, intuition, and creativity as well as on their understanding of the environment and of the art and science of warfare. They may have to select a COA, mentally war-game it, and confirm their decision to the staff in a short time. If so, they base their decision more on experience than on a formal, integrated staff process.

4-191. Effective commanders avoid changing their guidance unless a significantly changed situation requires major revisions. Making frequent, minor changes to the guidance can easily result in lost time as the staff constantly adjusts the plan with an adverse ripple effect throughout overall planning.

4-192. Commanders consult with subordinate commanders before making a decision, if possible. Subordinate commanders are closer to the operation and can more accurately describe enemy, friendly, and civilian situations. Additionally, consulting with subordinates gives commanders insight into the upcoming operation and allows parallel planning. White boards and collaborative digital means of communicating greatly enhance parallel planning.

4-193. In situations where commanders must decide quickly, they advise their higher headquarters of the selected COA, if time is available. However, commanders do not let an opportunity pass just because they cannot report their actions.

THE STAFF'S ROLE

4-194. Staff members keep their running estimates current. When time constraints exist, they can provide accurate, up-to-date assessments quickly and move directly into COA development. Under time-constrained conditions, commanders and staffs use as much of the previously analyzed information and products as possible. The importance of running estimates increases as time decreases. Decisionmaking in a time-constrained environment usually occurs after a unit has entered the AO and begun operations. This means that the IPB, an updated common operational picture, and some portion of running estimates should already exist. Civilian and military joint and multinational organizations operating in the AO should have well-developed plans and information to add insights to the operational environment. Detailed planning provides the basis for information that the commander and staff need to make decisions during execution.

TIME-SAVING TECHNIQUES

4-195. Paragraphs 4-196 through 4-200 discuss time-saving techniques to speed the planning process.

Increase Commander's Involvement

4-196. While commanders cannot spend all their time with the planning staff, the greater the commander's involvement in planning, the faster the staff can plan. In time-constrained conditions, commanders who participate in the planning process can make decisions (such as COA selection) without waiting for a detailed briefing from the staff.

Limit the Number of Courses of Action to Develop

4-197. Limiting the number of COAs developed and war-gamed can save planning time. If time is extremely short, the commander can direct development of only one COA. In this case, the goal is an acceptable COA that meets mission requirements in the time available. This technique saves the most time. The fastest way to develop a plan has the commander directing development of one COA with branches against the most likely enemy COA or most damaging civil situation or condition. However, this technique should be used only when time is severely limited. In such cases, this choice of COA is often intuitive, relying on the commander's experience and judgment. The commander determines which staff officers are essential to assist in COA development. Normally commanders require the intelligence officer, operations officer, plans officer, chief of fires (fire support officer), engineer officer, civil affairs operations officer, inform and influence activities officer, and COS (XO). They may also include subordinate commanders, if available, either in person or by a VTC. This team quickly develops a flexible COA that it feels will accomplish the mission. The commander mentally war-games this COA and gives it to the staff to refine.

Maximize Parallel Planning

4-198. Although parallel planning is the norm, maximizing its use in time-constrained environments is critical. In a time-constrained environment, the importance of WARNOs increases as available time decreases. A verbal WARNO now followed by a written order later saves more time than a written order one hour from now. The staff issues the same WARNOs used in the full MDMP when abbreviating the process. In addition to WARNOs, units must share all available information with subordinates, especially IPB products, as early as possible. The staff uses every opportunity to perform parallel planning with the higher headquarters and to share information with subordinates.

Increase Collaborative Planning

4-199. Planning in real time with higher headquarters and subordinates improves the overall planning effort of the organization. Modern information systems and a common operational picture shared electronically allow collaboration with subordinates from distant locations, can increase information sharing, and can improve the commander's visualization. Additionally, taking advantage of subordinates' input and knowledge of the situation in their AOs often results in developing better COAs faster.

Use Liaison Officers

4-200. Liaison officers posted to higher headquarters allow the commander to have representation in their higher headquarters' planning session. These officers assist in passing timely information to their parent headquarters and directly to the commander. Effective liaison officers have the commander's full confidence and the necessary rank and experience for the mission. Commanders may elect to use a single individual or a liaison team. As representatives, liaison officers must—

- Understand how their commander thinks and interpret their verbal and written guidance.
- Convey their commander's intent, planning guidance, mission, and concept of operations.
- Represent their commander's position.
- Know the unit's mission; tactics, techniques, and procedures; organization; capabilities; and communications equipment.
- Observe the established channels of command and staff functions.
- Be trained in their functional responsibilities.
- Be tactful.
- Possess the necessary language expertise.

Chapter 5

Troop Leading Procedures

Troop leading procedures provide small-unit leaders with a framework for planning and preparing for operations. Leaders of company and smaller units use troop leading procedures to develop plans and orders. This chapter describes the eight steps of troop leading procedures and their relationship to the military decisionmaking process. While this chapter explains troop leading procedures from a ground-maneuver perspective, it applies to all types of small units.

BACKGROUND AND COMPARISON TO THE MDMP

5-1. Troop leading procedures extend the military decisionmaking process (MDMP) to the small-unit level. The MDMP and troop leading procedures (TLP) are similar but not identical. They are both linked by the basic Army problem-solving process. Commanders with a coordinating staff use the MDMP as their primary planning process. Company-level and smaller units lack formal staffs and use TLP to plan and prepare for operations. This places the responsibility for planning primarily on the commander or small-unit leader.

5-2. *Troop leading procedures* are a dynamic process used by small-unit leaders to analyze a mission, develop a plan, and prepare for an operation (FM 5-0). These procedures enable leaders to maximize available planning time while developing effective plans and preparing their units for an operation. TLP consist of eight steps. TLP are also supported by composite risk management. (See FM 5-19.) The sequence of the steps of TLP is not rigid. Leaders modify the sequence to meet the mission, situation, and available time. Some steps are done concurrently while others may go on continuously throughout the operation:

- Step 1 – Receive the mission.
- Step 2 – Issue a warning order.
- Step 3 – Make a tentative plan.
- Step 4 – Initiate movement.
- Step 5 – Conduct reconnaissance.
- Step 6 – Complete the plan.
- Step 7 – Issue the order.
- Step 8 – Supervise and refine.

5-3. Leaders use TLP when working alone or with a small group to solve tactical problems. For example, a company commander may use the executive officer, first sergeant, fire support officer, supply sergeant, and communications sergeant to assist during TLP.

5-4. The type, amount, and timeliness of information passed from higher to lower headquarters directly impact the lower unit leader's TLP. Figure 5-1 (page 5-2) illustrates the parallel sequences of the MDMP of a battalion with the TLP of a company and a platoon. The solid arrows depict when a higher headquarters' planning event could start TLP of a subordinate unit. However, events do not always occur in the order shown. For example, TLP may start with receipt of a warning order (WARNO), or they may not start until the higher headquarters has completed the MDMP and issued an operation order (OPORD). WARNOs from higher headquarters may arrive at any time during TLP. Leaders remain flexible. They adapt TLP to fit the situation rather than try to alter the situation to fit a preconceived idea of how events should flow.

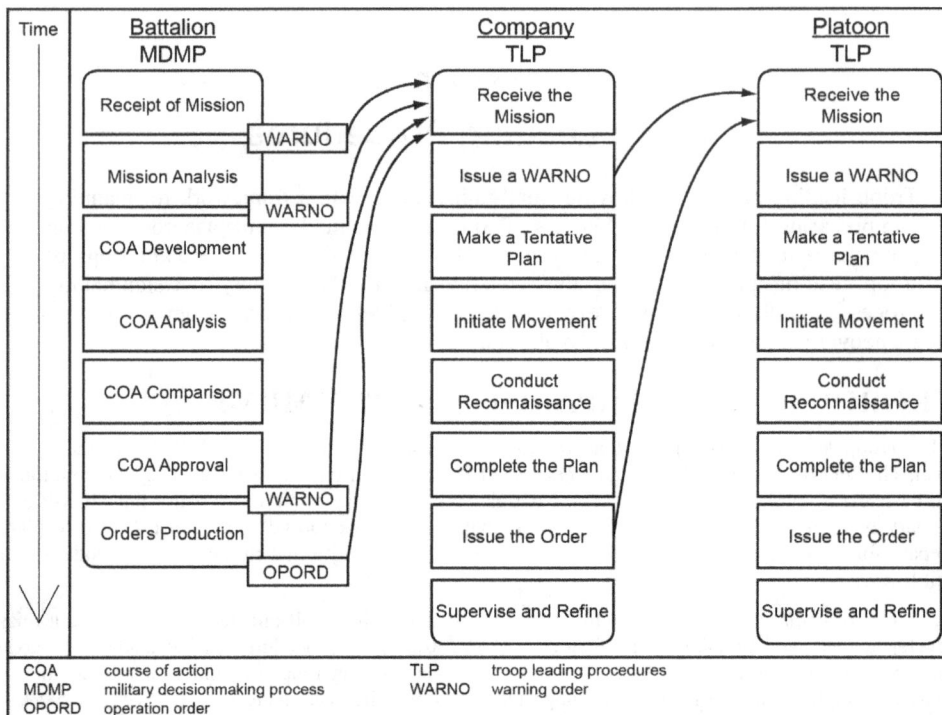

Figure 5-1. Parallel planning

5-5.   Normally, the first three steps (receive the mission, issue a WARNO, and make a tentative plan) of TLP occur in order. However, the sequence of subsequent steps is based on the situation. The tasks involved in some steps (for example, initiate movement and conduct reconnaissance) may occur several times. The last step, supervise and refine, occurs throughout.

5-6.   A tension exists between executing current operations and planning for future operations. The small-unit leader must balance both. If engaged in a current operation, leaders have less time for TLP. If in a lull, transition, or an assembly area, leaders have more time to use TLP thoroughly. In some situations, time constraints or other factors may prevent leaders from performing each step of TLP as thoroughly as they would like. For example, during the step, make a tentative plan, small-unit leaders often develop only one acceptable course of action (COA) vice multiple COAs. If time permits, leaders develop, compare, and analyze several COAs before deciding which one to execute.

5-7.   Ideally, a battalion headquarters issues at least three WARNOs to subordinates when conducting the MDMP as depicted in Figure 5-1. WARNOs are issued upon receipt of mission, completion of mission analysis, and when the commander approves a COA. However, the number of WARNOs is not fixed. WARNOs serve a function in planning similar to that of fragmentary orders (FRAGOs) during execution. Commanders may issue a WARNO whenever they need to disseminate additional planning information or initiate necessary preparatory action, such as movement or reconnaissance.

5-8.   Leaders begin TLP when they receive the initial WARNO or receive a new mission. As each subsequent order arrives, leaders modify their assessments, update tentative plans, and continue to supervise and assess preparations. In some situations, the higher headquarters may not issue the full sequence of WARNOs; security considerations or tempo may make it impractical. Commanders carefully consider decisions to eliminate WARNOs. Subordinate units always need to have enough information to plan and prepare for the operation. In other cases, leaders may initiate TLP before receiving a WARNO based on existing plans and orders (contingency plans or be-prepared missions) and on their understanding of the situation.

5-9. Parallel planning hinges on distributing information as it is received or developed. Leaders cannot complete their plans until they receive their unit mission. If each successive WARNO contains enough information, the higher headquarters' final order will confirm what subordinate leaders have already analyzed and put into their tentative plans. In other cases, the higher headquarters' order may change or modify the subordinate's tasks enough that additional planning and reconnaissance are required.

STEPS OF TROOP LEADING PROCEDURES

5-10. TLP provide small-unit leaders a framework for planning and preparing for operations. Figure 5-2 depicts TLP along with key planning tasks. The box on the left shows the steps of TLP. The box in the middle (METT-TC for mission, enemy, terrain and weather, troops and support available, time available, civil considerations) represents the initial METT-TC analysis that leaders conduct to develop an initial assessment. This occurs in steps 1 and 2 of TLP and is refined in plan development. The box on the right depicts plan development tasks. Plan development occurs in step 3 and is completed in step 6 of TLP. These tasks are similar to the steps of the MDMP.

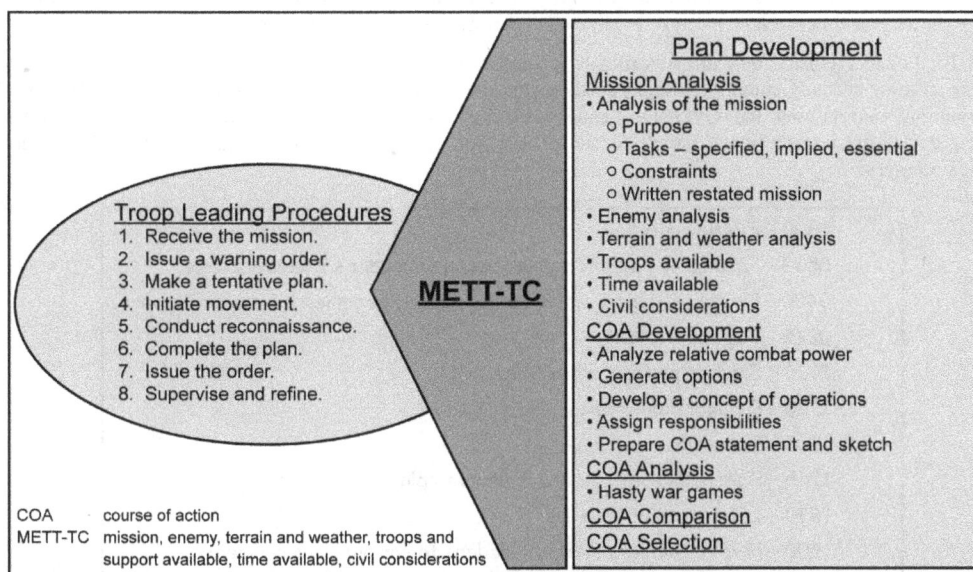

Troop Leading Procedures
1. Receive the mission.
2. Issue a warning order.
3. Make a tentative plan.
4. Initiate movement.
5. Conduct reconnaissance.
6. Complete the plan.
7. Issue the order.
8. Supervise and refine.

METT-TC

Plan Development
Mission Analysis
- Analysis of the mission
  o Purpose
  o Tasks – specified, implied, essential
  o Constraints
  o Written restated mission
- Enemy analysis
- Terrain and weather analysis
- Troops available
- Time available
- Civil considerations
COA Development
- Analyze relative combat power
- Generate options
- Develop a concept of operations
- Assign responsibilities
- Prepare COA statement and sketch
COA Analysis
- Hasty war games
COA Comparison
COA Selection

COA   course of action
METT-TC   mission, enemy, terrain and weather, troops and
                 support available, time available, civil considerations

Figure 5-2. Planning at company and below

STEP 1 – RECEIVE THE MISSION

5-11. Receive the mission may occur in several ways. It may begin when the initial WARNO or OPORD arrives from higher headquarters or when a leader anticipates a new mission. Frequently, leaders receive a mission in a FRAGO over the radio. Ideally, they receive a series of WARNOs, the OPORD, and a briefing from their commander. Normally after receiving an OPORD, leaders give a confirmation brief to their higher commander to ensure they understand the higher commander's intent and concept of operations. The leader obtains clarification on any portions of the higher headquarters plan as required.

5-12. When they receive the mission, leaders perform an initial assessment of the situation (mission analysis) and allocate the time available for planning and preparation. (Preparation includes rehearsals and movement.) This initial assessment and time allocation forms the basis of their initial WARNOs and addresses the factors of METT-TC. The order and detail in which leaders analyze the factors of METT-TC is flexible. It depends on the amount of information available and the relative importance of each factor. For example, leaders may concentrate on the mission, enemy, and terrain, leaving weather and civil considerations until they receive more detailed information.

5-13. Often, leaders do not receive their final unit mission until the WARNO is disseminated after COA approval or after the OPORD. Effective leaders do not wait until their higher headquarters completes planning to begin their planning. Using all information available, leaders develop their unit mission as completely as they can. They focus on the mission, commander's intent, and concept of operations of their higher and next higher headquarters. They pick major tasks their unit will probably be assigned and develop a mission statement based on information they have received. At this stage, the mission may be incomplete. For example, an initial mission statement could be, "First platoon conducts an ambush in the next 24 hours." While not complete, this information allows subordinates to start preparations. Leaders complete a formal mission statement during TLP step 3 (make a tentative plan) and step 6 (complete the plan).

5-14. Based on what they know, leaders estimate the time available to plan and prepare for the mission. They begin by identifying the times they must complete major planning and preparation events, including rehearsals. Reverse planning helps them do this. Leaders identify critical times specified by higher headquarters and work back from them, estimating how much time each event will consume. Critical times might include times to load aircraft, the line of departure, or the start point for movement.

5-15. Leaders ensure that all subordinate echelons have sufficient time for their own planning and preparation needs. Generally, leaders at all levels use no more than one-third of the available time for planning and issuing the OPORD. Leaders allocate the remaining two-thirds of it to subordinates. Figure 5-3 illustrates a time schedule for an infantry company. The company adjusts the tentative schedule as necessary.

```
0600 – Execute mission.
0530 – Finalize or adjust the plan based on leader's reconnaissance.
0400 – Establish the objective rallying point; begin leader reconnaissance.
0200 – Begin movement.
2100 – Conduct platoon inspections.
1900 – Conduct rehearsals.
1800 – Eat meals.
1745 – Hold backbriefs (squad leaders to platoon leaders).
1630 – Issue platoon OPORDs.
1500 – Hold backbriefs (platoon leaders to company commander).
1330 – Issue company OPORD.
1045 – Conduct reconnaissance.
1030 – Update company WARNO.
1000 – Receive battalion OPORD.
0900 – Receive battalion WARNO; issue company WARNO.
```

Figure 5-3. Sample schedule

STEP 2 – ISSUE A WARNING ORDER

5-16. As soon as leaders finish their initial assessment of the situation and available time, they issue a WARNO. Leaders do not wait for more information. They issue the best WARNO possible with the information at hand and update it as needed with additional WARNOs.

5-17. The WARNO contains as much detail as possible. It informs subordinates of the unit mission and gives them the leader's timeline. Leaders may also pass on any other instructions or information they think will help subordinates prepare for the new mission. This includes information on the enemy, the nature of the higher headquarters' plan, and any specific instructions for preparing their units. The most important thing is that leaders not delay in issuing the initial WARNO. As more information becomes available, leaders can—and should—issue additional WARNOs. By issuing the initial WARNO as quickly as possible, leaders enable their subordinates to begin their own planning and preparation.

5-18. WARNOs follow the five-paragraph OPORD format. Normally an initial WARNO issued below battalion level includes—

- The mission or nature of the operation.
- The time and place for issuing the OPORD.
- Units or elements participating in the operation.
- Specific tasks not addressed by unit standard operating procedures (SOPs).
- The timeline for the operation.

STEP 3 – MAKE A TENTATIVE PLAN

5-19. Once they have issued the initial WARNO, leaders develop a tentative plan. This step combines the MDMP steps 2 through 6: mission analysis, COA development, COA analysis, COA comparison, and COA approval. At levels below battalion, these steps are less structured than for units with staffs. Often, leaders perform them mentally. They may include their principal subordinates—especially during COA development, analysis, and comparison. However, leaders—not their subordinates—select the COA on which to base the tentative plan.

Mission Analysis

5-20. To frame the tentative plan, leaders perform mission analysis. This mission analysis follows the METT-TC format, continuing the initial assessment performed in TLP step 1. (FM 6-0 discusses the factors of METT-TC.)

Mission

5-21. Leaders analyze the higher headquarters' WARNO or OPORD to determine how their unit contributes to the higher headquarters' mission. They examine the following information that affects their mission:

- Higher headquarters' mission and commander's intent.
- Higher headquarters' concept of operations.
- Specified, implied, and essential tasks.
- Constraints.

5-22. Leaders determine the mission and commander's intent of their higher and next higher headquarters. When these are unavailable, leaders infer them based on available information. When they receive the actual mission and commander's intent, leaders revise their plan, if necessary.

5-23. Leaders examine their higher headquarters' concept of operations to determine how their unit's mission and tasks contribute to the higher mission's success. They determine details that will affect their operations, such as control measures and execution times.

5-24. Leaders extract the specified and implied tasks assigned to their unit from WARNOs and the OPORD. They determine why each task was assigned to their unit so to understand how it fits within the commander's intent and concept of operations. From the specified and implied tasks, leaders identify essential tasks. Leaders complete these tasks to accomplish the mission. Failure to complete an essential task results in mission failure.

5-25. Leaders also identify any constraints placed on their unit. Constraints can take the form of a requirement (for example, maintain a reserve of one platoon) or a prohibition on action (for example, no reconnaissance forward of Phase Line Bravo before H-hour).

5-26. The product of this part of the mission analysis is the restated mission. The restated mission is a simple, concise expression of the essential tasks the unit must accomplish and the purpose to be achieved. The mission statement states *who* (the unit), *what* (the task), *when* (either the critical time or on order), *where* (location), and *why* (the purpose of the operation).

Enemy

5-27. With the restated mission as the focus, leaders continue the analysis with the enemy. For small-unit operations, leaders need to know about the enemy's composition, disposition, strengths, recent activities, ability to reinforce, and possible COAs. Much of this information comes from higher headquarters. Additional information comes from adjacent units and other leaders. Some information comes from the leader's experience. Leaders determine how the available information applies to their operation. They also determine what they do not know about the enemy but should know. To obtain the necessary information, they identify these intelligence gaps to their higher headquarters or take action (such as sending out reconnaissance patrols).

Terrain and Weather

5-28. This aspect of mission analysis addresses the military aspects of terrain: observation and fields of fire, avenue of approach, key terrain, obstacles, and cover and concealment (known as OAKOC).

5-29. Observation the ability to see (or be seen by) the adversary either visually or through the use of surveillance devices. A field of fire is the area which a weapon or a group of weapons may cover effectively with fire from a given position. Observation and fields of fire apply to both enemy and friendly weapons. Leaders consider direct-fire weapons and the ability of observers to mass and adjust indirect fire.

5-30. An *avenue of approach* is an air or ground route of an attacking force of a given size leading to its objective or to key terrain in its path (JP 2-01.3). Avenues of approach include overland, air, and underground avenues. Underground avenues are particularly important in urban operations.

5-31. *Key terrain* is any locality, or area, the seizure or retention of which affords a marked advantage to either combatant (JP 2-01.3). Terrain adjacent to the area of operations (AO) may be key if its control is necessary to accomplish the mission.

5-32. An *obstacle* is any obstruction designed or employed to disrupt, fix, turn, or block the movement of an opposing force, and to impose additional losses in personnel, time, and equipment on the opposing force. Obstacles can exist naturally or can be man-made, or can be a combination of both (JP 3-15). Obstacles include military reinforcing obstacles, such as minefields.

5-33. Cover is protection from the effects of fires. Concealment is protection from observation and surveillance. Terrain that offers cover and concealment limits fields of fire. Leaders consider friendly and enemy perspectives. Although remembered as separate elements, leaders consider the military aspects of terrain together.

5-34. There are five military aspects of weather: visibility, winds, precipitation, cloud cover, and temperature and humidity. (See FM 2-01.3.) The consideration of their effects is an important part of the mission analysis. Leaders review the forecasts and considerations available from Army and Air Force weather forecast models and develop COAs based on the effects of weather on the mission. The analysis considers the effects on Soldiers, equipment, and supporting forces, such as air and artillery support. Leaders identify the aspects of weather that can affect the mission. They focus on factors whose effects they can mitigate. For example, leaders may modify the SOPs for uniforms and carrying loads based on the temperature. Small-unit leaders include instructions on mitigating weather effects in their tentative plan. They check for compliance during preparation, especially during rehearsals.

Troops and Support Available

5-35. Perhaps the most important aspect of mission analysis is determining the combat potential of one's own force. Leaders know the status of their Soldiers' morale, their experience and training, and the strengths and weaknesses of subordinate leaders. They realistically determine all available resources. This includes troops attached to, or in direct support of, the unit. The assessment includes knowing the strength and status of their equipment. It also includes understanding the full array of assets in support of the unit. Leaders know, for example, how much indirect fire will become available, and when it is available, they will know the type. They consider any new limitations based on the level of training or recent fighting.

Time Available

5-36. Leaders not only appreciate how much time is available, they understand the time-space aspects of preparing, moving, fighting, and sustaining. They view their own tasks and enemy actions in relation to time. They know how long it takes under such conditions to prepare for certain tasks (such as orders production, rehearsals, and subordinate element preparations). Most important, leaders monitor the time available. As events occur, they assess their impact on the unit timeline and update previous timelines for their subordinates. Timelines list all events that affect the unit and its subordinate elements.

Civil Considerations

5-37. *Civil considerations* are the influence of manmade infrastructure, civilian institutions, and activities of the civilian leaders, populations, and organizations within an area of operations on the conduct of military operations (FM 6-0). Rarely are military operations conducted in uninhabited areas. Most of the time, units are surrounded by noncombatants. These noncombatants include residents of the AO, local officials, and governmental and nongovernmental organizations. Based on information from higher headquarters and their own knowledge and judgment, leaders identify civil considerations that affect their mission. (See FM 6-0 and FM 3-05.401.) Commanders analyze civil considerations a using the six factors known by the memory aid ASCOPE: areas, structures, capabilities, organizations, people, and events.

Course of Action Development

5-38. Mission analysis provides information needed to develop COAs. COA development aims to determine one or more ways to accomplish the mission. At lower echelons, the mission may be a single task. Most missions and tasks can be accomplished in more than one way. Normally, leaders develop two or more COAs. However, in a time-constrained environment, they may develop only one. Leaders do not wait for a complete order before beginning COA development. Usable COAs are suitable, feasible, acceptable, distinguishable, and complete. Leaders develop COAs as soon as they have enough information to do so. To develop COAs, leaders focus on the actions the unit takes at the objective and conduct a reverse plan to the starting point.

Analyze Relative Combat Power

5-39. During COA development, leaders determine whether the unit has enough combat power to defeat the force (or accomplish a task in stability or civil support operations) against which it is arrayed by comparing the combat power of friendly and enemy forces. Leaders seek to determine where, when, and how friendly combat power (the elements of intelligence, movement and maneuver, fires, sustainment, protection, and mission command) can overwhelm the enemy. It is a particularly difficult process if the unit is fighting a dissimilar unit. For example, if the unit is attacking or defending against an enemy mechanized force as opposed to a similarly equipped light infantry force. Below battalion level, relative combat power comparisons are rough and generally rely on professional judgment instead of numerical analysis. When an enemy is not the object of a particular mission or tasks, leaders conduct a troop-to-task analysis to determine if they have enough combat power to accomplish the tasks. For example, a company commander assigned the task "establish civil control in town X" would need to determine if they had enough Soldiers and equipment (to include vehicles and barrier materials) to establish the necessary check points and security stations within the town to control the population in town X.

Generate Options

5-40. During this step, leaders brainstorm different ways to accomplish the mission. They determine the doctrinal requirements for the operation, including the tactical tasks normally assigned to subordinates. Doctrinal requirements give leaders a framework from which to develop COAs.

5-41. Next, leaders identify where and when the unit can mass overwhelming combat power to achieve specific results (with respect to enemy, terrain, time, or civil considerations) that accomplish the mission. Offensive and defensive operations focus on the destructive effects of combat power. Stability operations, on the other hand, emphasize constructive effects. Leaders identify any decisive points and determine what result they must achieve at the decisive points to accomplish the mission. This helps leaders determine the amount of combat power to apply at a decisive point and the required tasks.

5-42. After identifying the tasks, leaders next determine the purpose for each task. There is normally one primary task for each mission. The unit assigned this task is the main effort. The other tasks should support the accomplishment of the primary task.

Develop a Concept of Operations

5-43. The concept of operations describes how the leader envisions the operation unfolding from its start to its conclusion or end state. It determines how accomplishing each task leads to executing the next. It identifies the best ways to use available terrain and to employ unit strengths against enemy weaknesses. Fire support considerations make up an important part of the concept of operations. Planners identify essential stability tasks. Leaders develop the graphic control measures necessary to convey and enhance the understanding of the concept of operations, prevent fratricide, and clarify the task and purpose of the main effort.

Assign Responsibilities

5-44. Leaders assign responsibility for each task to a subordinate. Whenever possible, they depend on the existing chain of command. They avoid fracturing unit integrity unless the number of simultaneous tasks exceeds the number of available elements. Different command and support arrangements may be the distinguishing feature among COAs.

Prepare a Course of Action Statement and Sketch

5-45. Leaders base the COA statement on the concept of operations for that COA. The COA statement focuses on all significant actions, from the start of the COA to its finish. Whenever possible, leaders prepare a sketch showing each COA. One useful technique shows the time it takes to achieve each movement and task in the COA sketch. Doing this helps subordinate leaders gain an appreciation for how much time will pass as they execute each task of the COA. The COA contains the following information:

- Form of movement or defense to be used.
- Designation of the main effort.
- Tasks and purposes of subordinate units.
- Necessary sustaining operations.
- Desired end state.

5-46. Figure 5-4 provides a sample mission statement and COA statement for an infantry company in the defense.

Analyze Courses of Action (War Game)

5-47. For each COA, leaders think through the operation from start to finish. They compare each COA with the enemy's most probable COA. At the small-unit level, the enemy's most probable COA is what the enemy is most likely to do given what friendly forces are doing at that instant. The leader visualizes a set of actions and reactions. The object is to determine what can go wrong and what decision the leader will likely have to make as a result.

Mission Statement:	C Co/2-67 IN (L) defends NLT 281700(Z) AUG 2005 to destroy enemy forces from GL 375652 to GL 389650 to GL 394660 to GL 373665 to prevent the envelopment of A Co, the battalion main effort.
COA Statement:	The company defends with two platoons (PLTs) forward and one PLT in depth from PLT battle positions. The northern PLT (2 squads) destroys enemy forces to prevent enemy bypass of the main effort PLT on Hill 657. The southern PLT (3 squads, 2 Javelins) destroys enemy forces to prevent an organized company attack against the Co main effort on Hill 657. The main effort PLT (3 squads, 2 TOWS) retains Hill 657 (vic GL378659) to prevent the envelopment of Co A (BN main effort) from the south. The anti-armor section (1 squad, 4 Javelins) establishes ambush positions at the road junction (vic GL 377653) to destroy enemy recon to deny observation of friendly defensive position and to prevent a concentration of combat power against the main effort PLT. The company mortars establish a mortar firing point vic GL 377664 to suppress enemy forces to protect the main effort platoon.

Figure 5-4. Sample mission and COA statements

Course of Action Comparison and Selection

5-48. Leaders compare COAs by weighing the advantages, disadvantages, strengths, and weaknesses of each, as noted during the war game. They decide which COA to execute based on this comparison and on their professional judgment. They take into account—

- Mission accomplishment.
- Time available to execute the operation.
- Risks.
- Results from unit reconnaissance.
- Subordinate unit tasks and purposes.
- Casualties incurred.
- Posturing of the force for future operations.

STEP 4 – INITIATE MOVEMENT

5-49. Leaders conduct any movement directed by higher headquarters or deemed necessary to continue mission preparation or position the unit for execution. They do this as soon as they have enough information to do so or the unit is required to move to position itself for a task. This is also essential when time is short. Movements may be to an assembly area, a battle position, a new AO, or an attack position. They may include movement of reconnaissance elements, guides, or quartering parties.

STEP 5 – CONDUCT RECONNAISSANCE

5-50. Whenever time and circumstances allow, or as directed by higher headquarters, leaders personally observe the AO for the mission prior to execution. No amount of intelligence preparation of the battlefield can substitute for firsthand assessment of METT-TC from within the AO. Unfortunately, many factors can keep leaders from performing a personal reconnaissance. The minimum action necessary is a thorough map reconnaissance supplemented by imagery and intelligence products. As directed, subordinates or other elements (such as scouts) may conduct reconnaissance while the leader completes other TLP steps.

5-51. Leaders use results of the war game to identify information requirements. Reconnaissance operations seek to confirm or deny information that supports the tentative plan. They focus first on information gaps identified during mission analysis. Leaders ensure their leader's reconnaissance complements the higher headquarters' reconnaissance and surveillance plan. The unit may conduct additional reconnaissance operations as the situation allows. This step may also precede making a tentative plan if commanders lack enough information to begin planning. Reconnaissance may be the only way to develop the information required for planning.

STEP 6 – COMPLETE THE PLAN

5-52. During this step, leaders incorporate the results of reconnaissance into their selected COA to complete the plan or order. This includes preparing overlays, refining the indirect fire target list, coordinating sustainment with signal requirements, and updating the tentative plan because of the reconnaissance. At lower levels, this step may entail only confirming or updating information contained in the tentative plan. If time allows, leaders make final coordination with adjacent units and higher headquarters before issuing the order.

STEP 7 – ISSUE THE ORDER

5-53. Small-unit orders are normally issued verbally and supplemented by graphics and other control measures. An order follows the standard five-paragraph OPORD format. Typically, leaders below company level do not issue a commander's intent. They reiterate the intent of their higher and next higher commanders.

5-54. The ideal location for issuing the order is a point in the AO with a view of the objective and other aspects of the terrain. The leader may perform a leader's reconnaissance, complete the order, and then summon subordinates to a specified location to receive it. Sometimes security or other constraints make it infeasible to issue the order on the terrain. Then leaders use a sand table, detailed sketch, maps, and other products to depict the AO and situation.

STEP 8 – SUPERVISE AND REFINE

5-55. Throughout TLP, leaders monitor mission preparations, refine the plan, coordinate with adjacent units, and supervise and assess preparations. Normally, unit SOPs state individual responsibilities and the sequence of preparation activities. To ensure the unit is ready for the mission, leaders supervise subordinates and inspect their personnel and equipment.

5-56. A crucial component of preparation is the rehearsal. Rehearsals allow leaders to assess their subordinates' preparations. They may identify areas that require more supervision. Leaders conduct rehearsals to—
- Practice essential tasks.
- Identify weaknesses or problems in the plan.
- Coordinate subordinate element actions.
- Improve Soldier understanding of the concept of operations.
- Foster confidence among Soldiers.

5-57. Company and smaller sized units use four types of rehearsals discussed in Chapter 8:
- Backbrief.
- Combined arms rehearsal.
- Support rehearsal.
- Battle drill or SOP rehearsal.

Chapter 6

Running Estimates

This chapter defines running estimate and describes how the commander and staff build and maintain their running estimates throughout the operations process. This chapter provides a generic running estimate format that the commander and each staff section may modify to fit their functional area. See JP 5-0 for information on joint estimates.

TYPES OF RUNNING ESTIMATES

6-1. A *running estimate* is the continuous assessment of the current situation used to determine if the current operation is proceeding according to the commander's intent and if planned future operations are supportable (FM 5-0). The commander and each staff section maintain a running estimate. In their running estimates, the commander and each staff section continuously consider the effects of new information and update the following:

- Facts.
- Assumptions.
- Friendly force status.
- Enemy activities and capabilities.
- Civil considerations.
- Conclusions and recommendations.

6-2. Commanders maintain their running estimates to consolidate their understanding and visualization of an operation. The commander's running estimate summarizes the problem and integrates information and knowledge of the staff's and subordinate commanders' running estimates.

6-3. Each staff section builds and maintains running estimates. The running estimate helps the staff to track and record pertinent information as well as to provide recommendations to commanders. Running estimates represent the analysis and expert opinion of each staff section by functional area. Staffs maintain running estimates throughout the operations process to assist commanders in the exercise of mission command.

6-4. Each staff section and command post functional cell maintains a running estimate focused on how their specific areas of expertise are postured to support future operations. Because an estimate may be needed at any time, running estimates must be developed, revised, updated, and maintained continuously while in garrison and during operations. While in garrison, staffs must maintain a running estimate on friendly capabilities.

ESSENTIAL QUALITIES OF RUNNING ESTIMATES

6-5. A comprehensive running estimate addresses all aspects of operations and contains both facts and assumptions based on the staff's experience within a specific area of expertise. Figure 6-1 (page 6-2) provides the base format for a running estimate that parallels the planning process. Each staff section modifies it to account for their specific functional areas. All running estimates cover essential facts and assumptions including a summary of the current situation by the mission variables, conclusions, and recommendations. Once they complete the plan, commanders and staff sections continuously update their estimates.

```
1.  SITUATION AND CONSIDERATIONS.
    a.  Area of Interest. Identify and describe those factors of the area of interest that affect functional
        area considerations.
    b.  Characteristics of the Area of Operations.
        (1) Terrain. State how terrain affects staff functional area's capabilities.
        (2) Weather. State how weather affects staff functional area's capabilities.
        (3) Enemy Forces. Describe enemy disposition, composition, strength, and systems within a
        functional area as well as enemy capabilities and possible courses of action (COAs) with
        respect to their effects on a functional area.
        (4) Friendly Forces. List current functional area resources in terms of equipment, personnel,
        and systems. Identify additional resources available for the functional area located at higher,
        adjacent, or other units. List those capabilities from other military and civilian partners that may
        be available to provide support within the functional area. Compare requirements to current
        capabilities and suggest solutions for satisfying discrepancies.
        (5) Civilian Considerations. Describe civil considerations that may affect the functional area
        to include possible support needed by civil authorities from the functional area as well as
        possible interference from civil aspects.
    c.  Assumptions. List all assumptions that affect the functional area.
2.  MISSION. Show the restated mission resulting from mission analysis.
3.  COURSES OF ACTION.
    a.  List friendly COAs that were war-gamed.
    b.  List enemy actions or COAs that were templated that impact the functional area.
    c.  List the evaluation criteria identified during COA analysis. All staffs use the same criteria.
4.  ANALYSIS. Analyze each COA using the evaluation criteria from COA analysis. Review enemy
    actions that impact the functional area as they relate to COAs. Identify issues, risks, and
    deficiencies these enemy actions may create with respect to the functional area.
5.  COMPARISON. Compare COAs. Rank order COAs for each key consideration. Use a decision
    matrix to aid the comparison process.
6.  RECOMMENDATIONS AND CONCLUSIONS.
    a.  Recommend the most supportable COAs from the perspective of the functional area.
    b.  Prioritize and list issues, deficiencies, and risks and make recommendations on how to mitigate
        them.
```

Figure 6-1. Generic base running estimate format

6-6.   The base running estimate addresses information unique to each functional area. It serves as the staff section's initial assessment of the current readiness of equipment and personnel and of how the factors considered in the running estimate affect the staff's ability to accomplish the mission. Each staff section identifies functional area friendly and enemy strengths, systems, training, morale, leadership, and weather and terrain effects, and how all these factors impact both the operational environment and area of operations. Because the running estimate is a picture relative to time, facts, and assumptions, each staff section constantly updates the estimate as new information arises, as assumptions become facts or are invalidated, when the mission changes, or when the commander requires additional input. Running estimates can be presented verbally or in writing.

RUNNING ESTIMATES IN THE OPERATIONS PROCESS

6-7.   Commanders and staff sections immediately begin updating their running estimates upon receipt of mission. They continue to build and maintain their running estimates throughout out the operations process in planning, preparation, execution, and assessment as discussed in paragraphs 6-8 through 6-11.

RUNNING ESTIMATES IN PLANNING

6-8.   During planning, running estimates are key sources of information during mission analysis. Following mission analysis, commanders and staff sections update their running estimates throughout the rest of the military decisionmaking process. Based on the mission and the initial commander's intent, the staff develops one or more proposed courses of action (COAs) and continually refines its running estimates to account for the mission variables. The updated running estimates then support COA analysis (war-gaming) in which the staff identifies the strengths and weaknesses of each COA. The staff relies on its updated running estimate to provide input to the war game. Following COA analysis, the staff compares the proposed COAs against each other and recommends one of them to the commander for approval. During all these activities, each staff section continues to update and refine its running estimate to give commanders the best possible information available at the time to support their decisions. The selected COA provides each staff section an additional focus for its estimates and the key information it will need during orders production. Key information recorded in the running estimate is included in orders, particularly in the functional annexes.

RUNNING ESTIMATES IN PREPARATION

6-9. The commander and staff transition from planning to execution. As they transition, they use running estimates to identify the current readiness of the unit in relationship to its mission. The commander and staff also use running estimates to develop, then track, mission readiness goals and additional requirements.

RUNNING ESTIMATES IN EXECUTION

6-10. During execution, the commander and staff incorporate information included in running estimates into the common operational picture. This enables the commander and staff to depict key information from each functional area or warfighting function as it impacts current and future operations. This information directly supports the commander's visualization and rapid decisionmaking during operations.

RUNNING ESTIMATES IN ASSESSMENT

6-11. Each staff section continuously analyzes new information during operations to create knowledge and understand if operations are progressing according to plan. Staffs use their running estimates to develop measures of effectiveness and measures of performance to support their analyses. The assessment of current operations also supports validation or rejection of additional information that will help update the estimates and support further planning. At a minimum, a staff section's running estimate assesses the following:

- Friendly force capabilities with respect to ongoing and planned operations.
- Enemy capabilities as they affect the staff section's area of expertise for current operations and plans for future operations.
- Civil considerations as they affect the staff section's area of expertise for current operations and plans for future operations.

This page intentionally left blank.

Chapter 7

Formal Assessment Plans

This chapter provides guidelines to assist commanders and their staffs in developing formal assessment plans. It details each step.

ASSESSMENT PLAN DEVELOPMENT

7-1. Units with staffs develop formal assessment plans when appropriate. A critical element of the commander's planning guidance is determining which formal assessment plans to develop. An assessment plan focused on the end state often works well. It is also possible, and may be desirable, to develop an entire formal assessment plan for an intermediate objective, a named operation subordinate to the base operation plan, or a named operation focused solely on a single line of operations or geographic area. The time, resources, and added complexity involved in generating a formal assessment plan strictly limit the number of such efforts.

7-2. In units with an assessment cell, both the assessment cell and the appropriate staff principal present their findings to the commander. The assessment cell presents the assessment framework with current values and discusses key trends observed. This cell presents any relevant insights from the statistical analysis of the information. Then the staff principal either agrees or disagrees with the values provided in the formal model and discusses relevant insights and factors not considered or not explicit in the model. The staff principal then provides meaningful, actionable recommendations based on the assessment.

ASSESSMENT STEPS

7-3. Commanders and staffs develop assessment plans during planning using six steps:
- Step 1 – Gather tools and assessment data.
- Step 2 – Understand current and desired conditions.
- Step 3 – Develop assessment measures and potential indicators.
- Step 4 – Develop the collection plan.
- Step 5 – Assign responsibilities for conducting analysis and generating recommendations.
- Step 6 – Identify feedback mechanisms.

Once commanders and their staffs develop the assessment plan, they apply the assessment process of monitor, evaluate, and recommend or direct continuously throughout preparation and execution.

STEP 1 – GATHER TOOLS AND ASSESSMENT DATA

7-4. Planning begins with receipt of mission. The receipt of mission alerts the staffs to begin updating their running estimates and gather the tools necessary for mission analysis and continued planning. Specific tools and information gathered regarding assessment include, but are not limited to—
- The higher headquarters' plan or order, including the assessment annex if available.
- If replacing a unit, any current assessments and assessment products.
- Relevant assessment products (classified or open-source) produced by civilian and military organizations.
- The identification of potential data sources, including academic institutions and civilian subject matter experts.

STEP 2 – UNDERSTAND CURRENT AND DESIRED CONDITIONS

7-5. Fundamentally, assessment is about measuring progress toward the desired end state. Staffs compare current conditions in the area of operations against the desired conditions. Mission analysis and intelligence preparation of the battlefield help develop an understanding of the current situation. The commander and staff identify the desired conditions and key underlying assumptions for an operation during design and the military decisionmaking process.

7-6. Understanding current and desired conditions requires explicitly acknowledging the underlying assumptions. During the evaluation phase of the assessment process, staffs continually challenge assumptions they identified during planning. If they subsequently disprove assumptions, then reframing the problem may be appropriate.

7-7. Following mission analysis, commanders issue their initial commander's intent, planning guidance, and commander's critical information requirements. The end state in the initial commander's intent describes the desired conditions the commander wants to achieve. The staff section charged with responsibility for the assessment plan identifies each specific desired condition mentioned in the commander's intent. These individual desired conditions focus the overall assessment of the operation. Monitoring focuses on the corresponding conditions in the current situation. If the conditions that define the end state change during the planning process, the staff updates these changes for the assessment plan.

7-8. To measure progress effectively, the staff identifies both the current situation and the desired end state. For example, the commander provides the end state condition "Essential services restored to prehostility levels." The staff develops a plan to obtain indicators of this condition. These indicators also identify the current and prehostility levels of essential services across the area of operations. By taking these two actions, the staff establishes a mechanism to assess progress toward this condition.

STEP 3 – DEVELOP ASSESSMENT MEASURES AND POTENTIAL INDICATORS

7-9. A formal assessment plan has a hierarchical structure—known as the assessment framework—that begins with end state conditions, followed by measures of effectiveness (MOEs), and finally indicators. Commanders broadly describe the operation's end state in their commander's intent. The staff then identifies specific desired conditions from the commander's intent. Staffs measure each condition by MOEs. The MOEs are in turn informed by indicators.

7-10. A formal assessment plan focuses on measuring if the situation changed and whether units attained desired conditions while continually monitoring and evaluating assumptions to validate or invalidate them. Staffs use MOEs to measure this. Normally, formal assessment plans do not include measures of performance (MOPs). The current operations integration cell develops and tracks MOPs in the individual staff sections' running estimates. Occasionally staffs assess specific tasks as part of the assessment plan using the following hierarchical structure: tasks, MOPs, and indicators. Formal, detailed assessments of task completion tend to be the exception rather than the rule.

7-11. Developing assessment measures and potential indicators involves—
- Selecting and writing MOEs.
- Selecting and writing indicators.
- Building the assessment framework.

Selecting and Writing Measures of Effectiveness

7-12. Guidelines for selecting and writing MOEs consist of the following:
- Select only MOEs that measure the degree to which the desired outcome is achieved.
- Choose distinct MOEs.
- Include MOEs from different causal chains.
- Use the same MOE to measure more than one condition when appropriate.
- Avoid additional reporting requirements for subordinates.
- Structure MOEs so that they have measurable, collectable, and relevant indicators.

- Write MOEs as statements not questions.
- Maximize clarity.

7-13. Commanders select only MOEs that measure the degree to which the desired outcome is achieved. A good basis must exist for the theory that this MOE is expected to change if the condition is being achieved.

7-14. Commanders choose MOEs for each condition as distinct from each other as possible. Using similar MOEs can skew the assessment by containing virtually the same MOE twice.

7-15. Commanders include MOEs from differing relevant causal chains for each condition whenever possible. When MOEs have a cause and effect relationship with each other, either directly or indirectly, it decreases their value in measuring a particular condition. Measuring progress towards a desired condition by multiple means adds rigor to the assessment. For example, in Figure 7-1 under condition 1, MOE 1 and MOE 3 have no apparent cause and effect relationship with each other although both are valid measures of the condition. This adds rigor and validity to the measurement of that condition. MOE 2 does have a cause and effect relationship with MOE 1 and MOE 3 but is a worthwhile addition because of the direct relevancy and mathematical rigor of that particular source of data.

Condition 1: Enemy Division X forces prevented from interfering with corps decisive operation.
MOE 1: Enemy Division X forces west of phase line blue are defeated.
- **Indicator 1**: Friendly forces occupy OBJ Slam (Yes/No).
- **Indicator 2**: Number of reports of squad-sized or larger enemy forces in the division area of operations in the past 24 hours.
- **Indicator 3**: Current G-2 assessment of number of enemy Division X battalions west of phase line blue.
MOE 2: Enemy Division X forces indirect fire systems neutralized.
- **Indicator 1**: Number of indirect fires originating from enemy Division X's integrated fires command in the past 24 hours.
- **Indicator 2**: Current G-2 assessment of number of operational 240mm rocket launchers within enemy Division X's integrated fires command.
MOE 3: Enemy Division X communications systems disrupted.
- **Indicator 1**: Number of electronic transmissions from enemy Division X detected in the past 24 hours.
- **Indicator 2**: Number of enemy Division X battalion and higher command posts destroyed.

Figure 7-1. Sample of end state conditions for defensive operations

7-16. Commanders use the same MOE to measure more than one condition when appropriate. This sort of duplication in the assessment framework does not introduce significant bias unless carried to the extreme. The MOE duplication to be concerned about is among MOEs measuring the same condition.

7-17. Commanders avoid or minimize additional reporting requirements for subordinate units. In many cases, commanders use information requirements generated by other staff sections as MOEs and indicators in the assessment plan. With careful consideration, commanders and staffs can often find viable alternative MOEs without creating new reporting requirements. Excessive reporting requirements can render an otherwise valid assessment plan onerous and untenable.

7-18. Commanders structure MOEs so that measurable, collectable, and relevant indicators exist for them. A MOE is of no use if the staff cannot actually measure it.

7-19. Commanders write MOEs as statements not questions. They can express an MOE as a number. MOEs supply answers to questions rather than the questions themselves. (See Figure 7-1 and Figure 7-2, page 7-4, for examples.)

7-20. Commanders maximize clarity. A MOE describes the sought information precisely, including specifics on time, information, geography, or unit, if needed. Any staff member should be able to read the MOE and understand exactly what information it describes.

Selecting and Writing Indicators

7-21. Staffs develop indicators that provide insights into MOEs. Indicators must be measurable, collectable, and relevant.

7-22. Staffs can gauge a measurable indicator either quantitatively or qualitatively. Imprecisely defined indicators often pose a problem. For example, staffs cannot measure the indicator "Number of local nationals shopping." The information lacks clear parameters in time or geography. Staffs can measure the revised indicator "Average daily number of local nationals visiting main street market in city X this month." Additionally, staffs should design the indicator to minimize bias. This particularly applies when staffs only have qualitative indicators available for a given MOE. Many qualitative measures are easily biased, and Soldiers must use safeguards to protect objectivity in the assessment process.

Condition 1: Enemy defeated in the brigade area of operations.

MOE 1: Enemy kidnapping activity in the brigade area of operations disrupted.
- **Indicator 1**: Monthly reported dollars in ransom paid as a result of kidnapping operations.
- **Indicator 2**: Monthly number of reported attempted kidnappings.
- **Indicator 3**: Monthly poll question #23: "Have any kidnappings occurred in your neighborhood in the past 30 days?" Results for provinces ABC only.

MOE 2: Public perception of security in the brigade area of operations improved.
- **Indicator 1**: Monthly poll question #34: "Have you changed your normal activities in the past month because of concerns about your safety and that of your family?" Results for provinces ABC only.
- **Indicator 2**: Monthly K through12 school attendance in provinces ABC as reported by the host-nation ministry of education.
- **Indicator 3**: Monthly number of tips from local nationals reported to the brigade terrorism tips hotline.

MOE 3: Sniper events in the brigade area of operations disrupted.
- **Indicator 1**: Monthly decrease in reported sniper events in the brigade area of operations. (***Note:*** It is acceptable to have only one indicator that directly answers a given MOE. Avoid complicating the assessment needlessly when a simple construct suffices.)

Condition 2: Role 1 medical care available to the population in city X.

MOE 1: Public perception of medical care availability improved in city X.
- **Indicator 1**: Monthly poll question #42: "Are you and your family able to visit the hospital when you need to?" Results for provinces ABC only.
- **Indicator 2**: Monthly poll question #8: "Do you and your family have important health needs that are not being met?" Results for provinces ABC only.
- **Indicator 3**: Monthly decrease in number of requests for medical care received from local nationals by the brigade.

MOE 2: Battalion commander estimated monthly host-nation medical care availability in battalion area of operations.
- **Indicator 1**: Monthly average of reported battalion commander's estimates (scale of 1 to 5) of host-nation medical care availability in the battalion area of operation.

Figure 7-2. Sample of end state conditions for stability operations

7-23. A collectable indicator has reasonably obtained data associated with the indicator. In some cases, the data may not exist or the data may be prohibitively difficult to collect. For example, the indicator "Average daily number of local nationals visiting main street market in city X this month" is likely not collectable. This number exists, but unless a trusted source tracks and reports it, Soldiers cannot collect it. The revised indicator "Battalion commander's monthly estimate of market activity in city X on a scale of 1 to 5" is collectable. In this case, the staff did not have a quantitative indicator available, so they substituted a qualitative indicator.

7-24. An indicator is relevant if it provides insight into a supported MOE or MOP. Commanders must ask pertinent questions, such as does a change in this indicator actually indicate a change in the MOE? (Which is the cause and which is the effect is not the point here; what matters is that a correlation exists.) What factors unrelated to the MOE could cause this indicator to change? How reliable is the correlation between the indicator and the MOE? For example, the indicator "Decrease in monthly weapons caches found and cleared in the division area of operations" is not relevant to the MOE "Decrease in enemy activity in the division area of operations." This indicator could plausibly increase or decrease with a decrease in enemy activity. An increase in friendly patrols, particularly in areas not previously patrolled on a regular basis, could result in greater numbers of caches found and cleared. Staffs may also have difficulty determining when the enemy left the weapons, raising the question of when the enemy activity actually occurred. These factors, unrelated to enemy activity, could artificially inflate the indicator, creating a false impression of increased enemy activity within the assessment framework. In this example, staffs can reliably measure enemy activity levels without considering weapons caches or using the indicator for this MOE.

Building the Assessment Framework

7-25. A basic assessment framework typically quantifies end state conditions, MOEs, and indicators. In some cases, it may include an objective rather than the end state or MOPs rather than MOEs.

7-26. A formal assessment framework is simply a tool to assist commanders with estimating progress. Using a formal assessment framework does not imply that commanders mathematically determine the outcomes of military operations. Commanders and staff officers apply judgment to results of mathematical assessment to assess the progress holistically. For example, commanders in an enduring operation may receive a monthly formal assessment briefing from their staff. This briefing includes both the products of the formal assessment process as well as the expert opinions of members of the staff, subordinate commanders, and other partners. In this way, the commander receives both a mathematically rigorous analysis as well as expert opinions. Commanders combine what they find useful in those two viewpoints with their personal assessment of the operations, consider recommendations, and direct action as needed.

7-27. A significant amount of human judgment goes into designing an assessment framework. Choosing MOEs and indicators that accurately measure progress toward each desired condition is an art. Processing elements of the assessment framework requires establishing weights and thresholds for each MOE and indicator. Setting proper weights and thresholds requires operational expertise and judgment. Input from the relevant staff sections and subject matter experts are critical. Staffs record the logic of why the commander chose each MOE and indicator. This facilitates personnel turnover as well as understanding the assessment plan among all staff sections.

7-28. Each component of the assessment framework is standardized, assigned a weight, and given thresholds. Staffs mathematically combine them starting at the indicator's level, worked up through MOEs and conditions, arriving at the end state. (See Figure 7-3, page 7-6.)

7-29. Standardization means that each component is expressed as a number on a common scale such as 1 to 5 or 1 to 10. Setting a common scale aids understanding and comparing as well as running the mathematical model. For example, Indicator 1 for MOE 1 for Condition 1 in Figure 7-3 can report monthly dollars in ransom paid as a result of kidnapping operations. For the month of June, that number is $250,000. That number is normalized to a scale of 1 to 10, with 1 being bad and 10 being good. The value of that indicator within the framework is 6.8.

7-30. A weight is a number that expresses relative significance. Some indicators may have more significance than others for informing a given MOE. They count for more in the real world and should literally count for more in the mathematical assessment framework. Staffs use weights as multipliers for MOEs and indicators. The standard weight of 1.0 implies equal significance. A weight of 2.0 for an MOE (or indicator) implies that MOE carries twice the significance.

7-31. A threshold is a value above which one category is in effect and below which another category is in effect. Thresholds answer the question for a given indicator or MOE of what good and bad is. The categories can name whatever the commander finds useful, such as colors or numbers. Commonly used colors are red, yellow, and green. Mathematical thresholds are often set at plus or minus one standard deviation. Whatever category commanders use, they must define it in the assessment plan. They also must weigh the value of insight against the risk of bias.

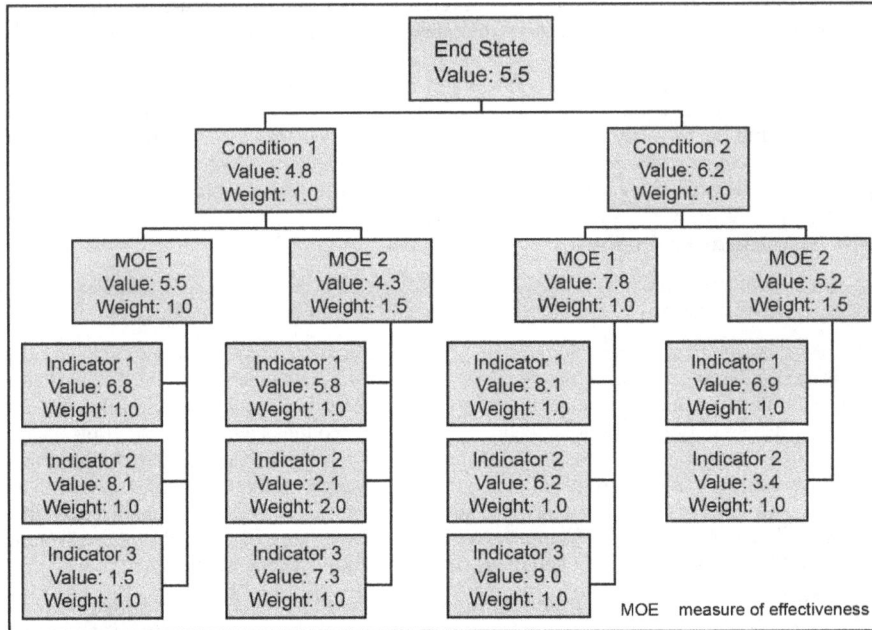

Figure 7-3. Sample assessment framework

7-32. Establishing a baseline for comparison is often useful in a formal assessment plan. A baseline is a time in the past against which the present is compared. The word baseline is a statistical term. In the context of assessment, do not use it to mean starting point. Often commanders choose the baseline from a time when conditions are similar to their desired conditions. However, the baseline must be recent enough to be relevant. In protracted operations, the baseline may represent conditions from which commanders are trying to move away. Baselines provide a focus for the commander and staff in comparing data across different blocks of time. Baselines are particularly useful when using standard deviations to establish thresholds. Staffs calculate the standard deviation over the baseline and use multiples of those values to set thresholds.

STEP 4 – DEVELOP THE COLLECTION PLAN

7-33. Each indicator represents an information requirement. In some instances, staffs feed these information requirements into the reconnaissance and surveillance synchronization process. Then, staffs task reconnaissance and surveillance assets to collect on these information requirements. In other instances, reports in the unit standard operating procedures may suffice. If not, the unit may develop a new report. Staffs may collect the information requirement from organizations external to the unit. For example, a host nation's central bank may publish a consumer price index for that nation. The assessment plan identifies the source for each indicator as well as the staff member who collects that information. Assessment information requirements compete with other information requirements for resources. When an information requirement is not resourced, staffs cannot collect the associated indicator and must remove it from the plan. Staffs then adjust the assessment framework to ensure that the MOE or MOP is properly worded.

STEP 5 – ASSIGN RESPONSIBILITIES FOR CONDUCTING ANALYSIS AND GENERATING RECOMMENDATIONS

7-34. In addition to assigning responsibility for collection, commanders assign staff members with responsibility for analyzing assessment data and developing recommendations. For example, the intelligence officer leads the assessment of enemy forces. The engineer leads the effort on assessing infrastructure development. The civil affairs operations officer leads assessment concerning the progress of local and provincial governments. The chief of staff aggressively requires staff principals and subject matter experts to participate in processing the formal assessment and in generating smart, actionable recommendations.

STEP 6 – IDENTIFY FEEDBACK MECHANISMS

7-35. A formal assessment with meaningful recommendations never heard by the appropriate decisionmaker wastes time and energy. The assessment plan identifies the who, what, when, where, and why of that presentation. The commander and staff discuss feedback leading up to and following that presentation as well. Feedback might include which assessment working groups the commander requires and how to act and follow up on recommendations.

This page intentionally left blank.

Chapter 8

Rehearsals

Rehearsing key actions before execution allows Soldiers to become familiar with the operation and translate the abstract ideas of the written plan into concrete actions. This chapter describes rehearsal types and techniques. It lists the responsibilities of those involved. It also contains guidelines for conducting rehearsals.

REHEARSAL BASICS

8-1. Rehearsals allow leaders and their Soldiers to practice executing key aspects of the concept of operations. These actions help Soldiers orient themselves to their environment and other units before executing the operation. Rehearsals help Soldiers to build a lasting mental picture of the sequence of key actions within the operation.

8-2. Rehearsals are the commander's tool to ensure staffs and subordinates understand the commander's intent and the concept of operations. They allow commanders and staffs to identify shortcomings (errors or omissions) in the plan not previously recognized. Rehearsals also contribute to external and internal coordination as the staff identifies additional coordinating requirements.

8-3. Effective and efficient units habitually rehearse during training. Commanders at every level routinely train and practice various rehearsal types and techniques. Local standard operating procedures (SOPs) identify appropriate rehearsal types, techniques, and standards for their execution. All leaders conduct periodic after action reviews to ensure their units conduct rehearsals to standard and correct substandard performances. After action reviews also enable leaders to incorporate lessons learned into existing plans and orders, or into subsequent rehearsals.

8-4. Adequate time is essential when conducting rehearsals. The time required varies with the complexity of the mission, the type and technique of rehearsal, and the level of participation. Units conduct rehearsals at the lowest possible level, using the most thorough technique possible, given the time available. Under time-constrained conditions, leaders conduct abbreviated rehearsals, focusing on critical events determined by reverse planning. Each unit will have different critical events based on the mission, unit readiness, and the commander's assessment.

8-5. Whenever possible, leaders base rehearsals on a completed operation order. However, a unit may rehearse a contingency plan to prepare for an anticipated deployment. The rehearsal is a coordination event, not an analysis. It does not replace war-gaming. Commanders war-game during the military decisionmaking process to analyze different courses of action to determine the optimal one. Rehearsals practice that selected course of action. Commanders avoid making major changes to operation orders during rehearsals. They make only those changes essential to mission success and risk mitigation.

REHEARSAL TYPES

8-6. Each rehearsal type achieves a different result and has a specific place in the preparation timeline. The four types of rehearsals are—

- Backbrief.
- Combined arms rehearsal.
- Support rehearsal.
- Battle drill or SOP rehearsal.

BACKBRIEF

8-7. A *backbrief* is a briefing by subordinates to the commander to review how subordinates intend to accomplish their mission. Normally, subordinates perform backbriefs throughout preparation. These briefs allow commanders to clarify the commander's intent early in subordinate planning. Commanders use the backbrief to identify any problems in the concept of operations.

8-8. The backbrief differs from the confirmation brief (a briefing subordinates give their higher commander immediately following receipt of an order) in that subordinate leaders are given time to complete their plan. Backbriefs require the fewest resources and are often the only option under time-constrained conditions. Subordinate leaders explain their actions from start to finish of the mission. Backbriefs are performed sequentially, with all leaders reviewing their tasks. When time is available, backbriefs can be combined with other types of rehearsals. Doing this lets all subordinate leaders coordinate their plans before performing more elaborate drills.

COMBINED ARMS REHEARSAL

8-9. A combined arms rehearsal is a rehearsal in which subordinate units synchronize their plans with each other. A maneuver unit headquarters normally executes a combined arms rehearsal after subordinate units issue their operation order. This rehearsal type helps ensure that subordinate commanders' plans achieve the higher commander's intent.

SUPPORT REHEARSAL

8-10. The support rehearsal helps synchronize each warfighting function with the overall operation. This rehearsal supports the operation so units can accomplish their missions. Throughout preparation, units conduct support rehearsals within the framework of a single or limited number of warfighting functions. These rehearsals typically involve coordination and procedure drills for aviation, fires, engineer support, or casualty evacuation. Support rehearsals and combined arms rehearsals complement preparations for the operation. Units may conduct rehearsals separately and then combine them into full-dress rehearsals. Although these rehearsals differ slightly by warfighting function, they achieve the same result.

BATTLE DRILL OR STANDARD OPERATING PROCEDURE REHEARSAL

8-11. A battle drill is a collective action rapidly executed without applying a deliberate decisionmaking process. A battle drill or SOP rehearsal ensures that all participants understand a technique or a specific set of procedures. Throughout preparation, units and staffs rehearse battle drills and SOPs. These rehearsals do not need a completed order from higher headquarters. Leaders place priority on those drills or actions they anticipate occurring during the operation. For example, a transportation platoon may rehearse a battle drill on reacting to an ambush while waiting to begin movement.

8-12. All echelons use these rehearsal types; however, they are most common for platoons, squads, and sections. They are conducted throughout preparation and are not limited to published battle drills. All echelons can rehearse such actions as a command post shift change, an obstacle breach lane-marking SOP, or a refuel-on-the-move site operation.

REHEARSAL TECHNIQUES

8-13. Techniques for conducting rehearsals are limited only by the commander's imagination and available resources. Generally, six techniques are used. (See Figure 8-1.) Resources required for each technique range from broad to narrow. As listed from left to right, each successive technique takes more time and more resources. Each rehearsal technique also imparts a different level of understanding to participants.

8-14. Paragraphs 8-15 through 8-51address these implications for each technique:
- **Time**–the amount of time required to conduct (plan, prepare, execute, and assess) the rehearsal.
- **Echelons involved**–the number of echelons that can participate in the rehearsal.

- **Operations security risk**–the ease by which adversary can exploit friendly actions from the rehearsal.
- **Terrain**–the amount of space needed for the rehearsal.

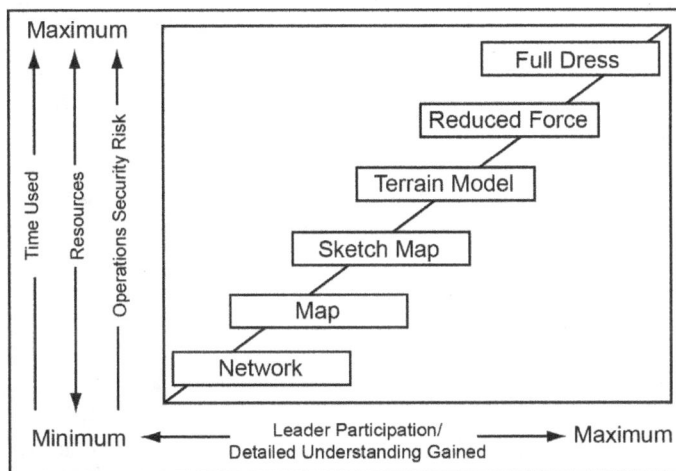

Figure 8-1. Rehearsal techniques

FULL-DRESS REHEARSAL

8-15. A full-dress rehearsal produces the most detailed understanding of the operation. It includes every participating Soldier and system. Leaders rehearse their subordinates on terrain similar to the area of operations (AO), initially under good light conditions, and then in limited visibility. Leaders repeat small-unit actions until executed to standard. Full-dress rehearsals help Soldiers to clearly understand what commanders expect of them. It helps them gain confidence in their ability to accomplish the mission. Supporting elements, such as aviation crews, meet and rehearse with Soldiers to synchronize the operation.

8-16. A unit may conduct full-dress rehearsals. The higher headquarters may conduct and support full-dress rehearsals. The full-dress rehearsal is the most difficult to accomplish at higher echelons. At those levels, commanders may develop an alternate rehearsal plan that mirrors the actual plan but fits the terrain available for the rehearsal.

8-17. Full-dress rehearsals consume more *time* than any other rehearsal type. For companies and smaller units, full-dress rehearsals most effectively ensure all units in the operation understand their roles. However, brigade and task force commanders consider how much time their subordinates need to plan and prepare when deciding whether to conduct a full-dress rehearsal.

8-18. All *echelons involved* in the operation participate in the full-dress rehearsal.

8-19. Moving a large part of the force may create an *operations security risk* by attracting unwanted enemy attention. Commanders develop a plan to protect the rehearsal from enemy reconnaissance and surveillance. Sometimes they develop an alternate plan, including graphics and radio frequencies, which rehearses selected actions without compromising the actual operation order. Commanders take care not to confuse subordinates when doing this.

8-20. *Terrain* management for a full-dress rehearsal proves challenging. Units identify, secure, clear, and maintain the rehearsal area throughout the rehearsal.

REDUCED-FORCE REHEARSAL

8-21. Circumstances may prohibit a rehearsal with all members of the unit. A reduced-force rehearsal involves only key leaders of the organization and its subordinate units. It normally takes fewer resources than a full-dress rehearsal. Terrain requirements mirror those of a full-dress rehearsal, even though fewer Soldiers participate. The commander first decides the level of leader involvement. Then the selected leaders rehearse the plan while traversing the actual or similar terrain. Often commanders use this technique to rehearse fire control measures for an engagement area during defensive operations. Commanders often use a reduced-force rehearsal to prepare key leaders for a full-dress rehearsal. It may require developing a rehearsal plan that mirrors the actual plan but fits the terrain of the rehearsal.

8-22. Often, small-scale replicas of terrain or buildings substitute for the actual AO. Leaders not only explain their plans, but also walk through their actions or move replicas across the rehearsal area or sand table. This is called a rock drill. It reinforces the backbrief given by subordinates since everyone can see the concept of operations and sequence of tasks.

8-23. A reduced-force rehearsal normally requires less *time* than a full-dress rehearsal. Commanders consider how much time their subordinates need to plan and prepare when deciding whether to conduct a reduced-force rehearsal.

8-24. A small unit from the *echelons involved* can perform a full-dress rehearsal as part of a larger organization's reduced-force rehearsal.

8-25. A reduced-force rehearsal is less likely to present *operations security risks* than a full-dress rehearsal because it has fewer participants. However, it requires the same number of radio transmissions as for a full-dress rehearsal.

8-26. *Terrain* management for the reduced-force rehearsal can be as difficult as for the full-dress rehearsal. Units identify, secure, clear, and maintain the rehearsal area throughout the rehearsal.

TERRAIN-MODEL REHEARSAL

8-27. The terrain-model rehearsal is the most popular rehearsal technique. It takes less time and fewer resources than a full-dress or reduced-force rehearsal. (A terrain-model rehearsal takes a proficient brigade between one to two hours to execute to standard.) An accurately constructed terrain model helps subordinate leaders visualize the commander's intent and concept of operations. When possible, commanders place the terrain model where it overlooks the actual terrain of the AO. However, if the situation requires more security, they place the terrain model on a reverse slope within walking distance of a point overlooking the AO. The model's orientation coincides with that of the terrain. The size of the terrain model can vary from small (using markers to represent units) to large (on which the participants can walk). A large model helps reinforce the participants' perception of unit positions on the terrain.

8-28. Often, constructing the terrain model consumes the most *time* during this technique. Units require a clear SOP that states how to build the model so it is accurate, large, and detailed enough to conduct the rehearsal. A good SOP also establishes staff responsibility for building the terrain model and a timeline for its completion.

8-29. Because a terrain model is geared to the *echelon* conducting the rehearsal, multiechelon rehearsals using this technique are difficult.

8-30. This rehearsal can present *operations security risks* if the area around the rehearsal site is not secured. Assembled commanders and their vehicles can draw enemy attention. Units must sanitize the terrain model after completing the rehearsal.

8-31. *Terrain* management is less difficult than with the previous techniques. A good site is easy for participants to find yet concealed from the enemy. An optimal location overlooks the terrain where the unit will execute the operation.

DIGITAL TERRAIN-MODEL REHEARSAL

8-32. With today's digital capabilities, users can construct terrain models in virtual space. Units drape high-resolution imagery over elevation data thereby creating a fly-through or walk-through. Holographic imagery produces the view in three dimensions. Often, the model hot links graphics, detailed information, unmanned aircraft systems, and ground imagery to key points providing more insight into the plan. Digital terrain models reduce the operations security risk because they do not use real terrain. The unit geospatial engineers or imagery analysts can assist in digital model creation. Detailed city models already exist for many world cities.

8-33. The *time* it takes to create the digital three-dimensional model depends on the amount of available data on the terrain being modeled.

8-34. Of all the *echelons involved*, this type of rehearsal best suits small units, although with a good local area network, a wider audience can view the graphics. All echelons may be provided copies of the digital model to take back to their headquarters for a more detailed examination.

8-35. If not placed on a computer network, there is limited *operations security risk* because no site is secured and the rehearsal can be conducted under cover. However, if placed on a computer network, digital terrain models can be subject to enemy exploitation due to inherent vulnerabilities of networks.

8-36. This space requires the least *terrain* of all rehearsals. Using tents or enclosed areas conceal the rehearsal from the enemy.

SKETCH-MAP REHEARSAL

8-37. Commanders can use the sketch-map technique almost anywhere, day or night. The procedures are the same as for a terrain-model rehearsal except the commander uses a sketch map in place of a terrain model. Large sketches ensure all participants can see as each participant walks through execution of the operation. Participants move markers on the sketch to represent unit locations and maneuvers.

8-38. Sketch-map rehearsals take less *time* than terrain-model rehearsals and more time than map rehearsals.

8-39. Units gear a sketch map to the *echelon* conducting the rehearsal. Multiechelon rehearsals using this technique are difficult.

8-40. This rehearsal can present *operations security risks* if the area around the rehearsal site is not secured. Assembled commanders and their vehicles can draw enemy attention. Units must sanitize, secure, or destroy the sketch map after use.

8-41. This technique requires less *terrain* than a terrain-model rehearsal. A good site ensures participants can easily find it yet stay concealed from the enemy. An optimal location overlooks the terrain where the unit will execute the operation.

MAP REHEARSAL

8-42. A map rehearsal is similar to a sketch-map rehearsal except the commander uses a map and operation overlay of the same scale used to plan the operation.

8-43. The map rehearsal itself consumes the most *time*. A map rehearsal is normally the easiest technique to set up since it requires only maps and graphics for current operations.

8-44. Units gear a map rehearsal's operation overlay to the *echelon* conducting the rehearsal. Multiechelon rehearsals using this technique are difficult.

8-45. This rehearsal can present *operations security risks* if the area around the rehearsal site is not secured. Assembled commanders and their vehicles can draw enemy attention.

8-46. This technique requires the least *terrain* of all rehearsals. A good site ensures participants can easily find it yet stay concealed from the enemy. An optimal location overlooks the terrain where the unit will execute the operation.

NETWORK REHEARSAL

8-47. Units conduct network rehearsals over wide-area networks or local area networks. Commanders and staffs practice these rehearsals by talking through critical portions of the operation over communications networks in a sequence the commander establishes. The organization rehearses only the critical parts of the operation. These rehearsals require all information systems needed to execute that portion of the operation. All participants require working information systems, the operation order, and overlays. Command posts can rehearse battle tracking during network rehearsals.

8-48. This technique can be *time* efficient if units provide clear SOPs. However, if the organization has unclear SOPs, has units not operating on the network, or has units without working communications, this technique can be time-consuming.

8-49. This technique lends itself to *multiechelon* rehearsals. Participation is limited only by the commander's intent and the capabilities of the command's information systems.

8-50. If a unit executes a network rehearsal from current unit locations, the *operations security risk* may increase. The enemy may monitor the increased volume of transmissions and potentially compromise information. To avoid such compromise, organizations use different frequencies from those planned for the operation. Using wire systems is an option but does not exercise the network systems, which is the strong point of this technique.

8-51. If a network rehearsal is executed from unit locations, *terrain* considerations are minimal. If a separate rehearsal area is required, considerations are similar to those of a reduced-force rehearsal.

REHEARSAL RESPONSIBILITIES

8-52. This discussion addresses responsibilities for conducting rehearsals based on the combined arms rehearsal. Responsibilities are the same for support rehearsals.

PLANNING

8-53. Commanders and chiefs of staff (executive officers at lower echelons) plan rehearsals.

Commander

8-54. Commanders provide certain information as part of the commander's guidance during the initial mission analysis. They may revise the following information when they select a course of action:
- Rehearsal type.
- Rehearsal technique.
- Location.
- Attendees.
- Enemy course of action to be portrayed.

Chief of Staff (Executive Officer)

8-55. The chief of staff or executive officer ensures all rehearsals are included in the organization's time-management SOP. The chief of staff or executive officer responsibilities include—
- Publishing the rehearsal time and location in the operation order or warning order.
- Conducting staff rehearsals.
- Determining rehearsal products, based on type, technique, and mission variables.
- Coordinating liaison officer attendance from adjacent units.

PREPARATION

8-56. Everyone involved in executing or supporting the rehearsal has responsibilities during preparation.

Commander

8-57. Commanders prepare to rehearse operations with events phased in proper order, from start to finish. Under time-constrained conditions, this often proves difficult. Commanders—
- Identify and prioritize key events to rehearse.
- Allocate time for each event.
- Perform personal preparation, including reviews of—
  - Task organization completeness.
  - Personnel and materiel readiness.
  - Organizational level of preparation.

Chief of Staff (Executive Officer)

8-58. The chief of staff or executive officer, through war-gaming and coordination with the commander—
- Prepares to serve as the rehearsal director.
- Coordinates time for key events requiring rehearsal.
- Establishes rehearsal time limits per the commander's guidance and mission variables.
- Verifies rehearsal site preparation. A separate rehearsal site may be required for some events, such as a possible obstacle site. A good rehearsal site includes—
  - Appropriate markings and associated training aids.
  - Parking areas.
  - Local security.
- Determines the method for controlling the rehearsal and ensuring its logical flow, such as a script. (See paragraphs 8-77 through 8-84.)

Subordinate Leaders

8-59. Subordinate leaders complete their planning. This planning includes—
- Completing unit operation orders.
- Identifying issues derived from the higher headquarters' operation order.
- Providing a copy of their unit operation order with graphics to the higher headquarters.
- Performing personal preparation similar to that of the commander.
- Ensuring they and their subordinates bring all necessary equipment.

Conducting Headquarters Staff

8-60. Conducting headquarters staff members—
- Develop an operation order with necessary overlays.
- Deconflict all subordinate unit graphics. Composite overlays are the first step for leaders to visualize the organization's overall plan.
- Publish composite overlays at the rehearsal including, at a minimum—
  - Movement and maneuver.
  - Intelligence.
  - Fires.
  - Sustainment.
  - Signal operations.
  - Protection.

EXECUTION

8-61. During execution, the commander, chief of staff, assistants, subordinate leaders, recorder, and staff from the conducting headquarters have specific responsibilities.

Commander

8-62. Commanders command the rehearsal just as they will command the operation. They maintain the focus and level of intensity, allowing no potential for subordinate confusion. Although the staff refines the operation order, it belongs to the commander. The commander uses the order to conduct operations. An effective rehearsal is not a commander's brief to subordinates. It validates synchronization—the what, when, and where—of tasks that subordinate units will perform to execute the operation and achieve the commander's intent.

Chief of Staff (Executive Officer)

8-63. Normally, the chief of staff or executive officer serves as the rehearsal director. This officer ensures each unit will accomplish its tasks at the right time and cues the commander to upcoming decisions. The chief of staff's or executive officer's script is the execution matrix and the decision support template. The chief of staff or executive officer as the rehearsal director—
- Starts the rehearsal on time.
- Has a formal roll call.
- Ensures everyone brings the necessary equipment, including organizational graphics and previously issued orders.
- Validates the task organization. Linkups must be complete or on schedule, and required materiel and personnel must be on hand. *The importance of this simple check cannot be overemphasized.*
- Ensures sustaining operations are synchronized with shaping operations and the decisive operation.
- Rehearses the synchronization of combat power from flank and higher organizations. These organizations often exceed communications range of the commander and G-3 (S-3) when they are away from the command post.
- Synchronizes the timing and contribution of each warfighting function.
- For each decisive point, defines conditions required to—
  - Commit the reserve or striking forces.
  - Move a unit.
  - Close or emplace an obstacle.
  - Fire at planned targets.
  - Move a medical unit, change a supply route, and alert specific observation posts.
- Disciplines leader movements, enforces brevity, and ensures completeness.
- Keeps within time constraints.
- Ensures that the most important events receive the most attention.
- Ensures that absentees and flank units receive changes to the operation order and transmits changes to them as soon as practical.
- Communicates the key civil considerations of the operation.

Assistant Chief of Staff, G-3 (S-3)

8-64. The G-3 (S-3) assists the commander with the rehearsal. The G-3 (S-3)—
- Portrays the friendly scheme of maneuver.
- Ensures subordinate unit actions comply with the commander's intent.
- Normally provides the recorder.

Assistant Chief of Staff, G-2 (S-2)

8-65. The G-2 (S-2) portrays the adversary forces and other variables of the operational environment during rehearsals. The G-2 (S-2) bases actions on the enemy course of action that the commander selected during the military decisionmaking process. The G-2 (S-2)—

- Provides participants with current intelligence.
- Portrays the best possible assessment of the enemy course of action.
- Communicates the adversary's presumed concept of operations, desired effects, and end state.
- Explains other factors of the operational environment that may hinder or complicate friendly actions.
- Communicates the key civil considerations of the operation.

Subordinate Leaders

8-66. Subordinate unit leaders, using an established format, effectively articulate their units' actions and responsibilities as well as record changes on their copies of the graphics or operation order.

Recorder

8-67. The recorder is normally a representative from the G-3 (S-3). During the rehearsal, the recorder captures all coordination made during execution and notes unresolved problems. At the end of the rehearsal, the recorder—

- Presents any unresolved problems to the commander for resolution.
- Restates any changes, coordination, or clarifications directed by the commander.
- Estimates when a written fragmentary order codifying the changes will follow.

Conducting Headquarters Staff

8-68. The staff updates the operation order, decision support template, and execution matrix based on the decisions of the commander.

ASSESSMENT

8-69. The commander establishes the standard for a successful rehearsal. A properly executed rehearsal validates each leader's role and how each unit contributes to the overall operation—what each unit does, when each unit does it relative to times and events, and where each unit does it to achieve desired effects. An effective rehearsal ensures commanders have a common vision of the enemy, their own forces, the terrain, and the relationship among them. It identifies specific actions requiring immediate staff resolution and informs the higher commander of critical issues or locations that the commander, chief of staff (executive officer), or G-3 (S-3) must personally oversee.

8-70. The commander (or rehearsal director in the commander's absence) assesses and critiques all parts of the rehearsal. Critiques center on how well the operation achieves the commander's intent and on the coordination necessary to accomplish that end. Usually, commanders leave the internal execution of tasks within the rehearsal to the subordinate unit commander's judgment and discretion.

REHEARSAL DETAILS

8-71. All participants have responsibilities before, during, and after a rehearsal. Before a rehearsal, the rehearsal director states the commander's expectations and orients the other participants on details of the rehearsal as necessary. During a rehearsal, all participants rehearse their roles in the operation. They make sure they understand how their actions support the overall operation and note any additional coordination required. After a rehearsal, participants ensure they understand any changes to the operation order and coordination requirements, and they receive all updated staff products.

8-72. Commanders do not normally address small problems that arise during rehearsals. Instead, the G-3 (S-3) recorder keeps a record of these problems. This ensures the commander does not interrupt the rehearsal's flow. If the problem remains at the end of the rehearsal, the commander resolves it then. If the problem jeopardizes mission accomplishment, the staff accomplishes the coordination necessary to resolve it before the participants disperse. Identifying and solving such problems is a major reason for conducting rehearsals. If commanders do not make corrections while participants are assembled, they may lose the opportunity to do so. Coordinating among dispersed participants and disseminating changes to them often proves more difficult than accomplishing these actions in person.

BEFORE THE REHEARSAL

8-73. Before the rehearsal, the rehearsal director calls the roll and briefs participants on information needed for execution. The briefing begins with an introduction, overview, and orientation. It includes a discussion of the rehearsal script and ground rules. The detail of this discussion is based on participants' familiarity with the rehearsal SOP.

8-74. Before the rehearsal, the staff develops an operation order with at least the basic five paragraphs and necessary overlays. The staff may not publish annexes; however, responsible staff officers should know their content.

Introduction and Overview

8-75. Before the rehearsal, the rehearsal director introduces all participants as needed. Then, the rehearsal director (normally the chief of staff or executive officer) gives an overview of the briefing topics, rehearsal subjects and sequence, and timeline, specifying the no-later-than ending time. The rehearsal director explains after action reviews, describes how and when they occur, and discusses how to incorporate changes into the operation order. The director explains any constraints, such as pyrotechnics use, light discipline, weapons firing, or radio silence. For safety, the rehearsal director ensures all participants understand safety precautions and enforces their use. Last, the director emphasizes results and states the commander's standard for a successful rehearsal. Subordinate leaders state any results of planning or preparation (including rehearsals) they have already conducted. If a subordinate recommends a change to the operation order, the rehearsal director acts on the recommendation before the rehearsal begins, if possible. If not, the commander resolves the recommendation with a decision before the rehearsal ends.

Orientation

8-76. The rehearsal director orients the participants to the terrain or rehearsal medium. The rehearsal director identifies orientation using magnetic north on the rehearsal medium and symbols representing actual terrain features. After explaining any graphic control measures, obstacles, and targets, the rehearsal director issues supplemental materials, if needed.

Rehearsal Script

8-77. An effective technique for controlling rehearsals is to use a script. It keeps the rehearsal on track. The script provides a checklist so the organization addresses all warfighting functions and outstanding issues. It has two major parts: the agenda and response sequence.

Agenda

8-78. An effective rehearsal follows a prescribed agenda that everyone knows and understands, including, but not limited to—

- Roll call.
- Participant orientation to the terrain.
- Location of local civilians.
- Enemy situation brief.
- Friendly situation brief.
- Description of expected adversary actions.
- Discussion of friendly unit actions.
- A review of notes made by the recorder.

8-79. The execution matrix, decision support template, and operation order outline the rehearsal agenda. These tools, especially the execution matrix, both drive and focus the rehearsal. The commander and staff use them to control the operation's execution. Any templates, matrixes, or tools developed within each of the warfighting functions should tie directly to the supported unit's execution matrix and decision support template. Examples include an intelligence synchronization matrix or fires execution matrix.

8-80. An effective rehearsal realistically and quickly portrays the enemy force and other variables of the operational environment without distracting from the rehearsal. One technique for doing this has the G-2 (S-2) preparing an actions checklist. It lists a sequence of events much like the one for friendly units but from the enemy or civilian perspective.

Response Sequence

8-81. Participants respond in a logical sequence: either by warfighting function or by unit as the organization deploys, from front to rear. The commander determines the sequence before the rehearsal. The staff posts the sequence at the rehearsal site, and the rehearsal director may restate it.

8-82. Effective rehearsals allow participants to visualize and synchronize the concept of operations. As the rehearsal proceeds, participants talk through the concept of operations. They focus on key events and the synchronization required to achieve the desired effects. The commander leads the rehearsal and gives orders during the operation. Subordinate commanders enter and leave the discussion at the time they expect to begin and end their tasks or activities during the operation. This practice helps the commander assess the adequacy of synchronization. They do not "re-war-game" unless absolutely necessary to ensure subordinate unit commanders understand the plan.

8-83. The rehearsal director emphasizes integrating fires, events that trigger different branch actions, and actions on contact. The chief of fires (fire support officer) or fires unit commander states when to initiate fires, who to fire them, from where the firing comes, the ammunition available, and the desired target effect. Subordinate commanders state when they initiate fires per their fire support plans. The rehearsal director speaks for any absent staff section and ensures the rehearsal addresses all actions on the synchronization matrix and decision support template at the proper time or event.

8-84. The rehearsal director ensures that the rehearsal includes key sustainment and protection actions at the appropriate times. (See Table 8-1.) Failure to do so reduces the value of the rehearsal as a coordination tool. The staff officer with coordinating staff responsibility inserts these items into the rehearsal. Special staff officers should brief by exception when a friendly or enemy event occurs within their area of expertise. Summarizing these actions at the end of the rehearsal can reinforce coordination requirements identified during the rehearsal. The staff updates the decision support template and gives a copy to each participant. Under time-constrained conditions, the conducting headquarters staff may provide copies before the rehearsal and rely on participants to update them with pen-and-ink changes.

Table 8-1. Example sustainment and protection actions for rehearsals

• Casualty evacuation routes	• Support area displacement times and locations
• Ambulance exchange point locations	• Enemy prisoner of war collection points
• Refuel-on-the-move points	• Aviation support
• Class IV and Class V resupply points	• Military police actions
• Logistics release points	

Ground Rules

8-85. After discussing the rehearsal script, the rehearsal director—
- States the standard (what the commander will accept) for a successful rehearsal.
- Ensures everyone understands the parts of the operation order to rehearse. If the unit will not rehearse the entire operation, the rehearsal director states the events to be rehearsed.
- Quickly reviews the rehearsal SOP if all participants are not familiar with it. An effective rehearsal SOP states—
  - Who controls the rehearsal.
  - Who approves the rehearsal venue and its construction.

- When special staff officers brief the commander.
- The relationship between how the execution matrix portrays events and how units rehearse events.

● Establishes the timeline that designates the rehearsal starting time in relation to H-hour. For example, begin the rehearsal by depicting the anticipated situation one hour before H-hour. One event executed before rehearsing the first event is deployment of forces.

● Establishes the time interval to begin and track the rehearsal. For example, specify a ten-minute interval equates to one hour of actual time.

● Updates friendly and adversary activities as necessary, for example, any ongoing reconnaissance.

The rehearsal director concludes the orientation with a call for questions.

DURING THE REHEARSAL

8-86. Once the rehearsal director finishes discussing the ground rules and answering questions, the G-3 (S-3) reads the mission statement, the commander reads the commander's intent, and the G-3 (S-3) establishes the current friendly situation. The rehearsal then begins, following the rehearsal script.

8-87. Paragraphs 8-88 through 8-101 outline a generic set of rehearsal steps developed for combined arms rehearsals. However, with a few modifications, these steps support any rehearsal technique. The products depend on the rehearsal type.

Step 1 – Enemy Forces Deployed

8-88. The G-2 (S-2) briefs the current enemy situation and operational environment and places markers on the map or terrain board (as applicable) indicating where enemy forces and other operationally significant groups or activities would be before the first rehearsal event. The G-2 (S-2) then briefs the most likely enemy course of action and operational context. The G-2 (S-2) also briefs the status of reconnaissance and surveillance operations (for example, citing any patrols still out or any observation post positions).

Step 2 – Friendly Forces Deployed

8-89. The G-3 (S-3) briefs friendly maneuver unit dispositions, including security forces, as they are arrayed at the start of the operation. Subordinate commanders and other staff officers brief their unit positions at the starting time and any particular points of emphasis. For example, the chemical, biological, radiological, and nuclear officer states the mission-oriented protective posture level, and the chief of fires (fire support officer) or fires unit commander states the range of friendly and enemy artillery. Other participants place markers for friendly forces, including adjacent units, at the positions they will occupy at the start of the operation. As participants place markers, they state their task and purpose, task organization, and strength.

8-90. Sustainment and protection units brief positions, plans, and actions at the starting time and at points of emphasis the rehearsal director designates. Subordinate units may include forward arming and refueling points, refuel-on-the-move points, communications checkpoints, security points, or operations security procedures that differ for any period during the operation. The rehearsal director restates the commander's intent, if necessary.

Step 3 – Initiate Action

8-91. The rehearsal director states the first event on the execution matrix. Normally this involves the G-2 (S-2) moving enemy markers according to the most likely course of action. The depiction must tie enemy actions to specific terrain or to friendly unit actions. The G-2 (S-2) portrays enemy actions based on the situational template developed for staff war-gaming. Portray the enemy as uncooperative but not invincible.

8-92. As the rehearsal proceeds, the G-2 (S-2) portrays the enemy and other operational factors and walks through the most likely enemy course of action (per the situational template). The G-2 (S-2) stresses reconnaissance routes, objectives, security force composition and locations, initial contact, initial fires (artillery, air, and attack helicopters), probable main force objectives or engagement areas, and likely commitment of reserve forces.

Step 4 – Decision Point

8-93. When the rehearsal director determines that a particular enemy movement or reaction is complete, the commander assesses the situation to determine if a decision point has been reached. Decision points are taken directly from the decision support template.

8-94. If the commander determines the unit is not at a decision point and not at the end state, the commander directs the rehearsal director to continue to the next event on the execution matrix. Participants use the response sequence (see paragraphs 8-81 through 8-84) and continue to act out and describe their units' actions.

8-95. When the rehearsal reaches conditions that establish a decision point, the commander decides whether to continue with the current course of action or by selecting a branch. If electing the current course of action, the commander directs the rehearsal director to move to the next event in the execution matrix. If selecting a branch, the commander states why that branch, states the first event of that branch, and continues the rehearsal until the organization has rehearsed all events of that branch. As the unit reaches decisive points, the rehearsal director states the conditions required for success.

8-96. When it becomes obvious that the operation requires additional coordination to ensure success, participants immediately begin coordinating. This is one of the key reasons for rehearsals. The rehearsal director ensures that the recorder captures the coordination and any changes and all participants understand the coordination.

Step 5 – End State Reached

8-97. Achieving the desired end state completes that phase of the rehearsal. In an attack, this will usually be when the unit is on the objective and has finished consolidation and casualty evacuation. In the defense, this will usually be after the decisive action (such as committing the reserve or striking force), the final destruction or withdrawal of the enemy, and casualty evacuation is complete. In a stability operation, this usually occurs when a unit achieves the targeted progress within a designated line of effort.

Step 6 – Reset

8-98. At this point, the commander states the next branch to rehearse. The rehearsal director resets the situation to the decision point where that branch begins and states the criteria for a decision to execute that branch. Participants assume those criteria have been met and then refight the operation along that branch until they attain the desired end state. They complete any coordination needed to ensure all participants understand and can meet any requirements. The recorder records any changes to the branch.

8-99. The commander then states the next branch to rehearse. The rehearsal director again resets the situation to the decision point where that branch begins, and participants repeat the process. This continues until the rehearsal addressed all decision points and branches that the commander wants to rehearse.

8-100. If the standard is not met and time permits, the commander directs participants to repeat the rehearsal. The rehearsal continues until participants are prepared or until the time available expires. (Commanders may allocate more time for a rehearsal but must assess the effects on subordinate commanders' preparation time.) Successive rehearsals, if conducted, should be more complex and realistic.

8-101. At the end of the rehearsal, the recorder restates any changes, coordination, or clarifications that the commander directed and estimates how long it will take to codify changes in a written fragmentary order.

AFTER THE REHEARSAL

8-102. After the rehearsal, the commander leads an after action review. The commander reviews lessons learned and makes the minimum required modifications to the existing plan. (Normally, a fragmentary order effects these changes.) Changes should be refinements to the operation order; they should not be radical or significant. Changes not critical to the operation's execution may confuse subordinates and hinder the synchronization of the plan. The commander issues any last minute instructions or reminders and reiterates the commander's intent.

8-103. Based on the commander's instructions, the staff makes any necessary changes to the operation order, decision support template, and execution matrix based on the rehearsal results. Subordinate commanders incorporate these changes into their units' operation orders. The chief of staff (executive officer) ensures the changes are briefed to all leaders or liaison officers who did not participate in the rehearsal.

8-104. A rehearsal provides the final opportunity for subordinates to identify and fix unresolved problems. The staff ensures that all participants understand any changes to the operation order and that the recorder captures all coordination done at the rehearsal. All changes to the published operation order are, in effect, verbal fragmentary orders. As soon as possible, the staff publishes these verbal fragmentary orders as a written fragmentary order that changes the operation order.

Chapter 9

Liaison

This chapter discusses liaison fundamentals and responsibilities of liaison officers and teams. It addresses requirements distinct to contingency operations and unified action. It includes liaison checklists and an example outline for a liaison officer handbook.

LIAISON FUNDAMENTALS

9-1. *Liaison* is that contact or intercommunication maintained between elements of military forces or other agencies to ensure mutual understanding and unity of purpose and action (JP 3-08). Liaison helps reduce uncertainty. Most commonly used for establishing and maintaining close communications, liaison continuously enables direct, physical communications between commands. Commanders use liaison during operations and normal daily activities to help facilitate communications between organizations, preserve freedom of action, and maintain flexibility. Effective liaison ensures commanders that subordinates understand implicit coordination. Liaison provides commanders with relevant information and answers to operational questions, thus enhancing the commander's confidence.

9-2. Liaison activities augment the commander's ability to synchronize and focus combat power. They include establishing and maintaining physical contact and communications between elements of military forces and nonmilitary agencies during unified action. Liaison activities ensure—

- Cooperation and understanding among commanders and staffs of different headquarters.
- Coordination on tactical matters to achieve unity of effort.
- Synchronization of lethal and nonlethal operations.
- Understanding of implied or inferred coordination measures to achieve synchronized results.

LIAISON OFFICER

9-3. A liaison officer (LNO) represents a commander or staff officer. LNOs transmit information directly, bypassing headquarters and staff layers. A trained, competent, trusted, and informed LNO (either a commissioned or a noncommissioned officer) is the key to effective liaison. LNOs must have the commander's full confidence and experience for the mission. At higher echelons, the complexity of operations often requires an increase in the rank required for LNOs. (See Table 9-1.)

Table 9-1. Senior liaison officer rank by echelon

Echelon	Recommended Rank
Corps	Lieutenant colonel
Division	Major
Brigade, regiment, group	Captain
Battalion	First lieutenant

9-4. The LNO's parent unit or unit of assignment is the sending unit; the unit to which the LNO is sent is the receiving unit. A LNO normally remains at the receiving unit until recalled. Because LNOs represent the commander, they—

- Understand how the commander thinks and interpret the commander's messages.
- Convey the commander's intent, guidance, mission, and concept of operations.
- Represent the commander's position.

9-5. As a representative, the LNO has access to the commander consistent with the duties involved. However, for routine matters, LNOs work for and receive direction from the chief of staff (COS) or the executive officer (XO). Using one officer to perform a liaison mission conserves manpower while guaranteeing a consistent, accurate flow of information. However, continuous operations require a liaison team.

9-6. The professional capabilities and personal characteristics of an effective LNO encourage confidence and cooperation with the commander and staff of the receiving unit. In addition to the above discussion, effective LNOs—

- Know the sending unit's mission; current and future operations; logistics status; organization; disposition; capabilities; and tactics, techniques, and procedures (TTP).
- Appreciate and understand the receiving unit's TTP, organization, capabilities, mission, doctrine, staff procedures, and customs.
- Are familiar with—
  - Requirements for and purpose of liaison.
  - The liaison system and its reports, documents, and records.
  - Liaison team training.
- Observe the established channels of command and staff functions.
- Are tactful.
- Possess the necessary language expertise.

LIAISON ELEMENTS

9-7. Commanders organize liaison elements based on the mission variables (known as METT-TC) and echelon of command. Common ways to organize liaison elements include—

- An LNO alone or with minimum support.
- A liaison team consisting of an LNO, a liaison noncommissioned officer in charge, clerical personnel, and communications personnel along with their equipment.
- A liaison detachment of several teams with expertise in specialized areas, such as intelligence, operations, civil affairs, and sustainment.
- Couriers (messengers) responsible for the secure physical transmission and delivery of documents and other materials.

LIAISON PRACTICES

9-8. When possible, liaison is reciprocal among higher, lower, supporting, supported, and adjacent organizations. Each organization sends a liaison element to the other. It must be reciprocal when U.S. forces are placed under control of a headquarters of a different nationality and vice versa, or when brigade-sized and larger formations of different nationalities are adjacent. When not reciprocal, the following practices apply to liaison:

- Higher-echelon units establish liaison with lower echelons.
- Units on the left establish liaison with units on their right.
- Supporting units establish liaison with units they support.
- Units of the same echelon and units in the rear establish liaison with those to their front.
- Units not in contact with the enemy establish liaison with units in contact with the enemy.
- During a passage of lines, the passing unit establishes liaison with the stationary unit.
- During a relief in place, the relieving unit establishes liaison with the unit being relieved.

If liaison is broken, both units act to reestablish it. However, the primary responsibility rests with the unit originally responsible for establishing liaison.

LIAISON RESPONSIBILITIES

9-9. Both sending and receiving units have liaison responsibilities before, during, and after operations.

SENDING UNIT

9-10. The sending unit's most important tasks include selecting and training the Soldiers best qualified for liaison duties. Liaison personnel should have the characteristics and qualifications discussed in paragraphs 9-3 through 9-6. Table 9-2 shows a sample outline for an LNO handbook that addresses knowledge and skills LNOs require.

Table 9-2. Example outline of a liaison officer handbook

Table of contents, with the sending unit's proponency statement.

Purpose statement.

Introduction statement.

Definitions.

Scope statement.

Responsibilities and guidelines for conduct.

Actions to take before departing from the sending unit.

Actions to take on arriving at the receiving unit.

Actions to take during liaison operations at the receiving unit.

Actions to take before departing from the receiving unit.

Actions to take upon returning to the sending unit.

Sample questions. LNOs should be able to answer the following questions:
- Does the sending unit have a copy of the receiving unit's latest operation plan, operation order, and fragmentary order?
- Does the receiving unit's plan support the plan of the higher headquarters? This includes sustainment as well as the tactical concept. Are main supply routes and required supply rates known? Can the controlled supply rate support the receiving unit's plan?
- What are the receiving unit's commander's critical information requirements (CCIRs)? At what time, phase, or event are they expected to change? Are there any items the CCIRs do not contain with which the sending unit can help?
- Which sending commander decisions are critical to executing the receiving unit operation?
- What are the "no-later-than" times for those decisions?
- What assets does the unit need to acquire to accomplish its mission? How would the unit use them? How do they support attaining the more senior commander's intent? From where can the unit obtain them? Higher headquarters? Other Services? Multinational partners?
- How do units use aviation assets?
- How can the LNOs communicate with the sending unit? Are telephones, radios, facsimile machines, computers, and other information systems available? Where are they located? Which communications are secure?
- What terrain did the unit designate as key? Decisive?
- What weather conditions would have a major impact on the operation?
- What effect would a chemical, biological, radiological, and nuclear environment have on the operation?
- What effect would large numbers of refugees or enemy prisoners of war have on the receiving unit's operations?
- What is the worst thing that could happen during execution of the current operation?
- How would a unit handle a passage of lines by other units through the force?
- What conditions would cause the unit to request operational control of a multinational force?
- If the unit is placed under operational control of a larger multinational force, or given operational control of a smaller such force, what special problems would it present?
- If going to a multinational force headquarters, how do the tactical principles and command concepts of that force differ from those of U.S. forces?

What host-nation support is available to the sending unit?

Required reports from higher and sending units' standard operating procedures.

Table 9-2. Example outline of a liaison officer handbook (continued)

Packing list:
- Credentials (including permissive jump orders, if qualified). Blank forms as required.
- References.
- Excerpts of higher and sending headquarters' operation orders and plans.
- Sending unit standard operating procedures.
- Sending unit's command diagrams and recapitulation of major systems.
- The unit modified table of equipment, unit status report (if its classification allows), and mission briefings. The G-3 (S-3) and the force modernization officer are excellent sources of these.
- Computers and other information systems required for information and data exchange.
- Signal operating instructions extract.
- Security code encryption device.
- Communications equipment.
- Sending unit telephone book.
- List of commanders and staff officers.
- Telephone calling (credit) card.
- Movement table.
- Administrative equipment (for example, pens, paper, scissors, tape, and hole punch).
- Map and chart equipment (for example, pens, pins, protractor, straight edge, scale, distance counter, acetate, and unit markers).
- Tent and accessories (camouflage net, cots, and stove, as appropriate).
- Foreign phrase book and dictionary.
- Local currency as required.
- Rations and water.
- Weapons and ammunition.

9-11. The sending unit describes the liaison team to the receiving unit providing number and types of vehicles and personnel, equipment, call signs, and frequencies. The LNO or liaison team also requires—
- Point-to-point transportation, as required.
- Identification and appropriate credentials for the receiving unit.
- Appropriate security clearance, courier orders, and information systems accredited for use on the receiving unit's network.
- The standard operating procedures (SOPs) outlining the missions, functions, procedures, and duties of the sending unit's liaison section.

9-12. Table 9-3 lists tasks for liaison personnel to perform before departing the sending unit.

Table 9-3. Liaison checklist—before departing the sending unit

- Understand what the sending commander wants the receiving commander to know.
- Receive a briefing from operations, intelligence, and other staff elements on current and future operations.
- Receive and understand the tasks from the sending unit staff.
- Obtain the correct maps, traces, and overlays.
- Arrange for transport, communications and cryptographic equipment, codes, signal instructions, and the challenge and password—including their protection and security. Arrange for replacement of these items, as necessary.
- Complete route-reconnaissance and time-management plans so the liaison team arrives at the designated location on time.
- Ensure that liaison team and interpreters have security clearances and access appropriate for the mission.

Table 9-3. Liaison checklist—before departing the sending unit (continued)

• Verify that the receiving unit received the liaison team's security clearances and will grant access to the level of information the mission requires.
• Verify courier orders.
• Know how to destroy classified information in case of an emergency during transit or at the receiving unit.
• Inform the sending unit of the LNO's departure time, route, arrival time, and, when known, the estimated time and route of return.
• Pick up all correspondence designated for the receiving unit.
• Conduct a radio check.
• Know the impending moves of the sending and receiving units.
• Bring accredited information systems needed to support liaison operations.
• Pack adequate rations and water for use in transit.
• Arrange for the liaison party's departure.

RECEIVING UNIT

9-13. The receiving unit—

- Provides the sending unit with the LNO's reporting time, place, point of contact, recognition signal, and password.
- Provides details of any tactical movement and logistics information relevant to the LNO's mission, especially while the LNO is in transit.
- Ensures that the LNO has access to the commander, the COS (XO), and other officers, as required.
- Gives the LNO an initial briefing of the unit battle rhythm and allows the LNO access necessary to remain informed of current operations.
- Protects the LNO while at the receiving unit.
- Publishes an SOP outlining the missions, functions, procedures to request information, information release restrictions and clearance procedures, and duties of the LNO or team at the receiving unit.
- Provides access to communications equipment (and operating instructions, as needed) when the LNO needs to communicate using the receiving unit's equipment.
- Provides adequate workspace for the LNO.
- Provides administrative and logistic support.

DURING THE TOUR

9-14. During the tour, LNOs have specific duties. (Table 9-4, page 9-6, summarizes those duties.) LNOs inform the receiving unit's commander or staff of the sending unit's needs or requirements. Due to the numbers of LNOs in the headquarters, sending units guard against inundating the receiving unit with formal requests for information. By virtue of their location in the headquarters and knowledge of the situation, LNOs can rapidly answer questions from the sending unit and keep the receiving unit from wasting planning time answering requests for information. During the liaison tour, LNOs—

- Arrive at the designated location on time.
- Promote cooperation between the sending and receiving units.
- Accomplish their mission without becoming overly involved in the receiving unit's staff procedures or actions; however, they may assist higher staffs in war-gaming.
- Follow the receiving unit's communications procedures.
- Actively obtain information without interfering with receiving unit's operations.
- Facilitate understanding of the sending unit's commander's intent.
- Help the sending unit's commander assess current and future operations.

- Remain informed of the sending unit's current situation and provide that information to the receiving unit's commander and staff.
- Quickly inform the sending unit of the receiving unit's upcoming missions, tasks, and orders.
- Ensure the sending unit has a copy of the receiving unit's SOP.
- Inform the receiving unit's commander or COS (XO) of the content of reports transmitted to the sending unit.
- Keep a record of their reports, listing everyone met (including each person's name, rank, duty position, and telephone number) as well as key staff members and their telephone numbers.
- Attempt to resolve issues within the receiving unit before involving the sending unit.
- Notify the sending unit promptly if unable to accomplish the liaison mission.
- Report their departure to the receiving unit's commander at the end of their mission.

Table 9-4. Liaison duties—during the liaison tour

• Arrive at least two hours before any scheduled briefings.
• Check in with security and complete any required documentation.
• Report to and present credentials to the COS (XO) or supervisor, as appropriate.
• Arrange for an office call with the commander.
• Meet coordinating and special staff officers.
• Notify the sending unit of arrival.
• Visit staff elements, brief them on the sending unit's situation, and collect information from them.
• Deliver all correspondence designated for the receiving unit.
• Annotate on all overlays the security classification, title, map scale, grid intersection points, and effective date-time group, when received, and from whom received.
• Pick up all correspondence for the sending unit when departing the receiving unit.
• Inform the receiving unit of LNO's departure time, return route, and expected arrival time at the sending unit.

AFTER THE TOUR

9-15. After returning to the sending unit, LNOs promptly transmit the receiving unit's requests to the sending unit's commander or staff, as appropriate. Table 9-5 lists tasks to perform after completing a liaison tour.

Table 9-5. Liaison duties—after the liaison tour

• Deliver all correspondence.
• Brief the COS (XO) and appropriate staff elements.
• Prepare the necessary reports.
• Clearly state what they did and did not learn from the mission.

9-16. Accuracy is paramount. Effective LNOs provide clear, concise, complete information. If the accuracy of information is in doubt, they quote the source and include the source in the report. LNOs limit their remarks to mission-related observations.

LIAISON DURING UNIFIED ACTION

9-17. Contingency, joint, interagency, and multinational operations require greater liaison efforts than most other operations.

CONTINGENCY OPERATIONS

9-18. Contingency operations create an increased need for liaison. Unfamiliarity with the area of operations requires extensive research for running estimates. Some operations require tight security, which restricts access or dissemination of information and affects the deployment schedule. Unfamiliar SOPs, unit equipment, and Soldiers typically slow new command and support relationships and newly task-organized units' staff coordination and actions. Effective liaison improves commanders' understanding and reduces the possibility of conflicting guidance, frequent planning changes, and inefficient execution of deployment tasks. During deployment, LNOs act as critical information conduits.

9-19. Effective LNOs understand their commander's information requirements, especially the CCIRs. Information requirements during deployment might include—

- The type of transportation the unit needs for deployment and resupply.
- The information systems and intelligence products available.
- The level and extent of protection the unit needs as it arrives, disembarks, and prepares for operations.
- Staging area requirements.
- The sustainment that the Army component of a joint force must provide to other Service components.
- Local tactical intelligence products otherwise unavailable.
- Unit movement officer responsibilities.

JOINT OPERATIONS

9-20. Current joint information systems do not meet all operational requirements. Few U.S. military information systems are interoperable. Army liaison teams require information systems that can rapidly exchange information between commands to ensure Army force operations are synchronized with operations of the joint force and its Service components.

INTERAGENCY OPERATIONS

9-21. Army forces may participate in interagency operations across the spectrum of conflict, especially when conducting stability or civil support operations. Frequently, Army forces conduct operations in cooperation with or in support of civilian government agencies. Relations in these operations are rarely based on standard military command and support relationships; rather, national laws or specific agreements for each given situation govern the specific relationships in interagency operations. For example, during civil support operations, the Federal Emergency Management Agency has overall charge of federal disaster relief within the United States, its territories, and possessions. Interagency operations may lack unity of command. All government agencies may work toward a common goal but not under a single authority. In such situations, achieving unity of effort requires effective liaison. (See FM 3-07.)

9-22. Some missions require coordination with nongovernmental organizations. No overarching interagency doctrine delineates or dictates the relationships and procedures governing all agencies, departments, and organizations in interagency operations. Effective liaison elements work toward establishing mutual trust and confidence, continuously coordinating actions to achieve cooperation and unity of effort. (See also JP 3-08.) In these situations, LNOs and their teams require a broader understanding of the interagency environment, responsibilities, motivations, and limitations of nongovernmental organizations, and the relationships these organizations have with the U.S. military.

MULTINATIONAL OPERATIONS

9-23. Army units often operate as part of a multinational force whose information systems may not be compatible. Some nations have little or no computerized information systems. Reciprocal liaison is especially important under these conditions. Mutual confidence makes these multinational operations successful. Liaison during multinational operations includes explicit coordination of doctrine and tactics, techniques, and procedures. It requires patience and tact during personal interactions. LNOs need to thoroughly understand the strategic, operational, and tactical aims of the international effort. Foreign disclosure limitations often require special communications and liaison arrangements to address cultural differences and sensitivities as well as ensure explicit understanding throughout the multinational force.

This page intentionally left blank.

Chapter 10

Military Briefings

This chapter describes the four types of military briefings presented to commanders, staffs, or other audiences. It also describes steps of the military briefings.

TYPES OF MILITARY BRIEFINGS

10-1. The Army uses four types of briefings: information, decision, mission, and staff.

INFORMATION BRIEFING

10-2. An information briefing presents facts in a form the audience can easily understand. It does not include conclusions or recommendations nor does it result in decisions. (See Figure 10-1.)

---

1. Introduction
- **Greeting**. Address the audience. Identify yourself and your organization.
- **Type and Classification of Briefing**. Identify the type and classification of the briefing. For example, "This is an information briefing. It is classified SECRET."
- **Purpose and Scope**. Describe complex subjects from general to specific.
- **Outline or Procedure**. Briefly summarize the key points and general approach. Explain any special procedures (such as demonstrations, displays, or tours). For example, "During my briefing, I will discuss the six phases of our plan. I will refer to maps of our area of operations. Then my assistant will bring out a sand table to show you the expected flow of battle." The key points may be placed on a chart that remains visible throughout the briefing.

2. Main Body
- Arrange the main ideas in a logical sequence.
- Use visual aids to emphasize main points.
- Plan effective transitions from one main point to the next.
- Be prepared to answer questions at any time.

3. Closing
- Ask for questions.
- Briefly recap main ideas and make a concluding statement.

Figure 10-1. Information briefing format

10-3. Briefers begin an information briefing by greeting the audience, identifying themselves and their organization, and then providing the classification of the briefing. The briefer states the purpose of the briefing is to inform the audience and no decision is required. The briefer then introduces the subject, orients the audience to any visual aids, and presents the information. Examples of appropriate topics for information briefings include, but are not limited to—

- High-priority information requiring immediate attention.
- Complex information such as complicated plans, systems, statistics or charts, or other items that require detailed explanations.
- Controversial information requiring elaboration and explanation.

DECISION BRIEFING

10-4. A decision briefing obtains the answer to a question or a decision on a course of action. The briefer presents recommended solutions from the analysis or study of a problem or problem area. (Chapter 4 discusses the military decisionmaking process and Chapter 11 discusses problem solving.) Decision briefings vary in formality and level of detail depending on the commander's or decisionmaker's knowledge on the subject.

10-5. If the decisionmaker is unfamiliar with the problem, the briefing format adheres to the decision briefing format. (See Figure 10-2.) Decision briefings should include all facts and assumptions relevant to the problem, a discussion of alternatives, analysis-based conclusions, and any coordination required.

---

1. Introduction
- **Greeting**. Address the decisionmaker. Identify yourself and your organization.
- **Type and Classification of Briefing**. Identify the type and classification of the briefing. For example, "This is a decision briefing. It is UNCLASSIFIED."
- **Problem Statement**. State the problem.
- **Recommendation**. State the recommendation.

2. Body
- **Facts**. Provide an objective presentation of both positive and negative facts bearing upon the problem.
- **Assumptions**. Identify necessary assumptions made to bridge any gaps in factual data.
- **Solutions**. Discuss the various options that can solve the problem.
- **Analysis**. List the criteria by which the briefer will evaluate how to solve the problem (screening and evaluation). Discuss relative advantages and disadvantages for each course of action.
- **Comparison**. Show how the courses of action rate against the evaluation criteria.
- **Conclusion**. Describe why the recommended solution is best.

3. Closing
- Ask for questions.
- Briefly recap main ideas and restate the recommendation.
- Request a decision.

Figure 10-2. Decision briefing format

10-6. When the decisionmaker is familiar with the subject or problem, the briefing format often resembles that of a decision paper: problem statement, essential background information, impacts, and recommended solution. In addition to this format, briefers must be prepared to present assumptions, facts, alternative solutions, reasons for recommendations, and any additional coordination required.

10-7. The briefer begins by stating, "This is a decision briefing." If no decision is provided upon conclusion of the decision briefing, the briefer will ask for one. The briefer ensures all participants clearly understand the decision and asks for clarification if necessary.

10-8. The briefer clearly states and precisely words a recommendation presented during decision briefings to prevent ambiguity and to translate it easily into a decision statement. If the decision requires an implementation document, briefers present that document at the time of the briefing for the decisionmaker to sign. If the chief of staff or executive officer is absent, the briefer informs the secretary of the general staff or designated authority of the decision upon conclusion of the briefing.

MISSION BRIEFING

10-9. Mission briefings are informal briefings that occur during operations or training. Briefers may be commanders, staffs, or special representatives.

10-10. Mission briefings serve to convey critical mission information not provided in the plan or order to individuals or small units. Mission briefings—
- Issue or enforce an order.
- Provide more detailed instructions or requirements.
- Instill a general appreciation for the mission.

- Review key points for an operation.
- Ensure participants know the mission objective, their contribution to the operation, problems they may confront, and ways to overcome them.

10-11. The nature and content of the information being provided determines the mission briefing format. Typically a briefer will use the operation plan or order as a format for a mission briefing.

STAFF BRIEFING

10-12. The staff uses a staff briefing to inform the commander and staff of the current situation to coordinate and synchronize efforts within the unit. The individual convening the staff briefing sets the briefing agenda. Each staff element presents relevant information from their functional areas. Staff briefings facilitate information exchange, announce decisions, issue directives, or provide guidance. The staff briefing format may include characteristics of the information briefing, decision briefing, and mission briefing.

10-13. The commander, deputies or assistants, chiefs of staff or executive officers, and coordinating, personal, and special staff officers often attend staff briefings. Representatives from major subordinate commands may also attend. The chief of staff or executive officer often presides over the briefing. The commander may take an active role during the briefing and normally concludes the briefing.

STEPS OF MILITARY BRIEFINGS

10-14. These four steps correspond to the operations process and lay the foundation for an effective briefing:

- **Plan**—analyze the situation and prepare a briefing outline.
- **Prepare**—collect information and construct the briefing.
- **Execute**—deliver the briefing.
- **Assess**—follow up as required.

ANALYZE THE SITUATION AND PREPARE A BRIEFING OUTLINE

10-15. Upon receipt of the task to conduct a briefing, the briefer analyzes the situation and determines the—

- Audience.
- Purpose and type.
- Subject.
- Classification.
- Physical facilities and support needed.
- Preparation timeline and schedule.

10-16. Based on the analysis, the briefer assembles a briefing outline. The briefing outline is the plan for the preparation, execution, and follow-up for the briefing. The briefer uses the timeline as a tool to manage preparations for the briefing and refine the briefing as new information becomes available.

10-17. Briefers consider many factors during planning (see Figure 10-3, page 10-4), and this includes, but is not limited to—

- Audience preferences for decision briefings, such as how the decisionmaker wants to see information presented.
- Time available.
- Facilities and briefing aids available.

10-18. The briefer then estimates suspense times for each task and schedules the preparation effort accordingly. The briefer alerts support personnel and any assistants as soon as possible.

---

1. Audience.
   - What is the size and composition? Single Service or joint? Civilians? Foreign nationals?
   - Who are the ranking members and their official duty positions?
   - How well do they know the subject?
   - Are they generalists or specialists?
   - What are their interests?
   - What is the anticipated reaction?
2. Purpose and Type.
   - Information briefing (to inform)?
   - Decision briefing (to obtain decision)?
   - Mission briefing (to review important details)?
   - Staff briefing (to exchange information)?
3. Subject.
   - What is the specific subject?
   - What is the desired depth of coverage?
   - How much time is allocated?
4. Classification.
   - What is the security classification?
   - Do all attendees meet this classification?
5. Physical Facilities and Support Needed.
   - Where is the briefing to be presented?
   - What support is needed?
   - What are the security requirements, if needed?
   - What are the equipment requirements? Computer? Projector? Screen?
6. Preparation Timeline and Schedule.
   - Prepare preliminary outline.
   - Determine requirements for training aids, assistants, and recorders.
   - Schedule rehearsals, facilities, and critiques.
   - Arrange for final review by responsible authority.

Figure 10-3. Considerations during planning

COLLECT INFORMATION AND CONSTRUCT THE BRIEFING

10-19. The briefing construction varies with type and purpose. (See Figure 10-4.) The analysis of the briefing determines the basis for this. Briefers follow these key steps to prepare a briefing:

- Collect materials needed.
- Prepare first draft.
- Revise first draft and edit.
- Plan use of visual aids.
- Practice.

DELIVER THE BRIEFING

10-20. The success of a briefing depends on a concise, objective, accurate, clearly enunciated, and forceful delivery. The briefer must also be confident and relaxed. The briefer should consider the following:

- The basic purpose is to present the subject as directed and ensure the audience understands it.
- Brevity precludes a lengthy introduction or summary.
- Conclusions and recommendations must flow logically from facts and assumptions.

1. Collect Materials Needed.
   - Use the Seven-Step Army Problem-Solving Process (See Chapter 11).
   - Research.
   - Become familiar with the subject.
   - Collect authoritative opinions and facts.
2. Prepare First Draft.
   - Prepare draft outline.
   - Include visual aids.
   - Review with appropriate authority.
3. Revise First Draft and Edit.
   - Verify facts, including those that are important and necessary.
   - Include answers to anticipated questions.
   - Refine materials.
4. Plan Use of Visual Aids.
   - Check for simplicity.
   - Check for readability.
5. Practice.
   - Rehearse (with assistants and visual aids).
   - Refine.
   - Isolate key points.
   - Memorize outline.
   - Develop transitions.
   - Anticipate and prepare for possible questions.

Figure 10-4. Considerations during preparation

10-21. Interruptions and questions may occur at any point. If they occur, briefers answer each question before continuing or indicate that they will answer the question later in the briefing. When briefers answer questions later in the briefing, they specifically reference the earlier question when they introduce material. They anticipate possible questions and are prepared to answer them.

FOLLOW UP AS REQUIRED

10-22. When the briefing is over, the briefer conducts a follow-up as required. To ensure understanding, the briefer prepares a memorandum for record. This memorandum for record records the subject, date, time, and location of the briefing as well as the ranks, names, and positions of audience members. The briefer concisely records the briefing's content to help ensure understanding. The briefer records the decision. The briefer records recommendations and their approval, disapproval, or approval with modification as well as instructions or directed actions. Recommendations can include who is to take action. When a decision is involved and any ambiguity exists about the commander's intent, the briefer submits a draft of the memorandum for record for correction before preparing the final document. Lastly, the briefer informs proper authorities. The briefer distributes the final memorandum for record to staff sections and agencies required to act on the decisions or instructions or whose plans or operations may be affected.

This page intentionally left blank.

Chapter 11

Problem Solving, Staff Studies, and Decision Papers

Problem solving is a daily activity for leaders. This chapter describes a standard, systematic approach for solving problems. It also discusses formats and instructions for preparing staff studies and decision papers—documents staff officer use to record their work and present recommendations develop during the problem solving process.

PROBLEM SOLVING

11-1. The ability to recognize and effectively solve problems is an essential skill for leaders (see FM 6-22). Not all problems require lengthy analysis. For simple problems, leaders often make quick decisions based on their experiences. However, for problems involving a variety of factors, leaders need a systematic problem-solving process. The objective of problem solving is not just to solve near-term problems, but to also do so in a way that forms the basis for long-term success. The Army's approach to problem solving includes the following steps:
- Identify the problem.
- Gather information.
- Develop criteria.
- Generate possible solutions.
- Analyze possible solutions.
- Compare possible solutions.
- Make and implement the decision.

IDENTIFY THE PROBLEM

11-2. Recognizing and defining the problem is an important first step in problem solving. However, identifying the problem is extremely difficult without also gathering information. Commanders and staffs implement both steps at the same time to ensure enough information exists for them to identify the problem properly and effectively.

11-3. This step is crucial, as the actual problem may not be obvious at first. Therefore, leaders seek to understand the situation and determine what the problem is by clearly defining its scope and limitations. Leaders should allow sufficient time and energy to gather enough information and to define the problem clearly before moving on to other steps of the problem-solving process.

11-4. A problem exists when the current state or condition differs from a desired end state or condition. Leaders identify problems from a variety of sources. These include—
- Higher headquarters' directives or guidance.
- Decisionmaker's guidance.
- Subordinates.
- Personal observations.

11-5. When identifying the problem, leaders actively seek to identify its root cause, not merely the symptoms on the surface. Symptoms may be the reason that the problem became visible. They are often the first things noticed and frequently require attention. However, focusing on a problem's symptoms may lead to false conclusions or inappropriate solutions. Using a systematic approach to identifying the real problem helps avoid the "solving symptoms" pitfall.

11-6. To identify the root cause of a problem, leaders do the following:

- Compare the current situation to the desired end state.
- Define the problem's scope or boundaries.
- Answer the following questions:
  - Who does the problem affect?
  - What is affected?
  - When did the problem occur?
  - Where is the problem?
  - Why did the problem occur?
- Determine the cause of obstacles between current and desired end state.
- Write a draft problem statement.
- Redefine the problem as necessary as staff acquires and assesses new information.

11-7. After identifying the root causes, leaders develop a problem statement—a statement that clearly describes the problem to be solved. When they base the problem under consideration upon a directive from a higher authority, it is best to submit the problem statement to the decisionmaker for approval. This ensures the problem solver has understood the decisionmaker's guidance before continuing.

11-8. Once leaders develop a problem statement, they make a plan to solve the problem. Leaders make the best possible use of available time and allocate time for each problem-solving step. Doing this provides a series of deadlines to meet in solving the problem. Leaders use reverse planning to prepare their problem-solving timeline. They use this timeline to periodically assess progress. They do not let real or perceived pressure cause them to abandon solving the problem systematically. They change time allocations as necessary, but they do not omit steps.

GATHER INFORMATION

11-9. After completing the problem statement, leaders continue to gather information relevant to the problem. Gathering information begins with defining the problem and continues throughout the problem-solving process. Leaders never stop acquiring and assessing the impact of new or additional information.

11-10. When gathering information, leaders define unfamiliar terms. Doing this is particularly important when dealing with technical information. Leaders consider the intended audience in deciding what to define. For example, a product for an audience that includes civilians may require definitions of all Army terms. A technical report prepared for a decisionmaker unfamiliar with the subject should include definitions the reader needs to know to understand the report.

11-11. Leaders gather information from primary sources whenever possible. Primary sources are people with first-hand knowledge of the subject under investigation, or documents produced by them. Methods of gathering information from primary sources include interviews, letters of request for specific information, and questionnaires.

11-12. Leaders require two types of information to solve problems: facts and assumptions. Fully understanding these types of information is critical to understanding problem solving. In addition, leaders need to know how to handle opinions and how to manage information when working in a group.

Facts

11-13. Facts are verifiable pieces of information or information presented that has objective reality. They form the foundation on which a solution to the problem is based. Regulations, policies, doctrinal publications, commander's guidance, plans and orders, and personal experience are just a few sources of facts.

Assumptions

11-14. An assumption is information accepted as true in the absence of facts; it is thought to be correct but cannot be verified. Appropriate assumptions used in decisionmaking have two characteristics:

- They are valid, that is, they are likely to be true.
- They are necessary, that is, they are essential to continuing the problem-solving process.

11-15. If the process can continue without making a particular assumption, leaders discard it. So long as an assumption is both valid and necessary, leaders treat it as a fact. Problem solvers continually seek to confirm or deny the validity of their assumptions.

Opinions

11-16. When gathering information, leaders evaluate opinions carefully. An opinion is a personal judgment that the leader or another individual makes. Opinions cannot be totally discounted. They are often the result of years of experience. Leaders objectively evaluate opinions to determine whether to accept them as facts, include them as opinions, or reject them. Leaders neither routinely accept opinions as facts nor reject them as irrelevant—regardless of their source.

Organizing Information

11-17. Leaders check each piece of information to verify its accuracy. If possible, two individuals should check and confirm the accuracy of facts and the validity of assumptions. Being able to establish whether a piece of information is a fact or an assumption is of little value if those working on the problem do not know the information exists. Leaders share information with the decisionmaker, subordinates, and peers, as appropriate. A proposed solution to a problem is only as good as the information that forms the basis of the solution. Sharing information among members of a problem-solving team increases the likelihood that a team member will uncover the information that leads to the best solution.

11-18. Organizing information includes coordination with units and agencies that may be affected by the problem or its solution. Leaders determine these as they gather information. They coordinate with other leaders as they solve problems, both to obtain assistance and to keep others informed of situations that may affect them. Such coordination may be informal and routine. For an informal example, a squad leader checks with the squad to the right to make sure their fields of fire overlap. For a formal example, a division action officer staffs a decision paper with the major subordinate commands. As a minimum, leaders always coordinate with units or agencies that might be affected by a solution they propose before they present it to the decisionmaker.

DEVELOP CRITERIA

11-19. The next step in the problem-solving process is developing criteria. A criterion is a standard, rule, or test by which something can be judged—a measure of value. Problem solvers develop criteria to assist them in formulating and evaluating possible solutions to a problem. Criteria are based on facts or assumptions. Problem solvers develop two types of criteria: screening and evaluation.

Screening Criteria

11-20. Leaders use screening criteria to ensure solutions they consider can solve the problem. Screening criteria defines the limits of an acceptable solution. They are tools to establish the baseline products for analysis. Leaders may reject a solution based solely on the application of screening criteria. Leaders commonly ask five questions of screening criteria to test a possible solution:

- **Is it suitable?**—Does it solve the problem and is it legal and ethical?
- **Is it feasible?**—Does it fit within available resources?
- **Is it acceptable?**—Is it worth the cost or risk?
- **Is it distinguishable?**—Does it differ significantly from other solutions?
- **Is it complete?**—Does it contain the critical aspects of solving the problem from start to finish?

Evaluation Criteria

11-21. After developing screening criteria, the problem solver develops the evaluation criteria in order to differentiate among possible solutions (see Figure 11-1). Well-defined evaluation criteria have five elements:

- **Short Title**—the criterion name.
- **Definition**—a clear description of the feature being evaluated.
- **Unit of Measure**—a standard element used to quantify the criterion. Examples of units of measure are U.S. dollars, miles per gallon, and feet.
- **Benchmark**—a value that defines the desired state or "good" for a solution in terms of a particular criterion.
- **Formula**—an expression of how changes in the value of the criterion affect the desirability of the possible solution. State the formula in comparative terms (for example, less is better) or absolute terms (for example, a night movement is better than a day movement).

Short Title: Cost

Definition: The maximum total cost of each truck.

Unit of Measure: Dollars

Benchmark: $38,600

Formula: ≤$38,600 is an advantage; >$38,600 is a disadvantage; less is better.

Figure 11-1. Sample evaluation criterion

11-22. A well thought-out benchmark is critical for meaningful analysis. Analysis judges a solution against a standard, telling whether that solution is good in an objective sense. It differs from comparison, which judges possible solutions against each other telling us whether it is better or worse in a relative sense. Benchmarks are the standards used in such analysis. They may be prescribed by regulations or guidance from the decisionmaker. Sometimes, a decisionmaker can infer the benchmark by the tangible return expected from the problem's solution. Often, however, leaders establish benchmarks themselves. Four common methods for doing this are—

- **Reasoning**—the benchmark is based on personal experience and judgment as to what is good.
- **Historical precedent**—the benchmark is based on relevant examples of prior success.
- **Current example**—the benchmark is based on an existing condition, which is considered desirable.
- **Averaging**—the benchmark is based on the mathematical average of the solutions being considered. Averaging is the least preferred of all methods because it essentially duplicates the process of comparison.

11-23. In practice, the criteria by which choices are made are almost never of equal importance. Because of this, it is often convenient to assign weights to each evaluation criterion. Weighting criteria establishes the relative importance of each one with respect to the others. Weighting should reflect the judgment of the decisionmaker or acknowledged experts as closely as possible. For example, a decisionmaker or expert might judge that two criteria are *equal* in importance, or that one criterion is *slightly favored* in importance, or *moderately* or *strongly favored*. If decisionmakers assign these verbal assessments numerical values, say from 1 to 4 respectively, they can use mathematical techniques to produce meaningful numerical criteria weights.

11-24. Additionally, pairwise comparison is an analytical tool that brings objectivity to the process of assigning criteria weights. In performing a pairwise comparison, the decisionmaker or expert methodically assesses each evaluation criterion against each of the others and judges its relative importance. A computer equipped with simple software easily performs the mathematical algorithms. This process does not diminish in any way the importance of the decisionmaker's judgment. Rather it enables problem solvers to bring that judgment to bear with greater precision and in problems of greater complexity than might otherwise be possible. Regardless of the method used to assign criteria weights, leaders state the rationale for each when recommending a solution to the decisionmaker.

GENERATE POSSIBLE SOLUTIONS

11-25. After gathering information relevant to the problem and developing criteria, leaders formulate possible solutions. They carefully consider the guidance provided by the commander or their superiors, and develop several alternatives to solve the problem. Too many possible solutions may result in wasted time on similar options. Experience and time available determine how many solutions to consider. Leaders should consider at least two solutions. Limiting solutions enables the problem solver to use both analysis and comparison as problem-solving tools. Developing only one solution to "save time" may produce a faster solution but risks creating more problems from factors not considered.

11-26. When developing solutions, leaders generate options and summarize the solution in writing, sketches, or both writing and sketches.

Generate Options

11-27. Leaders must use creativity to develop effective solutions. Often, groups can be far more creative than individuals However, those working on solutions should have some knowledge of or background in the problem area.

11-28. The basic technique for developing new ideas in a group setting is brainstorming. Brainstorming is characterized by unrestrained participation in discussion. While brainstorming, leaders—

- State the problem and make sure all participants understand it.
- Appoint someone to record all ideas.
- Withhold judgment of ideas.
- Encourage independent thoughts.
- Aim for quantity, not quality.
- Hitchhike ideas—combine one's thoughts with those of others.

At the conclusion of brainstorming, leaders may discard solutions that clearly miss the standards described by the screening criteria. If this informal screen leaves only one solution or none, then leaders need to generate more options.

Summarize the Solution in Writing and Sketches

11-29. After generating options, leaders accurately record each possible solution. The solution statement clearly portrays how the action or actions solve the problem. In some circumstances, the solution statement may be a single sentence (for example, "Provide tribal leader X with the means to dig a well"). In other circumstances, the solution statement may require more detail, including sketches or concept diagrams. For example, if the problem is to develop a multipurpose small-arms range, leaders may choose to portray each solution with a narrative and a separate sketch or blueprint of each proposed range.

ANALYZE POSSIBLE SOLUTIONS

11-30. Having identified possible solutions, leaders analyze each one to determine its merits and drawbacks. If criteria are well defined, to include a careful selection of benchmarks, analysis is greatly simplified.

11-31. Leaders use screening criteria and benchmarks to analyze possible solutions. They apply screening criteria to judge whether a solution meets minimum requirements. For quantitative criteria, they measure, compute, or estimate the raw data values for each solution and each criterion. In analyzing solutions that involve predicting future events, they use war-gaming, models, and simulations to visualize events and estimate raw data values for use in analysis. Once raw data values have been determined, the leader judges them against applicable screening criteria to determine if a possible solution merits further consideration. Leaders screen out any solution that fails to meet or exceeds the set threshold of one or more screening criteria.

11-32. After applying the screening criteria to all possible solutions, leaders use benchmarks to judge them with respect to the desired state. Data values that meet or exceed the benchmark indicate that the possible solution achieves the desired end state. Data values that fail to meet the benchmark indicate a poor solution that fails to achieve the desired end state. For each solution, leaders list the areas in which analysis reveals it to be good or not good. Sometimes the considered solutions fail to reach the benchmark. When this occurs, the leader points out the failure to the decisionmaker.

11-33. Leaders carefully avoid comparing solutions during analysis. To do so undermines the integrity of the process and tempts problem solvers to jump to conclusions. They examine each possible solution independently to identify its strengths and weaknesses. They are also careful not to introduce new criteria.

COMPARE POSSIBLE SOLUTIONS

11-34. During this step, leaders compare each solution against the others to determine the optimum one. Solution comparison identifies which solution best solves the problem based on the evaluation criteria. Leaders use any comparison technique that helps reach the best recommendation. The most common technique is a decision matrix (see Chapter 4).

11-35. Leaders use quantitative techniques (such as decision matrixes, select weights, and sensitivity analyses) to compare solutions. However, they are tools to support the analysis and comparison. They are not the analysis and comparison themselves. Leaders carefully summarize the quantitative techniques so the decisionmaker does not need to refer to an annex for the results.

MAKE AND IMPLEMENT THE DECISION

11-36. After completing their analysis and comparison, leaders identify the preferred solution. For simple problems, leaders may proceed straight to executing the solution. For more complex problems, a leader may need to form a design team (see FM 5-0). If a superior assigned the problem, leaders prepare the necessary products (verbal, written, or both) needed to present the recommendation to the decisionmaker. Before presenting the findings and a recommendation, leaders coordinate their recommendation with those affected by the problem or the solutions. In formal situations, leaders present their findings and recommendations to the decisionmaker as staff studies, decision papers, or decision briefings.

11-37. A good solution can be lost if the leader cannot persuade the audience that it is correct. Every problem requires both a solution and the ability to communicate the solution clearly. The writing and briefing skills a leader possesses may ultimately be as important as good problem-solving skills.

11-38. Based on the decisionmaker's decision and final guidance, leaders refine the solution and prepare necessary implementing instructions. Formal implementing instructions can be issued as a memorandum of instruction, policy letter, or command directive. Once leaders have given instructions, they monitor their implementation and compare results to the measure of success and the desired end state established in the approved solution. When necessary, they issue additional instructions.

11-39. A feedback system that provides timely and accurate information, periodic review, and the flexibility to adjust must also be built into the implementation plan. Leaders stay involved and carefully avoid creating new problems because of uncoordinated implementation of the solution. Army problem solving does not end with identifying the best solution or obtaining approval of a recommendation.

STAFF STUDIES

11-40. A staff study is a detailed formal report to a decisionmaker requesting action on a recommendation. It provides the information and methodology used to solve a problem. The staff study includes an official memorandum for the commander's signature that implements the action. The leader coordinates staff studies with all affected organizations. Staff studies include statements of nonconcurrence, if applicable, so that the decisionmaker clearly understands all staff members' support for the recommendation. A staff study is comprehensive; it includes all relevant information needed to solve the problem and a complete description of the methodology used to arrive at the recommended solution.

11-41. The staff study follows the seven-step Army problem-solving process. This ensures that the staff clearly identifies the problem, follows a logical sequence, and produces a justifiable solution.

11-42. The body of a completed staff study is a stand-alone document. While annexes are a part of most staff studies, a decisionmaker should not have to refer to them to understand the recommendation and the basis for it. Annexes contain details and supporting information and help keep the body of the study concise.

THE STAFF STUDY FORMAT

11-43. Staff studies are prepared as informal memorandums in the format at Figure 11-2, page 11-8 (see AR 25-50). Units may establish their own format to meet local requirements.

Memorandum For

11-44. Address the staff study to the decisionmaker. Include thru addressees if required.

Subject

11-45. Succinctly describe the subject to distinguish it from other documents as a courtesy to the decisionmaker. Do not simply state "Staff Study" as this does not provide sufficient detail, nor does it convey any information about the subject.

Problem

11-46. In paragraph 1, concisely state the problem as an infinitive phrase or question. An infinitive phrase uses a verb, but has no subject; for example, "To determine...", or, "How to...." Include in your problem statement *who*, *what*, *when*, and *where*, if pertinent.

Recommendation

11-47. In paragraph 2, recommend a solution or solutions based on the conclusion in paragraph 10. If there are several recommendations, state each one in a separate subparagraph.

Background

11-48. In paragraph 3, briefly state why the problem exists. Provide enough information to place the problem in context. This discussion may include the origin of the action and a summary of related events. If a tasking document is the source of the problem, place it in enclosure 2 and refer to it here.

Facts

11-49. In paragraph 4, state all facts that influence the problem or its solution. List each fact as a separate subparagraph. Make sure to state the facts precisely and attribute them correctly. Facts must stand-alone: either something is a generally accepted fact or it is attributed to a source that asserts it to be true. There is no limit to the number of facts as long as every fact is relevant. Include all facts relevant to the problem, not just facts used to support the study. The decisionmaker must have an opportunity to consider facts that do not support the recommendation. State any guidance given by the decisionmaker. Refer to annexes as necessary for amplification, references, mathematical formulas, or tabular data.

Office Symbol   Date

MEMORANDUM FOR

SUBJECT:

1. **PROBLEM.**

2. **RECOMMENDATION.**

3. **BACKGROUND.**

4. **FACTS.**

5. **ASSUMPTIONS.**

6. **POSSIBLE SOLUTION.**

7. **CRITERIA.**

a. Screening Criteria.

b. Evaluation Criteria.

c. Weighting of Criteria.

8. **ANALYSIS.**

a. Possible Solutions Screened Out.

b. Possible Solution 1.

(1) Advantages.

(2) Disadvantages.

c. Possible Solution 2. (Use the same sub-subparagraphs   in 8b.)

9. **COMPARISON.**

10. **CONCLUSION.**

11. **COORDINATION.**

ACofS, G-1   CONCUR/N NCON UR_____CMT_____DATE:_____

DPTM   CONCUR/NON   NCUR_____CMT_____DATE:_____

12. **APPROVAL/DISAPPROVAL.**

a. That the (state the approving authority and recommended solution).

APPROVED_____DISAPPROVED_____SEE ME_____

b. That the (approving authority) sign the implementing directive(s) (TAB A).

APPROVED_____DISAPPROVED_____SEE ME_____

13. **POINT OF CONTACT.**

[Signature Block]

[#] Encl
1. Implementing document
2. Tasking document
3. Coordination list
4. Nonconcurrences
5. Other supporting documents, listed as separate annexes

Figure 11-2. Sample format for a staff study

Assumptions

11-50.   In paragraph 5, identify assumptions necessary for a logical discussion of the problem. List each assumption as a separate subparagraph.

Possible Solution

11-51.   In paragraph 6, list all solutions considered. Place each solution in a separate subparagraph. List each solution by number and name or as a short sentence in the imperative (for example, "Increase physical security measures at key assets"). If a solution is not self-explanatory, include a brief description of it. Use enclosures to describe complex solutions.

Criteria

11-52.   In paragraph 7, list and define, in separate subparagraphs, the screening and evaluation criteria. A fact or an assumption in paragraph 4 or 5 should support each criterion. At a minimum, the number of facts and assumptions should exceed the number of criteria. In a third subparagraph, explain the rationale for how the evaluation criteria are weighted.

11-53.   **Screening Criteria**. In subparagraph 7a, list the screening criteria, each in its own sub-subparagraph. Screening criteria define the minimum and maximum characteristics of the solution to the problem. Answer each screening criterion: Is it suitable, feasible, acceptable, distinguishable, and complete? Screening criteria are not weighted. They are required, absolute standards. Reject courses of action that do not meet the screening criteria.

11-54.   **Evaluation Criteria**. In subparagraph 7b, list the evaluation criteria, each in its own sub-subparagraph. List them in order of their weight, from most to least important. Define each evaluation criterion in terms of five required elements: short title, definition, unit of measure, benchmark, and formula. (Refer to Figure 11-1.)

11-55.   **Weighting of Criteria**. In subparagraph 7c, state the relative importance of each evaluation criterion with respect to the others. Explain how each criterion compares to each of the other criteria (equal, slightly favored, favored, or strongly favored) or provide the values from the decision matrix and explain why the criterion is measured in that way. This subparagraph explains the order in which the evaluation criteria are listed in subparagraph 7b.

Analysis

11-56.   Paragraph 8 lists the courses of action that do not meet the screening criteria and the results of applying the evaluation criteria to the remaining ones.

11-57.   **Possible Solutions Screened Out.** In subparagraph 8a, list the courses of action that did not meet the screening criteria, each in its own subparagraph, and the screening criteria each did not meet. This subparagraph is particularly important if a solution the decisionmaker wanted to be considered does not meet the screening criteria.

11-58.   **Evaluated Solutions.** In subsequent subparagraphs, list the courses of action evaluated, each in a separate subparagraph. Discuss the advantages and disadvantages of each solution. For quantitative criteria, include the payoff value. Discuss or list advantages and disadvantages in narratives. Use the form that best fits the information. Avoid using bullets unless the advantage or disadvantage is self-evident.

Comparison

11-59.   In paragraph 9, compare the courses of action to each other, based on the analysis outlined in paragraph 8. Develop in a logical, orderly manner the rationale used to reach the conclusion stated in paragraph 10. If leaders use quantitative techniques in the comparison, summarize the results clearly enough that the reader does not have to refer to an enclosure. Include any explanations of quantitative techniques in enclosures. State only the results in paragraph 9.

Conclusion

11-60.   In paragraph 10, state the conclusion drawn based on the analysis (paragraph 8) and comparison (paragraph 9). The conclusion must answer the question or provide a possible solution to the problem. It must match the recommendation in paragraph 2.

Coordination

11-61.   In paragraph 11, list all organizations with which the study was coordinated ("staffed") in the format shown in Figure 11-2. If the list is long and space is a consideration, place it at enclosure 3. If the staffing list is placed in enclosure 3, indicate the number of nonconcurrences with the cross-reference (for example, "See enclosure 3; 2 nonconcurrences"; or "See enclosure 3; no nonconcurrences").

11-62.   A representative of each organization with which the study was staffed indicates whether the organization concurs with the study, nonconcurs, or concurs with comment. Representatives place their initials in the blank, followed by their rank, name, position, telephone number, and e-mail address. If separate copies were sent to each organization (rather than sending one copy to each organization in turn), this information may be typed into the final copy of the study and the actual replies placed in enclosure 4. Recommend this technique when using e-mail for staffing.

11-63.   Place all statements of nonconcurrence and considerations of nonconcurrence in enclosure 3, or in separate enclosures for each nonconcurrence. Concurrences with comment may be placed in enclosure 3 or in a separate enclosure or enclosures.

Approval or Disapproval Line

11-64.   In paragraph 12, restate the recommendation from paragraph 2 and provide a format for the approval authority to approve or disapprove the recommendation.

Point of Contact

11-65.   Use paragraph 13 to record the point of contact (or action officer) and contact information. Additional contact information may include the action officer's organization, a civilian telephone number, a unit address, and an e-mail address.

Signature Block

11-66.   Prepare the signature block as specified in chapter 2 of AR 25-50.

Enclosures

11-67.   All staff studies contain these first four enclosures:
- Enclosure 1 contains implementing memorandums, directives, or letters submitted for signature or approval. Since a staff study requests a decision, enclosure 1 contains the documents required to implement the decision.
- Enclosure 2 contains the document that directed the staff study or decision paper. If the requirement was given verbally, include the memorandum for record that documents the conversation. If no record exists, enter "Not used" in the annex list in the body.
- Enclosure 3 contains the staffing list if the list is too long for paragraph 11(paragraph 6 for the decision paper). If paragraph 11 contains the entire staffing list, enter "Not used" in the enclosure list in the body.
- Enclosure 4 contains statements of nonconcurrence and considerations of nonconcurrence. These documents may be placed in separate enclosures. Place concurrences with comment in either enclosure 4 or a separate enclosure. If there are no statements of nonconcurrence, enter "Not used" in the enclosure list in the body.

11-68.   Other enclosures contain detailed data, lengthy discussions, and bibliographies. Number the pages of each enclosure separately, except when an enclosure contains several distinct documents (such as, concurrences). Tab the enclosures.

COORDINATING STAFF STUDIES

11-69. Preparing a staff study normally involves coordinating with other staff officers and organizations. At a minimum, action officers obtain concurrences or nonconcurrences from agencies affected by the study's recommendations. Other aspects of the study may require coordination as well. Coordination should be as broad as time permits but should be limited to agencies that might be affected by possible recommendations or that have expertise in the subject of the study.

11-70. Action officers anticipate nonconcurrences and try to resolve as many as possible before staffing the final product. An action officer who cannot resolve a nonconcurrence has two options:

- Modify the staff study to satisfy the nonconcurrence, but only if the analysis and comparison supports the change. If this is done after the final draft has been staffed, the officer must re-staff the study.
- Prepare a consideration of nonconcurrence and include it and the statement of nonconcurrence in Annex C to the staff study as discussed in paragraphs 11-61 through 11-63 and paragraph 11-67.

Statements of Nonconcurrence

11-71. A statement of nonconcurrence is a recommendation that the decisionmaker reject all or part of the staff study. Statements of nonconcurrence are prepared in the memorandum format; e-mails may be accepted at the commander's discretion. They address specific points in the recommendations or the study, stating why they are wrong or unacceptable. When possible they offer an alternative or a constructive recommendation.

Considerations of Nonconcurrence

11-72. Action officers prepare considerations of nonconcurrence as a memorandum for record. They present the reasons for the nonconcurrence accurately and assess them objectively. Then they state why the study is correct and why the decisionmaker should reject the nonconcurrence.

Common Problems with Staff Studies

11-73. The following questions identify the most common problems found in staff studies. Review them before beginning a staff study and periodically thereafter:

- Is the subject too broad?
- Is the problem properly defined?
- Are facts or assumptions clear and valid?
- Are there any unnecessary facts or assumptions?
- Are there any facts that appear for the first time in the discussion?
- Are there a limited number of options or courses of action?
- Are evaluation criteria invalid or too restrictive?
- Is the discussion too long?
- Is the discussion complete?
- Must readers consult the enclosures to understand the staff study?
- Does the conclusion include a discussion?
- Is the logic flawed or incomplete?
- Does the conclusion follow from the analysis?
- Can the solution be implemented within resource and time constraints?
- Do the conclusions and recommendations solve the problem?
- Is there an implementing directive?
- Have new criteria been introduced in the analysis or comparison?

DECISION PAPERS

11-74. A decision paper is a piece of correspondence that requests the decisionmaker to act on its recommendation and provides the required implementing documents for signature. Action officers use a decision paper when they do not need a formal report or the decisionmaker does not require the details a staff study provides.

11-75. Decision papers are brief. Unlike staff studies, decision papers are not self-contained. For a decision paper, much of the material that would be included in a staff study is kept in the action officer's file. Decision papers contain the minimum information the decisionmaker needs to understand the action and make a decision. The action officer synthesizes the facts, summarizes the issues, presents feasible alternatives, and recommends one of them. Action officers attach essential explanations and other information as enclosures, which are always tabbed.

11-76. Action officers prepare decision papers as informal memorandums (see AR 25-50) in the format at Figure 11-3. This format also parallels the steps of the Army problem-solving process. Commands may establish format standards to meet local requirements. Decision papers should not exceed two pages, excluding the staffing list and supporting documentation. The coordination requirements for a decision paper are the same as those for a staff study. Follow the procedures in paragraphs 11-43 through 11-68.

Office Symbol (Marks Number)   Date

MEMORANDUM FOR

SUBJECT:

1. For DECISION.

2. PURPOSE.

3. RECOMMENDATION.

4. BACKGROUND AND DISCUSSION.

5. IMPACTS.

6. COORDINATION.

ACofS, G-1 CONCUR/NONCONCUR_____ CMT_____DATE: _____

DPTM   CONCUR/NONCONCUR____ _ ____CMT_____DATE: _____

7. APPROVAL/ DISAPPROVAL.
a. That the (state the approving authority and recommend d solution).

APPROVED_____**DISAPPROVED**_____**SEE ME**_____
b. That the (approving authority sig the implementing directive(s) (TAB A).

APPROVED_____**DISAPPROVED**_____**SEE ME**_____

8. POINT OF CONTACT.

[#] Encls   (Signature Block)
1. Implementing document (TAB A)
2. Tasking document (TAB B)
3. Coordination list (TAB C)
4. Nonconcurrences (TAB D)
5–[#]. Other supporting documents, listed as separate enclosures (TABS E through Z)

Figure 11-3. Sample format for a decision paper

MEMORANDUM FOR

11-77. Address the decision paper to the decisionmaker. Include thru addressees or on the routing slip, as specified by command policy.

SUBJECT

11-78. Briefly state the decision's subject. Be specific as the reader should not have to begin reading the body of the decision paper to figure out the subject. "Decision Paper" is not an acceptable subject.

FOR DECISION

11-79. Paragraph 1 states, "For DECISION." (Paragraph headings may be either underlined or bolded, according to command policy.) Indicate if the decision is time-sensitive, tied to an event, or has a suspense date to a higher headquarters. Show internal suspenses on the routing slip, if necessary. Do not show them in this paragraph.

PURPOSE

11-80. In paragraph 2, state clearly the decision required, as an infinitive phrase. An infinitive phrase uses a verb, but has no subject, for example, "To determine the...," or, "To obtain...." Include in the purpose statement *who*, *what*, *when*, and *where*, if pertinent.

RECOMMENDATION

11-81. In paragraph 3, recommend a solution or solutions to the problem. If there are several recommendations, state each one in a separate subparagraph.

BACKGROUND AND DISCUSSION

11-82. Paragraph 4 explains the origin of the action, why the problem exists, and a summary of events in chronological form. It helps put the problem in perspective and provides an understanding of the alternatives and the recommendation. If the decision paper is the result of a tasking document, refer to that document in paragraph 4 and place it at enclosure 2.

IMPACT

11-83. Paragraph 5 states the impact of the recommended decision. Address each affected area in a separate subparagraph, for example, personnel, equipment, funding, environment, and stationing. State parties affected by the recommendation and the extent to which they are affected.

COORDINATION, APPROVAL LINE, POINT OF CONTACT, SIGNATURE BLOCK, AND ENCLOSURES

11-84. The coordination, approval line, point of contact, signature block, and enclosures follow the same directions as for a staff study. See paragraphs 11-43 through 11-68.

STAFF STUDY ASSEMBLY

11-85. Action officers assemble a staff study in a manila folder. See Figure 11-4, page 11-4. Clipped to the front cover is the classification, if needed, and a routing slip. Assemble the decision paper inside the manila folder with the implementing memo, the tasker, the concurrences and nonconcurrences, and lastly any background information. Tab the staff actions and clip them to the inside of the back cover of the manila folder.

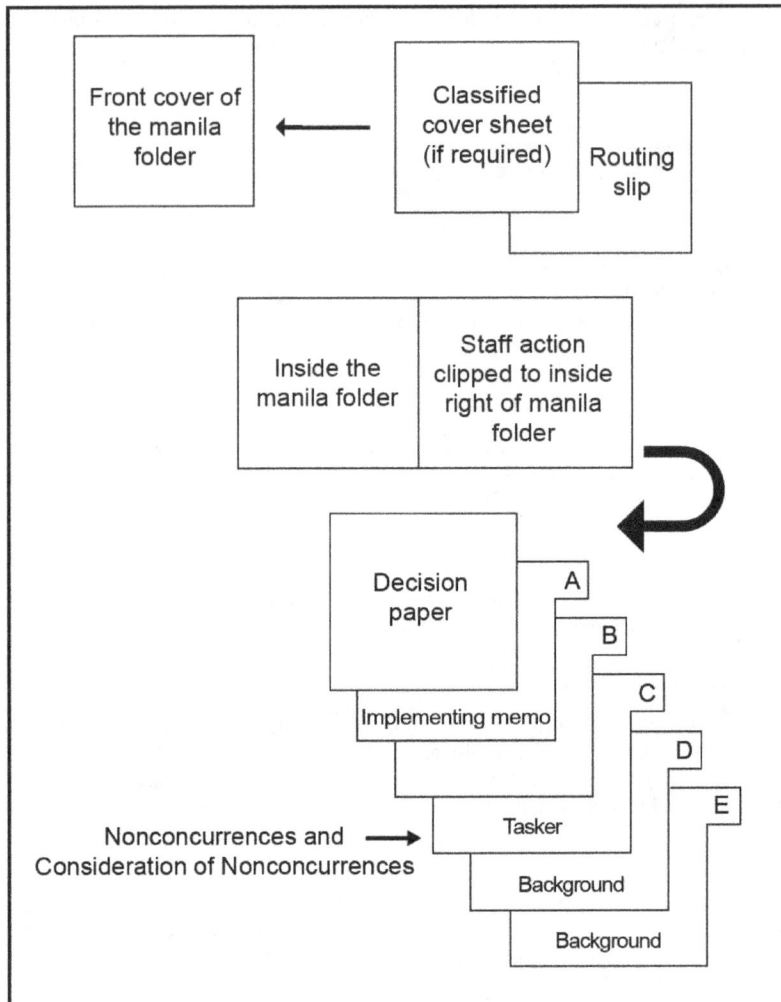

Figure 11-4. Assembling and tabbing staff action

Chapter 12

Plans and Orders

This chapter provides guidance for building simple, flexible plans through mission orders. It lists the different types of plans and orders to include those joint plans and orders that Army forces may receive from a joint force headquarters. Next, this chapter lists characteristics of good plans and orders and provides guidelines to ensure plans and orders are internally consistent and nested with the higher plan or order. This chapter concludes with administrative instructions for writing plans and orders. For detailed guidance on joint operation plans and orders, refer to JP 5-0.

GUIDANCE FOR PLANS

12-1. Planning is the art and science of understanding a situation, envisioning a desired future, and laying out an operational approach to achieve that future. Based on this understanding and operational approach, planning continues with the development of a fully synchronized operation plan or order that arranges potential actions in time, space, and purpose to guide the force during execution (see FM 5-0).

12-2. A product of planning is a plan or order—a directive for future action. Commanders issue plans and orders to subordinates to communicate their understanding of the situation and their visualization of an operation. Plans and orders direct, coordinate, and synchronize subordinate actions and inform those outside the unit how to cooperate and provide support. To properly understand and execute the joint commander's plan, Army commanders and staffs must be familiar with joint planning processes, procedures, and orders formats. (Refer to JP 3-33 and JP 5-0.)

BUILDING SIMPLE, FLEXIBLE PLANS

12-3. Simplicity is a principle of war and vital to effective planning. Effective plans and orders are simple and direct. Staffs prepare clear, concise, and complete plans and orders to ensure thorough understanding. They use doctrinally correct operational terms and graphics. Doing this minimizes chances of misunderstanding. Shorter rather than longer plans aid in simplicity. Shorter plans are easier to disseminate, read, and remember.

12-4. Complex plans have a greater potential to fail in execution since they often rely on intricate coordination. Operations are always subject to the fog of war and friction. The more detailed the plan, the greater the chances it will no longer be applicable as friendly, enemy, and civilian actions change the situation throughout an operation.

12-5. Simple plans require an easily understood concept of operations. Planners also promote simplicity by minimizing details where possible and by limiting the actions or tasks to what the situation requires. Subordinates can then develop specifics within the commander's intent. For example, instead of assigning a direction of attack, planners can designate an axis of advance.

12-6. Simple plans are not simplistic plans. Simplistic refers to something made overly simple by ignoring the situation's complexity. Good plans simplify complicated situations. However, some situations require more complex plans than others do. Commanders at all levels weigh the apparent benefits of a complex concept of operations against the risk that subordinates will be unable to understand or follow it adequately. Commanders prefer simple plans that are easy to understand and execute.

12-7. Flexible plans help units adapt quickly to changing circumstances. Commanders and planners build opportunities for initiative into plans by anticipating events that allow them to operate inside of the enemy's decision cycle or react promptly to deteriorating situations. Identifying decision points and designing branches ahead of time—combined with a clear commander's intent—help create flexible plans. Incorporating control measures to reduce risk also makes plans more flexible. For example, a commander may hold a large, mobile reserve to compensate for the lack of information concerning an anticipated enemy attack.

MISSION ORDERS

12-8. Commanders stress the importance of mission orders as a way of building simple, flexible plans. *Mission orders* are directives that emphasize to subordinates the results to be attained, not how they are to achieve them (FM 6-0). Mission orders focus on what to do and the purpose of doing it without prescribing exactly how to do it. Commanders establish control measures to aid cooperation among forces without imposing needless restrictions on freedom of action. Mission orders contribute to flexibility by allowing subordinates the freedom to seize opportunities or react effectively to unforeseen enemy actions and capabilities.

12-9. Mission orders follow the five-paragraph format (situation, mission, execution, sustainment, and command and signal) and are as brief and simple as possible. Mission orders clearly convey the unit's mission and commander's intent. They summarize the situation (current or anticipated starting conditions), describe the operation's objectives and end state (desired conditions), and provide a simple concept of operations to accomplish the unit's mission. When assigning tasks to subordinate units, mission orders include all components of a task statement: who, what, when, where, and why. However, commanders particularly emphasize the purpose (why) of the tasks to guide (along with the commander's intent) individual initiative. Effective plans and orders foster mission command by—

- Describing the situation to create a common situational understanding.
- Conveying the commander's intent and concept of operations.
- Assigning tasks to subordinate units and stating the purpose for conducting the task.
- Providing the control measures necessary to synchronize the operation while retaining the maximum freedom of action for subordinates.
- Task-organizing forces and allocating resources.
- Directing preparation activities and establishing times or conditions for execution.

12-10. Mission orders contain the proper level of detail; they are neither so detailed that they stifle initiative nor so general that they provide insufficient direction. The proper level depends on each situation and is not easy to determine. Some phases of operations require tighter control over subordinate elements than others require. An air assault's air movement and landing phases, for example, require precise synchronization. Its ground maneuver plan requires less detail. As a rule, the base plan or order contains only the specific information required to provide the guidance to synchronize combat power at the decisive time and place while allowing subordinates as much freedom of action as possible. Commanders rely on individual initiative and coordination to act within the commander's intent and concept of operations. The attachments to the plan or order contain details regarding the situation and instructions necessary for synchronization.

TYPES OF PLANS AND ORDERS

12-11. Generally, a plan is developed well in advance of execution and is not executed until directed. A plan becomes an order when directed for execution based on a specific time or an event. Some planning results in written orders complete with attachments. Other planning results in brief fragmentary orders issued verbally and followed in writing. Operation plans and orders follow the five-paragraph format (situation, mission, execution, sustainment, and command and signal).

TYPES OF PLANS

12-12. Plans come in many forms and vary in scope, complexity, and length of planning horizons. Strategic plans establish national and multinational military objectives and include ways to achieve those objectives. Operational-level or campaign plans cover a series of related military operations aimed at accomplishing a strategic or operational objective within a given time and space. Tactical plans cover the employment of units in operations, including the ordered arrangement and maneuver of units in relation to each other and to the enemy within the framework of an operational-level or campaign plan. There are several types of plans:

- Campaign plan.
- Operation plan.
- Supporting plan.
- Concept plan.
- Branch.
- Sequel.

12-13. A *campaign plan* is a joint operation plan for a series of related major operations aimed at achieving strategic or operational objectives within a given time and space (JP 5-0). Developing and issuing a campaign plan is appropriate when the contemplated simultaneous or sequential military operations exceed the scope of a single major operation. Only joint force commanders develop campaign plans.

12-14. An *operation plan* is plan for the conduct of military operations prepared in response to actual and potential contingencies (JP 5-0). An operation plan (OPLAN) may address an extended period connecting a series of objectives and operations, or it may be developed for a single part or phase of a long-term operation. An OPLAN becomes an operation order when the commander sets an execution time or designates an event that triggers the operation.

12-15. A *supporting plan* is an operation plan prepared by a supporting commander, a subordinate commander, or an agency to satisfy the requests or requirements of the supported commander's plan (JP 5-0). For example, the ARFOR commander develops a supporting plan as to how Army forces will support the joint force commander's campaign plan or OPLAN.

12-16. In the context of joint operation planning level 3 planning detail, a *concept plan* is an operation plan in an abbreviated format that may require considerable expansion or alteration to convert it into a complete operation plan or operation order (JP 5-0). Often branches and sequels are written as concept plans. As time and the potential allow for executing a particular branch or sequel, these concept plans are developed in detail into OPLANs.

TYPES OF ORDERS

12-17. An order is a communication—verbal, written, or signaled—which conveys instructions from a superior to a subordinate. Commanders issue orders verbally or in writing. The five-paragraph format (situation, mission, execution, sustainment, and command and signal) remains the standard for issuing orders. The technique used to issue orders (verbal or written) is at the discretion of the commander; each technique depends on time and the situation. Army organizations use three types of orders:

- Operation order (OPORD).
- Fragmentary order (FRAGO).
- Warning order (WARNO).

12-18. An *operation order* is a directive issued by a commander to subordinate commanders for the purpose of effecting the coordinated execution of an operation (JP 5-0). Commanders issue OPORDs to direct the execution of long-term operations as well as the execution of discrete short-term operations within the framework of a long-range OPORD.

12-19. A *fragmentary order* is an abbreviated form of an operation order issued as needed after an operation order to change or modify that order or to execute a branch or sequel to that order (JP 5-0). FRAGOs include all five OPORD paragraph headings and differ from OPORDs only in the degree of detail provided. An example of a proper naming convention for a FRAGO to an OPORD is, "FRAGO 11 to OPORD 3411." If a FRAGO contains an entire annex, then the proper naming convention would be, "Annex A (Task Organization) to FRAGO 12 to OPORD 3411."

12-20. A *warning order* is a preliminary notice of an order or action that is to follow (JP 3-33). WARNOs help subordinate units and staffs prepare for new missions by describing the situation, providing initial planning guidance, and directing preparation activities.

12-21. In addition to the above types of order, Army forces may receive the following types of orders from a joint headquarters:

● Planning order.
● Alert order.
● Execute order.
● Prepare-to-deploy order.

For clarification and guidance on planning orders, alert orders, execute orders, and prepare-to-deploy orders see JP 5-0.

VERBAL ORDERS

12-22. Commanders use verbal orders when operating in an extremely time-constrained environment. These orders offer the advantage of being distributed quickly but risk important information being overlooked or misunderstood. Verbal orders are usually followed by written FRAGOs.

WRITTEN ORDERS

12-23. Commanders issue written plans and orders that contain both text and graphics. Graphics convey information and instructions through military symbols. (FM 1-02 lists approved symbols.) They complement the written portion of a plan or an order and promote clarity, accuracy, and brevity. Staffs often develop and disseminate written orders electronically to shorten the time needed to gather and brief the orders group. Staffs can easily edit and modify electronically produced orders. They can send the same order to multiple recipients simultaneously. Using computer programs to develop and disseminate precise, corresponding graphics adds to the efficiency and clarity of the orders process.

12-24. Electronic editing makes importing text and graphics into orders easy. Unfortunately, such ease can result in orders becoming unnecessarily large without added operational value. Commanders need to ensure that orders contain only that information needed to facilitate effective execution. Orders should not regurgitate unit standard operating procedures (SOPs). They should be clear, concise, and relevant to the mission.

CHARACTERISTICS OF PLANS AND ORDERS

12-25. The amount of detail provided in a plan or order depends on several factors, including the cohesion and experience of subordinate units and complexity of the operation. Effective plans and orders encourage subordinate's initiative by providing the what and why of tasks to subordinate units; they leave how to perform the tasks to subordinates. To maintain clarity and simplicity, planners keep the base plan or order as short and concise as possible. They address detailed information and instructions in attachments as required.

12-26. Commanders issue written plans and orders that contain both text and graphics. Graphics convey information and instructions through military symbols. (FM 1-02 lists approved military symbols.) They complement the written portion of a plan or an order and promote clarity, accuracy, and brevity.

12-27. Good OPLANs and OPORDs—

● Possess simplicity.
● Possess authoritative expression.
● Possess positive expression.
● Avoid qualified directives.
● Possess brevity.
● Possess clarity.

- Contain assumptions.
- Incorporate flexibility.
- Exercise timeliness.

12-28.   Plans and orders are simple and direct to reduce misunderstanding and confusion. The situation determines the degree of simplicity required. Simple plans executed on time are better than detailed plans executed late. Commanders at all echelons weigh potential benefits of a complex concept of operations against the risk that subordinates will fail to understand it. Multinational operations mandate simplicity due to the differences in language, doctrine, and culture. The same applies to operations involving interagency and nongovernmental organizations.

12-29.   Authoritative expression through the commander's intent is reflected in plans and orders. As such, their language is direct. Effective plans and orders unmistakably state what the commander wants the unit and its subordinate units to do and why.

12-30.   Instructions in plans and orders are stated in the affirmative. For example, "Combat trains will remain in the assembly area" instead of "The combat trains will not accompany the unit."

12-31.   Plans and orders avoid meaningless expressions, such as "as soon as possible (ASAP)." Indecisive, vague, and ambiguous language leads to uncertainty and lack of confidence.

12-32.   Effective plans and orders are brief, clear, and concise. They use short words, sentences, and paragraphs. Use acronyms unless clarity is hindered. Do not include material covered in SOPs. Refer to those SOPs instead.

12-33.   Plans and orders possess clarity. They use doctrinally correct terms and symbols, avoid jargon, and eliminate every opportunity for misunderstanding the commander's exact, intended meaning.

12-34.   Effective plans and orders contain assumptions. This helps subordinates and others to better understand the logic behind a plan or order and facilitates the preparation of branches and sequels.

12-35.   Plans and orders incorporate flexibility. They leave room to adapt and make adjustments to counter unexpected challenges and seize opportunities. Effective plans and orders identify decision points and proposed options at those decision points to build flexibility.

12-36.   Plans and orders exercise timeliness. Plans and orders sent to subordinates promptly allow subordinates to collaborate, plan, and prepare their own actions.

PREPARATION OF THE PLAN OR ORDER

12-37.   The last step in the military decisionmaking process (MDMP) is orders production. Orders production is the next to last step in troop leading procedures. (See FM 5-0.) Within the MDMP, the staff prepares the plan or order by refining the commander's selected course of action into a clear, concise concept of operations and required supporting information that forms the base plan or order.

12-38.   Normally, the chief of staff (COS) or executive officer (XO) coordinates with staff principals to assist the G-3 (S-3) in developing the plan or order. Based on the commander's planning guidance, the COS (XO) dictates the type of order, sets and enforces the time limits and development sequence, and determines which staff section publishes which attachments.

12-39.   Prior to the commander approving the plan or order, the staff ensures the plan or order is internally consistent and is nested with the higher commander's intent. They do this through—

- Plans and orders reconciliation.
- Plans and orders crosswalk.

PLANS AND ORDERS RECONCILIATION

12-40.   Plans and orders reconciliation occurs internally as the staff conducts a detailed review of the entire plan or order. This reconciliation ensures that the base plan or order and all attachments are complete and in agreement. It identifies discrepancies or gaps in planning. If staff members find discrepancies or gaps, they take corrective actions. Specifically, the staff compares the commander's intent, mission, and commander's critical information requirements (CCIRs) against the concept of operations and the different schemes of support (such as scheme of fires or scheme of sustainment). The staff ensures attachments are consistent with the information in the base plan or order.

PLANS AND ORDERS CROSSWALK

12-41.   During the plans and orders crosswalk, the staff compares the plan or order with that of the higher and adjacent commanders to achieve unity of effort and ensure the plan meets the superior commander's intent. The crosswalk identifies discrepancies or gaps in planning. If staff members find discrepancies or gaps, they take corrective action.

APPROVING THE PLAN OR ORDER

12-42.   The final action in plan and order development is the approval of the plan or order by the commander. Commanders normally do not sign attachments; however, they should review them before signing the base plan or order.

ADMINISTRATIVE INSTRUCTIONS

12-43.   The following information pertains to administrative instructions for preparing all plans and orders. Unless otherwise stated, the term *order* refers to both plans and orders. The term *base order* refers to the main body of a plan or order without attachments.

12-44.   Regardless of echelon, all orders adhere to the same guidance. Show all paragraph headings on written orders. A paragraph heading with no text will state "None" or "See [attachment type] [attachment letter or number]." In this context, attachment is a collective term for annex, appendix, tab, and exhibit.

12-45.   The base order and all attachments follow a specific template for the paragraph layout. Every order follows the five-paragraph format. Title case, underline, and bold the titles of these five paragraphs: Situation, Mission, Execution, Sustainment, and Command and Signal. For example, "situation" is **Situation**. All subparagraphs and subtitles begin with capital letters and are underlined. For example, "concept of operations" is Concept of Operations.

12-46.   When a paragraph is subdivided, it must have at least two subdivisions. The tabs are 0.25 inches and the space is doubled between paragraphs. Subsequent lines of text for each paragraph may be flush left or equally indented at the option of the chief of staff or executive officer, as long as consistency is maintained throughout the order. (See Figure 12-1.)

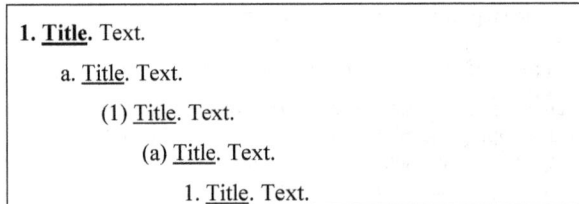

```
1. Title. Text.
     a. Title. Text.
          (1) Title. Text.
               (a) Title. Text.
                    1. Title. Text.
```

Figure 12-1. Paragraph layout for plans and orders

ACRONYMS AND ABBREVIATIONS

12-47.   Use acronyms and abbreviations to save time and space if they do not cause confusion. Do not sacrifice clarity for brevity. Keep acronyms and abbreviations consistent throughout the order and its attachments. Do not use acronyms and abbreviations not found in FM 1-02 or JP 1-02. Spell out the entire acronym or abbreviation and place the acronym or abbreviation between parentheses at first use in the document. After this first use, use the acronym or abbreviation throughout the document.

PLACE AND DIRECTION DESIGNATIONS

12-48. Describe locations or points on the ground by—

- Providing the map datum used throughout the order.
- Referring to military grid reference system coordinates.
- Referring to longitude and latitude if available maps do not have the military grid reference system.

12-49. Designate directions in one of two ways:

- As a point of the compass. For example, north or northeast.
- As a magnetic, grid, or true bearing, stating the unit of measure. For example, 85 degrees (magnetic).

12-50. When first mentioning a place or feature on a map, print the name in capital letters exactly as spelled on the map and show its complete grid coordinates (grid zone designator, 100-kilometer grid square, and four-, six-, eight-, or ten-digit grid coordinates) in parentheses after it. When first using a control measure (such as a contact point), print the name or designation of the point followed by its complete grid coordinates in parentheses. Thereafter, repeat the coordinates only for clarity; use names, planning names, or codes.

12-51. Describe areas by naming the northernmost (12 o'clock) point first and the remaining points in clockwise order. Describe positions from left to right and from front to rear, facing the enemy. To avoid confusion, identify flanks by compass directions, rather than right or left of the friendly force.

12-52. If the possibility of confusion exists when describing a route, add a compass direction for clarity. For example, "The route is northwest along the road LAPRAIRIE–DELSON." If a particular route already has a planning name, such as main supply route SPARTAN, refer to the route using only that designator.

12-53. Designate trails, roads, and railroads by the names of places along them or with grid coordinates. Precede place names with trail, road, or railroad. For example, "road GRANT–CODY." Designate the route for a movement by listing a sequence of grids from the start point to the release point. Otherwise, list the sequence of points from left to right or front to rear, facing the enemy.

12-54. Identify riverbanks as north, south, east, or west. In gap-crossing operations, identify riverbanks as either near or far.

NAMING CONVENTIONS

12-55. Unit SOPs normally designate naming conventions for graphics. Otherwise, planners select them. For clarity, avoid multiword names, such as "Junction City." Simple names are better than complex ones. To ensure operations security, avoid assigning names that could reveal unit identities, such as the commander's name or the unit's home station. Do not name sequential phase lines and objectives in alphabetical order. For memory aids, use sets of names designated by the type of control measure or subordinate unit. For example, the division might use colors for objective names and minerals for phase line names.

CLASSIFICATION MARKINGS

12-56. AR 380-5 contains a detailed description of marking techniques, transmitting procedures, and other classification instructions. Each page and portions of the text on that page will be marked with the appropriate abbreviation ("TS" for TOP SECRET, "S" for SECRET, "C" for CONFIDENTIAL, or "U for UNCLASSIFIED). Place classification markings at the top and bottom of each page. All paragraphs must have the appropriate classification marking immediately following the alphanumeric designation of the paragraph (preceding the first word if the paragraph is not numbered).

12-57. The abbreviation "FOUO" will be used in place of "U" when a portion is UNCLASSIFIED but contains "For Official Use Only" information. AR 25-55 contains the definition and policy application of FOUO markings.

EXPRESSING UNNAMED DATES AND HOURS

12-58. Use specific letters to designate unnamed dates and times in plans and orders. See Table 12-1.

Table 12-1. Designated letters for dates and times

Term	Definition
C-day	The unnamed day on which a deployment operation commences or is to commence. The deployment may be movement of troops, cargo, weapon systems, or a combination of these elements using any or all types of transport. The letter "C" will be the only one used to denote the above. The highest command or headquarters responsible for coordinating the planning will specify the exact meaning of C-day within the aforementioned definition. The command or headquarters directly responsible for the execution of the operation, if other than the one coordinating the planning, will do so in light of the meaning specified by the highest command or headquarters coordinating the planning (JP 1-02).
D-day	The unnamed day on which a particular operation commences or is to commence (JP 3-02).
F-hour	The effective time of announcement by the Secretary of Defense to the Military Departments of a decision to mobilize Reserve units (JP 1-02).
H-hour	The specific hour on D-day at which a particular operation commences (JP 1-02).
H-hour (amphibious operations)	For amphibious operations, the time the first assault elements are scheduled to touch down on the beach, or a landing zone, and in some cases the commencement of countermine breaching operations (JP 3-02).
P-hour (airborne operations)	In airborne assault operations, the specific hour on D-day at which a parachute assault commences with the exit of the first Soldier from an aircraft over a designated drop zone. P-hour may or may not coincide with H-hour (ATTP 5-0.1).
L-hour	The specific hour on C-day at which a deployment operation commences or is to commence (JP 1-02).
L-hour (amphibious operations)	In amphibious operations, the time at which the first helicopter of the helicopter-borne assault wave touches down in the landing zone (JP 3-02).
M-day	The term used to designate the unnamed day on which full mobilization commences or is due to commence (JP 1-02).
N-day	The unnamed day an active duty unit is notified for deployment or redeployment (JP 1-02).
R-day	Redeployment day. The day on which redeployment of major combat, combat support, and combat service support forces begins in an operation (JP 1-02).
S-day	The day the President authorizes Selective Reserve callup (not more than 200,000) (JP 1-02).
T-day	The effective day coincident with Presidential declaration of national emergency and authorization of partial mobilization (not more than 1,000,000 personnel exclusive of the 200,000 callup) (JP 1-02).
W-day	Declared by the President, W-day is associated with an adversary decision to prepare for war (unambiguous strategic warning) (JP 3-02.1).

12-59. C-, D-, and M-days end at 2400 hours, Universal Time (ZULU time). They are assumed to be 24-hours long for planning. Plans and orders state the letters used and their meanings. If a plan mentions more than one event, refer to the secondary event in terms of the time of the primary event. Staffs refer to days preceding or following C-, D-, or M-day by using a plus or minus sign and an Arabic number after the letter. For example, D – 3 is three days before D-day; D + 7 is seven days after D-day. When using a time element other than days, staffs spell it out. For example, D + 3 months.

12-60. Staffs refer to hours preceding or following (H- or L-hour) by a plus or minus sign and an Arabic number after the letter. For example, H – 3 is three hours before H-hour; H + 7 is seven hours after H-hour. When using a time element other than hours, staffs spell it out. For example, H + 30 minutes.

12-61.   Where it is necessary to identify a particular operation or exercise, staffs place a nickname or code words before the letter, such as BALD EAGLE (D-day) or ANVIL EXPRESS (M-day).

EXPRESSING TIME

12-62.   The effective time for implementing the plan or order is the same as the date-time group of the order. Express the date and time as a six-digit date-time group. The first two digits indicate the day of the month; the next four digits indicate the time. The letter at the end of the time indicates the time zone. Staffs add the month and year to the date-time group to avoid confusion. For example, a complete date-time group for 6 August 2012 at 1145 appears as 061145Z August 2012.

12-63.   If the effective time of any portion of the order differs from that of the order, staffs identify those portions at the beginning of the coordinating instructions (in paragraph 3). For example, "Effective only for planning on receipt" or "Task organization effective 261300Z May 20XX."

12-64.   Express all times in a plan or order in terms of one time zone, for example ZULU (Z) or LOCAL. (*Note:* Do not abbreviate local time as [L]. The abbreviation for the LIMA time is L.) Staffs include the appropriate time zone indicator in the heading data and mission statement. For example, the time zone indicator for Central Standard Time in the continental United States is SIERRA. When daylight savings time is in effect, the time zone indicator for Central Standard Time is ROMEO. The relationship of local time to ZULU time, not the geographic location, determines the time zone indicator to use.

12-65.   When using inclusive dates, staffs express them by writing both dates separated by an en dash (6–9 August 20XX or 6 August–6 September 20XX). They express times in the 24-hour clock system by means of four-digit Arabic numbers, including the time zone indicator.

IDENTIFYING PAGES

12-66.   Staffs identify pages following the first page of plans and orders with a short title identification heading located two spaces under the classification marking. Include the number (or letter) designation of the plan, the issuing headquarters. For example, OPLAN 09-15–23d AD (U) (base plan identification) or Annex B (Intelligence) to OPLAN 09-15–23d AD (U) (annex identification).

NUMBERING PAGES

12-67.   Use the following convention to indicate page numbers:

- Number the pages of the base order and each attachment separately beginning on the first page of each attachment. Use a combination of alphanumeric designations to identify each attachment.
- Use Arabic numbers only to indicate page numbers. Place page numbers after the alphanumeric designation that identifies the attachment. (Use Arabic numbers without any proceeding alphanumeric designation for base order page numbers.) For example, the designation of the third page to Annex C is C-3. Assign each attachment either a letter or Arabic number that corresponds to the letter or number in the attachment's short title. Assign letters to annexes, Arabic numbers to appendixes, letters to tabs, and Arabic numbers to exhibits. For example, the designation of the third page to Appendix 5 to Annex C is C-5-3.
- Separate elements of the alphanumeric designation with hyphens. For example, the designation of the third page of exhibit 2 to Tab B to Appendix 5 to Annex C is C-5-B-2-3.

ATTACHMENTS (ANNEXES, APPENDIXES, TABS, AND EXHIBITS)

12-68.   Attachments (annexes, appendixes, tables, and exhibits) are an information management tool. They simplify orders by providing a structure for organizing information. The organizational structure for attachments to Army OPLANS and OPORDs is in Table 12-2.

12-69.   Attachments are part of an order. Using them increases the base order's clarity and usefulness by keeping it short. Attachments include information (such as sustainment), administrative support details, and instructions that expand upon the base order.

12-70.   Commanders and staffs are not required to develop all attachments listed in Table 12-2. The number and type of attachments depend on the commander, level of command, and complexity or needs of a particular operation. Minimizing the number of attachments keeps the order consistent with completeness and clarity. If the information relating to an attachment's subject is brief, place the information in the base order and "omit" the attachment.

12-71. Staffs list attachments under an appropriate heading at the end of the document they expand. For example, they list annexes at the end of the base order, appendixes at the end of annexes, and so forth. Paragraph 12-73 shows the required sequence of attachments.

12-72. Army and joint OPLANs or OPORDs do not use Annexes I and O as attachments. Army orders label these annexes "not used." Annexes Q, T, W, X, and Y are available for use and are labeled as "Spare." When an attachment required by doctrine or an SOP is unnecessary, staffs indicate this by stating, "[Type of attachment and its alphanumeric identifier] omitted." For example "Annex R (Reports) omitted". If the situation requires an additional attachment not provided in Table 12-2, leaders can add to this structure. For example, if there is a requirement to add an additional tab to Appendix 1 (Intelligence Estimate), that addition would be labeled as Tab E.

12-73. Staffs refer to attachments by letter or number and title. They use the following convention:

- **Annexes**. Designate annexes with capital letters. For example, Annex D (Fires) to OPORD 09-06—1 ID.
- **Appendixes**. Designate appendixes with Arabic numbers. For example, Appendix 1 (Intelligence Estimate) to Annex B (Intelligence) to OPORD 09-06—1 ID.
- **Tabs**. Designate tabs with capital letters. For example, Tab B (Target Synchronization Matrix) to Appendix 3 (Targeting) to Annex D (Fires) to OPORD 09-06—1 ID.
- **Exhibits**. Designate exhibits with Arabic numbers; for example, Exhibit 1 (Traffic Circulation and Control) to Tab C (Transportation) to Appendix 1 (Logistics) to Annex F (Sustainment) to OPORD 09-06—1 ID.

12-74. If an attachment has wider distribution than the base order or is issued separately, the attachment requires a complete heading and acknowledgment instructions. When staffs distribute attachments with the base order, these elements are not required.

EXAMPLES AND PROCEDURES FOR CREATING PLANS, ORDERS, AND ANNEXES

12-75. All plans, orders, and attachments follow the five-paragraph order format. Exceptions are those attachments that are matrixes, overlays, and lists. Figure 12-2 provides formats and instruction for developing the base OPLAN or OPORD.

[CLASSIFICATION]

Place the classification at the top and bottom of every page of the OPLAN or OPORD. Place the classification marking (TS), (S), (C), or (U) at the front of each paragraph and subparagraph in parentheses. Refer to AR 380-5 for classification and release marking instructions.

Copy ## of ## copies
Issuing headquarters
Place of issue
Date-time group of signature
Message reference number

The first line of the heading is the copy number assigned by the issuing headquarters. Maintain a log of specific copies issued to addressees. The second line is the official designation of the issuing headquarters (for example, 1st Infantry Division). The third line is the place of issue. It may be a code name, postal designation, or geographic location. The fourth line is the date or date-time group that the plan or order was signed or issued and becomes effective unless specified otherwise in the coordinating instructions. The fifth line is a headquarters internal control number assigned to all plans and orders in accordance with unit standard operating procedures (SOPs).

OPERATION PLAN/ORDER [number] [(code name)] [(classification of title)]

Number plans and orders consecutively by calendar year. Include code name, if any.

(U) References: *List documents essential to understanding the OPLAN or OPORD. List references concerning a specific function in the appropriate attachments.*

(a) List maps and charts first. Map entries include series number, country, sheet names, or numbers, edition, and scale.

(b) List other references in subparagraphs labeled as shown.

(U) Time Zone Used Throughout the OPLAN/OPORD: *State the time zone used in the area of operations during execution. When the OPLAN or OPORD applies to units in different time zones, use Greenwich Mean (ZULU) Time.*

(U) Task Organization: *Describe the organization of forces available to the issuing headquarters and their command and support relationships. Refer to Annex A (Task Organization) if long or complicated.*

1. (U) <u>Situation</u>. *The situation paragraph describes the conditions of the operational environment that impact operations in the following subparagraphs:*

a. (U) <u>Area of Interest</u>. *Describe the area of interest. Refer to Annex B (Intelligence) as required.*

b. (U) <u>Area of Operations</u>. *Describe the area of operations (AO). Refer to the appropriate map by its subparagraph under references, for example, "Map, reference (b)." Refer to the Appendix 2 (Operation Overlay) to Annex C (Operations) as required.*

(1) (U) <u>Terrain</u>. *Describe the aspects of terrain that impact operations. Refer to Annex B (Intelligence) as required.*

(2) (U) <u>Weather</u>. *Describe the aspects of weather that impact operations. Refer to Annex B (Intelligence) as required.*

[page number]
[CLASSIFICATION]

Figure 12-2. Annotated Army OPLAN/OPORD format

[CLASSIFICATION]

OPLAN/OPORD [number] [(code name)]—[issuing headquarters] [(classification of title)]

Place the classification and title of the OPLAN or OPORD and the issuing headquarters at the top of the second and any subsequent pages of the base plan or order.

c. (U) <u>Enemy Forces</u>. *Identify enemy forces and appraise their general capabilities. Describe the enemy's disposition, location, strength, and probable courses of action. Identify known or potential terrorist threats and adversaries within the AO. Refer to Annex B (Intelligence) as required.*

d. (U) <u>Friendly Forces</u>. *Briefly identify the missions of friendly forces and the objectives, goals, and missions of civilian organizations that impact the issuing headquarters in following subparagraphs:*

(1) (U) <u>Higher Headquarters Mission and Intent</u>. *Identify and state the mission and commander's intent for headquarters two levels up and one level up from the issuing headquarters.*

(a) (U) <u>Higher Headquarters Two Levels Up</u>. *Identify the higher headquarters two levels up the paragraph heading (for example, Joint Task Force-18).*

1. (U) <u>Mission</u>.

2. (U) <u>Commander's Intent</u>.

(b) (U) <u>Higher Headquarters</u>. *Identify the higher headquarters one level up in the paragraph heading (for example, 1st [U.S.] Armored Division).*

1. (U) <u>Mission</u>.

2. (U) <u>Commander's Intent</u>.

(2) (U) <u>Missions of Adjacent Units</u>. *Identify and state the missions of adjacent units and other units whose actions have a significant impact on the issuing headquarters.*

e. (U) <u>Interagency, Intergovernmental, and Nongovernmental Organizations</u>. *Identify and state the objective or goals and primary tasks of those non-Department of Defense organizations that have a significant role within the AO. Refer to Annex V (Interagency Coordination) as required.*

f. (U) <u>Civil Considerations</u>. *Describe the critical aspects of the civil situation that impact operations. Refer to Appendix 1 (Intelligence Estimate) to Annex B (Intelligence) as required.*

g. (U) <u>Attachments and Detachments</u>. *List units attached to or detached from the issuing headquarters. State when each attachment or detachment is effective (for example, on order, on commitment of the reserve) if different from the effective time of the OPLAN or OPORD. Do not repeat information already listed in Annex A (Task Organization).*

h. (U) <u>Assumptions</u>. *List assumptions used in the development of the OPLAN or OPORD.*

2. (U) <u>Mission</u>. *State the unit's mission—a short description of the who, what (task), when, where, and why (purpose) that clearly indicates the action to be taken and the reason for doing so.*

3. (U) <u>Execution</u>. *Describe how the commander intends to accomplish the mission in terms of the commander's intent, an overarching concept of operations, schemes of employment for each warfighting function, assessment, specified tasks to subordinate units, and key coordinating instructions in the subparagraphs below.*

[page number]
[CLASSIFICATION]

Figure 12-2. Annotated Army OPLAN/OPORD format (continued)

[CLASSIFICATION]

OPLAN/OPORD [number] [(code name)]—[issuing headquarters] [(classification of title)]

a. (U) <u>Commander's Intent</u>. *Commanders develop their intent statement personally. The commander's intent is a clear, concise statement of what the force must do and conditions the force must establish with respect to the enemy, terrain, and civil considerations that represent the desired end state. It succinctly describes what constitutes the success of an operation and provides the purpose and conditions that define that desired end state. The commander's intent must be easy to remember and clearly understood two echelons down.*

b. (U) <u>Concept of Operations</u>. *The concept of operations is a statement that directs the manner in which subordinate units cooperate to accomplish the mission and establishes the sequence of actions the force will use to achieve the end state. It is normally expressed in terms of decisive, shaping, and sustaining operations. It states the principal tasks required, the responsible subordinate units, and how the principal tasks complement one another. Normally, the concept of operations projects the status of the force at the end of the operation. If the mission dictates a significant change in tasks during the operation, the commander may phase the operation. The concept of operations may be a single paragraph, divided into two or more subparagraphs, or if unusually lengthy, summarize here with details located in Annex C (Operations). If the concept of operations is phased, describe each phase in a subparagraph. Label these subparagraphs as "Phase" followed by the appropriate Roman numeral, for example, "Phase I." If the operation is phased, all paragraphs and subparagraphs of the base order and all annexes must mirror the phasing established in the concept of operations. The operation overlay and graphic depictions of lines of effort help portray the concept of operations and are located in Annex C (Operations).*

c. (U) <u>Scheme of Movement and Maneuver</u>. *Describe the employment of maneuver units in accordance with the concept of operations. Provide the primary tasks of maneuver units conducting the decisive operation and the purpose of each. Next, state the primary tasks of maneuver units conducting shaping operations, including security operations, and the purpose of each. For offensive operations, identify the form of maneuver. For defensive operations, identify the type of defense. For stability operations, describe the role of maneuver units by primary stability tasks. If the operation is phased, identify the main effort by phase. Identify and include priorities for the reserve. Refer to Annex C (Operations) as required.*

(1) (U) <u>Scheme of Mobility/Countermobility</u>. *State the scheme of mobility/countermobility including priorities by unit or area. Refer to Annex G (Engineer) as required.*

(2) (U) <u>Scheme of Battlefield Obscuration</u>. *State the scheme of battlefield obscuration, including priorities by unit or area. Refer to Appendix 9 (Battlefield Obscuration) to Annex C (Operations) as required.*

(3) (U) <u>Scheme of Reconnaissance and Surveillance</u>. *Describe how the commander intends to use reconnaissance and surveillance to support the concept of operations. Include the primary reconnaissance objectives. Refer to Annex L (Reconnaissance and Surveillance) as required.*

(**Note:** *Army forces do not conduct reconnaissance and surveillance within the United States and its territories. For domestic operations, this paragraph is titled "Information Awareness and Assessment" and the contents of this paragraph comply with Executive Order 12333.*)

[page number]
[CLASSIFICATION]

Figure 12-2. Annotated Army OPLAN/OPORD format (continued)

[CLASSIFICATION]

OPLAN/OPORD [number] [(code name)]—[issuing headquarters] [(classification of title)]

d. (U) <u>Scheme of Intelligence</u>. *Describe how the commander envisions intelligence supporting the concept of operations. Include the priority of effort to situation development, targeting, and assessment. State the priority of intelligence support to units and areas. Refer to Annex B (Intelligence) as required.*

e. (U) <u>Scheme of Fires</u>. *Describe how the commander intends to use fires to support the concept of operations with emphasis on the scheme of maneuver. State the fire support tasks and the purpose of each task. State the priorities for, allocation of, and restrictions on fires. Refer to Annex D (Fires) as required.*

f. (U) <u>Scheme of Protection</u>. *Describe how the commander envisions protection supporting the concept of operations. Include the priorities of protection by unit and area. Include survivability. Address the scheme of operational area security, including security for routes, bases, and critical infrastructure. Identify tactical combat forces and other reaction forces. Use subparagraphs for protection categories (for example, air and missile defense and explosive ordnance disposal) based on the situation. Refer to Annex E (Protection) as required.*

g. (U) <u>Stability Operations</u>. *Describe how the commander envisions the conduct of stability operations in coordination with other organizations through the primary stability tasks. (See FM 3-07.) If other organizations or the host nation are unable to provide for civil security, restoration of essential services, and civil control, then commanders with an assigned AO must do so with available resources, request additional resources, or request relief for these requirements from higher headquarters. Commanders assign specific responsibilities for stability tasks to subordinate units in paragraph 3i (Tasks to Subordinate Units) and paragraph 3j (Coordinating Instructions). Refer to Annex C (Operations) and Annex K (Civil Affairs Operations) as required.*

h. (U) <u>Assessment</u>. *Describe the priorities for assessment and identify the measures of effectiveness used to assess end state conditions and objectives. Refer to Annex M (Assessment) as required.*

i. (U) <u>Tasks to Subordinate Units</u>. *State the task assigned to each unit that reports directly to the headquarters issuing the order. Each task must include who (the subordinate unit assigned the task), what (the task itself), when, where, and why (purpose). Use a separate subparagraph for each unit. List units in task organization sequence. Place tasks that affect two or more units in paragraph 3j (Coordinating Instructions).*

j. (U) <u>Coordinating Instructions</u>. *List only instructions and tasks applicable to two or more units not covered in unit SOPs.*

(1) (U) <u>Time or condition when the OPORD becomes effective</u>.

(2) (U) <u>Commander's Critical Information Requirements</u>. *List commander's critical information requirements (CCIRs).*

(3) (U) <u>Essential Elements of Friendly Information</u>. *List essential elements of friendly information (EEFIs).*

(4) (U) <u>Fire Support Coordination Measures</u>. *List critical fire support coordination or control measures.*

[page number]
[CLASSIFICATION]

Figure 12-2. Annotated Army OPLAN/OPORD format (continued)

[CLASSIFICATION]

OPLAN/OPORD [number] [(code name)]—[issuing headquarters] [(classification of title)]

(5) (U) <u>Airspace Coordinating Measures</u>. *List critical airspace coordinating or control measures.*

(6) (U) <u>Rules of Engagement</u>. *List rules of engagement. Refer to Appendix 11 (Rules of Engagement) to Annex C (Operations) as required.*

*(***Note:** *For operations within the United States and its territories, title this paragraph "Rules for the Use of Force").*

(7) (U) <u>Risk Reduction Control Measures</u>. *State measures specific to this operation not included in unit SOPs. They may include mission-oriented protective posture, operational exposure guidance, troop-safety criteria, and fratricide avoidance measures. Refer to Annex E (Protection) as required.*

(8) (U) <u>Personnel Recovery Coordination Measures</u>. *Refer to Appendix 2 (Personnel Recovery) to Annex E (Protection) as required.*

(9) (U) <u>Environmental Considerations</u>. *Refer to Appendix 5 (Environmental Considerations) to Annex G (Engineer) as required.*

(10) (U) <u>Themes and Messages</u>. *List information themes and messages.*

(11) (U) <u>Other Coordinating Instructions</u>. *List in subparagraphs any additional coordinating instructions and tasks that apply to two or more units, such as the operational timeline and any other critical timing or events.*

4. (U) <u>Sustainment</u>. *Describe the concept of sustainment, including priorities of sustainment by unit or area. Include instructions for administrative movements, deployments, and transportation—or references to applicable appendixes—if appropriate. Use the following subparagraphs to provide the broad concept of support for logistics, personnel, and Army health system support. Provide detailed instructions for each sustainment sub-function in the appendixes to Annex F (Sustainment) listed in Table E-2.*

a. (U) <u>Logistics</u>. *Refer to Annex F (Sustainment) as required.*

b. (U) <u>Personnel</u>. *Refer to Annex F (Sustainment) as required.*

c. (U) <u>Army Health System Support</u>. *Refer to Annex F (Sustainment) as required.*

5. (U) <u>Command and Signal</u>.

a. (U) <u>Command</u>.

(1) (U) <u>Location of Commander</u>. *State where the commander intends to be during the operation, by phase if the operation is phased.*

(2) (U) <u>Succession of Command</u>. *State the succession of command if not covered in the unit's SOPs.*

(3) (U) <u>Liaison Requirements</u>. *State liaison requirements not covered in the unit's SOPs.*

[page number]
[CLASSIFICATION]

Figure 12-2. Annotated Army OPLAN/OPORD format (continued)

[CLASSIFICATION]

OPLAN/OPORD [number] [(code name)]—[issuing headquarters] [(classification of title)]

    b. (U) <u>Control</u>.

        (1) (U) <u>Command Posts</u>. *Describe the employment of command posts (CPs), including the location of each CP and its time of opening and closing, as appropriate. State the primary controlling CP for specific tasks or phases of the operation (for example, "Division tactical command post will control the air assault").*

        (2) (U) <u>Reports</u>. *List reports not covered in SOPs. Refer to Annex R (Reports) as required.*

    c. (U) <u>Signal</u>. *Describe the concept of signal support, including location and movement of key signal nodes and critical electromagnetic spectrum considerations throughout the operation. Refer to Annex H (Signal) as required.*

ACKNOWLEDGE: *Include instructions for the acknowledgement of the OPLAN or OPORD by addressees. The word "acknowledge" may suffice. Refer to the message reference number if necessary. Acknowledgement of a plan or order means that it has been received and understood.*

[Commander's last name]
[Commander's rank]

The commander or authorized representative signs the original copy. If the representative signs the original, add the phrase "For the Commander." The signed copy is the historical copy and remains in the headquarters' files.

OFFICIAL:

[Authenticator's name]
[Authenticator's position]

Use only if the commander does not sign the original order. If the commander signs the original, no further authentication is required. If the commander does not sign, the signature of the preparing staff officer requires authentication and only the last name and rank of the commander appear in the signature block.

ANNEXES: *List annexes by letter and title. Army and joint OPLANs or OPORDs do not use Annexes I and O as attachments and in Army orders label these annexes "Not Used." Annexes Q, T, W, X, and Y are available for use in Army OPLANs or OPORDs and are labeled as "Spare." When an attachment required by doctrine or an SOP is unnecessary, label it "Omitted."*

Annex A – Task Organization
Annex B – Intelligence
Annex C – Operations
Annex D – Fires
Annex E – Protection
Annex F – Sustainment
Annex G – Engineer
Annex H – Signal
Annex I   – Not Used
Annex J – Inform and Influence Activities
Annex K – Civil Affairs Operations
Annex L – Reconnaissance and Surveillance

[page number]
[CLASSIFICATION]

Figure 12-2. Annotated Army OPLAN/OPORD Format (continued)

[CLASSIFICATION]

OPLAN/OPORD [number] [(code name)]—[issuing headquarters] [(classification of title)]

Annex M – Assessment
Annex N – Space Operations
Annex O – Not Used
Annex P – Host-Nation Support
Annex Q – Spare
Annex R – Reports
Annex S – Special Technical Operations
Annex T – Spare
Annex U – Inspector General
Annex V – Interagency Coordination
Annex W – Spare
Annex X – Spare
Annex Y – Spare
Annex Z – Distribution

DISTRIBUTION: *Furnish distribution copies either for action or for information. List in detail those who are to receive the plan or order. Refer to Annex Z (Distribution) if lengthy.*

[page number]
[CLASSIFICATION]

Figure 12-2. Annotated Army OPLAN/OPORD format (continued)

12-76. Table 12-2 lists the attachments (annexes, appendixes, tabs, and exhibits) to the base OPLAN or OPORD and identifies the staff officers responsible for developing each attachment.

Table 12-2. List of attachments and responsible staff officers

ANNEX A – TASK ORGANIZATION (G-5 or G-3 [S-3])
ANNEX B – INTELLIGENCE (G-2 [S-2])
Appendix 1 – Intelligence Estimate
Tab A – Terrain (Engineer Officer)
Tab B – Weather (Staff Weather Officer)
Tab C – Civil Considerations
Tab D – Intelligence Preparation of the Battlefield Products
Appendix 2 – Counterintelligence
Appendix 3 – Signals Intelligence
Appendix 4 – Human Intelligence
Appendix 5 – Geospatial Intelligence
Appendix 6 – Measurement and Signature Intelligence
Appendix 7 – Open Source Intelligence
ANNEX C – OPERATIONS (G-5 or G-3 [S-3])
Appendix 1 – Design Concept
Appendix 2 – Operation Overlay
Appendix 3 – Decision Support Products
Tab A – Execution Matrix
Tab B – Decision Support Template and Matrix
Appendix 4 – Gap Crossing Operations
Tab A – Traffic Control Overlay
Appendix 5 – Air Assault Operations
Tab A – Pickup Zone Diagram
Tab B – Air Movement Table
Tab C – Landing Zone Diagram
Appendix 6 – Airborne Operations
Tab A – Marshalling Plan
Tab B – Air Movement Plan
Tab C – Drop Zone/Extraction Zone Diagram
Appendix 7 – Amphibious Operations
Tab A – Advance Force Operations
Tab B – Embarkation Plan
Tab C – Landing Plan
Tab D – Rehearsal Plan
Appendix 8 – Special Operations (G-3 [S-3])
Appendix 9 – Battlefield Obscuration (CBRN Officer)
Appendix 10 – Airspace Command and Control (G-3 [S-3] or Airspace Command and Control Officer)
Tab A – Air Traffic Services
Appendix 11 – Rules of Engagement (Staff Judge Advocate)
Tab A – No Strike List
Tab B – Restricted Target List (G-3 [S-3] with Staff Judge Advocate)
Appendix 12 – Law and Order Operations (Provost Marshal)
Tab A – Police Engagement
Tab B – Law Enforcement
Appendix 13 – Internment and Resettlement Operations (Provost Marshal)

Table 12-2. List of attachments and responsible staff officers (continued)

ANNEX D – FIRES (Chief of Fires/Fire Support Officer)
Appendix 1 – Fire Support Overlay
Appendix 2 – Fire Support Execution Matrix
Appendix 3 – Targeting
Tab A – Target Selection Standards
Tab B – Target Synchronization Matrix
Tab C – Attack Guidance Matrix
Tab D – Target List Worksheets
Tab E – Battle Damage Assessment (G-2 [S-2])
Appendix 4 – Field Artillery Support
Appendix 5 – Air Support
Appendix 6 – Naval Fire Support
Appendix 7 – Cyber/Electromagnetic Activities (Electronic Warfare Officer)
Tab A – Electronic Warfare
Tab B – Computer Network Operations
Tab C – Computer Network Attack
Tab D – Computer Network Exploitation

ANNEX E – PROTECTION (Chief of Protection/Protection Officer as designated by the commander)
Appendix 1 – Air and Missile Defense (Air and Missile Defense Officer)
Tab A – Enemy Air Avenues of Approach
Tab B – Enemy Air Order of Battle
Tab C – Enemy Theater Ballistic Missile Overlay
Tab D – Air and Missile Defense Protection Overlay
Tab E – Critical Asset List/Defended Asset List
Appendix 2 – Personnel Recovery (Personnel Recovery Officer)
Appendix 3 – Fratricide Avoidance (Safety Officer)
Appendix 4 – Operational Area Security (Provost Marshal)
Appendix 5 – Antiterrorism (Antiterrorism Officer)
Appendix 6 – Chemical, Biological, Radiological, and Nuclear Defense (CBRN Officer)
Appendix 7 – Safety (Safety Officer)
Appendix 8 – Operations Security (Operations Security Officer)
Appendix 9 – Explosive Ordnance Disposal (Explosive Ordnance Disposal Officer)
Appendix 10 – Force Health Protection (Surgeon)

Table 12-2. List of attachments and responsible staff officers (continued)

ANNEX F – SUSTAINMENT (Chief of Sustainment [S-4])
Appendix 1 – Logistics (G-4 [S-4])
Tab A – Sustainment Overlay
Tab B – Maintenance
Tab C – Transportation
Exhibit 1 – Traffic Circulation and Control (Provost Marshal)
Exhibit 2 – Traffic Circulation Overlay
Exhibit 3 – Road Movement Table
Exhibit 4 – Highway Regulation (Provost Marshal)
Tab D – Supply
Tab E – Field Services
Tab F – Distribution
Tab G – Contract Support Integration
Tab H – Mortuary Affairs
Tab I – Internment and Resettlement Support
Appendix 2 – Personnel Services Support (G-1 [S-1])
Tab A – Human Resources Support (G-1 [S-1])
Tab B – Financial Management (G-8)
Tab C – Legal Support (Staff Judge Advocate)
Tab D – Religious Support (Chaplain)
Tab E – Band Operations (G-1 [S-1])
Appendix 3 – Army Heath System Support (Surgeon)
ANNEX G – ENGINEER (Engineer Officer)
Appendix 1 – Mobility/Countermobility
Tab A – Obstacle Overlay
Appendix 2 – Survivability (Engineer Officer)
Appendix 3 – General Engineering
Appendix 4 – Geospatial Engineering
Appendix 5 – Environmental Considerations
Tab A – Environmental Assessments
Tab B – Environmental Assessment Exemptions
Tab C – Environmental Baseline Survey
ANNEX H – SIGNAL (G-6 [S-6])
Appendix 1 – Information Assurance
Appendix 2 – Voice and Data Network Diagrams
Appendix 3 – Satellite Communications
Appendix 4 – Foreign Data Exchanges
Appendix 5 – Electromagnetic Spectrum Operations
ANNEX I – Not Used
ANNEX J – INFORM AND INFLUENCE ACTIVITIES (G-7 [S-7])
Appendix 1 – Public Affairs (Public Affairs Officer)
Appendix 2 – Military Deception (Military Deception Officer)
Appendix 3 – Military Information Support Operations (Military Information Support Officer)
Appendix 4 – Soldier and Leader Engagement

Table 12-2. List of attachments and responsible staff officers (continued)

ANNEX K – CIVIL AFFAIRS OPERATIONS (G-9 [S-9])
Appendix 1 – Execution Matrix Appendix 2 – Populace and Resources Control Plan Appendix 3 – Civil Information Management Plan
ANNEX L – RECONNAISSANCE AND SURVEILLANCE (G-3 [S-3])
Appendix 1 – Reconnaissance and Surveillance Overlay Appendix 2 – Reconnaissance and Surveillance Tasking Matrix
ANNEX M – ASSESSMENT (G-5 [S-5] or G-3 [S-3])
Appendix 1 – Nesting of Assessment Efforts Appendix 2 – Assessment Framework Appendix 3 – Assessment Working Group
ANNEX N – SPACE OPERATIONS (Space Operations Officer)
ANNEX O – Not Used
ANNEX P – HOST-NATION SUPPORT (G-4 [S-4])
ANNEX Q – Spare
ANNEX R – REPORTS (G-3 [S-3], G-5 [S-5], G-7, and Knowledge Management Officer)
ANNEX S – SPECIAL TECHNICAL OPERATIONS (Special Technical Operations Officer)
Appendix 1 – Special Technical Operations Capabilities Integration Matrix Appendix 2 – Functional Area I Program and Objectives Appendix 3 – Functional Area II Program and Objectives
ANNEX T – Spare
ANNEX U – INSPECTOR GENERAL (Inspector General)
ANNEX V – INTERAGENCY COORDINATION (G-3 [S-3] and G-9 [S-9])
ANNEX W – Spare
ANNEX X – Spare
ANNEX Y – Spare
ANNEX Z – DISTRIBUTION (G-3 [S-3] and Knowledge Management Officer)

12-77.   Figure 12-3 provides formats and instructions for developing an attachment.

[CLASSIFICATION]

(Change from verbal orders, if any)

Copy ## of ## copies
Issuing headquarters
Place of issue
Date-time group of signature
Message reference number

Include heading if attachment is distributed separately from the base order or higher-level attachment.

[Attachment type and number/letter] [(attachment title)] TO [higher-level attachment type and number/letter, if applicable] [(higher-level attachment title, if applicable)] TO OPERATION PLAN/ORDER [number] [(code name)] [(classification of title)]

References: *Refer to higher headquarters' OPLAN or OPORD and identify map sheets for operation (Optional).*

Time Zone Used Throughout the Order:

1. (U) Situation. *Include information affecting the functional area that paragraph 1 of the OPLAN or OPORD does not cover or that needs expansion.*

a. (U) Area of Interest. *Refer to Annex B (Intelligence) as required.*

b. (U) Area of Operations. *Refer to Appendix 2 (Operation Overlay) to Annex C (Operations).*

(1) (U) Terrain. *Describe aspects of terrain that impact functional area operations. Refer to Annex B (Intelligence) as required.*

(2) (U) Weather. *Describe aspects of weather that impact functional area operations. Refer to Annex B (Intelligence) as required.*

c. (U) Enemy Forces. *List known and templated locations and activities of enemy functional area units for one echelon up and two echelons down. List enemy maneuver and other area capabilities that will impact friendly operations. State expected enemy courses of action and employment of enemy functional area assets. Refer to Annex B (Intelligence) as required.*

d. (U) Friendly Forces. *Outline the higher headquarters' plan as it pertains to the functional area. List designation, location, and outline of plan of higher, adjacent, and other functional area assets that support or impact the issuing headquarters or require coordination and additional support.*

e. (U) Interagency, Intergovernmental, and Nongovernmental Organizations. *Identify and describe other organizations in the area of operations that may impact the conduct of functional area operations or implementation of functional area-specific equipment and tactics.*

f. (U) Civil Considerations. *Describe critical aspects of the civil situation that impact functional area operations. Refer to Annex K (Civil Affairs Operations) as required.*

g. (U) Attachments and Detachments. *List units attached or detached only as necessary to clarify task organization. Refer to Annex A (Task Organization) as required.*

h. (U) Assumptions. *List any functional area-specific assumptions that support the annex development.*

[page number]
[CLASSIFICATION]

Figure 12-3. Annotated attachment format (general)

[CLASSIFICATION]

[Attachment type and number/letter] [(attachment title)] TO [higher-level attachment type and number/letter, if applicable] [(higher-level attachment title, if applicable)] TO OPERATION PLAN/ORDER [number] [(code name)]—[issuing headquarters] [(classification of title)]

2. (U) <u>Mission</u>. *State the mission of the functional area in support of the base plan or order.*

3. (U) <u>Execution</u>.

    a. (U) <u>Scheme of Support</u>. *Describe how the functional area supports the commander's intent and concept of operations. Establish the priorities of support to units for each phase of the operation. Refer to Annex C (Operations) as required.*

    b. (U) <u>Tasks to Subordinate Units</u>. *List functional area tasks assigned to specific subordinate units not contained in the base order.*

    c. (U) <u>Coordinating Instructions</u>. *List only instructions applicable to two or more subordinate units not covered in the base order.*

4. (U) <u>Sustainment</u>. *Identify priorities of sustainment for functional area key tasks and specify additional instructions as required. Refer to Annex F (Sustainment) as required.*

5. (U) <u>Command and Signal</u>.

    a. (U) <u>Command</u>. *State the location of key functional area leaders.*

    b. (U) <u>Control</u>. *State the functional area liaison requirements not covered in the base order.*

    c. (U) <u>Signal</u>. *Address any functional area-specific communications requirements or reports. Refer to Annex H (Signal) as required.*

ACKNOWLEDGE: *Include only if attachment is distributed separately from the base order.*

         [Commander's last name]
         [Commander's rank]

OFFICIAL:

[Authenticator's name]
[Authenticator's position]

Either the commander or coordinating staff officer responsible for the functional area may sign attachments.

ATTACHMENT: *List lower-level attachments.*

DISTRIBUTION: *Show only if distributed separately from the base order or higher-level attachments.*

[page number]
[CLASSIFICATION]

Figure 12-3. Annotated attachment format (general) (continued)

12-78.   Figure 12-4 provides formats and instructions for developing a WARNO.

[CLASSIFICATION]
(Change from verbal orders, if any) (Optional)

[Heading data is the same as for OPLAN/OPORD]

WARNING ORDER [number]

(U) References: *Refer to higher headquarters' OPLAN or OPORD and identify map sheets for operation (Optional).*

(U) Time Zone Used Throughout the OPLAN/OPORD: *(Optional).*

(U) Task Organization: *(Optional).*

1. (U) <u>Situation</u>. *The situation paragraph describes the conditions and circumstances of the operational environment that impact operations in the following subparagraphs:*

    a. (U) <u>Area of Interest</u>.

    b. (U) <u>Area of Operations</u>.

    c. (U) <u>Enemy Forces</u>.

    d. (U) <u>Friendly Forces</u>.

    e. (U) <u>Interagency, Intergovernmental, and Nongovernmental Organizations</u>.

    f. (U) <u>Civil Considerations</u>.

    g. (U) <u>Attachments and Detachments</u>. *Provide initial task organization.*

    h. (U) <u>Assumptions</u>. *List any significant assumptions for order development.*

2. (U) <u>Mission</u>. *State the issuing headquarters' mission.*

3. (U) <u>Execution</u>.

    a. (U) <u>Initial Commander's Intent</u>. *Provide brief commander's intent statement.*

    b. (U) <u>Concept of Operations</u>. *This may be "to be determined" for an initial WARNO.*

    c. (U) <u>Tasks to Subordinate Units</u>. *Include any known tasks at time of issuance of WARNO.*

    d. (U) <u>Coordinating Instructions</u>.

4. (U) <u>Sustainment</u>. *Include any known logistics, personnel, or Army health system preparation tasks.*

5. (U) <u>Command and Signal</u>. *Include any changes to the existing order or state "No change."*

ACKNOWLEDGE:

                      [Commander's last name]
                      [Commander's rank]

OFFICIAL:

[Authenticator's name]
[Authenticator's position]

ANNEXES: *List annexes by letter and title.*

DISTRIBUTION:

                      [page number]
                      [CLASSIFICATION]

Figure 12-4. Annotated WARNO format

12-79. Figure 12-5 provides formats for developing a FRAGO.

[CLASSIFICATION]
(Change from verbal orders, if any) (Optional)

Copy ## of ## copies
Issuing headquarters
Place of issue
Date-time group of signature
Message reference number

FRAGMENTARY ORDER [number] to OPERATION PLAN/ORDER [number] [(code name)]—[(classification of title)]

(U) References: Refer to the higher order being modified.

(U) Time Zone Used Throughout the OPLAN/OPORD:

1. (U) <u>Situation</u>. *Include any changes to the existing order or state "No change." For example, "No change to OPORD 03-XX."*

2. (U) <u>Mission</u>. *State "No change."*

3. (U) <u>Execution</u>. *Include any changes or state "No change."*

    a. (U) <u>Commander's Intent</u>. *Include any changes or state "No change."*

    b. (U) <u>Concept of Operations</u>. *Include any changes or state "No change."*

    c. (U) <u>Scheme Movement and Maneuver</u>. *Include any changes or state "No change."*

    d. (U) <u>Scheme of Intelligence</u>. *Include any changes or state "No change."*

    e. (U) <u>Scheme of Fires</u>. *Include any changes or state "No change."*

    f. (U) <u>Scheme of Protection</u>. *Include any changes or state "No change."*

    g. (U) <u>Stability Operations</u>. *Include any changes or state "No change."*

    h. (U) <u>Assessment</u>. *Include any changes or state "No change."*

    i. (U) <u>Tasks to Subordinate Units</u>. *Include any changes or state "No change."*

    j. (U) <u>Coordinating Instructions</u>. *Include any changes or state "No change"*

4. (U) <u>Sustainment</u>. *Include any changes or state "No change."*

5. (U) <u>Command and Signal</u>. *Include any changes or state "No change."*

ACKNOWLEDGE:

                [Commander's last name]
                [Commander's rank]

OFFICIAL:

[Authenticator's name]
[Authenticator's position]

ANNEXES: *List annexes by letter and title. Army and joint OPLANs or OPORDs do not use Annexes I and O as attachments and in Army orders label these annexes "Not Used." Annexes Q, T, W, X, and Y are available for use in Army OPLANs or OPORDs and are labeled as "Spare." When an attachment required by doctrine or an SOP is unnecessary, label it "Omitted."*

DISTRIBUTION:

[page number]
[CLASSIFICATION]

Figure 12-5. Annotated sample FRAGO

12-80. If, on occasion, a FRAGO has an annex as an attachment, use the naming convention for that attachment, such as, **"ANNEX A (TASK ORGANIZATION) to FRAGMENTARY ORDER [number] to OPERATION PLAN/ORDER [number] [(code name)]—[(classification of title)]."**

12-81. Figure 12-6 is a sample overlay order graphic with text.

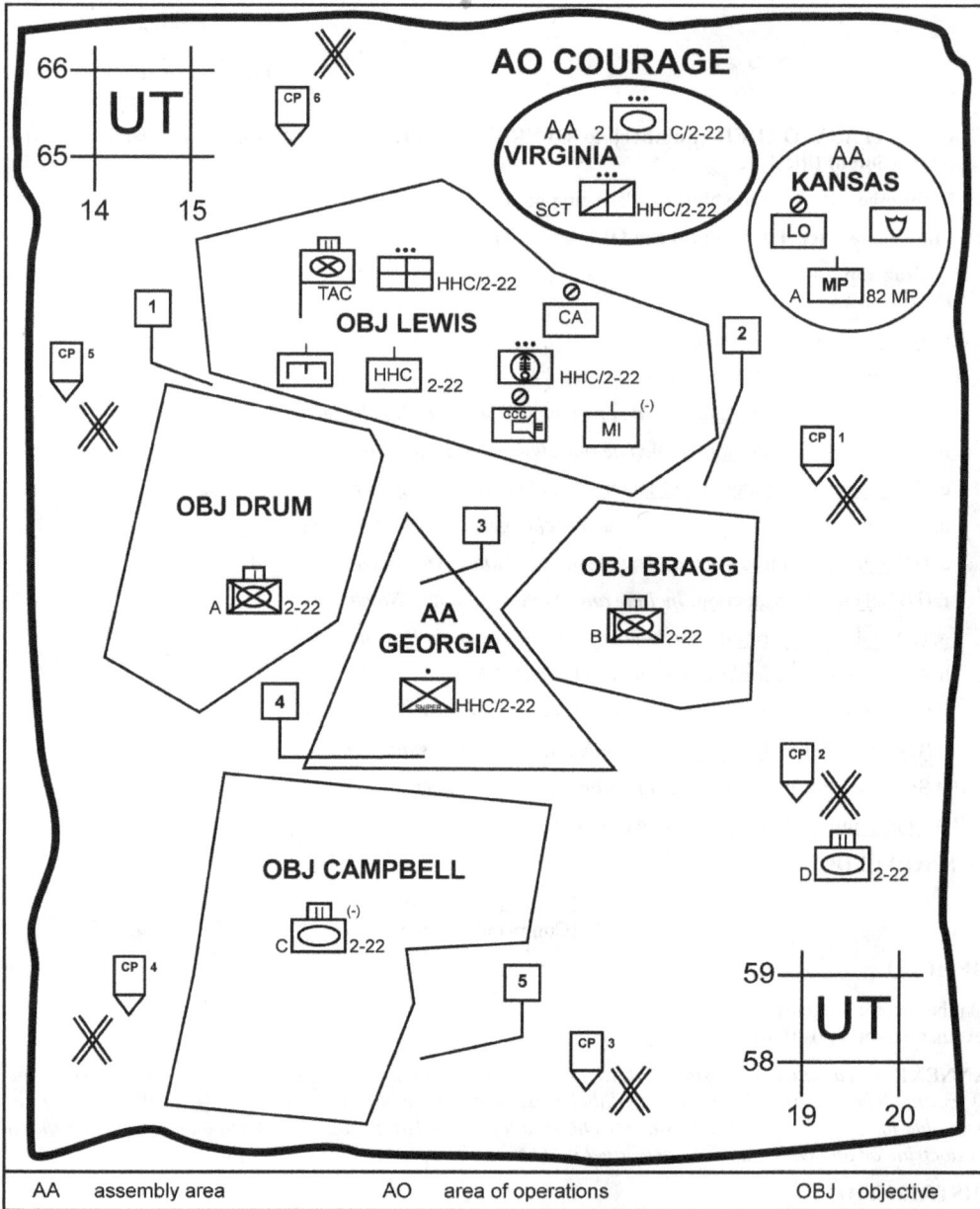

Figure 12-6. Example of overlay order graphic

TASK ORGANIZATION				
TF Control	A/2-22 IN	B/2-22 IN	C/2-22 AR	D/2-22 AR
Sniper Sqd/HHC/2-22	1/A/2-22 IN 2/A/2-22 IN 3/C/2-22 AR	1/B/2-22 IN 2/B/2-22 IN 3/D/2-22 AR	1/C/2-22 AR 2/C/2-22 AR 3/A/2-22 IN	1/D/2-22 AR 2/D/2-22 AR 3/B/2-22 IN
HHC	HN Civil Authorities (DIRLAUTH)			
Scout PLT/2-22 IN Mortars/HHC/2-22 Medical/HHC/2-22	None			

MISSION:

TF 2-22 conducts a cordon and search in AO COURAGE NLT 120900ZJAN07 to capture anti-coalition forces (ACF) and seize weapons caches in order to limit the attacks on coalition forces

COMMANDER'S INTENT:

Simultaneous occupation of outer cordon checkpoints (CKPs) to isolate search objectives and prevent ACF exfiltration or infiltration Lead with information dissemination of information themes and messages Exercise patience discipline and respect for host-nation population and property while conducting thorough searches Immediate evacuation of ACF personnel to BCT Detainee Collection Point for processing and evacuation End state is OBJs LEWIS DRUM BRAGG and CAMPBELL free of ACF and companies postured for future operations

EXECUTION – TASKS TO SUBORDINATE UNITS:

A/2-22 IN	**TF Decisive Operation:** Secure OBJ DRUM (inner cordon) and conduct search to capture ACF and seize weapons caches in order to limit the attacks on coalition forces
B/2-22 IN	Secure OBJ BRAGG (inner cordon) and conduct search to capture ACF and seize weapons caches in order to limit the attacks on coalition forces
C/2-22 AR	1 Secure OBJ CAMPBELL (inner cordon) and conduct search to capture ACF and seize weapons caches in order to limit the attacks on coalition forces
D/2-22 AR	1 Secure the outer cordon at CKPs 1-6 2 Secure AA KANSAS for HNCA occupation
HHC (-)/2-22	1 Secure TF tactical command post and TF Forward Aid Station in OBJ LEWIS
Sniper/HHC/2-22	1 Occupy AA GEORGIA and provide observation and surveillance of OBJs DRUM BRAGG and CAMPBELL 2 O/O deliver precision fires to destroy ACF

Acknowledge: A/2-22 IN B/2-22 IN C/2-22 AR D/2-22 AR HHC/2-22 Sniper/2-22 IN

Figure 12-6. Example of overlay order graphic (continued)

This page intentionally left blank.

Annex A

Task Organization Format and Instructions

This annex discusses the fundamentals of task organization, and provides the format and instructions for developing Annex A (Task Organization) to the base plan or order. This annex does not follow the five-paragraph attachment format. Unit standard operating procedures will dictate development and format for this annex.

FUNDAMENTAL CONSIDERATIONS

A-1. A *task organization* is a temporary grouping of forces designed to accomplish a particular mission (FM 3-0). *Task-organizing* is the act of designing an operating force, support staff, or logistic package of specific size and composition to meet a unique task or mission. Characteristics to examine when task-organizing the force include, but are not limited to, training, experience, equipage, sustainability, operating environment, enemy threat, and mobility. For Army forces, it includes allocating available assets to subordinate commanders and establishing their command and support relationships (FM 3-0). Command and support relationships provide the basis for unity of command in operations. The G-5 or G-3 (S-3) develops Annex A (Task Organization).

> *Note:* Army command relationships are similar but not identical to joint command authorities and relationships. Differences stem from the way Army forces task-organize internally and the need for a system of support relationships between Army forces. Another important difference is the requirement for Army commanders to handle the administrative control requirements.

A-2. Military units consist of organic components. Organic parts of a unit are those forming an essential part of the unit and are listed in its table of organization and equipment (TOE). Commanders can alter organizations' organic unit relationships to better allocate assets to subordinate commanders. They also can establish temporary command and support relationships to facilitate exercising mission command.

A-3. Establishing clear command and support relationships is fundamental to organizing any operation. These relationships establish clear responsibilities and authorities between subordinate and supporting units. Some command and support relationships (for example, tactical control) limit the commander's authority to prescribe additional relationships. Knowing the inherent responsibilities of each command and support relationship allows commanders to effectively organize their forces and helps supporting commanders to understand their unit's role in the organizational structure.

A-4. Commanders designate command and support relationships to weight the decisive operation and support the concept of operations. Task organization also helps subordinate and supporting commanders support the commander's intent. These relationships carry with them varying responsibilities to the subordinate unit by the parent and gaining units as discussed in paragraphs A-12 and A-13. Commanders consider two organizational principles when task-organizing forces:

- Maintain cohesive mission teams.
- Do not exceed subordinates' span of control capabilities.

A-5. When possible, commanders maintain cohesive mission teams. They organize forces based on standing headquarters, their assigned forces, and habitual associations when possible. When not feasible and ad hoc organizations are created, commanders arrange time for training and establishing functional working relationships and procedures. Once commanders have organized and committed a force, they keep its task organization unless the benefits of a change clearly outweigh the disadvantages. Reorganizations may result in a loss of time, effort, and tempo. Sustainment considerations may also preclude quick reorganization.

A-6. Commanders carefully avoid exceeding the span of control capabilities of subordinates. Span of control refers to the number of subordinate units under a single commander. This number is situation dependent and may vary. As a rule, commanders can effectively command two to six subordinate units. Allocating subordinate commanders more units gives them greater flexibility and increases options and combinations. However, increasing the number of subordinate units increases the number of decisions for commanders to make in a timely fashion. This slows down the reaction time among decisionmakers.

A-7. Running estimates and course of action (COA) analysis of the military decisionmaking process provide information that helps commanders determine the best task organization. An effective task organization—

- Facilitates the commander's intent and concept of operations.
- Retains flexibility within the concept of operations.
- Adapts to conditions imposed by mission variables.
- Accounts for the requirements to conduct essential stability tasks for populations within an area of operations.
- Creates effective combined arms teams.
- Provides mutual support among units.
- Ensures flexibility to meet unforeseen events and to support future operations.
- Allocates resources with minimum restrictions on their employment.
- Promotes unity of command.
- Offsets limitations and maximizes the potential of all forces available.
- Exploits enemy vulnerabilities.

A-8. Creating an appropriate task organization requires understanding—

- The mission, including the higher commander's intent and concept of operations.
- The fundamentals of full spectrum operations (see FM 3-0), basic tactical concepts (see FM 3-90), and the fundamentals of stability (see FM 3-07).
- The roles and relationships among the warfighting functions.
- The status of available forces, including morale, training, and equipment capabilities.
- Specific unit capabilities, limitations, strengths, and weaknesses.
- The risks inherent in the plan.

A-9. During COA analysis, commanders identify what resources they need, and where, when, and how frequently they will need them. Formal task organization and the change from generic to specific units begin after COA analysis when commanders assign tasks to subordinate commanders. Staffs assign tasks to subordinate headquarters and determine if subordinate headquarters have enough combat power, reallocating combat power as necessary. They then refine command and support relationships for subordinate units and decide the priorities of support. Commanders approve or modify the staff's recommended task organization based on their evaluation of the factors listed in paragraphs A-7 and A-8 and information from running estimates and COA analysis as part of the military decisionmaking process.

A-10. In allocating assets, the commander and staff consider—

- The task organization for the ongoing operation.
- Potentially adverse effects of breaking up cohesive teams by changing the task organization.
- Time necessary to realign the organization after receipt of the task organization.
- Limits on control over supporting units provided by higher headquarters.

ARMY COMMAND AND SUPPORT RELATIONSHIPS

A-11. Army commanders build combined arms organizations using command and support relationships. Command relationships define command responsibility and authority. Support relationships define the purpose, scope, and effect desired when one capability supports another.

ARMY COMMAND RELATIONSHIPS

A-12. Table A-1 lists the Army command relationships. Command relationships define superior and subordinate relationships between unit commanders. By specifying a chain of command, command relationships unify effort and enable commanders to use subordinate forces with maximum flexibility. Army command relationships identify the degree of control of the gaining Army commander. The type of command relationship often relates to the expected longevity of the relationship between the headquarters involved and quickly identifies the degree of support that the gaining and losing Army commanders provide.

Table A-1. Army command relationships

If relation-ship is:	Then inherent responsibilities:							
	Have command relation-ship with:	May be task-organized by:[1]	Unless modified, ADCON have responsi-bility through:	Are assigned position or AO by:	Provide liaison to:	Establish/ maintain communi-cations with:	Have priorities establish-ed by:	Can impose on gaining unit further command or support relationship of:
Organic	All organic forces organized with the HQ	Organic HQ	Army HQ specified in organizing document	Organic HQ	N/A	N/A	Organic HQ	Attached; OPCON; TACON; GS; GSR; R; DS
Assigned	Combatant command	Gaining HQ	Gaining Army HQ	OPCON chain of command	As required by OPCON	As required by OPCON	ASCC or Service-assigned HQ	As required by OPCON HQ
Attached	Gaining unit	Gaining unit	Gaining Army HQ	Gaining unit	As required by gaining unit	Unit to which attached	Gaining unit	Attached; OPCON; TACON; GS; GSR; R; DS
OPCON	Gaining unit	Parent unit and gaining unit; gaining unit may pass OPCON to lower HQ[1]	Parent unit	Gaining unit	As required by gaining unit	As required by gaining unit and parent unit	Gaining unit	OPCON; TACON; GS; GSR; R; DS
TACON	Gaining unit	Parent unit	Parent unit	Gaining unit	As required by gaining unit	As required by gaining unit and parent unit	Gaining unit	TACON;GS GSR; R; DS
Note: [1] In NATO, the gaining unit may not task-organize a multinational force. (See TACON.)								
ADCON administrative control AO area of operations ASCC Army Service component command DS direct support GS general support GSR general support–reinforcing				HQ headquarters N/A not applicable NATO North Atlantic Treaty Organization OPCON operational control R reinforcing TACON tactical control				

ARMY SUPPORT RELATIONSHIPS

A-13. Table A-2, page A-4, lists Army support relationships. Army support relationships are not a command authority and are more specific than the joint support relationships. Commanders establish support relationships when subordination of one unit to another is inappropriate. Commanders assign a support relationship when—

- The support is more effective if a commander with the requisite technical and tactical expertise controls the supporting unit rather than the supported commander.
- The echelon of the supporting unit is the same as or higher than that of the supported unit. For example, the supporting unit may be a brigade, and the supported unit may be a battalion. It would be inappropriate for the brigade to be subordinated to the battalion; hence, the echelon uses an Army support relationship.
- The supporting unit supports several units simultaneously. The requirement to set support priorities to allocate resources to supported units exists. Assigning support relationships is one aspect of mission command.

Table A-2. Army support relationships

If relation-ship is:	Then inherent responsibilities:							
	Have command relation-ship with:	May be task-organized by:	Receive sustain-ment from:	Are assigned position or an area of operations by:	Provide liaison to:	Establish/maintain communi-cations with:	Have priorities established by:	Can impose on gaining unit further command or support relation-ship by:
Direct support[1]	Parent unit	Parent unit	Parent unit	Supported unit	Supported unit	Parent unit; supported unit	Supported unit	See note[1]
Reinforc-ing	Parent unit	Parent unit	Parent unit	Reinforced unit	Reinforced unit	Parent unit; reinforced unit	Reinforced unit; then parent unit	Not applicable
General support–reinforc-ing	Parent unit	Parent unit	Parent unit	Parent unit	Reinforced unit and as required by parent unit	Reinforced unit and as required by parent unit	Parent unit; then reinforced unit	Not applicable
General support	Parent unit	Parent unit	Parent unit	Parent unit	As required by parent unit	As required by parent unit	Parent unit	Not applicable

Note: [1] Commanders of units in direct support may further assign support relationships between their subordinate units and elements of the supported unit after coordination with the supported commander.

A-14. Army support relationships allow supporting commanders to employ their units' capabilities to achieve results required by supported commanders. Support relationships are graduated from an exclusive supported and supporting relationship between two units—as in direct support—to a broad level of support extended to all units under the control of the higher headquarters—as in general support. Support relationships do not alter administrative control. Commanders specify and change support relationships through task organization.

FORMAT AND INSTRUCTIONS

A-15. Annex A does not follow the standard five-paragraph attachment format as described in Chapter 12. Task organization is typically displayed in an outline format following the unit listing convention in Table A-3.

Table A-3. Army unit listing convention

	Corps	Division	Brigade	Battalion	Company
Movement and Maneuver	Divisions Separate maneuver brigades or battalions Combat aviation brigades or battalions Special operations forces • Ranger • Special forces	Brigade-size ground units in alpha-numerical order • Infantry • Heavy • Stryker Battalion TF • Named TFs in alphabetical order • Numbered TFs in numerical order Combat aviation brigade Special operations forces	Battalion TFs Battalions or squadrons • Combined arms • Infantry • Reconnaissance Company teams Companies Air cavalry squadrons	Company teams • Named teams in alphabetical order • Letter designated teams in alphabetical order Companies or troops (in alphabetical order) • Rifle • Mechanized infantry • Armor	Organic platoons Attached platoons Weapons squads
Fires	Fires brigade USAF air support unit	Fires brigade USAF air support unit	Fires battalion USAF air support unit	FA batteries Fire support team Mortar platoon USAF air support unit	FA firing platoons Fire support team Mortar section
Intelligence	Battlefield surveillance brigade • MI • R&S squad • Human terrain team	Battlefield surveillance brigade • MI • R&S squad • Human terrain team	CI teams Ground sensor teams Human terrain team HUMINT teams Scout platoon TUAS platoon	CI teams Ground sensor teams HUMINT teams Scout platoon TUAS platoon	CI teams Ground sensor teams HUMINT teams
Protect	MEB Functional brigades • Air defense • CBRN • Engineer • EOD • Military police	MEB Functional brigades • Air defense • CBRN • Engineer • EOD • Military police	Functional battalions or companies or batteries and detachments • Air defense • CBRN • Engineer • EOD • Military police	Functional companies or batteries and detachments • Air defense • CBRN • Engineer • EOD • Military police	Functional platoons and detachments • Air defense • CBRN • Engineer • EOD • Military police

Table A-3. Army unit listing convention (continued)

	Corps	Division	Brigade	Battalion	Company
Sustainment	Sustainment brigade (attached functional units are listed in alpha-numerical order) • Contracting • Finance • Ordnance • Personnel services • Transportation • Quartermaster Medical brigade	Sustainment brigade (attached functional units are listed in alpha-numerical order) • Contracting • Finance • Ordnance • Personnel services • Transportation • Quartermaster Medical brigade	Brigade support battalion (attached or supporting functional units are listed first by branch in alphabetical order and then in numerical order)	Forward support company (attached or supporting functional units are listed first by branch in alphabetical order and then in numerical order)	Attached or supporting functional platoons and teams listed in alpha-numerical order
Mission Command	Signal Public affairs Civil affairs PRT MISO Space OGA, such as an FBI forensics team (listed in alphabetical order with reference to any applicable nonstandard command and support relationship)	Signal Public affairs Civil affairs PRT MISO Space OGA (listed in alphabetical order with reference to any applicable nonstandard command and support relationship)	Signal Public affairs Civil affairs PRT MISO OGA (listed in alphabetical order with reference to any applicable nonstandard command and support relationship)	Signal Public affairs Civil affairs PRT MISO OGA (listed in alphabetical order with reference to any applicable nonstandard command and support relationship)	

CBRN	chemical, biological, radiological, and nuclear	MISO	military information support operations
CI	counterintelligence	OGA	other governmental agencies
EOD	explosive ordnance disposal	PRT	provincial reconstruction team
FA	field artillery	R&S	reconnaissance and surveillance
HUMINT	human intelligence	TF	task force
MEB	maneuver enhancement brigade	TUAS	tactical unmanned aerial system
MI	military intelligence	USAF	United States Air Force

A-16. Group units by headquarters. List major subordinate maneuver units first (for example, 2d HBCT; 1-77th IN; A/4-52d CAV). Place them by size in alpha-numerical order. List brigade combat teams (BCTs) ahead of combat aviation brigades. In cases where two BCTs are numbered the same, use the division number by type. For example, 1st HBCT 1st Infantry Division (Mechanized) is listed before the 1st HBCT 1st Armored Division. In turn, the 1st HBCT 1st Armored Division is listed before the 1st HBCT 1st Cavalry Division. Combined arms battalions are listed before battalions, and company teams before companies. Follow maneuver units with multifunctional supporting units in the following order—fires, battlefield surveillance, maneuver enhancement, and sustainment. Following multifunctional supporting units are supporting units in alpha-numerical order. For example, a medical brigade is listed after a functional engineer brigade but before a functional military police brigade. The last listing should be any special troops units under the command of the force headquarters.

A-17. Use a plus (+) symbol when attaching one or more subordinate elements of a similar function to a headquarters. Use a minus symbol (−) when deleting one or more subordinate elements of a similar function to a headquarters. Always show the symbols in parenthesis. Do not use a plus symbol when the receiving headquarters is a combined arms task force or company team. Do not use plus and minus symbols together (as when a headquarters detaches one element and receives attachment of another); use the symbol that portrays the element's combat power with respect to other similar elements. Do not use either symbol when two units swap subordinate elements and their combat power is unchanged. Here are some examples:

- Within the 3-68th Combined Arms Battalion; C Company loses one platoon to A Company; the battalion task organization will show A Co. (+) and C Co. (–).
- Within the 3-68th Combined Arms Battalion; C Company swaps one platoon with A Company; the battalion task organization will show Team A and Team C. (The teams can also be named for their commanders, their unit nickname, or some other naming scheme.)
- 4-77th Infantry receives a tank company from 1-30th Armor; the BCT task organization will show TF 4-77 IN (+) and 1-30 AR (–).

Division and corps headquarters are always task organized. Therefore, do not show these headquarters with either the plus (+) or minus (–) symbol.

A-18. If applicable, list task organizations according to phases of the operation. When the effective attachment time of a nonorganic unit to another unit differs from the effective time of the plan or order, add the effective attachment time in parentheses after the attached unit—for example, 1-80 IN (OPCON 2 HBCT Phase II). List this information either in the task organization (preferred) or in paragraph 1c of the plan or order, but not both. For clarity, list subsequent command or support relationships under the task organization in parentheses following the affected unit—for example, "...on order, OPCON to 2 HBCT" is written (O/O OPCON 2 HBCT).

A-19. Long or complex task organizations are displayed in outline format in Annex A (Task Organization) of the operation plan or order in lieu of being placed in the base plan or order. Units are listed under the headquarters to which they are allocated or that they support in accordance with the organizational taxonomy previously provided in this chapter. The complete unit task organization for each major subordinate unit should be shown on the same page. Only show command or support relationship if it is other than organic or attached. Other Services and multinational forces recognize and understand this format. Planners should use it during joint and multinational operations.

A-20. List subordinate units under the higher headquarters to which they are assigned, attached, or in support. Place direct support (DS) units below the units they support. Indent subordinate and supporting units two spaces. Identify relationships other than attached with parenthetical terms—for example, (GS) or (DS).

A-21. Provide the numerical designations of units as Arabic numerals, except if shown as Roman numerals. An Army Corps is numbered in series beginning with Roman numeral "I"—for example, I Corps or XVIII Airborne Corps.

A-22. During multinational operations, insert the country code between the numeric designation and the unit name—for example, 3d (GE) Corps. (FM 1-02 contains authorized country codes.)

A-23. Use abbreviated designations for organic units. Use the full designation for nonorganic units—for example, 1-52 FA (MLRS) (GS), rather than 1-52 FA. Specify a unit's command or support relationship only if it differs from that of its higher headquarters.

A-24. Designate task forces with the last name of the task force commander (for example, TF WILLIAMS), a code name (for example, TF WARRIOR), or a number (for example, TF 47 or TF 1-77 IN).

A-25. For unit designation at theater army level, list major subordinate maneuver units first, placing them in alpha-numerical order, followed by multifunctional brigades in the following order: fires, intelligence, maneuver enhancement, sustainment, then followed by functional brigades in alpha-numerical order, and any units under the command of the force headquarters. For each function following maneuver, list headquarters in the order of commands, brigades, groups, battalions, squadrons, companies, detachments, and teams.

A-26. Figure A-1, page A-8, illustrates a sample Annex A (Task Organization) format. Figure A-2, page A-9, illustrates a sample acronym list for the task organization.

[CLASSIFICATION]

Place the classification at the top and bottom of every page of the attachments. Place the classification marking (TS), (S), (C), or (U) at the front of each paragraph and subparagraph in parentheses. Refer to AR 380-5 for classification and release marking instructions.

Copy ## of ## copies
Issuing headquarters
Place of issue
Date-time group of signature
Message reference number

Include the full heading if attachment is distributed separately from the base order or higher-level attachment.

ANNEX A (TASK ORGANIZATION) TO OPERATION PLAN/ORDER [number] [(code name)]— [issuing headquarters] [(classification of title)]

(U) References: *List documents essential to understanding Annex A (Task Organization).*

a. *List maps and charts first. Map entries include series number, country, sheet names, or numbers, edition, and scale.*

b. *List other references in subparagraphs labeled as shown.*

c. *Doctrinal references for task organization include FM 3-0, FM 5-0, JP 1, and JP 5-0.*

(U) Time Zone Used Throughout the OPLAN/OPORD: *Write the time zone established in the base plan or order.*

(U) Task Organization: *Use the outline format for listing units as show in the example below. A sample acronym list is at Figure A-2. (This is helpful if attached units are unfamiliar with Army acronyms.) If applicable, list task organization according to the phases of the operation during which it applies.*

2/52 HBCT	2/54 HBCT	116 HBCT (+)
1-77 IN (-)	4-77 IN	3-116 AR
1-30 AR (-)	2-30 AR	1-163 IN
1-20 CAV	3-20 CAV	2-116 AR
A/4-52 CAV (ARS) (DS)	2/C/4-52 CAV (ARS) (DS)	1-148 FA
2-606 FA (2x8)	2-607 FA	145 BSB
TACP/52 ASOS (USAF)	TACP/52 ASOS (USAF)	4/B/2-52 AV (GSAB) (TACON)
521 BSB	105 BSB	4/2/311 QM CO (MA)
2/2/311 QM CO (MA)	3/2/311 QM CO (MA)	4/577 MED CO (GRD AMB)
1/B/2-52 AV (GSAB) (TACON)	2/B/2-52 AV (GSAB) (TACON)	844 FST
2/577 MED CO (GRD AMB) (attached)	843 FST	116 BSTB
842 FST	3/577 MED CO (GRD AMB)	366 EN CO (SAPPER) (DS)
2 BSTB	3 BSTB	1/401 EN CO (ESC) (DS)
31 EN CO (MRBC) (DS)	A 388 CA BN	2/244 EN CO (RTE CL) (DS)
63 EOD	1/244 EN CO (RTE CL) (DS)	52 EOD
2/244 EN CO (RTE CL) (DS)	763 EOD	1/301 MP CO
1/2/1/55 SIG CO (COMCAM)	2/2/1/55 SIG CO (COMCAM)	1/3/1/55 SIG CO (COMCAM)
2D MP PLT	3D MP PLT	1/467 CM CO (MX) (S)
RTS TM 1/A/52 BSTB		C/388 CA BN
RTS TM 2/A/52 BSTB		116 MP PLT
RTS TM 3/A/52 BSTB		
RTS TM 4/A/52 BSTB		

Figure A-1. Sample task organization

```
87 IBCT                          52 CAB AASLT
1-80 IN                            HHC/52 CAB                    52 SUST BDE
2-80 IN                              1/B/1-77 IN (DIV QRF) (OPCON)  52 BTB
3-13 CAV                           1-52 AV (ARB) (-)             520 CSSB
A/3-52 AV (ASLT) (DS)              4-52 CAV (ARS) (-)            521 CSSB
B/1-52 AV (ARB) (DS)               3-52 AV (ASLT) (-)            10 CSH
C/4-52 CAV (ARS) (-) (DS)          2-52 AV (GSAB)                  168 MMB
2-636 FA                           1 (TUAS)/B/52 BSTB (-) (GS)
  A/3-52 FA (+)                    2/694 EN CO (HORIZ) (DS)      52 HHB
  TACP/52 ASOS (USAF)                                             A/1-30 AR (DIV RES)
  Q37 52 FA BDE (GS)             52 FIRES BDE                    35 SIG CO (-) (DS)
99 BSB                             HHB                           154 LTF
  845 FST                          TAB (-)                       2/1/55 SIG CO (-)
  1/577 MED CO (GRD AMB)           1-52 FA (MLRS)                14 PAD
  3/B/2-52 AV (GSAB) (TACON)       3-52 FA (-) (M109A6)          388 CA BN (-) (DS)
  1/2/311 QM CO (MA)               1/694 EN CO (HORIZ) (DS)
87 BSTB
  53 EOD                         17 MEB 52 ID
  3/2/1/55 SIG CO (COMCAM)         25 CM BN (-)
  B/420 CA BN                      700 MP BN
  2 HCT/3/B/52 BSTB                7 EN BN
  745 EN CO (MAC) (DS)             2/2/1/55 SIG CO (COMCAM)
  1/1/52 CM CO (R/D) (R)           11 ASOS (USAF)
  2/467 CM CO (MX) (S)
  1/1102 MP CO (CS) (DS)
```

Figure A-1. Sample task organization (continued)

AASLT	air assault	EOD	explosive ordnance disposal	MLRS	multiple launch rocket system
AR	armor	ESC	expeditionary sustainment command	MMB	multifunctional medical battalion
ARB	attack reconnaissance battalion	FA	field artillery	MP	military police
ARS	attack reconnaissance squadron	FST	forward surgical team	MRBC	multi-role bridge company
		GRD AMB	ground ambulance	MX	mechanized
ASLT	assault	GS	general support	OPCON	operational control
ASOS	air support operations squadron	GSAB	general support aviation battalion	PAD	public affairs detachment
AV	aviation	HBCT	heavy brigade combat team	PLT	platoon
BDE	brigade	HCT	human intelligence collection team	QM	quartermaster
BN	battalion			QRF	quick reaction force
BSB	brigade support battalion	HHB	headquarters and headquarters battalion	R	reinforcing
BSTB	brigade special troops battalion	HHC	headquarters and headquarters company	R/D	reconnaissance/ decontamination
BTB	brigade troop battalion	HORIZ	horizontal	RES	reserve
CA	civil affairs	IBCT	infantry brigade combat team	RTE CL	route clearance
CAB	combat aviation brigade			RTS	retransmission
CAV	cavalry	ID	infantry division	S	smoke
CM	chemical	IN	infantry	SIG	signal
CO	company	LTF	logistics task force	SUST	sustainment
COMCAM	combat camera	MA	mortuary affairs	TAB	target acquisition battery
CS	combat support	MAC	mobility augmentation company	TACON	tactical control
CSH	combat support hospital			TACP	tactical air control party
CSSB	combat sustainment support battalion	MEB	maneuver enhancement brigade	TM	team
DIV	division			TUAS	tactical unmanned aircraft system
DS	direct support	MED	medical	USAF	United States Air Force
EN	engineer				

Figure A-2. Sample acronym list

This page intentionally left blank.

Annex B

Intelligence Annex Format and Instructions

This annex provides fundamental considerations, formats, and instructions for developing Annex B (Intelligence) to the base plan or order.

HOW TO DEVELOP ANNEX B (INTELLIGENCE)

B-1. Commanders and staff use Annex B (Intelligence) to describe how intelligence supports the concept of operations described in the base plan or order. The G 2 (S-2) develops Annex B (Intelligence).

B-2. The purpose of Annex B (Intelligence) is to provide detailed information and intelligence on the characteristics of the operational environment and to direct intelligence and counterintelligence activities. Staffs use appendixes to provide detailed analysis of the operational environment and instructions from the various intelligence disciplines.

[CLASSIFICATION]

Place the classification at the top and bottom of every page of the attachments. Place the classification marking (TS), (S), (C), or (U) at the front of each paragraph and subparagraph in parentheses. Refer to AR 380-5 for classification and release marking instructions.

> **Copy ## of ## copies**
> **Issuing headquarters**
> **Place of issue**
> **Date-time group of signature**
> **Message reference number**

Include the full heading if attachment is distributed separately from the base order or higher-level attachment.

ANNEX B (INTELLIGENCE) TO OPERATION PLAN/ORDER [number] [(code name)]—[issuing headquarters] [(classification of title)]

(U) References: *List documents essential to understanding the attachment.*

a. *List maps and charts first. Map entries include series number, country, sheet names, or numbers, edition, and scale.*

b. *List other references in subparagraphs labeled as shown.*

c. *List FM 2-0 as the doctrinal reference for this annex.*

(U) Time Zone Used Throughout the Plan/Order: *Write the time zone established in the base plan or order.*

1. (U) <u>Situation</u>. *Include information affecting intelligence that paragraph 1 of the OPLAN or OPORD does not cover or that needs expansion.*

a. (U) <u>Area of Interest</u>. *Describe the area of interest as it relates to intelligence.*

b. (U) <u>Area of Operations</u>. *Refer to Appendix 2 (Operation Overlay) to Annex C (Operations) as required.*

[page number]
[CLASSIFICATION]

[CLASSIFICATION]

ANNEX B (INTELLIGENCE) TO OPERATION PLAN/ORDER [number] [(code name)]—[issuing headquarters] [(classification of title)]

(1) (U) <u>Terrain</u>. *Describe the aspects of terrain that impact intelligence operations. Refer to Tab A (Terrain) to Appendix 1 (Intelligence Estimate) to Annex B (Intelligence) as required.*

(2) (U) <u>Weather</u>. *Describe the aspects of weather that impact intelligence operations. Refer to Tab B (Weather) to Appendix 1 (Intelligence Estimate) to Annex B (Intelligence) as required.*

c. (U) <u>Enemy Forces</u>. *List known and templated locations and activities of enemy intelligence units for one echelon up and two echelons down. List enemy maneuver and other area capabilities that will impact friendly intelligence operations. State expected enemy courses of action and employment of enemy intelligence assets.*

d. (U) <u>Friendly Forces</u>. *Outline the higher headquarters' intelligence plan. List designation, location, and outline the plan of higher, adjacent, and other intelligence organizations and assets that support or impact the issuing headquarters or require coordination and additional support.*

e. (U) <u>Interagency, Intergovernmental, and Nongovernmental Organizations</u>. *Identify and describe other organizations in the area of operations that may impact the conduct of intelligence operations or implementation of intelligence-specific equipment and tactics. Refer to Annex V (Interagency Coordination) as required.*

f. (U) <u>Civil Considerations</u>. *Describe the aspects of the civil situation that impact intelligence operations. Refer to Tab C (Civil Considerations) to Appendix 1 (Intelligence Estimate) to Annex B (Intelligence) and Annex K (Civil Affairs Operations) as required.*

g. (U) <u>Attachments and Detachments</u>. *List units attached or detached only as necessary to clarify task organization. Refer to Annex A (Task Organization) as required.*

h. (U) <u>Assumptions</u>. *List any intelligence-specific assumptions that support the annex development.*

2. (U) <u>Mission</u>. *State the mission of intelligence in support of the base plan or order.*

3. (U) <u>Execution</u>.

a. (U) <u>Scheme of Intelligence Support</u>. *Outline the purpose of intelligence operations and summarize the means and agencies used in planning, directing, collecting, processing, exploiting, producing, disseminating, and evaluating intelligence in support of the concept of operations. When available and appropriate, integrate the resources of other Services and allied nations. Refer to the base plan or order and Annex C (Operations) as required.*

b. (U) <u>Tasks to Subordinate Units</u>. *List intelligence tasks assigned to specific subordinate units not contained in the base plan or order. Use subparagraphs to list detailed instructions for each unit performing intelligence functions.*

c. (U) <u>Counterintelligence</u>. *Refer to Appendix 2 (Counterintelligence) to Annex B (Intelligence).*

d. (U) <u>Coordinating Instructions.</u> *List only instructions applicable to two or more subordinate units not covered in the base plan or order.*

(1) (U) <u>Requirements</u>. *Provide guidance for determining intelligence requirements (including those of subordinate commanders), issuing orders, and issuing requests to information collection agencies.*

(a) (U) <u>Priority Intelligence Requirements</u>. *List the priority intelligence requirements (PIRs) along with the latest time intelligence of value for each PIR.*

(b) (U) <u>Friendly Force Information Requirements</u>. *List the friendly force information requirements.*

[page number]
[CLASSIFICATION]

[CLASSIFICATION]

ANNEX B (INTELLIGENCE) TO OPERATION PLAN/ORDER [number] [(code name)]—[issuing headquarters] [(classification of title)]

(c) (U) <u>Requests for Information</u>. *Provide separate, numbered subparagraphs applicable to each unit not organic or attached and from which intelligence support is requested, including multinational forces.*

(2) (U) <u>Measures for Handling Personnel, Documents, and Material</u>. *Describe in the following subparagraphs procedures for handling captured or detained personnel, captured documents, and materiel.*

(a) (U) <u>Prisoners of War, Deserters, Repatriates, Inhabitants, and Other Persons</u>. *State special handling, segregation instructions, and locations of the command's and next higher headquarters' enemy prisoners of war collection points.*

(b) (U) <u>Captured Documents</u>. *List instructions for handling and processing captured documents from time of capture to receipt by specified intelligence personnel.*

(c) (U) <u>Captured Materiel</u>. *Designate items or categories of enemy materiel required for examination. Include any specific instructions for processing and disposition. Give locations of the command's and next higher headquarters' captured materiel collection points.*

(d) (U) <u>Documents or Equipment Required</u>. *List in each category the conditions under which units can obtain or request certain documents or equipment. Items may include aerial photographs and maps, charts, and geodesy (satellite) products.*

(3) (U) <u>Distribution of Intelligence Products</u>. *Identify and list in the following subparagraphs any special request procedures for intelligence products in support of this operation. List in each category the conditions under which units can obtain or request certain documents or equipment.*

(a) (U) <u>Special Request for Reports</u>. *Identify, list, or describe the following: periods that routine reports and distribution address; updates to the threat and environment portions of the common operational picture; formats and methods for push and pull intelligence support; and distribution of special intelligence studies, such as defense overprints, photo intelligence reports, and order of battle overlays.*

(b) (U) <u>Special Request Liaison Requirements</u>. *Identify, list, or describe the following liaison requirements; periodic or special intelligence meetings and conferences; and special intelligence liaison, when indicated.*

(4) (U) <u>Other Instructions</u>. *Identify, list, or describe any other instructions not covered in the above paragraphs.*

4. (U) <u>Sustainment</u>. *Identify and list sustainment priorities for intelligence key tasks and specify additional sustainment instructions as necessary, to include contractor support. Refer to Annex F (Sustainment) as required.*

a. (U) <u>Logistics</u>. *Identify unique sustainment requirements, procedures, and guidance to support intelligence teams and operations. Specify procedures for specialized technical logistics support from external organizations as necessary. Use subparagraphs to identify priorities and specific instructions for maintenance, transportation, supply, field services, distribution, contracting, and general engineering support. Refer to Annex F (Sustainment) and Annex P (Host-Nation Support) as required.*

b. (U) <u>Personnel</u>. *Identify intelligence unique personnel requirements and concerns, including global sourcing support and contracted linguist requirements. Use subparagraphs to identify priorities and specific instructions for human resources support, financial management, legal support, and religious support. Refer to Annex F (Sustainment) as required.*

c. (U) <u>Army Health System Support</u>. *Identify availability, priorities, and instructions for medical care. Refer to Annex F (Sustainment) as required.*

[page number]
[CLASSIFICATION]

[CLASSIFICATION]

ANNEX B (INTELLIGENCE) TO OPERATION PLAN/ORDER [number] [(code name)]—[issuing headquarters] [(classification of title)]

5. (U) Command and Signal.

    a. (U) Command.

        (1) (U) Location of Commander. *State the location of key intelligence leaders.*

        (2) (U) Succession of Command. *State the succession of command if not covered in the unit's SOPs.*

        (3) (U) Liaison Requirements. *State the intelligence liaison requirements not covered in the base order or unit standard operating procedures (SOPs).*

    b. (U) Control.

        (1) (U) Command Posts. *Describe the employment of intelligence-specific command posts (CPs), including the location of each CP and its time of opening and closing.*

        (2) (U) Intelligence Coordination Line. *Identify the intelligence coordination line.*

        (3) (U) Special Security. *Identify special security office arrangements and coordination.*

        (4) (U) Reports. *List intelligence-specific reports not covered in SOPs. Refer to Annex R (Reports) as required.*

    c. (U) Signal. *Address any intelligence-specific communications requirements. Refer to Annex H (Signal) as required.*

ACKNOWLEDGE: *Include only if attachment is distributed separately from the base order.*

[Commander's last name]
[Commander's rank]

The commander or authorized representative signs the original copy of the attachment. If the representative signs the original, add the phrase "For the Commander." The signed copy is the historical copy and remains in the headquarters' files.

OFFICIAL:

[Authenticator's name]
[Authenticator's position]

Use only if the commander does not sign the original attachment. If the commander signs the original, no further authentication is required. If the commander does not sign, the signature of the preparing staff officer requires authentication and only the last name and rank of the commander appear in the signature block.

ATTACHMENTS: *List lower-level attachment (appendixes, tabs, and exhibits).*

Appendix 1 – Intelligence Estimate
Appendix 2 – Counterintelligence
Appendix 3 – Signals Intelligence
Appendix 4 – Human Intelligence
Appendix 5 – Geospatial Intelligence
Appendix 6 – Measurement and Signature Intelligence
Appendix 7 – Open Source Intelligence

DISTRIBUTION: *Show only if distributed separately from the base order or higher-level attachments.*

[page number]
[CLASSIFICATION]

Operations Annex Format and Instructions

This annex provides fundamental considerations, formats, and instructions for developing Annex C (Operations) to the base plan or order.

HOW TO DEVELOP ANNEX C (OPERATIONS)

C-1. Commanders and staff use Annex C (Operations) to describe and outline how this annex supports the concept of operations described in the base plan or order. The G-5 or G-3 (S-3) develops Annex C (Operations).

C-2. This annex describes the operations objectives. A complex operations concept of support may require a schematic to show the operations objectives and task relationships. It includes a discussion of the overall operations concept of support with specific details in element subparagraphs and attachments. It refers to the execution matrix to clarify timing relationships among various operations tasks. This annex also contains the information needed to synchronize timing relationships of each element related to operations. It includes operations-related constraints, if appropriate.

[CLASSIFICATION]

Place the classification at the top and bottom of every page of the attachments. Place the classification marking (TS), (S), (C), or (U) at the front of each paragraph and subparagraph in parentheses. Refer to AR 380-5 for classification and release marking instructions.

Copy ## of ## copies
Issuing headquarters
Place of issue
Date-time group of signature
Message reference number

Include the full heading if attachment is distributed separately from the base order or higher-level attachment.

ANNEX C (OPERATIONS) TO [OPERATION PLAN/ORDER [number] [(code name)]—[(classification of title)]

(U) References: *List documents essential to understanding the attachment.*

a. *List maps and charts first. Map entries include series number, country, sheet names, or numbers, edition, and scale.*

b. *List other references in subparagraphs labeled as shown.*

c. *Doctrinal references for this annex are FM 3-0, FM 5-0, and FM 6-0.*

(U) Time Zone Used Throughout the Order: *Write the time zone established in the base plan or order.*

1. (U) <u>Situation</u>. *Include information affecting operations that paragraph 1 of the OPLAN or OPORD does not cover or that needs expansion. If there is no new information from what is contained in the base order then indicate this by stating "See base order."*

a. (U) <u>Area of Interest</u>. *Describe the area of interest as it relates to operations. Reference the digital overlay(s) within systems such as command post of the future. Refer to Annex B (Intelligence) as required.*

[page number]
[CLASSIFICATION]

[CLASSIFICATION]

ANNEX C (OPERATIONS) TO [OPERATION PLAN/ORDER [number] [(code name)]— [(classification of title)]

 b. (U) <u>Area of Operations</u>. *Refer to Appendix 2 (Operation Overlay) to Annex C (Operations).*

  (1) (U) <u>Terrain</u>. *Describe the aspects of terrain that impact operations. Refer to Annex B (Intelligence) as required.*

  (2) (U) <u>Weather</u>. *Describe the aspects of weather that impact operations. Refer to Annex B (Intelligence) as required.*

 c. (U) <u>Enemy Forces</u>. *Identify and reference enemy overlays within digital command and control systems, such as command post of the future. First, list known and templated locations and activities of enemy units for two echelons down if not using digital command and control systems. For example, a U.S. division would address enemy battalions; a U.S. battalion would address enemy platoons. Second, list enemy maneuver and other capabilities that will impact friendly operations. Thirdly, state the enemy most likely and most dangerous courses of action and employment of enemy assets. A staff more easily understands these enemy courses of action when they are depicted in sketches. Fourth, include an assessment of terrorist or criminal activities directed against U.S. government interests in the area of operations. If conducting operations focused on stability or civil support, change the title of this subparagraph to "Terrorist/Criminal Threats." Refer to Annex B (Intelligence) and other sources as required.*

 d. (U) <u>Friendly Forces</u>. *Subparagraphs outline the mission, commander's intent, and concept of operations for headquarters one and two command echelons above. Subparagraphs also provide the missions and concept of operations of flank units, supported units, supporting units, and other units and organizations, such as special operations forces, whose actions have a significant effect on the issuing headquarters or require coordination. This subparagraph uses the same format as the base order and can be shortened by using the phrase "See Base Order" if there is no change.*

 e. (U) <u>Interagency, Intergovernmental, and Nongovernmental Organizations</u>. *Identify and describe other organizations in the area of operations that may impact the conduct of the unit's operations or require support not identified in the base order. Also identify nongovernmental organizations in the area of operations that want nothing to do with the U.S. military not identified in the base order. Refer to Annex V (Interagency Coordination) as required.*

 f. (U) <u>Civil Considerations</u>. *List all critical civil considerations that impact on the unit's operations, such as cultural or religious sensitivities to male Soldiers searching female civilians, searching civilian homes at night, or resolving injury or damage claims not established in base order. Refer to Annex B (Intelligence) and Annex K (Civil Affairs Operations) as required.*

 g. (U) <u>Attachments and Detachments</u>. *List units attached or detached only as necessary to clarify task organization. Do not repeat information already listed under Task Organization in the base order or in Annex A (Task Organization). Try to put all information in the task organization annex and state "See Annex A (Task Organization)." Otherwise, list units that are attached or detached to the issuing headquarters. State when attachment or detachment is effective, if different from the effective time of the operation plan or order, such as on-order, or commitment of reserve forces. Use the term "remains attached" when units will be or have been attached for some time. Refer to Annex A (Task Organization) as required.*

 h. (U) <u>Assumptions</u>. *List any operations-specific assumptions that support the annex development.*

2. (U) <u>Mission</u>. *Enter the unit's restated mission only if this annex is distributed separately from the base order. It should contain a short description of the who, what (task), when, where, and why (purpose) that clearly indicates the action to be taken and the reason for doing so. A mission statement contains no subparagraphs. The mission statement covers on-order missions, otherwise state "See base order."*

[page number]
[CLASSIFICATION]

[CLASSIFICATION]

ANNEX C (OPERATIONS) TO [OPERATION PLAN/ORDER [number] [(code name)]—[(classification of title)]

3. (U) <u>Execution.</u> *Describe how the commander intends to accomplish the mission in terms of the commander's intent, an overarching concept of operations, scheme of employing maneuver, assessment, specified tasks to subordinate units, and key coordinating instructions in the subparagraphs below only if this annex is distributed separately from the base order.*

Commanders ensure that their scheme of maneuver is consistent with their intent and that of the next two higher commanders. This paragraph and the operation overlay are complementary, each adding clarity to, rather than duplicating, the other. Do not duplicate information in unit subparagraphs and coordinating instructions contained in the base order. Provide the primary tasks of maneuver units conducting the decisive operation and the purpose of each. Next, state the primary tasks of maneuver units conducting shaping operations, including security operations, and the purpose of each. For offensive-focused operations, identify the form of maneuver. For defensive-focused operations, identify the type of defense. For stability-focused operations, describe the role of maneuver units by primary stability tasks. For civil support-focused operations, describe the role of maneuver units by primary civil support tasks. If the operation is phased, identify the main effort by phase. Identify and include priorities for the reserves. Refer to attached appendixes as required.

    a. (U) <u>Scheme of Movement and Maneuver.</u> *State the scheme of movement and maneuver by describing the employment of maneuver units, such as divisions, brigade combat teams, and combat aviation brigades in accordance with the concept of operations. Be sure this paragraph is consistent with the operation overlay (Appendix 2 [Operation Overlay]) to Annex C [Operations]). Describe how the actions of subordinate maneuver units fit together to accomplish the mission. The scheme of maneuver expands the commander's selected course of action and expresses how each maneuver element of the force will cooperate. As the commander's intent focuses on the end state, the scheme of maneuver focuses on the maneuver tactics and techniques employed during the operation as well as synchronizes the actions of each maneuver element.*

        (1) (U) <u>Scheme of Mobility/Countermobility.</u> *State the scheme of mobility/countermobility including priorities by unit or area. Refer to Annex G (Engineer) as required.*

        (2) (U) <u>Scheme of Battlefield Obscuration.</u> *State the scheme of battlefield obscuration, including priorities by unit or area. Refer to Appendix 9 (Battlefield Obscuration) to Annex C (Operations) as required.*

        (3) (U) <u>Scheme of Reconnaissance and Surveillance.</u> *Describe how the commander intends to use reconnaissance and surveillance to support the concept of operations. Include the primary reconnaissance objectives. Refer to Annex L (Reconnaissance and Surveillance) as required.*

    b. (U) <u>Assessment.</u> *Describe the priorities for assessment and identify the measures of performance and effectiveness used to assess end state conditions and objectives. Refer to Annex M (Assessment) as required.*

    c. (U) <u>Tasks to Subordinate Units.</u> *List movement and maneuver tasks assigned to specific subordinate units not contained in the base order. Each task must include who (the subordinate unit assigned the task), what (the task itself), when, where, and why (purpose). Use a separate subparagraph for each unit. List units in sequence of task organization. Place tasks that affect two or more units in paragraph 3d (Coordinating Instructions).*

    d. (U) <u>Coordinating Instructions.</u> *List only instructions applicable to two or more subordinate units not covered in the base plan or order.*

[page number]
[CLASSIFICATION]

[CLASSIFICATION]

ANNEX C (OPERATIONS) TO [OPERATION PLAN/ORDER [number] [(code name)]—[(classification of title)]

4. (U) <u>Sustainment</u>. *Describe priorities of sustainment by unit or area. Highlight subordinate allocations of command-regulated classes of supply that impact movement and maneuver, such as controlled supply rates. Include instructions for deployment or redeployment. Identify priorities of sustainment for operations key tasks and specify additional instructions as required. Refer to Annex F (Sustainment) as required.*

a. (U) <u>Logistics</u>. *Use subparagraphs to identify priorities and specific instructions for maintenance, transportation, supply, field services, distribution, contracting, and general engineering support. Refer to Annex F (Sustainment) and Annex P (Host-Nation Support) as required.*

b. (U) <u>Personnel</u>. *Use subparagraphs to identify priorities and specific instructions for human resources support, financial management, legal support, and religious support. Refer to Annex F (Sustainment) as required.*

c. (U) <u>Army Health System Support</u>. *Identify availability, priorities, and instructions for medical care. Refer to Annex F (Sustainment) as required.*

5. (U) <u>Command and Signal</u>. *List information in this paragraph and its subparagraphs only if annex distributed separately from base order, otherwise state "Same as base order."*

a. (U) <u>Command</u>.

(1) (U) <u>Location of Commander</u>. *State the location of key leaders.*

(2) (U) <u>Succession of Command</u>. *State the succession of command if not covered in the unit's SOPs.*

(3) (U) <u>Liaison Requirements</u>. *State the liaison requirements not covered in the base order.*

b. (U) <u>Control</u>.

(1) (U) <u>Command Posts</u>. *Describe the employment of command posts (CPs), including the location of each CP and its time of opening and closing.*

(2) (U) <u>Reports</u>. *List reports not covered in standard operating procedures (SOPs). Refer to Annex R (Reports) as required.*

c. (U) <u>Signal</u>. *Address any communications requirements. Refer to Annex H (Signal) as required.*

ACKNOWLEDGE: *Include only if attachment is distributed separately from the base order.*

[Commander's last name]
[Commander's rank]

The commander or authorized representative signs the original copy of the attachment. If the representative signs the original, add the phrase "For the Commander." The signed copy is the historical copy and remains in the headquarters' files.

OFFICIAL:

[Authenticator's name]
[Authenticator's position]

Use only if the commander does not sign the original attachment. If the commander signs the original, no further authentication is required. If the commander does not sign, the signature of the preparing staff officer requires authentication and only the last name and rank of the commander appear in the signature block.

[page number]
[CLASSIFICATION]

[CLASSIFICATION]

ANNEX C (OPERATIONS) TO [OPERATION PLAN/ORDER [number] [(code name)]— [(classification of title)]

ATTACHMENT: *List lower-level attachment (appendixes, tabs, and exhibits).*

Appendix 1   – Design Concept
Appendix 2   – Operation Overlay
Appendix 3   – Decision Support Products
Appendix 4   – Gap Crossing Operations
Appendix 5   – Air Assault Operations
Appendix 6   – Airborne Operations
Appendix 7   – Amphibious Operations
Appendix 8   – Special Operations
Appendix 9   – Battlefield Obscuration
Appendix 10 – Airspace Command and Control
Appendix 11 – Rules of Engagement
Appendix 12 – Law and Order Operations
Appendix 13 – Internment and Resettlement Operations

DISTRIBUTION: *Show only if distributed separately from the base order or higher-level attachments.*

[page number]
[CLASSIFICATION]

This page intentionally left blank.

Annex D

Fires Annex Format and Instructions

This annex provides fundamental considerations, format, and instructions for developing Annex D (Fires) to the base plan or order.

HOW TO DEVELOP ANNEX D (FIRES)

D-1. Commanders and staff use Annex D (Fires) to describe how fires supports the concept of operations described in the base plan or order. The chief of fires (fire support officer) develops Annex D (Fires).

D-2. This annex describes the fires concept of support objectives. A complex fires concept of support may require a schematic to show the fires objectives and task relationships. It includes a discussion of the overall fires concept of support with the specific details in element subparagraphs and attachments. It refers to the execution matrix to clarify timing relationships among various fires tasks. This annex also contains the information needed to synchronize timing relationships of each element related to fires. It includes fires-related constraints, if appropriate.

[CLASSIFICATION]

Place the classification at the top and bottom of every page of the attachments. Place the classification marking (TS), (S), (C), or (U) at the front of each paragraph and subparagraph in parentheses. Refer to AR 380-5 for classification and release marking instructions.

Copy ## of ## copies
Issuing headquarters
Place of issue
Date-time group of signature
Message reference number

Include the full heading if attachment is distributed separately from the base order or higher-level attachment.

ANNEX D (FIRES) TO OPERATION PLAN/ORDER [number] [(code name)]—[issuing headquarters] [(classification of title)]

 (U) References: *List documents essential to understanding the attachment.*

a. *List maps and charts first. Map entries include series number, country, sheet names, or numbers, edition, and scale.*

b. *List other references in subparagraphs labeled as shown.*

c. *Doctrinal references for this annex include the FM 3-09 series, FM 3-36, FM 3-60, FM 6-20-40, and FM 6-20-50.*

(U) Time Zone Used Throughout the Plan/Order: *Write the time zone established in the base plan or order.*

1. (U) Situation. *Include information affecting fires that paragraph 1 of the OPLAN or OPORD does not cover or that needs expansion.*

a. (U) Area of Interest. *Describe the area of interest as it relates to fires. Refer to Annex B (Intelligence) as required.*

b. (U) Area of Operations. *Refer to Annex C (Operations) as required.*

[page number]
[CLASSIFICATION]

[CLASSIFICATION]

ANNEX D (FIRES) TO OPERATION PLAN/ORDER [number] [(code name)]—[issuing headquarters] [(classification of title)]

(1) (U) <u>Terrain</u>. *Describe the aspects of terrain that impact fires. Refer to Annex B (Intelligence) as required.*

(2) (U) <u>Weather</u>. *Describe the aspects of weather that impact fires. Refer to Annex B (Intelligence) as required.*

c. (U) <u>Enemy Forces</u>. *List known and templated locations and activities of enemy fires units for one echelon up and two echelons down. List enemy maneuver, indirect fire/counterfire, air, and electronic warfare threats and other capabilities that will impact friendly fires operations. State expected enemy courses of action and employment of enemy fires assets. Refer to Annex B (Intelligence) as required.*

d. (U) <u>Friendly Forces</u>. *Outline the higher headquarters' fires plan. List designation, location, and outline the plan of higher, adjacent, and other fires organizations and assets that support or impact the issuing headquarters or require coordination and additional support.*

e. (U) <u>Interagency, Intergovernmental, and Nongovernmental Organizations</u>. *Identify and describe other organizations in the area of operations that may impact the conduct of fires or implementation of fires-specific equipment and tactics. Refer to Annex V (Interagency Coordination) as required.*

f. (U) <u>Civil Considerations</u>. *Describe the aspects of the civil situation that impact fires. Refer to Annex B (Intelligence) and Annex K (Civil Affairs Operations) as required.*

g. (U) <u>Attachments and Detachments</u>. *List fires resources attached or under operational control to the unit by higher headquarters and any units detached or under operational control to other headquarters. Refer to Annex A (Task Organization) as required.*

h. (U) <u>Assumptions</u>. *List any fires-specific assumptions that support the annex development.*

2. (U) <u>Mission</u>. *State the mission of fires in support of the base plan or order.*

3. (U) <u>Execution</u>.

a. (U) <u>Scheme of Fires</u>. *Describe how fires support the commander's intent and concept of operations. Establish the priorities of fires to units for each phase of the operation. The scheme of fires must be concise but specific enough to clearly state what fires are to accomplish in the operation. The scheme of fires must answer the "who, what, when, where, and why" of the fires to be provided, but provide enough flexibility to allow subordinate commanders to determine the "how" to the maximum extent possible by ensuring necessary procedural and positive control. The scheme of fires may include a general narrative for the entire operation that should address the fire support task and purpose, allocation of assets, positioning guidance for fire support assets and observers, and attack guidance to include the entire scalable range of effects (lethal to nonlethal effects). Add subparagraphs addressing fire support tasks for each phase of the operation use the following format: task, purpose, execution, and assessment in matrix form. Refer to the base plan or order and Annex C (Operations) as required.*

(1) <u>Task, Purpose, Execution, and Assessment</u>: *Below is an example of the task, purpose, execution, and assessment matrix (to be used at the discretion of the commander):*

[page number]
[CLASSIFICATION]

[CLASSIFICATION]

ANNEX D (FIRES) TO OPERATION PLAN/ORDER [number] [(code name)]—[issuing headquarters] [(classification of title)]

PHASE: State the phase of the operation	

TASK(what)= State the type(s) of fire the "FIRES" warfighting function must provide for that phase of the operation (suppressive, neutralization, interdiction, counterfire, destruction, obscuration, screening, etc.)
PURPOSE(why)= Targeting objective (disrupt, delay, degrade, deceive, limit, destroy, etc.)+ enemy formation/ function/ capability
* **May have more than 1 task/purpose per phase**

EXECUTION: This part of a fire support task continues to answer three of the required five "Ws" required of every mission task (**who, when, and where**). But most importantly it describes *how* the task will be accomplished in detailed terms. The execution plan ties the detect function or "looker" or "acquisition asset" (executor / observer / TA sensor) with the deliver function or "shooters" (lethal and non lethal fire support assets) in time and space and describes how to achieve the task. A method to use in describing the execution is: TTLODAC. In addition to TTLODAC for each target in the phase, include additional information as necessary such as: POF, allocation of additional assets, positioning guidance to subordinate units/ assets, and restrictions/ FSCMs for the phase.

POF: State Priority of Fire to subordinate units for all FS assets under the units command/ control

FST	T	T	L	O	D	A	C
List the task number the target supports	List the target number or target type	State the trigger (tactical/technical) for the target	Give the location of the target	State the Observer of the target (pri/alt)	State the delivery system for the target (pri/alt)	State the attack guidance/ method of engagement for the target	State the frequency and commo net the target will be called in on (Primary, Alternate, Contingency, Emergency; PACE)

ALLOCATIONS: List any additional assets assigned to subordinates for planning (ex. Pri targets, radar zones, ATK AVN, etc.)

POSITIONING GUIDANCE: Guidance to assets such as mortars or observers required for execution

RESTRICTIONS/ FSCM: List all restrictions/ FSCMs for the phase

ASSESSMENT: As you determine a Fire Support Task, you must define success of the Fire Support Tasks purpose/objective. By quantifying success, the delivery assets and observation/acquisition assets understand what qualifies as successful completion of the task. It also provides the basis for the assess function in D³A and the decision to re-attack or not. Assessments should be quantified in terms of measures of performance (MOP), measures of effectiveness (MOE) or BDA. Often times, but not always, MOPs are task standards for the delivery assets and MOEs are task standards for acquisition assets.

b. (U) Scheme of Field Artillery Support. *Describe the scheme of cannon, rocket, and missile fires in support of decisive, shaping, and sustaining operations. Include specific tasks to subordinate field artillery headquarters. Address any potential requirements for massing fires that may affect organic, direct support, or reinforcing fires units. Identify the timing and duration of specific identified fire plans, such as counterfire, preparations, suppression of enemy air defenses, or joint suppression of enemy air defenses. Refer to Appendix 4 (Field Artillery Support) to Annex D (Fires) as required.*

(1) (U) Organization for Combat. *Provide direction for the proper organization for combat, to include the unit designation, nomenclature, and tactical task.*

(2) (U) Miscellaneous. *Provide any other information necessary for planning not already mentioned. Other information in this subparagraph may include changes to the targeting numbering system, the use of pulse repetition frequency codes, positioning restrictions, and a position area overlay.*

c. (U) Scheme of Air Support. *Briefly describe the maneuver commander's guidance for the use of air power. Refer to Appendix 5 (Air Support) to Annex D (Fires) as required.*

(1) (U) Organization for Combat. *Provide direction for the proper organization for combat, to include the unit designation, nomenclature, and tactical task.*

(2) (U) Air Interdiction Operations. *Briefly describe the joint force air component commander's intent for air interdiction. Describe the maneuver commander's air interdiction concept and priorities for target attack within the area of operations.*

(3) (U) Close Air Support Operations. *Provide the allocation and distribution of close air support sorties by subordinate unit. Provide the desired method for planning close air support (immediate or pre-planned) or any special control arrangements.*

[page number]
[CLASSIFICATION]

[CLASSIFICATION]

ANNEX D (FIRES) TO OPERATION PLAN/ORDER [number] [(code name)]—[issuing headquarters] [(classification of title)]

(4) (U) <u>Electronic Warfare Operations</u>. *Provide the concept for use of electronic warfare aircraft and if the joint force air component commander can provide the resources.*

(5) (U) <u>Air Reconnaissance Operations</u>. *Provide the concept for use of reconnaissance aircraft if resources are provided by the joint force air component commander. Refer to Annex L (Reconnaissance and Surveillance).*

(6) (U) <u>Miscellaneous</u>. *Provide any other information necessary for planning not already mentioned to include the following:*

(a) *The air tasking order's effective time.*

(b) *Deadlines for submission of air interdiction, close air support, reconnaissance aircraft, and electronic warfare aircraft requests.*

(c) *The mission request numbering system as it relates to the target numbering system.*

(d) *The joint suppression of enemy air defenses tasking from the joint force land component commander.*

(e) *Reference to essential airspace command and control measures (coordinating altitude, target areas, low level transit route requirements, and so on) identified in Annex C (Operations).*

d. (U) <u>Scheme of Naval Fire Support</u>. *Describe the concept for use of naval fire support. Include specific tasks to supporting units. Include trajectory limitations or minimum safe distances. Refer to Appendix 6 (Naval Fire Support) to Annex D (Fires) as required.*

(1) (U) <u>Organization for Combat</u>. *List the grouping or organization for combat, including the following:*

(a) (U) *Identify and list the allocation of observers and spotters.*

(b) (U) *Identify and list the allocation of ships to units.*

(2) (U) <u>Miscellaneous</u>. *Provide any other information necessary for planning not already mentioned.*

e. (U) <u>Scheme of Cyber/Electromagnetic Activities</u>. *Describe the concept for use of electronic warfare (electronic attack). Include specific tasks to supporting units. Refer to the Appendix 7 (Cyber/Electromagnetic Activities) to Annex D (Fires) as required.*

f. (U) <u>Battlefield Obscuration Support</u>. *Describe the concept for use of artillery smoke and battlefield obscuration. Refer to Annex C (Operations) as required.*

g. (U) <u>Target Acquisition</u>. *Provide information pertaining to the employment and allocation of fires target acquisition systems and assets. Refer to Appendix 3 (Targeting) and Appendix 4 (Field Artillery Support) to Annex D (Fires) as required.*

h. (U) <u>Tasks to Subordinate Units</u>. *List fires tasks assigned to specific subordinate units not contained in the base order.*

i. (U) <u>Coordinating Instructions</u>. *List only instructions applicable to two or more subordinate units not covered in the base plan or order. Provide subordinates and adjacent units the following information to coordinate fires:*

(1) *A clear definition of the boundary of the operational area if not specified in the basic plan. This area may be identified by phase if it is a phased operation.*

(2) *Targeting products.*

[page number]
[CLASSIFICATION]

[CLASSIFICATION

ANNEX D (FIRES) TO OPERATION PLAN/ORDER [number] [(code name)]—[issuing headquarters] [(classification of title)]

(3) *Fire support coordination measures.*

(4) *The time of execution of program of fires relative to H-hour (counterfire, preparations or counter-preparations, joint suppression of enemy air defenses), if needed.*

(5) *Rules of engagement specific to fires.*

4. (U) Sustainment. *Identify sustainment priorities for fires key tasks and specify additional sustainment instructions as necessary. Describe critical or unusual sustainment actions that might occur before, during, and after the battle to support the commander's scheme of fires. Refer to Annex F (Sustainment) as required.*

a. (U) Logistics. *Use subparagraphs to identify priorities and specific instructions for maintenance, transportation, supply, field services, distribution, contracting, and general engineering support. Refer to Annex F (Sustainment) and Annex P (Host-Nation Support) as required.*

(1) (U) Supply. *Identify the location of ammunition transfer points and ammunition supply points. Refer to Annex F (Sustainment) as required.*

(2) (U) Allocation of Ammunition. *List the allocation of cannon, rocket, and missile ammunition for each phase of the operation based on the amount of Class V available. Refer to Annex F (Sustainment) as required.*

b. (U) Personnel. *Use subparagraphs to identify priorities and specific instructions for human resources support, financial management, legal support, and religious support. Refer to Annex F (Sustainment) as required.*

c. (U) Army Health System Support. *Identify availability, priorities, and instructions for medical care. Refer to Annex F (Sustainment) as required.*

5. (U) Command and Signal.

a. (U) Command.

(1) (U) Location of Commander. *State the location of key fires leaders.*

(2) (U) Succession of Command. *State the succession of command if not covered in the unit's SOPs.*

(3) (U) Liaison Requirements. *State the fires liaison requirements not covered in the base order.*

b. (U) Control.

(1) (U) Command Posts. *Describe the employment of maneuver units and fires-specific command posts, including the location of each command post and its time of opening and closing.*

(2) (U) Reports. *List fires-specific reports not covered in standard operating instructions. Refer to Annex R (Reports) as required.*

c. (U) Signal. *Address any fires-specific communications requirements. Identify the current standard operating instructions edition. Refer to Annex H (Signal) as required.*

[Commander's last name]
[Commander's rank]

ACKNOWLEDGE: *Include only if attachment is distributed separately from the base order.*

The commander or authorized representative signs the original copy of the attachment. If the representative signs the original, add the phrase "For the Commander." The signed copy is the historical copy and remains in the headquarters' files.

[page number]
[CLASSIFICATION]

[CLASSIFICATION]

ANNEX D (FIRES) TO OPERATION PLAN/ORDER [number] [(code name)]—[issuing headquarters] [(classification of title)]

OFFICIAL:

[Authenticator's name]
[Authenticator's position]

Use only if the commander does not sign the original attachment. If the commander signs the original, no further authentication is required. If the commander does not sign, the signature of the preparing staff officer requires authentication and only the last name and rank of the commander appear in the signature block.

ATTACHMENTS: *List lower-level attachment (appendixes, tabs, and exhibits).*

Appendix 1 – Fire Support Overlay
Appendix 2 – Fire Support Execution Matrix
Appendix 3 – Targeting
Appendix 4 – Field Artillery Support
Appendix 5 – Air Support
Appendix 6 – Naval Fire Support
Appendix 7 – Cyber/Electromagnetic Activities

DISTRIBUTION: *Show only if distributed separately from the base order or higher-level attachments.*

[page number]
[CLASSIFICATION]

Annex E

Protection Annex Format and Instructions

This annex provides fundamental considerations, formats, and instructions for developing Annex E (Protection) to the base plan or order.

HOW TO DEVELOP ANNEX E (PROTECTION)

E-1. Commanders and staff use Annex E (Protection) to describe how protection supports the concept of operations described in the base plan or order. This annex describes how the commander intends to preserve the force through the protection tasks (listed in this annex's appendixes). The chief of protection or a designated staff officer (engineer, chemical, air and missile defense officer or provost marshal) develops Annex E (Protection).

E-2. This annex describes the protection concept of support objectives. A complex protection concept of support may require a schematic to show the protection objectives and task relationships. This annex includes a discussion of the overall protection concept of support, with the specific details in element subparagraphs and attachments. It refers to the execution matrix to clarify timing relationships among various protection tasks. This annex also contains information needed to synchronize timing relationships of each element related to protection. It includes protection-related constraints, if appropriate.

[CLASSIFICATION]

Place the classification at the top and bottom of every page of the attachments. Place the classification marking (TS), (S), (C), or (U) at the front of each paragraph and subparagraph in parentheses. Refer to AR 380-5 for classification and release marking instructions.

Copy ## of ## copies
Issuing headquarters
Place of issue
Date-time group of signature
Message reference number

Include the full heading if attachment is distributed separately from the base order or higher-level attachment.

ANNEX E (PROTECTION) TO OPERATION PLAN/ORDER [number] [(code name)]—[issuing headquarters] [(classification of title)]

(U) References: *List documents essential to understanding the attachment.*

a. *List maps and charts first. Map entries include series number, country, sheet names, or numbers, edition, and scale.*

b. *List other references in subparagraphs labeled as shown.*

c. *Doctrinal references for protection include FM 3-0, FM 3-01, FM 3-11, FM 3-11.21, FM 3-13, FM 3-37, FM 3-50.1, FM 3-90, FM 4-02.7, FM 4-02.17, FM 4-30.51, FM 5-103, AR 385-10, AR 525-13, AR 530-1, and DA Pamphlet 385-10.*

[page number]
[CLASSIFICATION]

[CLASSIFICATION]

ANNEX E (PROTECTION) TO OPERATION PLAN/ORDER [number] [(code name)]—[issuing headquarters] [(classification of title)]

(U) **Time Zone Used Throughout the Plan/Order:** *Write the time zone established in the base plan or order.*

1. (U) <u>Situation</u>. *Provide situational information affecting the protection tasks and systems that paragraph 1 of the OPLAN or OPORD does not cover or that needs expansion.*

    a. (U) <u>Area of Interest</u>. *Describe the area of interest as it impacts protection. Identify area of interest characteristics and hazards that require coordinated protection actions to preserve the force. Refer to Annex B (Intelligence) as required.*

    b. (U) <u>Area of Operations</u>. *Identify and describe the area of operation's characteristics and hazards that require coordinated protection actions to preserve the force. Refer to Annex C (Operations) as required.*

        (1) (U) <u>Terrain</u>. *Describe the aspects of terrain that impact protection operations. Identify terrain features in the area of interest and area of operations that create a hazard or enhance the threat. Specify protection action that may be required as a result of the terrain. Identify terrain that may benefit protection capabilities. Refer to Annex B (Intelligence) as required.*

        (2) (U) <u>Weather</u>. *Describe the aspects of weather that impact protection operations, tasks, and systems. Refer to Appendix 7 (Safety) to Annex E (Protection) and Annex B (Intelligence) as required.*

    c. (U) <u>Enemy Forces</u>. *List known and templated locations and activities of enemy protection units for one echelon up and two echelons down. List enemy maneuver and other area capabilities that will impact friendly operations. State expected enemy courses of action and employment of enemy protection assets. Include consideration of civil disturbances and criminal acts. Narrow the focus to offensive minded threats that require planning, resources, and actions to protect the force. Refer to Annex B (Intelligence) as required.*

    d. (U) <u>Friendly Forces</u>. *Outline the higher headquarters' protection plan. List designation, location, and outline of plan of higher, adjacent, and other protection assets that support or impact the issuing headquarters or require coordination and additional support. List areas of the operation most vulnerable to enemy attack or adverse influence.*

    e. (U) <u>Interagency, Intergovernmental, and Nongovernmental Organizations</u>. *Identify and describe other organizations in the area of operations that may impact the conduct of protection operations or impact protection specific equipment and tactics. Outline the results of the composite risk management process to mitigate the risk of fratricide. Enhance continual situational awareness by frequently updating data of friendly forces. Describe the method and timing of the data updates. Refer to Annex V (Interagency Coordination) as required.*

    f. (U) <u>Civil Considerations</u>. *Describe the aspects of the civil situation that impact protection operations. Refer to Annex B (Intelligence) and Annex K (Civil Affairs Operations) as required.*

    g. (U) <u>Attachments and Detachments</u>. *List units attached or detached only as necessary to clarify task organization. Refer to Annex A (Task Organization) as required.*

    h. (U) <u>Assumptions</u>. *List any protection-specific assumptions that support the annex development.*

2. (U) <u>Mission</u>. *State the protection mission in support of the base plan or order.*

3. (U) <u>Execution</u>.

[page number]
[CLASSIFICATION]

[CLASSIFICATION]

ANNEX E (PROTECTION) TO OPERATION PLAN/ORDER [number] [(code name)]—[issuing headquarters] [(classification of title)]

a. (U) <u>Scheme of Protection</u>. *Describe how the protection tasks and systems support the commander's intent and concept of operations. Establish the priorities of support to units for each phase of the operation. If required information for a specific protection task or system is brief, include it in this paragraph and eliminate the associated appendix. Refer to the base order and Annex C (Operations) as required.*

(1) (U) <u>Air and Missile Defense</u>. *Describe how air and missile defense supports the commander's intent and concept of operations. Establish the priorities of air and missile defense support to units for each phase of the operation. Refer to Appendix 1 (Air and Missile Defense) to Annex E (Protection) as required.*

(2) (U) <u>Personnel Recovery</u>. *Describe the manner in which subordinate units execute personnel recovery operations in support of the mission, including phasing and the principal tasks to accomplish. Describe this in terms of shaping, decisive, and sustaining operations. This narrative of how the operation will proceed includes support from host-nation, coalition, and multinational forces and capabilities. Discuss the roles of specialized personnel recovery assets from other Services and special operations forces (for unconventional assisted recovery). Refer to Appendix 2 (Personnel Recovery) to Annex E (Protection) as required.*

(3) (U) <u>Fratricide Avoidance</u>. *Describe how fratricide avoidance supports the commander's intent and concept of operations. Refer to Appendix 3 (Fratricide Avoidance) to Annex E (Protection) as required.*

(4) (U) <u>Operational Area Security</u>. *State the scheme of operational area security and overall area security objective. Describe how operational area security supports the commander's intent the maneuver plan and protection priorities. Direct how each element of the force will cooperate to accomplish operational area security and tie that to support of the operation with the task and purpose statement. Discuss how operational area security orients on the force, installation, route, area, or asset to be protected. Discuss how operational area security is often an economy of force role assigned in some manner to many organizations. Discuss how operational area security is often designed to ensure the continued conduct of sustainment operations and to support decisive and shaping operations. Describe how forces engaged in area security operations saturate an area or position on key terrain to provide protection through early warning, reconnaissance, or surveillance and guard against unexpected enemy attack with an active response. Discuss the role of response forces in the operational area security scheme. Refer to Appendix 4 (Operational Area Security) to Annex E (Protection) as required.*

(5) (U) <u>Antiterrorism</u>. *State the overall antiterrorism objective. Describe how the commander envisions antiterrorism measures in support of the scheme of protection that supports the concept of operations in the base order. It should stress detection, deterrence, and mitigation of the terrorist threat in the applicable environment (in-transit, on a base, during operations, and in protection of host-nation and local civilians). Refer to Appendix 5 (Antiterrorism) to Annex E (Protection) as required.*

(6) (U) <u>Chemical, Biological, Radiological, and Nuclear Defense</u>. *Describe how the chemical, biological, radiological, and nuclear (CBRN) defense unit supports the commander's intent and concept of operations. Establish the priorities of support to units or the concept for employing CBRN defense units for each phase of the operation. Detail the priority of CBRN defense reconnaissance and obscuration support to the maneuver forces based on the mission and CBRN defense threat. Focus on the commander's guidance, mission, and intent. Emphasize how CBRN defense operations affect readiness and warfighting capability. Refer to Appendix 6 (Chemical, Biological, Radiological, and Nuclear Defense) to Annex E (Protection) as required.*

(7) (U) <u>Safety</u>. *Describe how mission-dictated safety program requirements support the commander's intent and concept of operations. Describe how safety tasks and function are prioritized to eliminate or mitigate hazards on a greatest risk first basis to support the unit. Refer to Appendix 7 (Safety) to Annex E (Protection) as required.*

[page number]
[CLASSIFICATION]

[CLASSIFICATION]

ANNEX E (PROTECTION) TO OPERATION PLAN/ORDER [number] [(code name)]—[issuing headquarters] [(classification of title)]

(8) (U) <u>Operations Security</u>. *Describe how operations security supports the commander's intent and concept of operations. Describe the general concept for implementing planned operations security measures. Describe by phase and functional area (movement and maneuver, fires, protection, sustainment, intelligence, information, and mission command), if appropriate. Refer to Appendix 8 (Operations Security) to Annex E (Protection) as required.*

(9) (U) <u>Explosive Ordnance Disposal</u>. *Describe how explosive ordnance disposal supports the commander's intent and concept of operations. Establish the priorities of explosive ordnance disposal support to units for each phase of the operation. Refer to Appendix 9 (Explosive Ordnance Disposal) to Annex E (Protection) as required.*

(10) (U) <u>Force Health Protection</u>. *Describe how force health protection supports the commander's intent and concept of operations. Establish the priorities of support to units for each phase of the operation. Refer to Appendix 10 (Force Health Protection) to Annex E (Protection) as required.*

(11) (U) <u>Survivability</u>. *Describe how survivability operations support the commander's intent and concept of operations. Establish the priorities of survivability support to units for each phase of the operation. Refer to Annex G (Engineer) as required.*

(12) (U) <u>Information Protection</u>. *Describe how information assurance supports the commander's concept of operations. Outline procedures to ensure proper security of information on the Nonsecure Internet Protocol Router Network, SECRET Internet Protocol Router Network, and Joint Worldwide Intelligence Communications System. Refer to Annex H (Signal) as required.*

b. (U) <u>Tasks to Subordinate Units</u>. *List protection tasks assigned to specific subordinate units not contained in the base order.*

c. (U) <u>Coordinating Instructions</u>. *List only instructions applicable to two or more subordinate units not covered in the base plan or order. Identify any nonstandard operating procedure type of information that will enhance protection by coordinated actions. Examples include personnel identification, vehicle identification, and control measures. Provide additional coordinating instructions for the following:*

(1) (U) <u>Critical Assets</u>. *Identify, assess, and prioritize all critical assets and develop a critical asset for given area of responsibility.*

(2) (U) <u>Mitigate Threats</u>. *Develop measures (forces and procedures) to mitigate threats against critical assets.*

(3) (U) <u>Monitor and Report</u>. *Monitor and report threats to critical assets and forces.*

(4) (U) <u>Report Actions</u>. *Report all vulnerability mitigation and remediation actions to critical assets.*

(5) (U) <u>Essential Elements of Friendly Information</u>.

(a) (U) *Date-time group, location, size, disposition, and flight path of aviation units in the area of responsibility.*

(b) (U) *Date-time group, location, size, disposition, and mobility of units in the area of responsibility.*

(c) (U) *Location and disposition of command nodes.*

(d) (U) *Sustainment plans and sustainment operations.*

[page number]
[CLASSIFICATION]

[CLASSIFICATION]

ANNEX E (PROTECTION) TO OPERATION PLAN/ORDER [number] [(code name)]—[issuing headquarters] [(classification of title)]

(e) (U) *Methods of locating and neutralizing enemy weapons of mass destruction and tactical ballistic missile capabilities.*

(f) (U) *Logistics, operational, intelligence, command, control, and communication limitations and vulnerabilities.*

(g) (U) *Vulnerabilities that could be exploited to recue or eliminate international support of ongoing operations.*

(6) (U) Risk Reduction Control Measures. *Provide the required information.*

(a) (U) *Air and Missile Defense Warning.*

(b) (U) *Air and Missile Defense Weapon Control Status.*

(c) (U) *Operational Exposure Guidance.*

(d) (U) *Mission-Oriented Protective Posture.*

(e) (U) *Force Protection Level.*

(f) (U) *Information Operations Condition Level.*

(g) (U) *Operations Security.*

4. (U) Sustainment. *Identify priorities of sustainment for key protection tasks and specify additional instructions as required. Refer to Annex F (Sustainment) as required.*

a. (U) Logistics. *Use subparagraphs to identify priorities and specific instructions for maintenance, transportation, supply, field services, distribution, contracting, and general engineering support. Refer to Annex F (Sustainment) and Annex P (Host-Nation Support) as required.*

b. (U) Personnel. *Use subparagraphs to identify priorities and specific instructions for human resources support, financial management, legal support, and religious support. Refer to Annex F (Sustainment) as required.*

c. (U) Army Health System Support. *Identify availability, priorities, and instructions for medical care. Refer to Annex F (Sustainment) as required.*

5. (U) Command and Signal.

a. (U) Command.

(1) (U) Location of Commander. *State the location of key protection leaders.*

(2) (U) Succession of Command. *State the succession of command if not covered in the unit's SOPs.*

(3) (U) Liaison Requirements. *State the protection liaison requirements not covered in the unit's standard operating procedures.*

b. (U) Control.

(1) (U) Command Posts. *Describe the employment of protection-specific command posts (CPs), including the location of each CP and its time of opening and closing.*

(2) (U) Reports. *List protection-specific reports not covered in standard operating procedures. Refer to Annex R (Reports) as required.*

[page number]
[CLASSIFICATION]

[CLASSIFICATION]

ANNEX E (PROTECTION) TO OPERATION PLAN/ORDER [number] [(code name)]—[issuing headquarters] [(classification of title)]

    c. (U) <u>Signal</u>. *Address any protection-specific communications requirements. Refer to Annex H (Signal) as required.*

[Commander's last name]
[Commander's rank]

ACKNOWLEDGE: *Include only if attachment is distributed separately from the base order.*

The commander or authorized representative signs the original copy of the attachment. If the representative signs the original, add the phrase "For the Commander." The signed copy is the historical copy and remains in the headquarters' files.

OFFICIAL:

[Authenticator's name]
[Authenticator's position]

Use only if the commander does not sign the original attachment. If the commander signs the original, no further authentication is required. If the commander does not sign, the signature of the preparing staff officer requires authentication and only the last name and rank of the commander appear in the signature block.

ATTACHMENTS: *List lower-level attachment (appendixes, tabs, and exhibits). If a particular attachment is not used, place "not used" beside the attachment number. Unit standard operating procedures will dictate attachment development and format. Common attachments include the following:*

Appendix 1 – Air and Missile Defense
Appendix 2 – Personnel Recovery
Appendix 3 – Fratricide Avoidance
Appendix 4 – Operational Area Security
Appendix 5 – Antiterrorism
Appendix 6 – Chemical, Biological, Radiological, and Nuclear Defense
Appendix 7 – Safety
Appendix 8 – Operations Security
Appendix 9 – Explosive Ordnance Disposal
Appendix 10 – Force Health Protection

DISTRIBUTION: *Show only if distributed separately from the base order or higher-level attachments.*

[page number]
[CLASSIFICATION]

Annex F

Sustainment Annex Format and Instructions

This annex provides fundamental considerations, formats, and instructions for developing Annex F (Sustainment) to the base plan or order.

HOW TO DEVELOP ANNEX F (SUSTAINMENT)

F-1. Commanders and staff use Annex F (Sustainment) to describe how sustainment operations support the concept of operations described in the base plan or order. The chief of sustainment (S-4) develops Annex F (Sustainment).

[CLASSIFICATION]

Place the classification at the top and bottom of every page of the attachments. Place the classification marking (TS), (S), (C), or (U) at the front of each paragraph and subparagraph in parentheses. Refer to AR 380-5 for classification and release marking instructions.

Copy ## of ## copies
Issuing headquarters
Place of issue
Date-time group of signature
Message reference number

Include the full heading if attachment is distributed separately from the base order or higher-level attachment.

ANNEX F (SUSTAINMENT) TO OPERATION PLAN/ORDER [number] [(code name)]—[issuing headquarters] [(classification of title)]

(U) References: List documents essential to understanding the attachment.

a. *List maps and charts first. Map entries include series number, country, sheet names, or numbers, edition, and scale.*

b. *List other references in subparagraphs labeled as shown.*

c. *Doctrinal references for sustainment include the FM 4-0 series.*

(U) Time Zone Used Throughout the Order: *Write the time zone established in the base plan or order.*

1. (U) <u>Situation</u>**.** *Include information affecting the sustainment operations that paragraph 1 of the OPLAN or OPORD does not cover or that needs expansion.*

a. (U) <u>Area of Interest</u>. *Describe the area of interest as it relates to the sustainment. Refer to Annex B (Intelligence) as required.*

b. (U) <u>Area of Operations</u>. *Refer to Appendix 2 (Operation Overlay) to Annex C (Operations) as required.*

(1) (U) <u>Terrain</u>. *Describe the aspects of terrain that impact sustainment operations. Refer to Annex B (Intelligence) as required.*

(2) (U) <u>Weather</u>. *Describe the aspects of weather that impact sustainment operations. Refer to Annex B (Intelligence) as required.*

[page number]
[CLASSIFICATION]

[CLASSIFICATION]

ANNEX F (SUSTAINMENT) TO OPERATION PLAN/ORDER [number] [(code name)]—[issuing headquarters] [(classification of title)]

    c. (U) <u>Enemy Forces</u>. *List known and templated locations and activities of enemy sustainment units for one echelon up and two echelons down. List enemy maneuver and other capabilities that will impact friendly sustainment operations. State expected enemy sustainment courses of action and employment of enemy sustainment assets. Refer to Annex B (Intelligence) as required.*

    d. (U) <u>Friendly Forces</u>. *Outline the higher headquarters' sustainment plan. List designation, location, and outline of plan of higher, adjacent, and other sustainment assets that support or impact the issuing headquarters or require coordination and additional support.*

    e. (U) <u>Interagency, Intergovernmental, and Nongovernmental Organizations</u>. *Identify and describe other organizations in the area of operations that may impact the conduct of sustainment operations or implementation of sustainment-specific equipment and tactics. Refer to Annex V (Interagency Coordination) as required.*

    f. (U) <u>Civil Considerations</u>. *Describe the aspects of the civil situation that impact sustainment operations. Refer to Annex B (Intelligence) and Annex K (Civil Affairs Operations) as required.*

    g. (U) <u>Attachments and Detachments</u>. *List units attached or detached only as necessary to clarify task organization. Refer to Annex A (Task Organization) as required.*

    h. (U) <u>Assumptions</u>. *List any sustainment-specific assumptions that support the annex development.*

2. (U) <u>Mission</u>. *State the mission of sustainment in support of the base plan or order.*

3. (U) <u>Execution</u>.

    a. (U) <u>Scheme of Sustainment Support</u>. *Describe how sustainment supports the commander's intent and concept of operations. Establish the priorities of sustainment support to units for each phase of the operation. Refer to Annex C (Operations) as required.*

    b. (U) <u>Tasks to Subordinate Units</u>. *List sustainment tasks assigned to specific subordinate units not contained in the base order.*

    c. (U) <u>Coordinating Instructions</u>. *List only instructions applicable to two or more subordinate units not covered in the base plan or order.*

4. (U) <u>Sustainment</u>. *Identify priorities of sustainment for key tasks and specify additional instructions as required.*

    a. (U) <u>Materiel and Services</u>. *Provide materiel and services information in the following subparagraphs.*

      (1) (U) <u>Maintenance</u>. *Provide maintenance information for each subparagraph, to include priority of maintenance, location of facilities and collection points, repair time limits at each level of maintenance, and evacuation procedures. Post maintenance collection points and command posts to the sustainment overlay at Tab A (Sustainment Overlay) to Appendix 1 (Logistics) to Annex F (Sustainment). Refer to Tab B (Maintenance) to Appendix 1 (Logistics) to Annex F (Sustainment) as required.*

        (a) (U) <u>Ground</u>. *Identify the proper procedures to request ground recovery and maintenance.*

        (b) (U) <u>Watercraft</u>. *Identify the proper procedures to request watercraft recovery and maintenance.*

        (c) (U) <u>Aircraft</u>. *Identify the proper procedures to request aircraft recovery and maintenance.*

[page number]
[CLASSIFICATION]

[CLASSIFICATION]

ANNEX F (SUSTAINMENT) TO OPERATION PLAN/ORDER [number] [(code name)]—[issuing headquarters] [(classification of title)]

(d) (U) <u>Field Maintenance</u>. *Identify, list, and describe the recovery plan and types of recovery vehicles available; Class IX parts support; the locations of maintenance collection points; logistics civil augmentation program (LOGCAP) capabilities and availability; and field maintenance support relationships at each phase of the operation.*

(e) (U) <u>Sustainment Maintenance</u>. *Identify, list, and describe the location of sustainment maintenance units and services; the locations of maintenance collection points; the LOGCAP capabilities and availability; and sustainment maintenance support relationships at each phase of the operation.*

(2) (U) <u>Transportation</u>. *Provide transportation information for each subparagraph. Identify facility locations, traffic control, regulation measures, main supply routes, alternate supply routes, transportation critical shortages, and other essential transportation data not provided elsewhere. Post main supply routes, alternate supply routes, and transportation facilities to the logistics synchronization matrix and the overlay at Tab A (Sustainment Overlay) to Appendix 1 (Logistics) to Annex F (Sustainment). Identify and list transportation request procedures. Refer to Tab C (Transportation) to Appendix 1 (Logistics) to Annex F (Sustainment) as required.*

(a) (U) <u>Ground</u>. *Identify the proper procedures to request ground transportation.*

(b) (U) <u>Sea/River/Water</u>. *Identify the proper procedures to request sea, river, and water transportation.*

(c) (U) <u>Air</u>. *Identify the proper procedures to request air transportation.*

(d) (U) <u>Container Management</u>. *Describe the container management plan.*

(3) (U) <u>Supply</u>. *Provide information by class of supply in each subparagraph. Identify and list maps, water, special supplies, and excess and salvage materiel, as applicable. For each subparagraph, list supply point locations and state supply plan and procedures. Post supply points and facilities to the logistics synchronization matrix and the overlay at Tab A (Sustainment Overlay) to Appendix 1 (Logistics) to Annex F (Sustainment). Refer to Tab D (Supply) to Appendix 1 (Logistics) to Annex F (Sustainment) as required.*

(a) (U) <u>Class I Rations</u>. *Identify and list the issue and ration cycle, ration stockage objectives, and the bulk water locations.*

(b) (U) <u>Class II Organizational Clothing and Individual Equipment and Maps</u>. *Identify and list organizational clothing and individual equipment available for this operation. Submit classified map requests through G-2 (S-2) channels.*

(c) (U) <u>Class III Bulk Fuel; Class III Package Petroleum, Oils, and Lubricants</u>. *Identify and list quantities of petroleum, oil, and lubricant; locations of the retail and bulk fuel points; and types of products available at each site available to support the operation.*

(d) (U) <u>Class IV Construction and Fortification Material</u>. *Identify and list construction and fortification or barrier material available for this operation including command-controlled items.*

(e) (U) <u>Class V Munitions</u>. *Identify and list available ammunition and the controlled supply rates. List the procedures to request explosive ordnance disposal support. Refer to Annex E (Protection) as required for explosive ordnance disposal support.*

(f) (U) <u>Class VI Personal Demand Items</u>. *Describe the Class VI plan. Identify and list items available.*

(g) (U) <u>Class VII Major End Items</u>. *Identify and list major end items available for this operation.*

[page number]
[CLASSIFICATION]

[CLASSIFICATION]

ANNEX F (SUSTAINMENT) TO OPERATION PLAN/ORDER [number] [(code name)]—[issuing headquarters] [(classification of title)]

(h) (U) <u>Class VIII Medical Supply</u>. *Identify and list medical supplies available for this operation.*

(i) (U) <u>Class IX Repair Parts</u>. *Identify and list all critical shortage, repair parts, and command-controlled items available for this operation. State the approving authority for controlled exchange of parts.*

(j) (U) <u>Class X Material for Nonmilitary or Civil Affairs Operations</u>. *Identify and list material available for this operation.*

(k) (U) <u>Miscellaneous</u>. *Identify and list any other available materiel and supplies not mentioned in the above subparagraphs available for this operation.*

(4) (U) <u>Field Services</u>. *Identify and list key field services available during this operation. At a minimum, this paragraph and subparagraphs must contain the location and the responsible unit for each separate field service activity. Identify and list locations and operating hours for laundry facilities, shower facilities, clothing repair facilities, food services facilities, billeting facilities, and field sanitation facilities. Highlight field sanitation requirements for each service, such as water purification and trash removal. Post field service facilities to the logistics synchronization matrix and the overlay at Tab A (Sustainment Overlay) to Appendix 1 (Logistics) to Annex F (Sustainment). Refer to Tab E (Field Services) to Appendix 1 (Logistics) to Annex F (Sustainment) as required.*

(a) (U) <u>Construction</u>. *Identify and list available construction material. Provide essential information as appropriate.*

(b) (U) <u>Light Textile Repair and Showers, Laundry, and Clothing Repair</u>. *Identify and list locations of showers, laundry, and clothing repair available for this operation.*

(c) (U) <u>Food Preparation</u>. *Identify and list food preparation available for this operation.*

(d) (U) <u>Water Purification</u>. *Identify and list water purification locations and units available for this operation.*

(e) (U) <u>Aerial Delivery</u>. *Identify and list aerial delivery available for this operation.*

(f) (U) <u>Installation Services</u>. *Identify and list installation services available for this operation.*

(5) (U) <u>Distribution</u>. *Provide information about distribution support. Refer to Tab F (Distribution) to Appendix 1 (Logistics) to Annex F (Sustainment) as required.*

(a) (U) <u>Distribution Nodes' Locations</u>. *Identify and list the location of distribution nodes (seaport of debarkation and arrival/departure airfield control group).*

(b) (U) <u>Tracking Procedures</u>. *Identify and discuss the tracking procedures.*

(c) (U) <u>Distribution Modes</u>. *Identify and list the various distribution modes: land, sea, or air.*

(d) (U) <u>Movement Request Format</u>. *Discuss the movement request format and processing requirements.*

(e) (U) <u>Container Operations</u>. *Discuss container management and operations.*

(f) (U) <u>Movement Control Responsibility</u>. *Identify units at each level responsible for movement control.*

[page number]
[CLASSIFICATION]

[CLASSIFICATION]

ANNEX F (SUSTAINMENT) TO OPERATION PLAN/ORDER [number] [(code name)]—[issuing headquarters] [(classification of title)]

(6) (U) Contract Support Integration. *Identify and list key contract support integration functions for this operation. Identify the location and contract support unit responsible at each level. Identify contract support capabilities, limitations, and priority of support. Refer to Tab G (Contract Support Integration) to Appendix 1 (Logistics) to Annex F (Sustainment) as required.*

(7) (U) Mortuary Affairs. *Provide information about mortuary affairs support. Refer to Tab H (Mortuary Affairs) to Appendix 1 (Logistics) to Annex F (Sustainment) as required.*

(8) (U) Internment and Resettlement Support. *Identify and list the location and the unit responsible for each level of internment and resettlement operations. Identify all major capabilities and known limitations that may affect the operation. Discuss the procedures for internment and resettlement, to include transportation, field service, personnel processing, mortuary affairs, and health services. Refer to Tab I (Internment and Resettlement) to Appendix 1 (Logistics) to Annex F (Sustainment) and Appendix 13 (Internment and Resettlement Operations) to Annex C (Operations) as required.*

(9) (U) Labor. *Provide information about contract labor. Refer to Appendix 1 (Logistics) to Annex F (Sustainment) and Annex P (Host-Nation Support) as required.*

b. (U) Personnel. *Provide personnel information. Outline plans for unit-strength maintenance; personnel management; morale development and maintenance; discipline, law, and order; headquarters management; force provider; religious support; and legal and finance support. Post personnel services unit locations to the logistics synchronization matrix and the overlay at Tab A (Sustainment Overlay) to Appendix 1 (Logistics) to Annex F (Sustainment). Refer to Appendix 2 (Personnel Services Support) to Annex F (Sustainment) as required.*

(1) (U) Human Resources Support. *Provide human resources support information. Refer to Tab A (Human Resources Support) to Appendix 2 (Personnel Services Support) to Annex F (Sustainment) as required.*

(2) (U) Financial Management. *Provide financial management support information. Refer to Tab B (Financial Management) to Appendix 2 (Personnel Services Support) to Annex F (Sustainment) as required.*

(3) (U) Legal Support. *Provide legal support information. Refer to Tab C (Legal Support) to Appendix 2 (Personnel Services Support) to Annex F (Sustainment) as required.*

(4) (U) Religious Support. *Provide religious support information. Refer to Tab D (Religious Support) to Appendix 2 (Personnel Services Support) to Annex F (Sustainment) as required.*

(5) (U) Band Operations. *Provide band operations support information. Refer to Tab E (Band Operations) to Appendix 2 (Personnel Services Support) to Annex F (Sustainment) as required.*

c. (U) Army Health System Support. *Provide Army Health System Support information. Identify availability, priorities, and instruction for medical care. Describe the plan for collection and medical treatment of sick, injured, or wounded U.S., multinational, and joint force soldiers, enemy prisoners of war, detainees, and, when authorized, civilians. Describe support requirements for health service logistics (including blood management), combat operational stress control, preventive medicine, dental services, medical laboratory support, and veterinary services. Post hospital and medical treatment facility locations to the logistics synchronization matrix and the overlay at Tab A (Sustainment Overlay) to Appendix 1 (Logistics) to Annex F (Sustainment). Refer to Appendix 3 (Army Health System Support) to Annex F (Sustainment) as required.*

[page number]
[CLASSIFICATION]

[CLASSIFICATION]

ANNEX F (SUSTAINMENT) TO OPERATION PLAN/ORDER [number] [(code name)]—[issuing headquarters] [(classification of title)]

(1) (U) <u>Medical Evacuation</u>. *Provide medical evacuation information. Address the theater evacuation policy, en route care, medical regulating (if appropriate), casualty evacuation, and the medical evacuation of casualties contaminated with chemical, biological, radiological, and nuclear ordnance.*

(2) (U) <u>Hospitalization</u>. *Provide hospitalization information and guidelines. List the locations of medical treatment facilities. Identify and list area units without organic medical resources requiring support and describe how to support these units. Describe the procedures for mass casualty operations and patient decontamination operations. Identify and list levels of medical care (I, II, III, and IV) by treatment facility and location. Refer to Tab A (Sustainment Overlay) to Appendix 1 (Logistics) to Annex F (Sustainment) and Appendix 3 (Army Health System Support) to Annex F (Sustainment) as required.*

d. (U) <u>Foreign Nation and Host-Nation Support</u>. *Provide host-nation support information. Refer to Annex P (Host-Nation Support) as required.*

e. (U) <u>Resource Availability</u>. *Identify significant competing demands for sustainment resources where expected requirements may exceed resources.*

f. (U) <u>Miscellaneous</u>. *Provide any general miscellaneous information not covered in this annex.*

5. (U) Command and Signal.

a. (U) <u>Command</u>.

(1) (U) <u>Location of Commander</u>. *State the location of sustainment area leaders.*

(2) (U) <u>Succession of Command</u>. *State the succession of command if not covered in the unit's SOPs.*

(3) (U) <u>Liaison Requirements</u>. *State the sustainment liaison requirements not covered in the base order.*

b. (U) <u>Control</u>.

(1) (U) <u>Command Posts</u>. *Describe the employment of sustainment-specific command posts (CPs), including the location of each CP and its time of opening and closing.*

(2) (U) <u>Reports</u>. *List sustainment-specific reports not covered in standard operating procedures. Refer to Annex R (Reports) as required.*

c. (U) <u>Signal</u>. *Address any sustainment-specific communications requirements. Refer to Annex H (Signal) as required.*

ACKNOWLEDGE: *Include only if attachment is distributed separately from the base order.*

[Commander's last name]
[Commander's rank]

The commander or authorized representative signs the original copy of the attachment. If the representative signs the original, add the phrase "For the Commander." The signed copy is the historical copy and remains in the headquarters' files.

OFFICIAL:

[Authenticator's name]
[Authenticator's position]

[page number]
[CLASSIFICATION]

[CLASSIFICATION]

ANNEX F (SUSTAINMENT) TO OPERATION PLAN/ORDER [number] [(code name)]—[issuing headquarters] [(classification of title)]

Use only if the commander does not sign the original attachment. If the commander signs the original, no further authentication is required. If the commander does not sign, the signature of the preparing staff officer requires authentication and only the last name and rank of the commander appear in the signature block.

ATTACHMENTS: *List lower-level attachments (appendixes, tabs, and exhibits).*

Appendix 1 – Logistics
Appendix 2 – Personnel Services Support
Appendix 3 – Army Health System Support

DISTRIBUTION: *Show only if distributed separately from the base order or higher-level attachments.*

[page number]
[CLASSIFICATION]

This page intentionally left blank.

Annex G

Engineer Annex Format and Instructions

This annex provides fundamental considerations, formats, and instructions for developing Annex G (Engineer) to the base plan or order.

HOW TO DEVELOP ANNEX G (ENGINEER)

G-1. Commanders and staff use Annex G (Engineer) to describe how the engineer plan supports the concept of operations described in the base plan or order. The engineer officer develops Annex G (Engineer).

G-2. This annex follows the five-paragraph (situation, mission, execution, sustainment, and command and signal) format of the base plan or order. Engineers use this annex to define engineer support to the maneuver commander's intent, coordinating instructions to subordinate commanders, and essential tasks for mobility, countermobility, and survivability. This annex is not intended to function as the internal order for an engineer organization, where the engineer commander will articulate intent, concept of operations, and coordinating instructions to subordinate, supporting, and supported commanders. This annex seeks to clarify engineer support to the base plan or order. Guidance to maneuver units on obstacle responsibilities should be listed in the body of the base plan or order, not in this annex.

[CLASSIFICATION]

Place the classification at the top and bottom of every page of the attachments. Place the classification marking (TS), (S), (C), or (U) at the front of each paragraph and subparagraph in parentheses. Refer to AR 380-5 for classification and release marking instructions.

Copy ## of ## copies
Issuing headquarters
Place of issue
Date-time group of signature
Message reference number

Include the full heading if attachment is distributed separately from the base order or higher-level attachment.

ANNEX G (ENGINEER) TO OPLAN/OPORD [number] [(code name)]—[issuing headquarters] [(classification of title)]

(U) References: *List documents essential to understanding this attachment.*

    a. *List maps and charts first. Map entries include series number, country, sheet names, or numbers, edition, and scale.*

    b. *List other references in subparagraphs List other references in subparagraphs labeled as shown.*

    c. *Doctrinal references for this annex are FM 3-34, FM 3-34.5, FM 3-34.170, FM 3-34.400, FM 5-34, FM 5-102, FM 5-103, ATTP 3-34.23, and ATTP 3-34.80.*

(U) Time Zone Used Throughout the OPLAN/OPORD: *Write the time zone established in the base plan or order.*

[page number]
[CLASSIFICATION]

[CLASSIFICATION]

ANNEX G (ENGINEER) TO OPLAN/OPORD [number] [(code name)]—[issuing headquarters] [(classification of title)]

1. (U) Situation. *Include information affecting engineer support that paragraph 1 of the OPLAN or OPORD does not cover or that needs expansion.*

    a. (U) <u>Area of Interest</u>. *Describe the area of interest as it relates to engineer operations. Refer to Annex B (Intelligence) as required.*

    b. (U) <u>Area of Operations</u>. *Refer to Appendix 2 (Operation Overlay) to Annex C (Operations) as required.*

        (1) (U) <u>Terrain</u>. *Describe the aspects of terrain that impact engineer operations. Refer to Annex B (Intelligence) as required.*

        (2) (U) <u>Weather</u>. *Describe the aspects of weather that impact engineer operations. Refer to Annex B (Intelligence) as required.*

    c. (U) <u>Enemy Forces</u>. *List known and templated locations and activities of enemy engineer units for one echelon up and two echelons down. List enemy maneuver and other capabilities that will impact engineer operations. State expected enemy courses of action and employment of enemy engineer assets. Give a detailed description of enemy engineer units, assets, and any known obstacles. Refer to Annex B (Intelligence) as required.*

    d. (U) <u>Friendly Forces</u>. *Outline the higher headquarters' engineer operations plan. List designation, location, and outline of plan of higher, adjacent, and other engineer assets that support or impact the issuing headquarters or require coordination and additional support.*

    e. (U) <u>Interagency, Intergovernmental, and Nongovernmental Organizations</u>. *Identify and describe other organizations in the area of operations that may impact the conduct of engineer operations or implementation of engineer-specific equipment and tactics. Refer to Annex V (Interagency Coordination) as required.*

    f. (U) <u>Civil Considerations</u>. *Describe the critical aspects of the civil situation that impact engineer operations. Refer to Annex B (Intelligence) and Annex K (Civil Affairs Operations) as required.*

    g. (U) <u>Attachments and Detachments</u>. *List all engineer assets with a command support relationship with higher headquarters. List any units detached or under the operational control of other headquarters. Refer to Annex A (Task Organization) as required.*

    h. (U) <u>Assumptions</u>. *List any engineer-specific assumptions that support the annex development.*

2. (U) <u>Mission</u>. *State the engineer mission in support of the base plan or order.*

3. (U) <u>Execution</u>.

    a. (U) <u>Scheme of Engineer Support</u>. *Describe how engineer operations support the commander's intent and concept of operations. Establish the priorities of engineer support to units for each phase of the operation. Refer to the base plan or order and Annex C (Operations) as required.*

        (1) (U) <u>Assured Mobility</u>. *Describe the plan to maintain freedom of movement and maneuver. Refer to Appendix 1 (Mobility/Countermobility) to Annex G (Engineer) as required.*

            (a) (U) <u>Mobility Support</u>. *State the scheme of mobility operations to include task and purpose. This includes breaching (proofing, marking lanes, providing guides, and maintaining and clearing routes), relative location (route or objective), priority for reduction assets used (use plows first, then mine-clearing line charge), priority of clearance assets, and unit responsible. For gap crossing operations, refer to Appendix 4 (Gap Crossing Operations) to Annex C (Operations).*

[page number]
[CLASSIFICATION]

[CLASSIFICATION]

ANNEX G (ENGINEER) TO OPLAN/OPORD [number] [(code name)]—[issuing headquarters] [(classification of title)]

(b) (U) <u>Countermobility Support</u>. *State the scheme of countermobility operations to include task and purpose, unit responsible for task, priority of effort, intent, target number assignments (by unit) and planned grid coordinates. Operations requiring obstacle emplacement will also be required to include a Tab A (Obstacle Overlay) to Appendix 1 (Mobility/Countermobility) to Annex G (Engineer).*

(2) (U) <u>Survivability</u>. *Describe how survivability operations support the commander's intent and concept of operations. Establish the priorities of survivability support to units for each phase of the operation. Refer to the base plan or order, Annex C (Operations) and Appendix 2 (Survivability) to Annex G (Engineer) as required.*

(3) (U) <u>General Engineering</u>. *Describe how general engineer assets support the commander's intent and concept of operations. Establish the priorities of support to subordinate units for each phase of the operation. Refer to the base plan or order and Annex C (Operations) and refer to Appendix 3 (General Engineering) to Annex G (Engineer) as required.*

(4) (U) <u>Geospatial Engineering</u>. *Describe how geospatial engineering capabilities will support the operation. Expand the scheme of engineer operations in Annex G (Engineer) with any additional information that clarifies the geospatial engineering tasks, purposes, and priorities in support of each phase of the scheme of maneuver. The four primary functions of geospatial engineering (generate, analyze, manage, and disseminate) may be used to structure this narrative. Refer to Appendix 4 (Geospatial Engineering) to Annex G (Engineer) as required.*

(5) (U) <u>Environmental Considerations</u>. *Summarize the commander's concept of environmental actions required to support the OPLAN or OPORD, or concept plan. Identify issues and actions that should be addressed during all phases of the operation. Refer to Appendix 5 (Environmental Considerations) to Annex G (Engineer) as required.*

(6) (U) <u>Engineer Reconnaissance</u>. *State the scheme of engineer reconnaissance by task and purpose for engineer tactical and technical reconnaissance including infrastructure reconnaissance requirements.*

b. (U) <u>Tasks to Subordinate Units</u>. *List engineering tasks to specific units that are not assigned in the base plan or order. List tasks specific to engineering and mobility, countermobility, and survivability assets only as necessary to ensure unity of effort. Specific and detailed task descriptions should be done in each respective appendix as applicable.*

c. (U) <u>Coordinating Instructions</u>. *List only instructions applicable to two or more subordinate units not covered in the base plan or order. Provide additional coordinating instructions for the following:*

(1) (U) *Identify and list the times or events when obstacle control measures become effective.*

(2) (U) *List supported unit information requirements focused on mobility, countermobility, and survivability that must be considered by subordinate engineer staff officers or that the supported unit requires. This includes engineer-related commander's critical information requirements and perhaps the requests for information that have already been submitted to higher.*

(3) (U) *Explain and describe the countermobility and survivability timelines.*

4. (U) <u>Sustainment</u>. *Identify sustainment priorities for engineer key tasks and specify additional sustainment instructions as necessary, and at a minimum address engineer Class IV and V locations. Refer to Annex F (Sustainment) as required.*

[page number]
[CLASSIFICATION]

[CLASSIFICATION]

ANNEX G (ENGINEER) TO OPLAN/OPORD [number] [(code name)]—[issuing headquarters] [(classification of title)]

a. (U) <u>Logistics</u>. *Use subparagraphs to identify priorities and specific instruction for maintenance, transportation, supply, field services, distribution, contracting, and general engineering support. Refer to Annex F (Sustainment) and Annex P (Host-Nation Support) as required.*

(1) (U) <u>Command-Regulated Classes of Supply</u>. *Identify command-regulated classes of supply. Highlight supported unit allocations that affect engineer support (such as Class IV barrier material allocated to other efforts).*

(2) (U) <u>Supply Distribution Plan</u>. *Establish Class IV and Class V (obstacle) supply distribution plan. State method of supply for each class and for each supported unit subordinate element. List supply linkup points. Identify and list all allocations of Class IV and Class V by support unit element by obstacle control measure or combination. Summarize in a matrix or table as necessary.*

(3) (U) <u>Transportation</u>. *List any transportation coordination to include supported, troop movements, Class IV building materials, and Class V materials.*

b. (U) <u>Personnel</u>. *Use subparagraphs to identify priorities and specific instructions for human resources support, financial management, legal support, and religious support. Refer to Annex F (Sustainment) as required.*

c. (U) <u>Army Health System Support</u>. *Identify availability, priorities, and instructions for medical care. Refer to Annex F (Sustainment) as required.*

5. (U) <u>Command and Signal</u>.

a. (U) <u>Command</u>.

(1). (U) <u>Location of Key Leaders</u>. *State the location of key engineer leaders. Designate the headquarters that controls the mobility, countermobility, and survivability effort within work lines on an area basis. Clearly identify release authority for special munitions, such as the Intelligent Munitions System (Scorpion).*

(2) (U) <u>Succession of Command</u>. *State the succession of command or leadership if not covered in the unit's standard operating procedures (SOPs).*

(3) (U) <u>Liaison Requirements</u>. *State engineer liaison requirements not covered in the unit's SOPs.*

b. (U) <u>Control</u>.

(1) (U) <u>Command Posts</u>. *Describe the employment of command posts (CPs), including the location of each CP and state the primary controlling CP for specific tasks or phases of the operation.*

(2) (U) <u>Reports</u>. *Identify critical engineer reporting requirements of subordinates if not covered in SOPs. Refer to Annex R (Reports) as required.*

c. (U) <u>Signal</u>. *Describe the concept of signal support as it pertains to engineer support operations. Refer to Annex H (Signal) as required.*

[page number]
[CLASSIFICATION]

[CLASSIFICATION]

ANNEX G (ENGINEER) TO OPLAN/OPORD [number] [(code name)]—[issuing headquarters] [(classification of title)]

ACKNOWLEDGE: *Include only if attachment is distributed separately from the base order.*

[Commander's last name]
[Commander's rank]

The commander or authorized representative signs the original copy of the attachment. If the representative signs the original, add the phrase "For the Commander." The signed copy is the historical copy and remains in the headquarters' files.

OFFICIAL:

[Authenticator's name]
[Authenticator's position]

Use only if the commander does not sign the original attachment. If the commander signs the original, no further authentication is required. If the commander does not sign, the signature of the preparing staff officer requires authentication and only the last name and rank of the commander appear in the signature block.

ATTACHMENTS: *List lower-level attachment (appendixes, tabs, and exhibits). If a particular attachment is not used, place "not used" beside the attachment number. Unit SOPs will dictate attachment development and format. Common attachments include the following:*

Appendix 1 – Mobility/Countermobility
Appendix 2 – Survivability
Appendix 3 – General Engineering
Appendix 4 – Geospatial Engineering
Appendix 5 – Engineer Task Organization and Execution Matrix
Appendix 6 – Environmental Considerations

DISTRIBUTION: *Show only if distributed separately from the base order or higher-level attachments.*

[page number]
[CLASSIFICATION]

This page intentionally left blank.

Annex H

Signal Annex Format and Instructions

This annex provides fundamental considerations, formats, and instructions for developing Annex H (Signal) to the base plan or order.

HOW TO DEVELOP ANNEX H (SIGNAL)

H-1. Commanders and staff use Annex H (Signal) to describe how signal supports the concept of operations described in the base plan or order. The G-6 (S-6) develops Annex H (Signal).

[CLASSIFICATION]

Place the classification at the top and bottom of every page of the attachments. Place the classification marking (TS), (S), (C), or (U) at the front of each paragraph and subparagraph in parentheses. Refer to AR 380-5 for classification and release marking instructions.

Copy ## of ## copies
Issuing headquarters
Place of issue
Date-time group of signature
Message reference number

Include the full heading if attachment is distributed separately from the base order or higher-level attachment.

ANNEX H (SIGNAL) TO OPERATION PLAN/ORDER [number] [(code name)]—[issuing headquarters] [(classification of title)]

(U) References: *List documents essential to understanding the attachment.*

a. *List maps and charts first. Map entries include series number, country, sheet names, or numbers, edition, and scale.*

b. *List other references in subparagraphs labeled as shown.*

c. *Doctrinal references for signal operations include FM 6-02.40, FM 6-02.43, FM 6-02.53, FM 6-02.70, and FM 6-02.71.*

(U) Time Zone Used Throughout the Order: *Write the time zone established in the base plan or order.*

1. (U) <u>Situation</u>. *Include information affecting signal operations that paragraph 1 of the OPLAN or OPORD does not cover or that needs expansion.*

a. (U) <u>Area of Interest</u>. *Describe the area of interest. Refer to Annex B (Intelligence) as required.*

b. (U) <u>Area of Operations</u>. *Refer to Appendix 2 (Operation Overlay) to Annex C (Operations).*

(1) (U) <u>Terrain</u>. *Describe the aspects of terrain that impact signal operations. Refer to Annex B (Intelligence) as required.*

(2) (U) <u>Weather</u>. *Describe all critical weather aspects that impact signal operations such as (rain, flooding, windstorms, and snow) that also may impact network availability or reliability in the area of operations. Refer to Annex B (Intelligence) as required.*

[page number]
[CLASSIFICATION]

[CLASSIFICATION]

ANNEX H (SIGNAL) TO OPERATION PLAN/ORDER [number] [(code name)]—[issuing headquarters] [(classification of title)]

c. (U) <u>Enemy Forces</u>. *List known and templated locations and activities of enemy signal units for one echelon up and two echelons down. List enemy maneuver and other area capabilities that will impact friendly signal operations. State expected enemy courses of action and employment of enemy signal assets. Refer to Annex B (Intelligence) as required.*

d. (U) <u>Friendly Forces</u>. *Briefly identify the signal mission of friendly forces and the objectives, goals and mission of civilian organizations that impact signal operations. Refer to Annex A (Task Organization) and Annex C (Operations) as required.*

(1) (U) <u>Higher Headquarters' Signal Operations Mission</u>. *Identify and state the signal mission of the higher headquarters.*

(2) (U) <u>Signal Operations Impact of Adjacent Units</u>. *Identify and state the missions of adjacent units and other units whose actions have a significant impact on the issuing headquarters' signal operations.*

e. (U) <u>Interagency, Intergovernmental, and Nongovernmental Organizations</u>. *Identify and state the objectives or goals and primary tasks of those non-Department of Defense organizations that may impact the conduct of signal operations or implementation of signal-specific equipment and tactics in the area of operations. Refer to Annex V (Interagency Coordination) as required.*

f. (U) <u>Civil Considerations</u>. *Describe the critical aspects of the civil situation that impact voice and data network operations using the memory aid ASCOPE (areas, structures, capabilities, organizations, people, and events). Refer to Annex B (Intelligence) and Annex K (Civil Affairs Operations) as required.*

g. (U) <u>Attachments and Detachments</u>. *List units attached or detached only as necessary to clarify task organization that impact signal operations. Refer to Annex A (Task Organization) as required.*

h. (U) <u>Assumptions</u>. *List key assumptions that pertain to signal operations which support development of the annex.*

2. (U) <u>Mission</u>. *State the mission of signal in support of the base plan or order.*

3. (U) <u>Execution</u>.

a. (U) <u>Scheme of Signal Operations</u>. *Describe how signal operations supports the commander's intent and concept of operations described in the base plan or order. Establish the priorities of support to units for each phase of the operation. Refer to Annex C (Operations) as required.*

(1) (U) <u>Scheme of Information Assurance</u>. *Describe how information assurance supports the commander's intent and concept of operations described in the base plan or order. Outline procedures to ensure proper security of information on Nonsecure Internet Protocol Router Network, SECRET Internet Protocol Router Network, and Joint Worldwide Intelligence Communications System. Refer to Appendix 1 (Information Assurance) to Annex H (Signal) as required.*

(2) (U) <u>Scheme of Voice and Data Network Diagrams</u>. *Describe how voice and data network diagrams support the commander's intent and concept of operations described in the base plan or order. Establish the priorities of support to units for each phase of the operation. Refer to Appendix 2 (Voice and Data Network Diagrams) to Annex H (Signal) as required.*

(3) (U) <u>Scheme of Satellite Communications</u>. *Describe how satellite communications support the commander's intent and concept of operations described in the base plan or order. Establish the priorities of support to units for each phase of the operation. Refer to Appendix 3 (Satellite Communications) to Annex H (Signal) as required.*

[page number]
[CLASSIFICATION]

[CLASSIFICATION]

ANNEX H (SIGNAL) TO OPERATION PLAN/ORDER [number] [(code name)]—[issuing headquarters] [(classification of title)]

(4) (U) <u>Scheme of Foreign Data Exchanges</u>. *Describe how foreign data exchanges support the commander's intent and concept of operations described in the base plan or order. Outline procedures to prevent unauthorized disclosure and release of classified information on the SECRET Internet Protocol Router Network and the Joint Worldwide Intelligence Communications System. Outline the information to be disclosed to, released to, or received from foreign entities and the planned approach, including safe guarding steps to be taken. Refer to Appendix 4 (Foreign Data Exchanges) to Annex H (Signal) as required.*

(5) (U) <u>Electromagnetic Spectrum Operations</u>. *Describe how electromagnetic spectrum operations supports the commander's intent and concept of operations described in the base plan or order. Outline the effects the commander wants to achieve while prioritizing tasks for electromagnetic spectrum operations. List objectives and the primary tasks to achieve those objectives. Refer to Appendix 5 (Electromagnetic Spectrum Operations) to Annex H (Signal) as required.*

(6) (U) <u>Network Diagram</u>. *Provide a detailed network diagram including the internet protocol (IP) scheme of the satellite communications (SATCOM) network being established. Provide a chart for all required frequencies, access times, access dates, and in the case of IP-based SATCOM systems, provide the IP scheme for the modem, as well as the Nonsecure Internet Protocol Router Network and SECRET Internet Protocol Router Network routers. (This subparagraph will serve as a reference to units along with attachments.)*

b. (U) <u>Tasks to Subordinate Units</u>. *List signal operations tasks assigned to subordinate signal units not contained in the base order. Each task must include who (the subordinate unit assigned the task), what (the task itself), when, where, and why (purpose). Include tasks for supporting interagency, intergovernmental, and nongovernmental organizations. Use a separate subparagraph for each unit. List units in task organization sequence. Place tasks that affect two or more units in paragraph 3c (Coordinating Instructions).*

c. (U) <u>Coordinating Instructions</u>. *List only instructions applicable to two or more subordinate units not covered in the base plan or order.*

4. (U) <u>Sustainment</u>. *Identify priorities of sustainment for signal operations key tasks and specify additional instructions as required in the paragraph below. Refer to Annex F (Sustainment) as required.*

a. (U) <u>Logistics</u>. *Use subparagraphs to identify priorities and specific instructions for maintenance, transportation, supply, field services, distribution, contracting, and general engineering support. Refer to Annex F (Sustainment) and Annex P (Host-Nation Support) as required.*

b. (U) <u>Personnel</u>. *Use subparagraphs to identify priorities and specific instructions for human resources support, financial management, legal support, and religious support. Refer to Annex F (Sustainment) as required.*

c. (U) <u>Army Health System Support</u>. *Identify availability, priorities, and instruction for medical care. Refer to Annex F (Sustainment) as required.*

5. (U) <u>Command and Signal</u>.

a. (U) <u>Command</u>.

(1) (U) <u>Location of Commander</u>. *State the location of key signal unit commanders and staff officers.*

(2) (U) <u>Succession of Command</u>. *State the succession of command if not covered in the unit's standard operating procedures (SOPs).*

(3) (U) <u>Liaison Requirements</u>. *State the signal liaison requirements not covered in unit SOPs.*

[page number]
[CLASSIFICATION]

[CLASSIFICATION]

ANNEX H (SIGNAL) TO OPERATION PLAN/ORDER [number] [(code name)]—[issuing headquarters] [(classification of title)]

b. (U) <u>Control</u>.

(1) (U) <u>Command Posts</u>. *Describe the employment of signal command posts (CPs), including the location of each CP and its time of opening and closing.*

(2) (U) <u>Reports</u>. *List reports not covered in SOPs. Describe signal operations reporting requirements for subordinate units. Refer to Annex R (Reports) as required.*

c. (U) <u>Signal</u>. *List signal operating instructions for signal operations as needed, as well as primary and alternate means of communications with both military and nonmilitary organizations conducting signal operations. Consider operations security requirements.*

(1) (U) *Describe the networks to monitor for reports.*

(2) (U) *Address any signal operations communications or digitization connectivity requirements or coordination necessary to meet functional responsibilities (consider telephone listing).*

ACKNOWLEDGE: *Include only if attachment is distributed separately from the base order.*

[Commander's last name]
[Commander's rank]

The commander or authorized representative signs the original copy of the attachment. If the representative signs the original, add the phrase "For the Commander." The signed copy is the historical copy and remains in the headquarters' files.

OFFICIAL:

[Authenticator's name]
[Authenticator's position]

Use only if the commander does not sign the original attachment. If the commander signs the original, no further authentication is required. If the commander does not sign, the signature of the preparing staff officer requires authentication and only the last name and rank of the commander appear in the signature block.

ATTACHMENTS: *List lower-level attachment (appendixes, tabs, and exhibits). If a particular attachment is not used, place "not used" beside the attachment number. Unit SOPs will dictate attachment development and format. Common attachments include the following:*

Appendix 1 – Information Assurance
Appendix 2 – Voice and Data Network Diagrams
Appendix 3 – Satellite Communications
Appendix 4 – Foreign Data Exchanges
Appendix 5 – Electromagnetic Spectrum Operations

DISTRIBUTION: *Show only if distributed separately from the base order or higher-level attachments.*

[page number]
[CLASSIFICATION]

Annex I

Not Used

This page intentionally left blank.

Annex J

Inform and Influence Activities Annex Format and Instructions

This annex provides fundamental considerations, formats, and instructions for developing Annex J (Inform and Influence Activities) to the base plan or order.

HOW TO DEVELOP ANNEX J (INFORM AND INFLUENCE ACTIVITIES)

J-1.   Commanders and staff use Annex J (Inform and Influence Activities) to describe how inform and influence activities support the concept of operations described in the base plan or order. The G-7 (S-7) develops Annex J (Inform and Influence Activities).

[CLASSIFICATION]

Place the classification at the top and bottom of every page of the attachments. Place the classification marking (TS), (S), (C), or (U) at the front of each paragraph and subparagraph in parentheses. Refer to AR 380-5 for classification and release marking instructions.

Copy ## of ## copies
Issuing headquarters
Place of issue
Date-time group of signature
Message reference number

Include the full heading if attachment is distributed separately from the base order or higher-level attachment.

ANNEX J (INFORM AND INFLUENCE ACTIVITIES) TO OPERATION PLAN/ORDER [number] [(code name)]—[(classification of title)]

(U) References: *List documents essential to understanding the attachment.*

a. *List maps and charts first. Map entries include series number, country, sheet names, or numbers, edition, and scale.*

b. *List other references in subparagraphs labeled as shown.*

c. *Doctrinal references for inform and influence activities include FM 3-61.1, FM 46-1, and JP 3-61.*

(U) Time Zone Used Throughout the Plan/Order: *Write the time zone established in the base plan or order.*

1. (U) <u>Situation</u>. *Include information affecting inform and influence activities that paragraph 1 of the OPLAN or OPORD does not cover or that needs expansion.*

a. (U) <u>Area of Interest</u>. *Describe the area of interest as it relates to inform and influence activities. Refer to Annex B (Intelligence) as required.*

b. (U) <u>Area of Operations</u>. *Refer to Appendix 2 (Operation Overlay) to Annex C (Operations).*

[page number]
[CLASSIFICATION]

[CLASSIFICATION]

ANNEX J (INFORM AND INFLUENCE ACTIVITIES) TO OPERATION PLAN/ORDER [number] [(code name)]—[(classification of title)]

(1) (U) <u>Terrain</u>. *Describe the aspects of terrain that impact inform and influence activities. Refer to Annex B (Intelligence) as required.*

(2) (U) <u>Weather</u>. *Describe the aspects of weather that impact inform and influence activities. Refer to Annex B (Intelligence) as required.*

c. (U) <u>Enemy Forces</u>. *List known and templated locations and activities of enemy units for inform and influence activities for one echelon up and two echelons down. List enemy maneuver and other capabilities that will impact friendly inform and influence activities. Identify enemy situation, force disposition, intelligence elements, and possible actions. Describe those aspects of the information environment that favor the enemy. Refer to Annex B (Intelligence) as required.*

(1) (U) <u>Enemy Centers of Gravity</u>. *List the enemy strategic and operational centers of gravity.*

(2) (U) <u>Enemy Courses of Action</u>. *Describe key enemy objectives and activities for inform and influence activities. State expected enemy courses of action, employment of enemy assets for inform and influence activities, and enemy courses of action through the perceived end state. Identify how the enemy will deploy information systems and to what extent the enemy will conduct deliberate, coordinated inform and influence activities to affect the information environment.*

(3) (U) <u>Identify Enemy Inform and Influence Activities Elements</u>. *Describe the enemy elements for inform and influence activities including the decisionmaking structure and characteristics. Identify decisionmakers and their personal attributes.*

(4) (U) <u>Enemy Inform and Influence Activities Vulnerabilities</u>. *Identify and list enemy inform and influence activities and command and control vulnerabilities.*

(5) (U) <u>Enemy Inform and Influence Activities Capabilities</u>. *Identify and list enemy capabilities to degrade friendly command and control. List required enemy assets and systems needed to execute inform and influence activities.*

d. (U) <u>Friendly Forces</u>. *Outline the higher headquarters' inform and influence activities plan. List designation, location, and outline of plan of higher, adjacent, and other assets for inform and influence activities that support or impact the issuing headquarters or require coordination and additional support.*

(1) (U) <u>Friendly Inform and Influence Activities</u>. *Summarize the situation of friendly forces for inform and influence activities including supporting agencies such as the Defense Intelligence Agency, the Department of State, and any other national agencies or departments that address inform and influence activities.*

(2) (U) <u>Friendly Centers of Gravity</u>. *List the friendly strategic and operational centers of gravity.*

(3) (U) <u>Multinational Forces</u>. *List the friendly multinational inform and influence activities forces.*

(4) (U) <u>Inform and Influence Activities Capabilities</u>. *Identify and list friendly inform and influence activities capabilities, inform and influence activities assets to attack enemy targets, friendly forces that will directly affect inform and influence activities, and critical limitations of planned inform and influence activities. Identify and list each unit's inform and influence activities capabilities and vulnerabilities.*

(5) (U) <u>Potential Conflicts</u>. *Identify and list potential conflicts with friendly inform and influence activities especially if conducting joint or multinational operations. Identify methods to deconflict and list the priority of information dissemination.*

(6) (U) <u>Constraints</u>. *Identify and list constraints on friendly inform and influence activities.*

[page number]
[CLASSIFICATION]

[CLASSIFICATION]

ANNEX J (INFORM AND INFLUENCE ACTIVITIES) TO OPERATION PLAN/ORDER [number] [(code name)]—[(classification of title)]

(7) (U) <u>Vulnerabilities</u>. *Identify and list friendly vulnerabilities to enemy and third-party inform and influence activities.*

e. (U) <u>Interagency, Intergovernmental, and Nongovernmental Organizations</u>. *Identify and describe other organizations in the area of operations that may impact the conduct of operations of inform and influence activities or implementation of inform and influence activities-specific equipment and tactics. Refer to Annex V (Interagency Coordination) as required.*

f. (U) <u>Civil Considerations</u>. *Identify, list, and describe civil organizations in the area of operations that may impact inform and influence activities. Refer to Annex B (Intelligence) and Annex K (Civil Affairs Operations) as required.*

(1) (U) <u>Key Elements</u>. *Identify key people, organizations, and groups in the area of operations that conduct inform and influence activities. Identify how this will affect friendly and enemy inform and influence activities.*

(2) (U) <u>Key Elements' Objectives</u>. *Describe likely objectives and activities of these key people, organizations, and groups in the area of operations that will affect inform and influence activities.*

g. (U) <u>Information Environment</u>. *Identify significant characteristics of the information environment: populace and civil infrastructure; information content, flow, and distribution; and populace and third-party perceptions, awareness, and understanding. Identify those aspects of inform and influence activities that favor all other persons in the area of operations.*

h. (U) <u>Attachments and Detachments</u>. *List units attached or detached only as necessary to clarify task organization.*

i. (U) <u>Assumptions</u>. *List any additional inform and influence activities-specific assumptions or information not included in the general situation that will impact inform and influence activities operations.*

2. (U) <u>Mission</u>. *State the mission of inform and influence activities in support of the base plan or order.*

3. (U) <u>Execution</u>.

a. (U) <u>Scheme of Inform and Influence Activities</u>. *Describe how inform and influence activities support the commander's intent and concept of operations. Summarize how the commander visualizes executing inform and influence activities. Establish the priorities of support to units for each phase of inform and influence activities operations. Explain how inform and influence activities will assist in achieving an operational advantage at the operation's decisive points. Refer to Annex C (Operations) as required.*

(1) (U) <u>Inform and Influence Activities Objectives</u>. *Describe the clearly defined inform and influence activities objective and the obtainable effects that the commander intends to achieve.*

(2) (U) <u>Inform and Influence Activities Tasks</u>. *Describe the tasks developed to support the accomplishment of one or more inform and influence activities objectives.*

(a) (U) <u>Public Affairs</u>. *Describe how public affairs supports inform and influence activities in this operation. Establish the priorities of support for each phase of the operation. Refer to Appendix 1 (Public Affairs) to Annex J (Inform and Influence Activities) as required.*

(b) (U) <u>Military Deception</u>. *Describe how military deception supports the commander's intent and concept of operations. Establish the priorities of support to units for each phase of the operation. State how military deception tasks will deceive and influence the enemy. State how military deception supports the accomplishment of the operation. Synchronize this element with the other military deception elements. Refer to Appendix 2 (Military Deception) to Annex J (Inform and Influence Activities) as required.*

[page number]
[CLASSIFICATION]

ANNEX J (INFORM AND INFLUENCE ACTIVITIES) TO OPERATION PLAN/ORDER [number] [(code name)]—[(classification of title)]

    (c) (U) <u>Military Information Support Operations</u>. *Summarize how the commander visualizes executing military information support operations (MISO). Establish the priorities of support for military information support elements during each phase of the operation. Describe how MISO will meet the commander's intent and the concept of operations during each phase of the operation. State how tasks assigned to military information support elements will degrade, disrupt, deny, or influence the enemy to support the accomplishment of the commander's objectives. Synchronize MISO with the other inform and influence activities. Refer to Appendix 3 (Military Information Support Operations) to Annex J (Inform and Influence Activities) as required. Appendix 3 must include a military information support program approved by the Under Secretary of Defense for Policy. This program provides the necessary guidelines for the planning, development, and delivery of products and actions. Appendix 3 includes key components of the program to delineate the approval authorities and parameters for using MISO. An approved OPORD that accurately reflects the program guidance and the commander's intent ensures the effective integration and execution of MISO. It also serves as the authorization for the approval by the supported commander of timely military information support products and actions.*

    (d) (U) <u>Soldier and Leader Engagement</u>. *Describe how Soldier and leader engagement support the commander's intent and concept of operations. Summarize how the commander visualizes executing Soldier and leader engagement. Establish the priorities of support to units for each phase of the Soldier and leader engagement operation. Explain how Soldier and leader engagement will assist in achieving an operational advantage at the operation's decisive points. Describe how units will conduct Soldier and leader engagements to meet the commander's intent and higher headquarters' engagement criteria. Identify and list any Soldier and leader engagement criteria and tasks. Refer to Appendix 4 (Soldier and Leader Engagement) to Annex J (Inform and Influence Activities) as required.*

    (3) (U) <u>Combat Camera</u>. *State how combat camera operations support inform and influence activities in this operation. Identify and list the priority of tasks, imagery collection, and events documentation.*

    b. (U) <u>Tasks to Subordinate Units</u>. *Identify and list tasks of inform and influence activities assigned to specific subordinate units not contained in the base order including maneuver units, MISO units, electronic warfare units, and counterintelligence units.*

    c. (U) <u>Inform and Influence Activities Cell</u>. *Identify and list tasks to the combat camera units and state nonstandard operating procedures tasks assigned to the inform and influence activities cell.*

    d. (U) <u>Coordinating Instructions</u>. *List only instructions applicable to two or more subordinate units not covered in the base plan or order. Address any mutual support issues relating to the elements of inform and influence activities.*

4. (U) <u>Sustainment</u>. *Identify priorities of sustainment for inform and influence activities key tasks and specify additional instructions as required in the paragraph below. Refer to Annex F (Sustainment) as required.*

    a. (U) <u>Logistics</u>. *Use subparagraphs to identify priorities and specific instructions for maintenance, transportation, supply, field services, distribution, contracting, and general engineering support. Refer to Annex F (Sustainment) and Annex P (Host-Nation Support) as required.*

    b. (U) <u>Personnel</u>. *Use subparagraphs to identify priorities and specific instructions for human resources support, financial management, legal support, and religious support. Refer to Annex F (Sustainment) as required.*

[CLASSIFICATION]

ANNEX J (INFORM AND INFLUENCE ACTIVITIES) TO OPERATION PLAN/ORDER [number] [(code name)]—[(classification of title)]

c. (U) <u>Army Health System Support</u>. *Identify availability, priorities, and instructions for medical care. Refer to Annex F (Sustainment) as required.*

5. (U) <u>Command and Signal</u>.

a. (U) <u>Command</u>.

(1) (U) <u>Location of Commander</u>. *State the location of inform and influence activities area leaders.*

(2) (U) <u>Succession of Command</u>. *State the succession of command or leadership for key inform and influence activities units and staff if not covered in unit standard operating procedures (SOPs).*

(3) (U) <u>Liaison Requirements</u>. *State the inform and influence activities liaison requirements not covered in the unit's SOPs.*

b. (U) <u>Control</u>.

(1) (U) <u>Command Posts</u>. *Describe the employment of inform and influence activities-specific command posts (CPs), including the location of each CP and its time of opening and closing.*

(2) (U) <u>Reports</u>. *List inform and influence activities-specific reports not covered in SOPs. Refer to Annex R (Reports) as required.*

c. (U) <u>Signal</u>. *Address any inform and influence activities-specific communications requirements. Refer to Annex H (Signal) as required.*

ACKNOWLEDGE: *Include only if attachment is distributed separately from the base order.*

[Commander's last name]
[Commander's rank]

The commander or authorized representative signs the original copy of the attachment. If the representative signs the original, add the phrase "For the Commander." The signed copy is the historical copy and remains in the headquarters' files.

OFFICIAL:

[Authenticator's name]
[Authenticator's position]

Use only if the commander does not sign the original attachment. If the commander signs the original, no further authentication is required. If the commander does not sign, the signature of the preparing staff officer requires authentication and only the last name and rank of the commander appear in the signature block.

ATTACHMENTS: *List lower-level attachment (appendixes, tabs, and exhibits).*

Appendix 1 – Public Affairs
Appendix 2 – Military Deception
Appendix 3 – Military Information Support Operations
Appendix 4 – Soldier and Leader Engagement

DISTRIBUTION: *Show only if distributed separately from the base order or higher-level attachments.*

[page number]
[CLASSIFICATION]

This page intentionally left blank.

Annex K

Civil Affairs Operations Annex Format and Instructions

This annex provides fundamental considerations, formats, and instructions for developing Annex K (Civil Affairs Operations) to the base plan or order.

HOW TO DEVELOP ANNEX K (CIVIL AFFAIRS OPERATIONS)

K-1. Commanders and staff use Annex K (Civil Affairs Operations) to describe how civil affairs operations, in coordination with other military and civil organizations, support the concept of operations described in the base plan or order. The G-9 (S-9) is responsible for developing Annex K (Civil Affairs Operations).

[CLASSIFICATION]

Place the classification at the top and bottom of every page of the attachments. Place the classification marking (TS), (S), (C), or (U) at the front of each paragraph and subparagraph in parentheses. Refer to AR 380-5 for classification and release marking instructions.

Copy ## of ## copies
Issuing headquarters
Place of issue
Date-time group of signature
Message reference number

Include the full heading if attachment is distributed separately from the base order or higher-level attachment.

ANNEX K (CIVIL AFFAIRS OPERATIONS) TO OPLAN/OPORD [number] [(code name)]— [issuing headquarters] [(classification of title)]

(U) References: *List documents essential to understanding this attachment.*

a. *List maps and charts first. Map entries include series number, country, sheet names, or numbers, edition, and scale.*

b. *List other references in subparagraphs such as the civil affairs operations annex of higher headquarters, relevant civilian agency operations guides and standard documents, relevant plans of participating civilian organizations, coordinated transition plans, international treaties and agreements, and civil information management plans.*

c. *Doctrinal references for civil affairs operations include FM 3-05.40, FM 3-05.401, and JP 3-57.*

(U) Time Zone Used Throughout the OPLAN/OPORD: *Write the time zone established in the base plan or order.*

1. **(U) <u>Situation</u>.** *Include information affecting civil affairs operations that paragraph 1 of the OPLAN or OPORD does not cover or that needs expansion.*

a. (U) <u>Area of Interest</u>. *Describe the area of interest as it relates to civil affairs operations. Refer to Annex B (Intelligence) as required.*

b. (U) <u>Area of Operations</u>. *Refer to Appendix 2 (Operation Overlay) to Annex C (Operations).*

[page number]
[CLASSIFICATION]

[CLASSIFICATION]

ANNEX K (CIVIL AFFAIRS OPERATIONS) TO OPLAN/OPORD [number] [(code name)]— [issuing headquarters] [(classification of title)]

   (1) (U) <u>Terrain</u>. *Describe the aspects of terrain that impact civil affairs operations such as population centers, likely movement corridors of dislocated civilians, and terrain that channels dislocated civilians. Refer to Annex B (Intelligence) as required.*

   (2) (U) <u>Weather</u>. *Describe the aspects of weather that impact civil affairs operations such as seasonal events (rain, flooding, wind storms, and snow) that may impact commercial mobility, agricultural production, farmer to market access, and populace and resources control in the area of operations. Refer to Annex B (Intelligence) as required.*

   c. (U) <u>Enemy Forces</u>. *List known and templated locations and activities of enemy civil affairs operations units for one echelon up and two echelons down. Identify enemy forces and appraise their general capabilities and impacts on the indigenous population and civil affairs operations. State expected enemy courses of action and employment of enemy civil affairs operations assets. Refer to Annex B (Intelligence) as required.*

   d. (U) <u>Friendly Forces</u>. *Outline the higher headquarters' civil affairs operations plan. Briefly identify the mission of friendly forces and the objectives, goals, and mission of civilian organization that impact civil affairs operations. List designation, location, and outline of plan of higher, adjacent, and other civil affairs organizations and assets that support or impact the issuing headquarters or require coordination and additional support.*

   (1) (U) <u>Higher Headquarters' Civil Affairs Operations Mission</u>. *Identify and state the civil affairs operations mission of the higher headquarters.*

   (2) (U) <u>Civil Affairs Operations Missions of Adjacent Units</u>. *Identify and state the civil affairs operations missions of adjacent units and other units whose actions have a significant impact on the issuing headquarters.*

   e. (U) <u>Interagency, Intergovernmental, and Nongovernmental Organizations</u>. *Identify and state the objectives or goals and primary tasks of those non-Department of Defense organizations that have a significant role within the civil situation in the area of operations or implementation of civil affairs operations-specific equipment and tactics. Refer to Annex V (Interagency Coordination) as required.*

   (1) (U) <u>Interagency Organizations</u>. *Identify and state the objectives and primary tasks of those interagency organizations that impact the unit's civil affairs operations mission. Briefly describe the capabilities and capacity of each organization if not listed in Annex V (Interagency Coordination).*

   (2) (U) <u>Intergovernmental Organizations</u>. *Identify and state the objectives and primary tasks of those intergovernmental organizations that impact the unit's civil affairs operations mission. Briefly describe the capabilities and capacities of each organization.*

   (3) (U) <u>Nongovernmental Organizations</u>. *Identify and state the objectives and primary tasks of those nongovernmental organizations that impact the unit's civil affairs operations mission. Briefly describe the capabilities and capacities of each organization.*

   f. (U) <u>Civil Considerations</u>. *Describe the critical aspects of the civil situation that impact civil affairs operations using the memory aid ASCOPE (areas, structures, capabilities, organizations, people, and events). Refer to Annex B (Intelligence) as required.*

   (1) (U) <u>Areas</u>. *List the key civilian areas such as political boundaries; locations of government centers; social, political, religious, or criminal enclaves; agricultural and mining regions; trade routes; possible sites for the temporary settlement of dislocated civilians in the area of interest. Describe how these civilian areas affect the mission and how military operations may affect these areas.*

[page number]
[CLASSIFICATION]

ANNEX K (CIVIL AFFAIRS OPERATIONS) TO OPLAN/OPORD [number] [(code name)]—[issuing headquarters] [(classification of title)]

(2) (U) <u>Structures</u>. *List the locations of existing civil structures (critical infrastructure) such as ports, air terminals, transportation networks, bridges, communications towers, power plants, and dams. Identify churches, mosques, national libraries, hospitals, and other cultural sites generally protected by international law or other agreements. Other infrastructure includes governance and public safety structures (national, regional, and urban government facilities, record archives, judiciary, police, fire, and emergency medical services) and economic and environmental structures (banking, stock and commodity exchanges, toxic industrial facilities, and pipelines). Identify facilities with practical applications—such as jails, warehouses, schools, television stations, radio stations, and print plants—which may be useful for military purposes.*

(3) (U) <u>Capabilities</u>. *Describe civil capabilities by assessing the populace capabilities of sustaining itself through public safety, emergency services, and food and agriculture. Include whether the populace needs assistance with public works and utilities, public health, public transportation, economics, and commerce. Refer to the civil affairs preliminary area assessment.*

(4) (U) <u>Organizations</u>. *Identify and list civil organizations that may or may not be affiliated with government agencies, such as church groups, ethnic groups, multinational corporations, fraternal organizations, patriotic or service organizations, intergovernmental organizations, or nongovernmental organizations. Do not repeat those listed in Annex V (Interagency Coordination) or paragraph 1e. (Interagency, Intergovernmental, and Nongovernmental Organizations) of this annex. Include host-nation organizations capable of forming the nucleus for humanitarian assistance programs, interim-governing bodies, civil defense efforts, and other activities.*

(5) (U) <u>People</u>. *List key personnel and their linkage to the population, leaders, figureheads, clerics, and subject matter experts such as plant operators and public utility managers. (**Note:** This list may extend to personnel outside of the area of operations [AO] whose actions, opinions, and influence can affect the commander's AO.) Categorize groups of civilians using local nationals (town and city dwellers, farmers and other rural dwellers, and nomads), local civil authorities (elected and traditional leaders at all levels of government), expatriates, tribal or clan figure heads and religious leaders, third-nation government agency representatives, foreign employees of intergovernmental organizations or nongovernmental organizations, contractors (American citizens, local nationals, and third-nation citizens providing contract services), the media (journalists from print, radio, and visual media), and dislocated civilians (refugees, displaced persons, evacuees, migrants, and stateless persons).*

(6) (U) <u>Events</u>. *Determine what events, military and civilian, are occurring and analyze the events for their political, economic, psychological, environmental, moral, and legal implications. Categorize civilian events that may affect military missions. Events may include harvest seasons, elections, riots, voluntary evacuations, involuntary evacuations, holidays, school year, and religious periods.*

g. (U) <u>Attachments and Detachments</u>. *List units attached to or detached from the issuing headquarters only as necessary to clarify task organization that impact civil affairs operations. Refer to Annex A (Task Organization) as required.*

h. (U) <u>Assumptions</u>. *List key assumptions that pertain to civil affairs operations that were used to form the civil affairs operations running estimate and develop the OPLAN or OPORD and this annex.*

2. (U) <u>Mission</u>. *State the mission of civil affairs operations in support of the base plan or order.*

3. (U) <u>Execution</u>.

a. (U) <u>Scheme of Civil Affairs Operations</u>. *Describe how civil affairs operations support the commander's intent and concept of operations described in the base plan or order. Outline the effects the commander wants civil affairs operations to achieve while prioritizing civil affairs tasks. Identify and list civil-military objectives and the primary tasks to achieve those objectives.*

[CLASSIFICATION]

ANNEX K (CIVIL AFFAIRS OPERATIONS) TO OPLAN/OPORD [number] [(code name)]—[issuing headquarters] [(classification of title)]

(1) (U) <u>Execution Matrix</u>. *Provide the execution matrix. Refer to Appendix 1 (Execution Matrix) to Annex K (Civil Affairs Operations).*

(2) (U) <u>Populace and Resources Control Plan</u>. *Provide the populace and resources control plan. Refer to Appendix 2 (Populace and Resources Control Plan) to Annex K (Civil Affairs Operations).*

(3) (U) <u>Civil Information Management Plan</u>. *Provide the civil information management plan. Refer to Appendix 3 (Civil Information Management Plan) to Annex K (Civil Affairs Operations).*

b. (U) <u>Tasks to Subordinate Units</u>. *State the civil affairs operations tasks assigned to each unit that report directly to the headquarters issuing the order. Each task must include* who *(the subordinate unit assigned the task),* what *(the task itself),* when, where, *and* why *(purpose). Include interagency, intergovernmental organization, or nongovernmental organization supporting tasks. Use a separate subparagraph for each unit. List units in task organization sequence. Place tasks that affect two or more units in paragraph 3c (Coordinating Instructions) of this annex.*

c. (U) <u>Coordinating Instructions</u>. *List only instructions applicable to two or more subordinate units not covered in the base plan or order.*

(1) (U) <u>Environmental Considerations</u>. *Review environmental planning guidance and, if available, the Environmental Management Support Plan for implied civil affairs operations tasks that support environmental activities. For example, establishing and supporting camps for dislocated civilians may require air and water purification, hazardous waste and material disposal, and identification of hazards such as pesticides, toxic chemicals, and historic or cultural resources for preservation. Refer to Annex G (Engineer) as required.*

(2) (U) <u>Stability Operations</u>. *Describe how civil affairs operations support the command's identified minimum-essential stability operations tasks—civil control, civil security, and restoration of essential services. Units responsible for an area of operations must execute the minimum-essential tasks with available resources if no civilian agency or organization is capable. Address course of action support to governance and economic stability if required by mission taskings of the higher headquarters.*

4. (U) <u>Sustainment</u>. *Identify priorities of sustainment for civil affairs operations key tasks and specify additional instructions as required. Refer to Annex F (Sustainment) as required.*

a. (U) <u>Logistics</u>. *Identify unique sustainment requirements, procedures, and guidance to support civil affairs teams and operations. Specify procedures for specialized technical logistics support from external organizations as necessary. Use subparagraphs to identify priorities and specific instructions for maintenance, transportation, supply, field services, distribution, contracting, and general engineering support pertaining to civil affairs operations. Refer to Annex F (Sustainment) and Annex P (Host-Nation Support) as required.*

b. (U) <u>Personnel</u>. *Identify unique personnel requirements and concerns, associated with civil affairs operations, including global sourcing support and contracted linguist requirements. Use subparagraphs to identify priorities and specific instructions for human resources support, financial management, legal support, and religious support. Refer to Annex F (Sustainment) as required.*

c. (U) <u>Army Health System Support</u>. *Identify availability, priorities, and instructions for medical care. Refer to Annex F (Sustainment) as required. Provide additional information on the following:*

(1) (U) *Identify and list locations, capabilities, and capacity of nonmilitary medical facilities that can or will support civil affairs operations.*

(2) (U) *Identify and list unique problems, challenges, and legal considerations of providing medical system support to the indigenous population.*

[page number]
[CLASSIFICATION]

[CLASSIFICATION]

ANNEX K (CIVIL AFFAIRS OPERATIONS) TO OPLAN/OPORD [number] [(code name)]— [issuing headquarters] [(classification of title)]

(3) (U) *Identify and list host-nation medical support capabilities if not addressed in Annex P (Host-Nation Support).*

5. (U) Command and Signal.

a. (U) Command.

(1). (U) Location of Key Leaders. *List the location of key civil affairs unit commanders and staff officers G-9 (S-9).*

(2) (U) Succession of Command. *State the succession of command if not covered in the unit's SOPs.*

(3) (U) Liaison Requirements. *State civil affairs liaison requirements not covered in the unit's SOPs.*

b. (U) Control.

(1) (U) Command Posts. *Describe the employment of command posts (CPs), including the location of each CP and its time of opening and closing, as appropriate. State the primary controlling CP for specific tasks or phases of the operation (for example, "Civil-military operations center (CMOC) will be co-located with division main CP").*

(a) (U) *Location and alternate locations of civil affairs command post or CMOC.*

(b) (U) *Location and alternate locations of higher, adjacent, and subordinate CMOCs.*

(c) (U) *Location of key civil affairs operations leaders G-9 (S-9).*

(2) (U) Reports. *List reports not covered in SOPs. Describe civil affairs operations reporting requirements for subordinate units. Refer to Annex R (Reports) as required.*

c. (U) Signal. *List signal operating instructions for civil affairs operations as needed, as well as primary and alternate means of communications with both military and nonmilitary organizations conducting civil affairs operations. Consider operations security requirements. Refer to Annex H (Signal) as required.*

(1) (U) *Describe the networks to monitor for reports.*

(2) (U) *Address any civil affairs operations specific communications or digitization connectivity requirements or coordination necessary to meet functional responsibilities (consider telephone listing). Provide instructions regarding maintenance and update of the civil information management database.*

ACKNOWLEDGE: *Include only if attachment is distributed separately from the base order.*

[Commander's last name]
[Commander's rank]

The commander or authorized representative signs the original copy of attachment. If the representative signs the original, add the phrase "For the Commander." The signed copy is the historical copy and remains in the headquarters' files.

OFFICIAL:

[Authenticator's name]
[Authenticator's position]

[page number]
[CLASSIFICATION]

[CLASSIFICATION]

ANNEX K (CIVIL AFFAIRS OPERATIONS) TO OPLAN/OPORD [number] [(code name)]— [issuing headquarters] [(classification of title)]

Use only if the commander does not sign the original attachment. If the commander signs the original, no further authentication is required. If the commander does not sign, the signature of the preparing staff officer requires authentication and only the last name and rank of the commander appear in the signature block.

ATTACHMENTS: *List lower-level attachment (appendixes, tabs, and exhibits).*

Appendix 1 – Execution Matrix
Appendix 2 – Populace and Resources Control Plan
Appendix 3 – Civil Information Management Plan

DISTRIBUTION: *Show only if distributed separately from the base order or higher-level attachment.*

[page number]
[CLASSIFICATION]

Annex L

Reconnaissance and Surveillance Format and Instructions

This annex provides fundamental considerations, formats, and instructions for developing Annex L (Reconnaissance and Surveillance) to the base plan or order.

HOW TO DEVELOP ANNEX L (RECONNAISSANCE AND SURVEILLANCE)

L-1. Commanders and staff use Annex L (Reconnaissance and Surveillance) to describe how reconnaissance and surveillance support the concept of operations described in the base plan or order. The G-3 (S-3) is responsible for developing Annex L (Reconnaissance and Surveillance).

[CLASSIFICATION]

Place the classification at the top and bottom of every page of the attachments. Place the classification marking (TS), (S), (C), or (U) at the front of each paragraph and subparagraph in parentheses. Refer to AR 380-5 for classification and release marking instructions.

Copy ## of ## copies
Issuing headquarters
Place of issue
Date-time group of signature
Message reference number

Include the full heading if attachment is distributed separately from the base order or higher-level attachment.

ANNEX L (RECONNAISSANCE AND SURVEILLANCE) TO OPERATION PLAN/ORDER [number] [(code name)]—[issuing headquarters] [(classification of title)]

(U) References: *List documents essential to understanding Annex L.*

   a. *List maps and charts first. Map entries include series number, country, sheet names, or numbers, edition, and scale.*

   b. *List other references in subparagraphs labeled as shown.*

   c. *A doctrinal reference for this annex includes FM 2-0.*

(U) Time Zone Used Throughout the Plan/Order: *Write the time zone established in the base plan or order.*

1. (U) Situation. *Include information affecting reconnaissance and surveillance that paragraph 1 of the OPLAN or OPORD does not cover or that needs expansion.*

   a. (U) <u>Area of Interest</u>. *Describe the area of interest as it relates to reconnaissance and surveillance. Refer to Annex B (Intelligence) as required.*

   b. (U) <u>Area of Operations</u>. *Refer to Appendix 2 (Operation Overlay) to Annex C (Operations) as required.*

[page number]
[CLASSIFICATION]

[CLASSIFICATION]

ANNEX L (RECONNAISSANCE AND SURVEILLANCE) TO OPERATION PLAN/ORDER [number] [(code name)]—[issuing headquarters] [(classification of title)]

(1) (U) <u>Terrain</u>. *Describe the aspects of terrain that impact reconnaissance and surveillance operations. Refer to Annex B (Intelligence) as required.*

(2) (U) <u>Weather</u>. *Describe the aspects of weather that impact reconnaissance and surveillance operations. Refer to Annex B (Intelligence) as required.*

c. (U) <u>Enemy Forces</u>. *List known and templated locations and activities of enemy reconnaissance and surveillance units for one echelon up and two echelons down. List enemy maneuver and other area capabilities that will impact friendly reconnaissance and surveillance operations. State expected enemy courses of action and employment of enemy reconnaissance and surveillance assets. Refer to Annex B (Intelligence) as required.*

d. (U) <u>Friendly Forces</u>. *Outline the higher headquarters' reconnaissance and surveillance plan. List designation, location, and outline of plan of higher, adjacent, and other reconnaissance and surveillance organizations and assets that support or impact the issuing headquarters or require coordination and additional support.*

e. (U) <u>Interagency, Intergovernmental, and Nongovernmental Organizations</u>. *Identify and describe other organizations in the area of operations that may impact the conduct of reconnaissance and surveillance operations or implementation of reconnaissance and surveillance-specific equipment and tactics. Refer to Annex V (Interagency Coordination) as required.*

f. (U) <u>Civil Considerations</u>. *Describe the aspects of the civil situation that impact reconnaissance and surveillance operations. Refer to Annex B (Intelligence) and Annex K (Civil Affairs Operations) as required.*

g. (U) <u>Attachments and Detachments</u>. *List units or assets attached to or detached from the issuing headquarters that impact reconnaissance and surveillance. State when each attachment or detachment is effective (for example, on order, on commitment of the reserve) if different from the effective time of the base plan or order. Do not repeat information already listed in Annex A (Task Organization). Refer to Annex A (Task Organization) as required.*

h. (U) <u>Assumptions</u>. *List any reconnaissance and surveillance-specific assumptions that support the annex development.*

2. (U) <u>Mission</u>. *State the mission of the reconnaissance and surveillance in support of the base plan or order.*

3. (U) <u>Execution</u>.

a. (U) <u>Scheme of Reconnaissance and Surveillance Operations</u>. *State the overall reconnaissance objective or objectives. Describe how the scheme of reconnaissance and surveillance supports the commander's intent, concept of operations, and commander's critical information requirements. Direct the manner in which each element of the force will cooperate to accomplish the key reconnaissance and surveillance tasks and tie that to support of the operation with task and purpose statement. Describe, at a minimum, the overall reconnaissance and surveillance scheme of maneuver and scheme of fires. Refer to Appendix 1 (Reconnaissance and Surveillance Overlay) and Appendix 2 (Reconnaissance and Surveillance Tasking Matrix) to Annex L (Reconnaissance and Surveillance) as required.*

(1) (U) <u>Movement and Maneuver</u>. *State the scheme of movement and maneuver for reconnaissance and surveillance units. Refer to Annex C (Operations) as required.*

[page number]
[CLASSIFICATION]

[CLASSIFICATION]

ANNEX L (RECONNAISSANCE AND SURVEILLANCE) TO OPERATION PLAN/ORDER [number] [(code name)]—[issuing headquarters] [(classification of title)]

(2) (U) <u>Mobility/Countermobility</u>. *State the scheme of engineer support for reconnaissance and surveillance operations. Indicate priority of effort for mobility and countermobility assets. Refer to Annex G (Engineer) as required.*

(3) (U) <u>Battlefield Obscuration</u>. *State the scheme of battlefield obscuration in support of reconnaissance and surveillance including priorities by unit or area. Refer to Annex C (Operations) as required.*

(4) (U) <u>Intelligence</u>. *Describe the intelligence concept for supporting reconnaissance and surveillance. Refer to Annex B (Intelligence) as required.*

(5) (U) <u>Fires</u>. *State the scheme of fires in support of reconnaissance and surveillance operations. Identify which reconnaissance and surveillance assets have priority of fires and the coordinating purpose of, priorities for, allocation of, and restrictions on fire support and fire support coordination measures. Refer to Annex D (Fires) as required.*

(6) (U) <u>Protection</u>. *State the protection support to reconnaissance and surveillance. Include air and missile defense and explosive ordnance disposal support and priorities of support to reconnaissance and surveillance operations. Identify reactionary forces available in the operational area. Refer to Annex E (Protection) as required.*

b. (U) <u>Tasks to Subordinate Units</u>. *State the reconnaissance and surveillance collection tasks and tasks to support reconnaissance and surveillance for each subordinate unit not identified in the base order. List units by task organization sequence per the base order or Annex A (Task Organization). Address the function or support roles of military intelligence units. Refer to Appendix 2 (Reconnaissance and Surveillance Tasking Matrix) to Annex L (Reconnaissance and Surveillance) as required.*

c. (U) <u>Coordinating Instructions</u>. *List only instructions applicable to two or more subordinate units not covered in the base plan or order.*

4. (U) Sustainment. *Identify priorities of sustainment for reconnaissance and surveillance key tasks and specify additional instructions as required. Refer to Annex F (Sustainment) as required.*

a. (U) <u>Logistics</u>. *Identify unique sustainment requirements, procedures, and guidance to support reconnaissance and surveillance teams and operations. Specify procedures for specialized technical logistics support from external organizations as necessary. Use subparagraphs to identify priorities and specific instructions for maintenance, transportation, supply, field services, distribution, contracting, and general engineering support pertaining to reconnaissance and surveillance operations. Refer to Annex F (Sustainment) and Annex P (Host-Nation Support) as required.*

b. (U) <u>Personnel</u>. *Identify reconnaissance and surveillance unique personnel requirements and concerns, including global sourcing support and contracted linguist requirements. Use subparagraphs to identify priorities and specific instructions for human resources support, financial management, legal support, and religious support pertaining to reconnaissance and surveillance operations. Refer to Annex F (Sustainment) as required.*

c. (U) <u>Army Health System Support</u>. *Identify availability, priorities, and instructions for medical care. Refer to Annex F (Sustainment) as required.*

5. (U) Command and Signal.

a. (U) <u>Command</u>.

[page number]
[CLASSIFICATION]

[CLASSIFICATION]

ANNEX L (RECONNAISSANCE AND SURVEILLANCE) TO OPERATION PLAN/ORDER [number] [(code name)]—[issuing headquarters] [(classification of title)]

        (1) (U) <u>Location of Commander</u>. *State the location of key reconnaissance and surveillance leaders.*

        (2) (U) <u>Succession of Command</u>. *State the succession of command if not covered in the unit's standard operating procedures.*

        (3) (U) <u>Liaison Requirements</u>. *State the reconnaissance and surveillance liaison requirements not covered in the unit's standard operating procedures.*

b. (U) <u>Control</u>.

        (1) (U) <u>Command Posts</u>. *Describe the employment of reconnaissance and surveillance specific command posts (CPs), including the location of each CP and its time of opening and closing.*

        (2) (U) <u>Reports</u>. *List reconnaissance and surveillance-specific reports not covered in standard operating procedures. Refer to Annex R (Reports) as required.*

        c. (U) <u>Signal</u>. *Address any reconnaissance and surveillance-specific communications requirements. Refer to Annex H (Signal) as required.*

ACKNOWLEDGE: *Include only if attachment is distributed separately from the base plan or order.*

                 [Commander's last name]
                 [Commander's rank]

The commander or authorized representative signs the original copy. If the representative signs the original, add the phrase "For the Commander." The signed copy is the historical copy and remains in the headquarters' files.

OFFICIAL:

[Authenticator's name]
[Authenticator's position]

Use only if the commander does not sign the original plan or order. If the commander signs the original, no further authentication is required. If the commander does not sign, the signature of the preparing staff officer requires authentication and only the last name and rank of the commander appear in the signature block.

ATTACHMENTS: *List lower-level attachment (appendixes, tabs, and exhibits).*

Appendix 1 – Reconnaissance and Surveillance Overlay
Appendix 2 – Reconnaissance and Surveillance Tasking Matrix

DISTRIBUTION: *Show only if attachment is distributed separately from the base plan or order.*

[page number]
[CLASSIFICATION]

Annex M

Assessment Annex Format and Instructions

This annex provides fundamental considerations, formats, and instructions for developing Annex M (Assessment) to the base plan or order.

HOW TO DEVELOP ANNEX M (ASSESSMENT)

M-1. Commanders and staff use Annex M (Assessment) to as a means to quantify and qualify mission success or task accomplishment. The G-3 (S-3) or G-5 (S-5) is responsible for the development of Annex M (Assessment).

M-2. This annex describes the assessment concept of support objectives. A complex assessment concept of support may require a schematic to show the space operations objectives and task relationships. This annex includes a discussion of the overall assessment concept of support, with the specific details in element subparagraphs and attachments. It includes space operations-related constraints, if appropriate.

[CLASSIFICATION]

Place the classification at the top and bottom of every page of the attachments. Place the classification marking (TS), (S), (C), or (U) at the front of each paragraph and subparagraph in parentheses. Refer to AR 380-5 for classification and release marking instructions.

Copy ## of ## copies
Issuing headquarters
Place of issue
Date-time group of signature
Message reference number

Include the full heading if attachment is distributed separately from the base order or higher-level attachment.

ANNEX M (ASSESSMENT) TO OPERATION PLAN/ORDER [number] [(code name)]—[issuing headquarters] [(classification of title)]

(U) References: *List documents essential to understanding the attachment.*

a. *List maps and charts first. Map entries include series number, country, sheet names, or numbers, edition, and scale.*

b. *List other references in subparagraphs labeled as shown. List available assessment products that are produced external to this unit. This includes classified and open source assessment products of the higher headquarters, adjacent units, key government organizations (such as the State Department or other government agency), and any other relevant military or civilian organizations.*

c. *A doctrinal reference for assessment includes FM 5-0.*

(U) Time Zone Used Throughout the Plan/Order: *Write the time zone established in the base plan or order.*

1. (U) Situation. *See the base order or use the following subparagraphs. Include information affecting assessment that paragraph 1 of the OPLAN or OPORD does not cover or that needs expansion.*

a. (U) <u>Area of Interest</u>. *Describe the area of interest as it relates to assessment. Refer to Annex B (Intelligence) as required.*

[page number]
[CLASSIFICATION]

[CLASSIFICATION]

ANNEX M (ASSESSMENT) TO OPERATION PLAN/ORDER [number] [(code name)]—[issuing headquarters] [(classification of title)]

b. (U) <u>Area of Operations</u>. *Refer to Appendix 2 (Operation Overlay) to Annex C (Operations).*

(1) (U) <u>Terrain</u>. *Describe the aspects of terrain that impact assessment. Refer to Annex B (Intelligence) as required.*

(2) (U) <u>Weather</u>. *Describe the aspects of weather that impact assessment. Refer to Annex B (Intelligence) as required.*

c. (U) <u>Enemy Forces</u>. *List known and templated locations and activities of enemy assessment units for one echelon up and two echelons down. List enemy maneuver and other area capabilities that will impact friendly operations. State expected enemy courses of action and employment of enemy assessment assets. Refer to Annex B (Intelligence) as required.*

d. (U) <u>Friendly Forces</u>. *Outline the higher headquarters' assessment plan. List designation, location, and outline of plans of higher, adjacent, and other assessment organizations and assets that support or impact the issuing headquarters or require coordination and additional support.*

e. (U) <u>Interagency, Intergovernmental, and Nongovernmental Organizations</u>. *Identify and describe other organizations in the area of operations that may impact assessment. Refer to Annex V (Interagency Coordination) as required.*

f. (U) <u>Civil Considerations</u>. *Describe the aspects of the civil situation that impact assessment. Refer to Annex B (Intelligence) and Annex K (Civil Affairs Operations) as required.*

g. (U) <u>Attachments and Detachments</u>. *List units attached or detached only as necessary to clarify task organization. Refer to Annex A (Task Organization) as required.*

h. (U) <u>Assumptions</u>. *List any assessment-specific assumptions that support the annex development.*

2. (U) <u>Mission</u>. *State the mission of assessment in support of the base plan or order.*

3. (U) <u>Execution</u>.

a. (U) <u>Scheme of Operational Assessment</u>. *State the overall concept for assessing the operation. Include priorities of assessment, quantitative and qualitative indicators, and the general concept for how the recommendations produced by the assessment process will reach decisionmakers at the relevant time and place.*

(1) (U) <u>Nesting with Higher Headquarters</u>. *Provide the concept of nesting of unit assessment practices with lateral and higher headquarters (include military and interagency organizations, where applicable). Use Appendix 1 (Nesting of Assessment Efforts) to Annex M (Assessment) to provide a diagram or matrix that depicts the nesting of headquarters assessment procedures.*

(2) (U) <u>Information Requirements (Data Collection Plan)</u>. *Information requirements for assessment are synchronized through the reconnaissance and surveillance synchronization process and may be commander's critical information requirements. Provide a narrative that describes the plan to collect the data needed to inform the status on metrics and indicators developed. The data collection plan should include a consideration to minimize impact on subordinate unit operations. Provide diagrams or matrixes that depict the hierarchy of assessment objectives with the underlying measures of effectiveness, measures of performance, indicators, and metrics. Provide measures of effectiveness with the underlying data collection requirements and responsible agency for collecting the data.*

(3) (U) <u>Battle Rhythm</u>. *Establish the sequence of regularly occurring assessments activities. Explicitly state frequency of data collection for each data element. Include requirements to higher units, synchronization with lateral units, and products provided to subordinate units.*

[page number]
[CLASSIFICATION]

[CLASSIFICATION]

ANNEX M (ASSESSMENT) TO OPERATION PLAN/ORDER [number] [(code name)]—[issuing headquarters] [(classification of title)]

(4) (U) <u>Reframing Criteria</u>. *Identify key assumptions, events, or conditions that staffs will periodically assess to refine understanding of the existing problem and, if appropriate, trigger a reframe.*

b. (U) <u>Tasks to Subordinate Units</u>. *Identify the unit, agency, or staff section assigned responsibility for collecting data, conducting analysis, and generating recommendations for each condition or measure of effectiveness. Refer to paragraph 3a(2) (Information Requirements) of this annex as necessary.*

c. (U) <u>Coordinating Instructions</u>. *List only instructions applicable to two or more subordinate units not covered in the base plan or order. Use Appendix 3 (Assessment Working Group) to Annex M (Assessment) to include quad charts that provide details about meeting location, proponency, members, agenda, and inputs or outputs.*

4. (U) <u>Sustainment</u>. *Identify priorities of sustainment assessment key tasks and specify additional instructions as required. Refer to Annex F (Sustainment) as required.*

a. (U) <u>Logistics</u>. *Identify unique sustainment requirements, procedures, and guidance to support assessment teams. Use subparagraphs to identify priorities and specific instructions for maintenance, transportation, supply, field services, distribution, contracting, and general engineering support. Refer to Annex F (Sustainment) and Annex P (Host-Nation Support) as required.*

b. (U) <u>Personnel</u>. *Use subparagraphs to identify priorities and specific instructions for human resources support, financial management, legal support, and religious support. Refer to Annex F (Sustainment) as required.*

c. (U) <u>Army Health System Support</u>. *Identify availability, priorities, and instructions for medical care. Refer to Annex F (Sustainment) as required.*

5. (U) <u>Command and Signal</u>.

a. (U) <u>Command</u>. *State the location of key assessment cells. State assessment liaison requirements not covered in the unit's standard operating procedures (SOPs).*

(1) (U) <u>Location of Commander</u>. *State the location of key assessment leaders.*

(2) (U) <u>Succession of Command</u>. *State the succession of command if not covered in the unit's SOPs.*

(3) (U) <u>Liaison Requirements</u>. *State the assessment liaison requirements not covered in the unit's SOPs.*

b. (U) <u>Control</u>.

(1) (U) <u>Command Posts</u>. *Describe the employment of assessment-specific command posts (CPs), including the location of each CP and its time of opening and closing.*

(2) (U) <u>Reports</u>. *List assessment-specific reports not covered in SOPs. Refer to Annex R (Reports) as required.*

c. (U) <u>Signal</u>. *Address any assessment-specific communications requirements. Refer to Annex H (Signal) as required.*

[page number]
[CLASSIFICATION]

[CLASSIFICATION]

ANNEX M (ASSESSMENT) TO OPERATION PLAN/ORDER [number] [(code name)]—[issuing headquarters] [(classification of title)]OFFICIAL:

ACKNOWLEDGE: *Include only if attachment is distributed separately from the base order.*

[Commander's last name]
[Commander's rank]

The commander or authorized representative signs the original copy of the attachment. If the representative signs the original, add the phrase "For the Commander." The signed copy is the historical copy and remains in the headquarters' files.

[Authenticator's name]
[Authenticator's position]

Use only if the commander does not sign the original attachment. If the commander signs the original, no further authentication is required. If the commander does not sign, the signature of the preparing staff officer requires authentication and only the last name and rank of the commander appear in the signature block.

ATTACHMENTS: *List lower-level attachment (appendixes, tabs, and exhibits).*

Appendix 1 – Nesting of Assessment Efforts
Appendix 2 – Assessment Framework
Appendix 3 – Assessment Working Group

DISTRIBUTION: *Show only if distributed separately from the base order or higher-level attachments.*

[page number]
[CLASSIFICATION]

Annex N

Space Operations Format and Instructions

This annex provides fundamental considerations, formats, and instructions for developing Annex N (Space Operations) to the base plan or order.

HOW TO DEVELOP ANNEX N (SPACE OPERATIONS)

N-1. Commanders and staff use Annex N (Space Operations) to describe how space operations support the concept of operations described in the base plan or order. The space operations officer develops the Annex N (Space Operations).

N-2. This annex is used to coordinate early with the staff, to include the G-2 (S-2), G-6 (S-6), air defense artillery officer, and the special technical operations cell to synchronize efforts and avoid duplication of information. While the G-2 (S-2) may want to produce and include the enemy space assessment portion in Annex B (Intelligence), there are products space professionals may uniquely contribute. This annex requests space orders of battle through the Joint Space Operations Center prior to deployment.

[CLASSIFICATION]

Place the classification at the top and bottom of every page of the attachments. Place the classification marking (TS), (S), (C), or (U) at the front of each paragraph and subparagraph in parentheses. Refer to AR 380-5 for classification and release marking instructions.

(Change from verbal orders, if any)

> **Copy ## of ## copies**
> **Issuing headquarters**
> **Place of issue**
> **Date-time group of signature**
> **Message reference number**

Include heading if attachment is distributed separately from the base order or higher-level attachment.

ANNEX N (SPACE OPERATIONS) TO OPLAN/OPORD [number] [(code name)]—[issuing headquarters] [(classification of title)]

(U) References: *List documents essential to understanding the attachment.*

a. *List maps and charts first. Map entries include series number, country, sheet names, or numbers, edition, and scale.*

b. *List other references in subparagraphs labeled as shown.*

c. *Doctrinal references for space operations include FM 3-14, JP 3-14, Professional Reference Guide, and U.S. National Space Policy.*

(U) Time Zone Used Throughout the Order: *Write the time zone established in the base plan or order.*

1. (U) Situation. *Include information affecting space operations that paragraph 1 of the OPLAN or OPORD does not cover or that needs expansion.*

[page number]
[CLASSIFICATION]

[CLASSIFICATION]

ANNEX N (SPACE OPERATIONS) TO OPLAN/OPORD [number] [(code name)]—[issuing headquarters] [(classification of title)]

a. (U) <u>Area of Interest</u>. *Describe the area of interest as it relates to space operations. Refer to Annex B (Intelligence) as required.*

b. (U) <u>Area of Operations</u>. *Refer to Appendix 2 (Operation Overlay) to Annex C (Operations).*

(1) (U) <u>Terrain</u>. *Describe the aspects of terrain that impact space operations such as terrain masking. Refer to Annex B (Intelligence) as required.*

(2) (U) <u>Weather</u>. *Describe the aspects of space and terrestrial weather that impact space operations. Refer to Annex B (Intelligence) as required.*

c. (U) <u>Enemy Forces</u>. *List known locations and activities of enemy space capable assets and units. List enemy space capabilities that can impact friendly operations. State expected enemy courses of action and employment of enemy and commercial space assets. Refer to Annex B (Intelligence) as required.*

d. (U) <u>Friendly Forces</u>. *Outline the higher headquarters' plan for space operations and space support teams including but not limited to space support elements, Army space support teams, and an organic space weapons officer. List designation, location, and outline of plans of higher, adjacent, and other space operations-related assets that support or impact the issuing headquarters or require coordination and additional support. For example, the space coordinating authority and specified processes established for the area of responsibility.*

e. (U) <u>Interagency, Intergovernmental, and Nongovernmental Organizations</u>. *Identify and describe other organizations in the area of operations that may impact the conduct of space operations or implementation of space-specific equipment, tactics, and capabilities. Consider all multinational, civil, and nongovernmental organizations such as civilian relief agencies and other customers and providers of space-based capabilities. Refer to Annex V (Interagency Coordination) as required.*

f. (U) <u>Civil Considerations</u>. *Describe the aspects of the civil situation that impact space operations. Refer to Annex B (Intelligence) and Annex K (Civil Affairs Operations) as required.*

g. (U) <u>Attachments and Detachments</u>. *List units attached or detached only as necessary to clarify task organization. Refer to Annex A (Task Organization) as required.*

h. (U) <u>Assumptions</u>. *List space operations-specific assumptions that support the annex development.*

2. (U) <u>Mission</u>. *State the mission of space operations in support of the base plan or order.*

3. (U) <u>Execution</u>.

a. (U) <u>Scheme of Space Operations</u>. *Describe how space capabilities support the commander's intent and concept of operations. Establish the priorities of space support to units for each phase of the operation. For example, electromagnetic interference resolution and defended asset list. Also address unique space reliances or vulnerabilities related to unit systems and capabilities. Refer to Annex C (Operations) as required.*

(1) (U) <u>Space Force Enhancement</u>. *Identify space activities required to support the operation plan, including the following specific areas as applicable:*

[page number]
[CLASSIFICATION]

[CLASSIFICATION]

ANNEX N (SPACE OPERATIONS) TO OPLAN/OPORD [number] [(code name)]—[issuing headquarters] [(classification of title)]

(a) (U) <u>Satellite Communication</u>. *Describe the space operations communications plan. Ensure defensive space priorities for satellite communication links are established and coordinated based on operational priorities. Refer to Annex H (Signal) as required.*

(b) (U) <u>Remote Sensing/Environmental Monitoring</u>. *Identify and list meteorological, oceanographic, geodetic, and other environmental support information provided by space assets that affect space, air, surface, or subsurface activities and assets. Refer to Annex G (Engineer) as required.*

(c) (U) <u>Position, Navigation, and Timing</u>. *Provide navigational capabilities that would aid the transit of ships, aircraft, personnel, or ground vehicles and determine the course and distance traveled or position location. Provide global positioning system (GPS) accuracy to support GPS-aided munitions.*

(d) (U) <u>Reconnaissance and Surveillance</u>. *Provide information pertaining to friendly and enemy forces in or external to the operational areas that would aid in operations and force positioning. Refer to Annex L (Reconnaissance and Surveillance) as required.*

(e) (U) <u>Theater Missile Warning</u>. *Provide information on the notification of enemy ballistic missile or space-weapon attacks evaluated from available sensor and intelligence sources and the possible affect on the operational area. Provide notification of friendly ballistic missile launches and the impacts on the operational areas that would require early warning of affected friendly forces and an estimated point of impact for each launch. Establish provisions, in coordination with the air defense artillery officer, to disseminate information quickly throughout the operational areas. Refer to Annex B (Intelligence) and Annex E (Protection) as required.*

(2) (U) <u>Space Control</u>. *Provide information on space-related activities, whether performed by space, air, or surface assets that ensure friendly forces and deny enemy forces the unrestricted use of space and space assets. Identify targetable enemy assets and limitations of targeting. Address all capabilities and effects related to offensive or defensive space control and space situational awareness requirements.*

(3) (U) <u>Nuclear Detonation</u>. *Provide information on the notification of detected nuclear detonations that might affect the operation and require evaluation as to yield and location. Refer to Annex B (Intelligence) as required.*

(4) (U) <u>Cyber/Electromagnetic Operations</u>. *Integrate cyber/electromagnetic plans and capabilities to optimally synchronize their effects. Refer to Annex D (Fires) as required.*

(5) (U) <u>Special Technical Programs</u>. *Provide information on the organization and synchronization of the integrated joint special technical operations and alternate compensatory control measures plans in support of the commander's objectives. Refer to Annex S (Special Technical Operations) as required.*

(6) (U) <u>Mission Command</u>. *Provide information and an assessment on friendly space reliances upon satellite communications, missile warning, and network architectures. Determine how organic unit systems and equipment rely upon these communications paths (architectures).*

[page number]
[CLASSIFICATION]

ANNEX N (SPACE OPERATIONS) TO OPLAN/OPORD [number] [(code name)]—[issuing headquarters] [(classification of title)]

b. (U) <u>Tasks to Subordinate Units</u>. *List space tasks assigned to specific subordinate units not contained in the base plan or order. Refer to any tasks in base order.*

c. (U) <u>Coordinating Instructions</u>. *List only instructions applicable to two or more subordinate units not covered in the base plan or order. Document coordination and reachback support requests in accordance with space coordinating authority guidance such as "Space Coordinating Plans" and other directives for the area of responsibility; include unique equipment sustainment and technical points of contact.*

4. (U) <u>Sustainment</u>. *Identify priorities of sustainment for space operations key tasks and specify additional instructions as required. Refer to Annex F (Sustainment) as required.*

a. (U) <u>Logistics</u>. *Identify unique sustainment requirements, procedures, and guidance to support space operations teams and operations. Specify procedures for specialized technical logistics support from external organizations as necessary. Use subparagraphs to identify priorities and specific instructions for maintenance, transportation, supply, field services, distribution, contracting, and general engineering support. Refer to Annex F (Sustainment) and Annex P (Host-Nation Support) as required.*

b. (U) <u>Personnel</u>. *Use subparagraphs to identify priorities and specific instructions for human resources support, financial management, legal support, and religious support. Refer to Annex F (Sustainment) as required.*

c. (U) <u>Army Health System Support</u>. *Identify availability, priorities, and instructions for medical care. Refer to Annex F (Sustainment) as required.*

5. (U) <u>Command and Signal</u>.

a. (U) **<u>Command</u>.**

(1) (U) <u>Location of the Commander</u>. *State the location of key space leaders such as the space coordinating authority, director of space forces), Joint Space Operations Center, electronic warfare officers, and other key reachback leaders.*

(2) (U) <u>Succession of Command</u>. *State the succession of command if not covered in the unit's SOPs.*

(3) (U) <u>Liaison Requirements</u>. *State the space liaison requirements not covered in the unit's standard operating procedures (SOPs), such as air component coordination element or coalition space officers.*

b. (U) <u>Control</u>.

(1) (U) <u>Command Posts</u>. *Describe the employment of space command, control, and functional chains including their location and contact information.*

(2) (U) <u>Reports</u>. *List space related reports not covered in SOPs. Refer to any space coordinating authority concept of operations or guidance and Annex R (Reports) as required.*

c. (U) <u>Signal</u>. *Address any space-specific communications requirements such as secure chat communications applications. These often require a lengthy approval process to tunnel through existing networks and should be specified well in advance. Refer to Annex H (Signal) as required.*

ACKNOWLEDGE: *Include only if attachment is distributed separately from the base order.*

[Commander's last name]
[Commander's rank]

[page number]
[CLASSIFICATION]

[CLASSIFICATION]

ANNEX N (SPACE OPERATIONS) TO OPLAN/OPORD [number] [(code name)]—[issuing headquarters] [(classification of title)]

The commander or authorized representative signs the original copy of attachment. If the representative signs the original, add the phrase "For the Commander." The signed copy is the historical copy and remains in the headquarters' files.

OFFICIAL:

[Authenticator's name]
[Authenticator's position]

Use only if the commander does not sign the original attachment. If the commander signs the original, no further authentication is required. If the commander does not sign, the signature of the preparing staff officer requires authentication and only the last name and rank of the commander appear in the signature block.

ATTACHMENT: *List lower-level attachments (appendixes, tabs, and exhibits).*

DISTRIBUTION: *Show only if distributed separately from the base order or higher-level attachments.*

[page number]
[CLASSIFICATION]

This page intentionally left blank.

Annex O

Not Used

This page intentionally left blank.

Annex P

Host-Nation Support Annex Format and Instructions

This annex provides fundamental considerations, formats, and instructions for developing Annex P (Host-Nation Support) to the base plan or order.

HOW TO DEVELOP ANNEX P (HOST-NATION SUPPORT)

P-1.   Commanders and staff use Annex P (Host-Nation Support) to describe how sustainment operations support the concept of operations described in the base plan or order. The G-4 (S-4) is the staff officer responsible for Annex P (Host-Nation Support).

P-2.   Host-nation support is the civil and military assistance provided by host nation to the forces located in or transiting through that host nation's territory. Efficient use of available host-nation support can greatly aid forces and augment the deployed sustainment structure.

[CLASSIFICATION]

Place the classification at the top and bottom of every page of the attachments. Place the classification marking (TS), (S), (C), or (U) at the front of each paragraph and subparagraph in parentheses. Refer to AR 380-5 for classification and release marking instructions.

(Change from verbal orders, if any)

Copy ## of ## copies
Issuing headquarters
Place of issue
Date-time group of signature
Message reference number

Include heading if attachment is distributed separately from the base order or higher-level attachment.

ANNEX P (HOST-NATION SUPPORT) TO OPLAN/OPORD [number] [(code name)]—[issuing headquarters] [(classification of title)]

(U) References: *List documents essential to understanding the attachment.*

   a. *List maps and charts first. Map entries include series number, country, sheet names, or numbers, edition, and scale.*

   b. *List other references in subparagraphs labeled as shown.*

   c. *A doctrinal reference for host-nation support includes FM 3-16.*

(U) Time Zone Used Throughout the Order: *Write the time zone established in the base plan or order.*

1. (U) Situation. *Include information affecting host-nation support that paragraph 1 of the OPLAN or OPORD does not cover or that needs expansion.*

   a. (U) Area of Interest. *Describe the area of interest as it relates to host-nation support. Refer to Annex B (Intelligence) as required.*

[page number]
[CLASSIFICATION]

[CLASSIFICATION]

ANNEX P (HOST-NATION SUPPORT) TO OPLAN/OPORD [number] [(code name)]—[issuing headquarters] [(classification of title)]

b. (U) <u>Area of Operations</u>. *Refer to Appendix 2 (Operation Overlay) to Annex C (Operations).*

(1) (U) <u>Terrain</u>. *Describe the aspects of terrain that impact host-nation support operations. Refer to Annex B (Intelligence) as required.*

(2) (U) <u>Weather</u>. *Describe the aspects of weather that impact host-nation support operations. Refer to Annex B (Intelligence) as required.*

c. (U) <u>Enemy Forces</u>. *List known and templated locations and activities of enemy host-nation support for one echelon up and two echelons down. List enemy maneuver and other area capabilities that will impact friendly host-nation support operations. State expected enemy courses of action and employment of enemy host-nation support assets. Refer to Annex B (Intelligence) as required.*

d. (U) <u>Friendly Forces</u>. *Outline the higher headquarters' host-nation support plan. List designation, location, and outline of plans of higher, adjacent, and other host-nation support assets that support or impact the issuing headquarters or require coordination and additional support.*

e. (U) <u>Interagency, Intergovernmental, and Nongovernmental Organizations</u>. *Identify and describe other organizations in the area of operations that may impact the conduct of host-nation support operations or implementation of host-nation support-specific equipment and tactics. Refer to Annex V (Interagency Coordination) as required.*

f. (U) <u>Civil Considerations</u>. *Describe the aspects of the civil situation that impact host-nation support operations. Refer to Annex B (Intelligence) and Annex K (Civil Affairs Operations) as required.*

g. (U) <u>Attachments and Detachments</u>. *List units attached or detached only as necessary to clarify task organization. Refer to Annex A (Task Organization) as required.*

h. (U) <u>Assumptions</u>. *List any host-nation support-specific assumptions that support the annex development. State assumptions concerning host-nation support and the operational impact if the assumptions are inaccurate.*

i. (U) <u>Host-Nation Support Agreements</u>. *List host-nation support agreements, unreliable or doubtful agreements, and presumed host-nation support agreements.*

2. (U) <u>Mission</u>. *State the mission of host-nation support in support of the base plan or order.*

3. (U) <u>Execution</u>.

a. (U) <u>Scheme of Host-Nation Support</u>. *Describe how the commander's intent and concept of operations is supported by host-nation support. Cover the overall status of negotiations and agreements, to include customs requirements, by country or treaty organization, presumed host-nation support and the reliability of host-nation support. Identify peacetime and pre-conflict military information support operations that would develop support in foreign countries for the provision of host-nation support. Establish the priorities of support to units for each phase of the operation. Refer to Annex C (Operations) as required.*

b. (U) <u>Host Nation Support Considerations</u>. *The subparagraphs below are not an all inclusive list. Each host-nation agreement is unique. Refer to Annex F (Sustainment) as required.*

(1) (U) <u>Accommodations</u>. *Describe host-nation accommodation considerations for the following: billeting; offices; stores and warehouses; workshops, vehicle parks, gun parks; medical; hardstands; fuel; weapons and ammunition; transportation to include aircraft; firing ranges; training areas and facilities; recreational areas and facilities; and laundry and dry-cleaning facilities.*

[page number]
[CLASSIFICATION]

[CLASSIFICATION]

ANNEX P (HOST-NATION SUPPORT) TO OPLAN/OPORD [number] [(code name)]—[issuing headquarters] [(classification of title)]

(2) (U) <u>Ammunition and Weapons</u>. *Describe host-nation considerations for ammunition and weapons security, storage, and collection or delivery.*

(3) (U) <u>Communications</u>. *Describe host-nation considerations for local and international communications, and security.*

(4) (U) <u>Finance</u>. *Describe host-nation considerations and payment for accommodations, supplies, communications, equipment, local labor, maintenance, medical and movement facilities, emergency facilities, and personal facilities.*

(5) (U) <u>Fuel</u>. *Describe host-nation fuel considerations for aircraft, vehicles, ships, method of delivery, storage, interoperability of refueling equipment, and common use of refueling installations.*

(6) (U) <u>Local Labor</u>. *Describe host-nation local labor considerations for method of hiring, method of payment, and administration.*

(7) (U) <u>Maintenance</u>. *Describe host-nation maintenance considerations for accommodations, vehicles, ships, equipment, roads, fixed and rotary wing aircraft, provision of assembly areas, damage control, emergency facilities for visitors' vehicles and equipment, and evacuation of disabled vehicles and equipment.*

(8) (U) <u>Medical</u>. *Describe host-nation medical considerations for hospital facilities, emergency facilities, reciprocal national health agreements, and casualty evacuation.*

(9) (U) <u>Movement</u>. *Describe host-nation movement considerations for airheads (facilities, alternates, equipment, and refueling), ports (facilities, alternates, ships, draft, bunkering/fueling, and repair), road and rail movement (personnel, equipment, security, and traffic control), and pipeline movement.*

(10) (U) <u>Rations</u>. *Describe host-nation rations considerations for fresh food, packaged foods, and potable water.*

(11) (U) <u>Supplies and Equipment</u>. *Describe host-nation supplies and equipment considerations for common use items other than ammunition, fuel, or rations.*

(12) (U) <u>Translation</u>. *Describe host-nation translation considerations for interpreters, linguists, language specialists, and document translation.*

(13) (U) <u>Transportation Equipment</u>. *Describe host-nation transportation equipment considerations for use of host-nation military vehicles, equipment, ships, and aircraft; locally hired vehicles and equipment, ships, and aircraft; and the policy on drivers and handlers of the military and locally hired vehicles.*

(14) (U) <u>Water</u>. *Describe host-nation water considerations for production and purification capability (municipal and other water treatment systems), distribution capability (trucks, pipeline, and hose line), storage capability, receipt and issue capability, available water sources (wells, surface, and sub-surface), and host-nation water quality standards.*

c. (U) <u>Tasks to Subordinate Units</u>. *List host-nation support tasks assigned to specific subordinate units not contained in the base order. Identify the office of primary responsibility for each type of host-nation support managed separately within the command.*

d. (U) <u>Coordinating Instructions</u>. *List only instructions applicable to two or more subordinate units not covered in the base plan or order.*

[page number]
[CLASSIFICATION]

[CLASSIFICATION]

ANNEX P (HOST-NATION SUPPORT) TO OPLAN/OPORD [number] [(code name)]—[issuing headquarters] [(classification of title)]

4. (U) Sustainment. *Identify priorities of sustainment for host-nation support key tasks and specify additional instructions as required. Outline support limitations that are due to lack of host-nation water agreements, operational impact, status of any current negotiations, and prospects for availability of the required support on a emergency basis. Refer to Annex F (Sustainment) as required.*

a. (U) Logistics. *Identify unique sustainment requirements, procedures, and guidance to support host-nation support teams and operations. Specify procedures for specialized technical logistics support from external organizations as necessary. Use subparagraphs to identify priorities and specific instructions for maintenance, transportation, supply, field services, distribution, contracting, and general engineering support. Refer to Annex F (Sustainment) as required.*

b. (U) Personnel. *Identify host-nation support unique personnel requirements and concerns, including global sourcing support and contracted linguist requirements. Use subparagraphs to identify priorities and specific instructions for human resources support, financial management, legal support, and religious support. Refer to Annex F (Sustainment) as required.*

c. (U) Army Health System Support. *Identify availability, priorities, and instructions for medical care. Refer to Annex F (Sustainment) as required.*

5. (U) Command and Signal.

a. (U) Command.

(1) (U) Location of the Commander. *State the location of host-nation support area leaders.*

(2) (U) Succession of Command. *State the succession of command if not covered in the unit's standard operating procedures.*

(3) (U) Liaison Requirements. *State the host-nation support liaison requirements not covered in the base order.*

b. (U) Control.

(1) (U) Command Posts. *Describe the employment of host-nation support-specific command posts (CPs), including the location of each CP and its time of opening and closing.*

(2) (U) Reports. *List host-nation support-specific reports not covered in standard operating procedures. Refer to Annex R (Reports) as required.*

c. (U) Signal. *Address any host-nation support-specific communications requirements or reports. Refer to Annex H (Signal) as required.*

ACKNOWLEDGE: *Include only if attachment is distributed separately from the base order.*

[Commander's last name]
[Commander's rank]

The commander or authorized representative signs the original copy of attachment. If the representative signs the original, add the phrase "For the Commander." The signed copy is the historical copy and remains in the headquarters' files.

[page number]
[CLASSIFICATION]

[CLASSIFICATION]

ANNEX P (HOST NATION SUPPORT) TO OPLAN/OPORD [number] [(code name)]—[issuing headquarters] [(classification of title)]

OFFICIAL:

[Authenticator's name]
[Authenticator's position]

Use only if the commander does not sign the original attachment. If the commander signs the original, no further authentication is required. If the commander does not sign, the signature of the preparing staff officer requires authentication and only the last name and rank of the commander appear in the signature block.

ATTACHMENT: *List lower-level attachments (appendixes, tabs, and exhibits).*

DISTRIBUTION: *Show only if distributed separately from the base order or higher-level attachments.*
[page number]
[CLASSIFICATION]

This page intentionally left blank.

Annex Q
Spare

This page intentionally left blank.

Annex R

Reports Annex Format and Instructions

This annex provides fundamental considerations, formats, and instructions for developing Annex R (Reports) to the base plan or order.

HOW TO DEVELOP ANNEX R (REPORTS)

R-1. Commanders and staff use Annex R (Reports) to list and catalog all unit reports and their respective formats. This annex does not follow the five-paragraph attachment format. Unit standard operating procedures dictate development and format for this annex. The G-3 (S-3), G-5 (S-5), or G-7, in coordination with the knowledge management officer, develops Annex R (Reports).

[CLASSIFICATION]

Place the classification at the top and bottom of every page of the attachments. Place the classification marking (TS), (S), (C), or (U) at the front of each paragraph and subparagraph in parentheses. Refer to AR 380-5 for classification and release marking instructions.

Copy ## of ## copies
Issuing headquarters
Place of issue
Date-time group of signature
Message reference number

Include heading if attachment is distributed separately from the base order or higher-level attachment.

ANNEX R (REPORTS) TO OPERATION PLAN/ORDER [number] [(code name)]—[issuing headquarters] [(classification of title)]

(U) References: *List documents essential to understanding the attachment.*

  a. *List maps and charts first. Map entries include series number, country, sheet names, or numbers, edition, and scale.*

  b. *List other references in subparagraphs labeled as shown.*

  c. *A doctrinal reference for this annex includes FM 6-99.2.*

(U) Time Zone Used Throughout the Order: *Write the time zone established in the base plan or order.*

 (U) Reports. *List all reports (formats, submission standards and times) not covered in unit standard operating procedures. Ensure to specify reporting requirements for all assigned, attached, operational control, and tactical control command relationships.*

ACKNOWLEDGE: *Include only if attachment is distributed separately from the base order.*

[Commander's last name]
[Commander's rank]

[page number]
[CLASSIFICATION]

[CLASSIFICATION]

ANNEX R (REPORTS) TO OPERATION PLAN/ORDER [number] [(code name)]—[issuing headquarters] [(classification of title)]

The commander or authorized representative signs the original copy of attachment. If the representative signs the original, add the phrase "For the Commander." The signed copy is the historical copy and remains in the headquarters' files.

OFFICIAL:

[Authenticator's name]
[Authenticator's position]

Use only if the commander does not sign the original attachment. If the commander signs the original, no further authentication is required. If the commander does not sign, the signature of the preparing staff officer requires authentication and only the last name and rank of the commander appear in the signature block.

ATTACHMENTS: *List lower-level attachment (appendixes, tabs, and exhibits).*

DISTRIBUTION: *Show only if distributed separately from the base order or higher-level attachments.*

[page number]
[CLASSIFICATION]

Annex S

Special Technical Operations Annex Format and Instructions

This annex provides fundamental considerations, formats, and instructions for developing Annex S (Special Technical Operations) to the base plan or order.

HOW TO DEVELOP ANNEX S (SPECIAL TECHNICAL OPERATIONS)

S-1. Commanders and staff use Annex S (Special Technical Operations) to expand the plan or order and provide the mission, scheme, and tasks to units for special technical operations. Annex S (Special Technical Operations) follows the five-paragraph order format. The special technical operations officer is the staff officer responsible for developing Annex S (Special Technical Operations).

[CLASSIFICATION]

Place the classification at the top and bottom of every page of the attachments. Place the classification marking (TS), (S), (C), or (U) at the front of each paragraph and subparagraph in parentheses. Refer to AR 380-5 for classification and release marking instructions.

Copy ## of ## copies
Issuing headquarters
Place of issue
Date-time group of signature
Message reference number

Include heading if attachment is distributed separately from the base order or higher-level attachment.

ANNEX S (SPECIAL TECHNICAL OPERATIONS) TO OPLAN/OPORD [number] [(code name)]—[issuing headquarters] [(classification of title)]

(U) References: *List documents essential to understanding the attachment*

   a. *List maps and charts first. Map entries include series number, country, sheet names, or numbers, edition, and scale.*

   b. *List other references in subparagraphs labeled as shown.*

   c. *Doctrinal references for this attachment include the CJCSM 3122 series.*

(U) Time Zone Used Throughout the Order: *Write the time zone established in the base plan or order.*

1. (U) Situation. *Include information affecting special technical operations that paragraph 1 of the OPLAN or OPORD does not cover or that needs expansion.*

   a. (U) Area of Interest. *Describe the area of interest as it relates to special technical operations. Refer to Annex B (Intelligence) as required.*

   b. (U) Area of Operations. *Refer to Appendix 2 (Operation Overlay) to Annex C (Operations).*

[page number]
[CLASSIFICATION]

[CLASSIFICATION]

ANNEX S (SPECIAL TECHNICAL OPERATIONS) TO OPLAN/OPORD [number] [(code name)]—[issuing headquarters] [(classification of title)]

(1) (U) <u>Terrain</u>. *Describe the aspects of terrain that impact special technical operations. Refer to Annex B (Intelligence) as required.*

(2) (U) <u>Weather</u>. *Describe the aspects of weather that impact special technical operations. Refer to Annex B (Intelligence) as required.*

c. (U) <u>Enemy Forces</u>. *List known and templated locations and activities of enemy special technical operations units for one echelon up and two echelons down. List enemy maneuver and other area capabilities that will impact friendly operations. State expected enemy courses of action and employment of enemy special technical operations assets. Refer to Annex B (Intelligence) as required.*

d. (U) <u>Friendly Forces</u>. *Outline the higher headquarters' special technical operations plan. List designation, location, and outline of plans of higher, adjacent, and other special technical operations assets that support or impact the issuing headquarters or require coordination and additional support.*

e. (U) <u>Interagency, Intergovernmental, and Nongovernmental Organizations</u>. *Identify and describe other organizations in the area of operations that may impact the conduct of special technical operations. Refer to Annex V (Interagency Coordination) as required.*

f. (U) <u>Civil Considerations</u>. *Describe the aspects of the civil situation that impact special technical operations. Refer to Annex B (Intelligence) and Annex K (Civil Affairs Operations) as required.*

g. (U) <u>Attachments and Detachments</u>. *List units attached or detached only as necessary to clarify task organization. Refer to Annex A (Task Organization) as required.*

h. (U) <u>Assumptions</u>. *List any special technical operations-specific assumptions that support the annex development.*

2. (U) Mission. *State the mission of special technical operations in support of the base plan or order.*

3. (U) Execution.

a. (U) <u>Scheme of Special Technical Operations</u>. *Describe how the special technical operations support the commander's intent and concept of operations. List and describe the commander's objective for each special technical operations target set or functional area in separate number subparagraphs. Establish the priorities of support to units for each phase of the operation. Refer to Annex C (Operations) as required.*

(1) (U) <u>Capabilities Integration Matrix</u>. *Refer to Appendix 1 (Special Technical Operations Capabilities Integration Matrix) to Annex S (Special Technical Operations) as required.*

(2) (U) <u>Objective for Functional Area I</u>. *Describe commander's objective for this functional area. Refer to Appendix 2 (Functional Area I Program and Objectives) to Annex S (Special Technical Operations) as required.*

(3) (U) <u>Objective for Functional Area II</u>. *Describe commander's objective for this functional area. Refer to Appendix 3 (Functional Area II Program and Objectives) to Annex S (Special Technical Operations) as required.*

b. (U) <u>Tasks to Subordinate Units</u>. *List special technical operations tasks assigned to specific subordinate units not contained in the base order.*

c. (U) <u>Coordinating Instructions</u>. *List only instructions applicable to two or more subordinate units not covered in the base order.*

page number]
[CLASSIFICATION]

[CLASSIFICATION]

ANNEX S (SPECIAL TECHNICAL OPERATIONS) TO OPLAN/OPORD [number] [(code name)]—[issuing headquarters] [(classification of title)]

4. (U) Sustainment. *Identify priorities of sustainment for special technical operations key tasks and specify additional instructions as required. Provide general instructions concerning the movement, support, and maintenance of special technical operations capabilities. Provide additional information on equipment to support special technical operations planning and operations. Provide any additional guidance on special technical operations-specific administrative matters. Refer to Annex F (Sustainment) as required.*

    a. (U) Logistics. *Identify unique sustainment requirements, procedures, and guidance to support special technical operations teams and operations. Specify procedures for specialized technical logistics support from external organizations as necessary. Use subparagraphs to identify priorities and specific instructions for maintenance, transportation, supply, field services, distribution, contracting, and general engineering support. Refer to Annex F (Sustainment) and Annex P (Host-Nation Support) as required.*

    b. (U) Personnel. *Use subparagraphs to identify priorities and specific instructions for human resources support, financial management, legal support, and religious support. Refer to Annex F (Sustainment) as required.*

    c. (U) Army Health System Support. *Identify availability, priorities, and instructions for medical care. Refer to Annex F (Sustainment) as required.*

5. (U) Command and Signal.

    a. (U) Command.

        (1) (U) Location of the Commander. *State the location of key special technical operations leaders. Provide guidance on specific approval authorities for deployment and employment of special technical operations capabilities.*

        (2) (U) Succession of Command. *State the succession of command if not covered in the unit's standard operating procedures.*

        (3) (U) Liaison Requirements. *State the special technical operations liaison requirements not covered in the base order.*

    b. (U) Control.

        (1) (U) Command Posts. *Describe the employment of special technical operations-specific command posts (CPs), including the location of each CP and its time of opening and closing.*

        (2) (U) Reports. *List special technical operations-specific reports not covered in standard operating procedures. Refer to Annex R (Reports) as required.*

    c. (U) Signal. *Address any special technical operations-specific communications requirements or reports. Provide guidance on the communication methods authorized to transmit planning, coordination, deconfliction, deployment, and employment information for special technical operations capabilities included in this annex. Refer to Annex H (Signal) as required.*

ACKNOWLEDGE: *Include only if attachment is distributed separately from the base order.*

[Commander's last name]
[Commander's rank]

[page number]
[CLASSIFICATION]

[CLASSIFICATION]

ANNEX S (SPECIAL TECHNICAL OPERATIONS) TO OPLAN/OPORD [number] [(code name)]—[issuing headquarters] [(classification of title)]

The commander or authorized representative signs the original copy of attachment. If the representative signs the original, add the phrase "For the Commander." The signed copy is the historical copy and remains in the headquarters' files.

OFFICIAL:

[Authenticator's name]
[Authenticator's position]

Use only if the commander does not sign the original attachment. If the commander signs the original, no further authentication is required. If the commander does not sign, the signature of the preparing staff officer requires authentication and only the last name and rank of the commander appear in the signature block.

ATTACHMENT: *List lower-level attachments (appendixes, tabs, and exhibits).*

Appendix 1 – Special Technical Operations Capabilities Integration Matrix
Appendix 2 – Functional Area I Program and Objectives
Appendix 3 – Functional Area II Program and Objectives

DISTRIBUTION: *Show only if distributed separately from the base order or higher-level attachments.*

[page number]
[CLASSIFICATION]

Annex T

Spare

This page intentionally left blank.

Annex U

Inspector General Annex Format and Instructions

This annex provides fundamental considerations, formats, and instructions for developing Annex U (Inspector General) to the base plan or order.

HOW TO DEVELOP ANNEX U (INSPECTOR GENERAL)

U-1. The inspector general uses Annex U (Inspector General) to describe and outline the inspector general support to the concept of operations described in the base plan or order. Staffs include this annex when they need to expand the inspector general functions beyond the base plan or order. The inspector general is responsible for developing Annex U (Inspector General).

[CLASSIFICATION]

Place the classification at the top and bottom of every page of the attachments. Place the classification marking (TS), (S), (C), or (U) at the front of each paragraph and subparagraph in parentheses. Refer to AR 380-5 for classification and release marking instructions.

Copy ## of ## copies
Issuing headquarters
Place of issue
Date-time group of signature
Message reference number

Include heading if attachment is distributed separately from the base order or higher-level attachment.

ANNEX U (INSPECTOR GENERAL) TO OPLAN/OPORD [number] [(code name)]—[issuing headquarters] [(classification of title)]

(U) References: *List documents essential to understanding the attachment.*

a. *List maps and charts first. Map entries include series number, country, sheet names, or numbers, edition, and scale.*

b. *List other references in subparagraphs labeled as shown.*

c. *Policy references for this attachment include AR 1-201 and AR 20-1.*

(U) Time Zone Used Throughout the Order: *Write the time zone established in the base plan or order.*

1. (U) <u>Situation</u>. *Include information affecting inspector general operations that paragraph 1 of the OPLAN or OPORD does not cover or that needs expansion.*

a. (U) <u>Area of Interest</u>. *Describe the area of interest as it relates to inspector general operations. Refer to Annex B (Intelligence) as required.*

b. (U) <u>Area of Operations</u>. *Refer to Appendix 2 (Operation Overlay) to Annex C (Operations).*

(1) (U) <u>Terrain</u>. *Describe the aspects of terrain that impact inspector general operations. Refer to Annex B (Intelligence) as required.*

[page number]
[CLASSIFICATION]

[CLASSIFICATION]

ANNEX U (INSPECTOR GENERAL) TO OPLAN/OPORD [number] [(code name)]—[issuing headquarters] [(classification of title)]

(2) (U) <u>Weather</u>. *Describe the aspects of weather that impact inspector general operations. Refer to Annex B (Intelligence) as required.*

c. (U) <u>Enemy Forces</u>. *Refer to the base order. Describe the possible or anticipated impact of enemy activities and courses of action on inspector general operations. Refer to Annex B (Intelligence) as required.*

d. (U) <u>Friendly Forces</u>. *Outline the higher headquarters' inspector general plan. List designation, location, and outline of plan of higher, adjacent, and other inspector general assets that support or impact the issuing headquarters or require coordination and additional support.*

e. (U) <u>Interagency, Intergovernmental, and Nongovernmental Organizations</u>. *Identify and describe other organizations in the area of operations that may impact the conduct of inspector general operations. Refer to Annex V (Interagency Coordination) as required.*

f. (U) <u>Civil Considerations</u>. *Describe the aspects of the civil situation that impact inspector general operations. Refer to Annex B (Intelligence) and Annex K (Civil Affairs Operations) as required.*

g. (U) <u>Attachments and Detachments</u>. *List units attached or detached only as necessary to clarify task organization. Refer to Annex A (Task Organization) as required.*

h. (U) <u>Assumptions</u>. *List inspector general-specific assumptions that support the annex development.*

2. (U) Mission. *State the mission of the inspector general in support of the base plan or order. For example, "On order, the inspector general provides the full range of inspector general functions (inspections, assistance, investigations, teaching, and training) in support of assigned and attached units of (unit name) for the duration of this operation."*

3. (U) Execution.

a. (U) <u>Scheme of Inspector General Support</u>. *Describe how the inspector general supports the commander's intent and concept of operations. Establish the priorities of support to units, or the concept for inspector general employment, for each phase of the operation. Focus on the commander's guidance, mission, and intent, and emphasize how inspector general operations reduce friction that affects readiness and warfighting capability. List any general areas the commander has asked the inspector general to assess in any travels. Refer to Annex C (Operations) as required.*

(1) (U) <u>Inspections</u>. *Outline inspection plan by phase based on the commanding general's guidance and the compressed inspection plan for unanticipated inspection topics when directed. Inspection plans should focus on high-payoff issues for the commander related to each phase of the operation (such as mobilization, deployment, employment, and sustainment). Include command guidance on requirements for the Organizational Inspection Program in theater, to include command inspections, staff inspections, inspector general inspections, intelligence oversight inspections, and audits. Include request and tasking procedures for subject-matter experts to serve as temporary assistant inspectors general. List upcoming outside agency assessments—Government Accountability Office and Department of Defense—that may impact the command's resources.*

[page number]
[CLASSIFICATION]

[CLASSIFICATION]

ANNEX U (INSPECTOR GENERAL) TO OPLAN/OPORD [number] [(code name)]—[issuing headquarters] [(classification of title)]

(2) (U) <u>Assistance and Investigations</u>. *Develop assistance coverage plan for subordinate units with considerations for geographically dispersed units and split-based operations. Description of coverage should include unit visitation plans and plans for use of acting inspectors general for assistance. Emphasize the inspector general's role of underwriting the chain of command in addressing issues and allegations, to include handling of law of war violations. The inspector general assistance plan should also address support for units under the operational control or direct-supporting role of the inspector general's organization (such as assistance support on an area-support basis).*

(3) (U) <u>Teaching and Training</u>. *Detail plans for deliberate teaching and training tools, such as deployment and reception briefs, inspector general bulletins and newsletters, and new commander orientations.*

b. (U) <u>Tasks to Subordinate Units</u>. *List inspector general tasks assigned to specific subordinate units not contained in the base order, and areas of responsibility for inspectors general and acting inspector general elements geographically separated from the command inspector general.*

c. (U) <u>Coordinating Instructions</u>. *List only instructions applicable to two or more subordinate units not covered in the base order. Include instructions for coordination between inspector general elements conducting split-based operations and coordination for reachback assistance from nondeployed supporting inspectors general at home station. List coordination and reporting requirements to the higher command inspector general and other inspector general technical channels. List the unit's reporting process for intelligence oversight procedure 15 reports, law of war violations, whistle-blower reprisals, and other Department of Defense-level critical information requirements. List the standard "before you see the inspector general" checklist.*

4. (U) <u>Sustainment</u>. *Identify priorities of sustainment for inspector general key tasks and specify additional instructions as required. Refer to Annex F (Sustainment) as required.*

a. (U) <u>Logistics</u>. *Identify unique sustainment requirements, procedures, and guidance to support inspector general teams and operations. Specify procedures for specialized technical logistics support from external organizations as necessary. Use subparagraphs to identify priorities and specific instructions for maintenance, transportation, supply, field services, distribution, contracting, and general engineering support. Refer to Annex F (Sustainment) and Annex P (Host-Nation Support) as required.*

b. (U) <u>Personnel</u>. *Identify inspector general-unique personnel requirements and concerns, including global sourcing support and contracted linguist requirements. Use subparagraphs to identify priorities and specific instructions for human resources support, financial management, legal support, and religious support. Refer to Annex F (Sustainment) as required.*

c. (U) <u>Army Health System Support</u>. *Identify availability, priorities, and instructions for medical care. Refer to Annex F (Sustainment) as required.*

5. (U) <u>Command and Signal</u>.

a. (U) <u>Command</u>.

(1) (U) <u>Location of the Commander</u>. *Identify current or future command post locations or map coordinate locations of inspectors general. Identify the inspector general chain of command if not addressed in the unit standard operating procedures (SOPs).*

[page number]
[CLASSIFICATION]

[CLASSIFICATION]

ANNEX U (INSPECTOR GENERAL) TO OPLAN/OPORD [number] [(code name)]—[issuing headquarters] [(classification of title)]

        (2) (U) <u>Succession of Leadership</u>. *State the succession of leadership if not covered in the unit's SOPs.*

        (3) (U) <u>Liaison Requirements</u>. *State the inspector general liaison requirements not covered in the base order.*

    b. (U) <u>Control</u>.

        (1) (U) <u>Command Posts</u>. *Describe the employment of inspector general-specific command posts (CPs), including the location of each CP and its time of opening and closing.*

        (2) (U) <u>Reports</u>. *List inspector general-specific reports not covered in SOPs. Refer to Annex R (Reports) as required.*

    c. (U) <u>Signal</u>. *Address any inspector general-specific communications requirements or reports. List signal instructions and network-centric instructions, to include call signs, phone numbers, and addresses to reach the inspector general. Address unique digitization connectivity requirements or coordination to meet functional responsibilities. Refer to Annex H (Signal) as required.*

ACKNOWLEDGE: *Include only if attachment is distributed separately from the base order.*

[Commander's last name]
[Commander's rank]

The commander or authorized representative signs the original copy of attachment. If the representative signs the original, add the phrase "For the Commander." The signed copy is the historical copy and remains in the headquarters' files.

OFFICIAL:

[Authenticator's name]
[Authenticator's position]

Use only if the commander does not sign the original attachment. If the commander signs the original, no further authentication is required. If the commander does not sign, the signature of the preparing staff officer (normally the command inspector general) requires authentication and only the last name and rank of the commander appear in the signature block.

ATTACHMENT: *List lower-level attachments (appendixes, tabs, and exhibits).*

DISTRIBUTION: *Show only if distributed separately from the base order or higher-level attachments.*

[page number]
[CLASSIFICATION]

Annex V

Interagency Coordination Annex Format and Instructions

This annex provides fundamental considerations, formats, and instructions for developing Annex V (Interagency Coordination) to the base plan or order.

HOW TO DEVELOP ANNEX V (INTERAGENCY COORDINATION)

V-1. Annex V (Interagency Coordination) provides military and interagency personnel with detailed information (mission, scheme, and tasks) to direct the necessary coordination and interaction between Army forces and interagency organizations. It describes how the commander intends to cooperate, provide support, and receive support from interagency organizations throughout the operation. This annex follows the five-paragraph order format; however, some subparagraphs are modified to accommodate communication with the interagency. The G-3 (S-3), in conjunction with the G-9 (S-9), develops Annex V (Interagency Coordination).

V-2. Interagency organizations of the United States government include the following:
- Central Intelligence Agency.
- Department of Commerce.
- Department of Defense.
- Department of Energy.
- Department of Homeland Security.
- Department of Justice.
- Department of State.
- Department of the Treasury.
- Department of Transportation.
- Environmental Protection Agency.
- National Security Council.
- Peace Corps.
- United States Agency for International Development/Office of Foreign Disaster Assistance.
- United States Department of Agriculture.

[CLASSIFICATION]

Place the classification at the top and bottom of every page of the attachments. Place the classification marking (TS), (S), (C), or (U) at the front of each paragraph and subparagraph in parentheses. Refer to AR 380-5 for classification and release marking instructions.

Copy ## of ## copies
Issuing headquarters
Place of issue
Date-time group of signature
Message reference number

Include heading if attachment is distributed separately from the base order or higher-level attachment.

ANNEX V (INTERAGECY COORDINATION) TO OPLAN [number] [(code name)]—[issuing headquarters] [(classification of title)]

(U) References: *List documents essential to understanding the attachment.*

    a. *List maps and charts first. Map entries include series number, country, sheet names, or numbers, edition, and scale.*

    b. *List other references in subparagraphs labeled as shown.*

    c. *Doctrinal references for interagency coordination include FM 3-07 and JP 3-08.*

(U) Time Zone Used Throughout the Order: *Write the time zone established in the base plan or order.*

1. (U) Situation. *Include information affecting interagency coordination that paragraph 1 of the OPLAN or OPORD does not cover or that needs expansion.*

    a. (U) <u>Area of Interest</u>. *Describe the area of interest as it relates to interagency coordination. Refer to Annex B (Intelligence) as required.*

    b. (U) <u>Area of Operations</u>. *Refer to Appendix 2 (Operation Overlay) to Annex C (Operations).*

      (1) (U) <u>Terrain</u>. *Describe the aspects of terrain that impact interagency coordination. Refer to Annex B (Intelligence) as required.*

      (2) (U) <u>Weather</u>. *Describe the aspects of weather that impact interagency coordination. Refer to Annex B (Intelligence) as required.*

    c. (U) <u>Political-Military Situation</u>. *Describe the political-military situation in the area of interest and area of operations. Identify U.S. national security objectives and interests applicable to the plan or order.*

    d. (U) <u>Enemy Forces</u>. *Summarize the threat to interagency personnel. Identify enemy forces and appraise their general capabilities and impacts on interagency coordination operations. Refer to Annex B (Intelligence) as required.*

    e. (U) <u>Friendly Forces</u>. *Outline the higher headquarters' interagency coordination plan. Identify and state the objectives or goals and primary tasks of those interagency organizations involved in the operations in subparagraphs below.*

    f. (U) <u>Civil Considerations</u>. *Describe the aspects of the civil situation that impact interagency coordination. Refer to Annex B (Intelligence) and Annex K (Civil Affairs Operations) as required.*

    g. (U) <u>Attachments and Detachments</u>. *List units attached or detached only as necessary to clarify task organization. Refer to Annex A (Task Organization) as required.*

    h. (U) <u>Assumptions</u>. *List any interagency coordination-specific assumptions that support the annex development.*

[page number]
[CLASSIFICATION]

[CLASSIFICATION]

ANNEX V (INTERAGECY COORDINATION) TO OPLAN [number] [(code name)]—[issuing headquarters] [(classification of title)]

    i. (U) <u>Legal Considerations</u>. *List any legal considerations that may affect interagency participation, such as applicable international law or the authorities established under USC titles 10, 34, or 50.*

2. (U) <u>Mission</u>. *State the mission of interagency coordination in support of the concept of operations in the base plan or order.*

3. (U) <u>Execution</u>.

    a. (U) <u>Scheme of Interagency Coordination</u>. *Summarize the concept of operations in the base plan or order including an outline of the primary objectives and desired effects of each phase. Describe the concept of interagency coordination and how it supports the concept of operations. Describe the areas of responsibility from United States government agencies by major areas of response: humanitarian, economic, political or diplomatic, and others as required. The operational variables (known as PMESII-PT) are another method to organize major areas of response: political, military, economic, social, information, infrastructure, physical environment, and time.*

    (1) (U) <u>Humanitarian</u>. *Define, in broad terms, the desired actions and responsibilities for United States government agencies in rebuilding and shaping the humanitarian structure and health of the affected nation. Coordinate these requested actions with the commander's phase development.*

    (2) (U) <u>Economic</u>. *Define, in broad terms, the desired actions and responsibilities for United States government agencies in rebuilding and shaping the economic structure and health of the affected nation. Coordinate these requested actions with the supported commander's phase.*

    (3) (U) <u>Political/Diplomatic</u>. *Define, in broad terms, the desired actions and responsibilities for United States government agencies in rebuilding and shaping the political and diplomatic structure and health of the affected nation. Coordinate these requested actions with the supported commander's phase development.*

    (4) (U) <u>Others</u>. *As required.*

    b. (U) <u>Tasks to Subordinate Units and Milestones</u>. *Identify tasks and required milestones of the issuing headquarters and interagency organizations during the conduct of operations.*

    c. (U) <u>Coordinating Instructions</u>. *List only instructions applicable to two or more subordinate units not covered in the base plan or order. Identify and list general instructions applicable to other United States government agencies, such as agreements with the host country and allied forces.*

4. (U) <u>Sustainment</u>. *Identify priorities of sustainment for interagency coordination key tasks and specify additional instructions as required. Refer to Annex F (Sustainment) as required.*

    a. (U) <u>Logistics</u>. *Use subparagraphs to identify availability, priorities, and specific instructions for maintenance, transportation, supply, field services, distribution, contracting, and general engineering support. Refer to Annex F (Sustainment) and Annex P (Host-Nation Support) as required.*

    b. (U) <u>Personnel</u>. *Use subparagraphs to identify availability, priorities, and specific instructions for human resources support, financial management, legal support, and religious support. Refer to Annex F (Sustainment) as required.*

    c. (U) <u>Army Health System Support</u>. *Identify availability, priorities, and instructions for medical care. Refer to Annex F (Sustainment) as required.*

5. (U) <u>Command and Signal</u>.

[page number]
[CLASSIFICATION]

[CLASSIFICATION]

ANNEX V (INTERAGECY COORDINATION) TO OPLAN [number] [(code name)]—[issuing headquarters] [(classification of title)]

a. (U) <u>Command</u>. *Identify any unique command relationships established for the purpose of interagency coordination. Identify any interagency coordination forms or bodies such as an interagency coordination working group.*

(1) (U) <u>Location of Interagency Coordination Leadership</u>. *Identify current or future locations of the interagency coordination leadership.*

(2) (U) <u>Succession of Command</u>. *State the succession of leadership if not covered in the unit's standard operating procedures.*

(3) (U) <u>Liaison Requirements</u>. *State the interagency coordination liaison requirements not covered in the base order.*

b. (U) <u>Control</u>. *List the locations of key interagency leaders and contact information.*

(1) (U) <u>Command Posts</u>. *Describe the employment of interagency coordination command posts (CPs), including the location of each CP and its time of opening and closing.*

(2) (U) <u>Reports</u>. *List interagency coordination specific reports not covered in standard operating procedures. Refer to Annex R (Reports) as required.*

c. (U) <u>Signal</u>. *Describe the communication plan used among the issuing force and interagency organizations to include the primary and alternate means of communications. Consider operations security requirements. Refer to Annex H (Signal) as required.*

ACKNOWLEDGE: *Include only if attachment is distributed separately from the base order.*

[Commander's last name]
[Commander's rank]

The commander or authorized representative signs the original copy of attachment. If the representative signs the original, add the phrase "For the Commander." The signed copy is the historical copy and remains in the headquarters' files.

OFFICIAL:

[Authenticator's name]
[Authenticator's position]

Either the commander or coordinating staff officer responsible for the functional area may sign attachments.

ATTACHMENT: *List lower-level attachments (appendixes, tabs, and exhibits).*

DISTRIBUTION: *Show only if distributed separately from the base order or higher-level attachments.*

[page number]
[CLASSIFICATION]

Annex W
Spare

This page intentionally left blank.

Annex X

Spare

This page intentionally left blank.

Annex Y

Spare

This page intentionally left blank.

Annex Z

Distribution Annex Format and Instructions

This annex provides fundamental considerations, formats, and instructions for developing Annex Z (Distribution) to the base plan or order.

HOW TO DEVELOP ANNEX Z (DISTRIBUTION)

Z-1. Commanders and staff use Annex Z (Distribution) to track the distribution of the operation plan and order and attachments. The G-3 (S-3), in coordination with the knowledge management officer, is responsible for developing Annex Z (Distribution).

Z-2. An important information management task is determining what organizations receive copies of the unit's operation plan and order (see FM 6-01.1). Normally, the distribution list is located at the end of the base plan or order. If the distribution plan is lengthy or complicated, use Annex Z (Distribution). This annex does not follow the five-paragraph attachment format. Unit standard operating procedures dictate development and format.

[CLASSIFICATION]

Place the classification at the top and bottom of every page of the attachments. Place the classification marking (TS), (S), (C), or (U) at the front of each paragraph and subparagraph in parentheses. Refer to AR 380-5 for classification and release marking instructions.

Copy ## of ## copies
Issuing headquarters
Place of issue
Date-time group of signature
Message reference number

Include heading if attachment is distributed separately from the base order or higher-level attachment.

ANNEX Z (DISTRIBUTION) TO OPLAN/OPORD [number] [(code name)]—[issuing **headquarters**] [(classification of title)]References:

(U) References: *List documents essential to understanding Annex Z.*

a. List maps and charts first. Map entries include series number, country, sheet names, or numbers, edition, and scale.

b. List other references in subparagraphs labeled as shown.

c. Doctrinal references include AR 25-50, AR 380-10, CJCSM 3122.03C, and FM 6-01.1.

Time Zone Used Throughout the Order: *Write the time zone established in the base plan or order.*

(U) Distribution: *Furnish distribution copies either for action or for information. List in detail those who are to receive the plan or order. When referring to a standard distribution list, also show distribution to reinforcing, supporting, and adjacent units, since that list does not normally include these units. Refer to Annex A (Task Organization) as a guide to major subordinate commands involved in the operation and the base operation order for description of adjacent units. When units from coalition partners or host-nation forces are involved, ensure distribution is in accordance with theater foreign disclosure policies and AR 380-10.*

[page number]
[CLASSIFICATION]

[CLASSIFICATION]

ANNEX Z (DISTRIBUTION) TO OPLAN/OPORD [number] [(code name)]—[issuing headquarters] [(classification of title)]References:

Distribution lists for paper copies should include the following information:

Duty Position, Unit, Location, Copy Number(s)

Example: CDR, C/1-503/173 ABN, Patrol Base Rock, #10-11

Electronic distribution and posting on a secure unit Web-portal (such as SECRET Internet Protocol Router Network) may also be used. Ensure all recipients have required privileges to access Web-portal and acknowledge in accordance with instructions provided in the base order.

ACKNOWLEDGE: *Include only if attachment is distributed separately from the base order.*

[Commander's last name]
[Commander's rank]

The commander or authorized representative signs the original copy of attachment. If the representative signs the original, add the phrase "For the Commander." The signed copy is the historical copy and remains in the headquarters' files.

OFFICIAL:

[Authenticator's name]
[Authenticator's position]

Either the commander or coordinating staff officer responsible for distribution may sign attachments.

DISTRIBUTION: *Show only if distributed separately from the base order or higher-level attachments.*

[page number]
[CLASSIFICATION]

Glossary

The glossary lists acronyms and terms with Army or joint definitions, and other selected terms. Where Army and joint definitions are different, *(Army)* precedes the definition. Terms for which ATTP 5-0.1 is the proponent manual (the authority) are marked with an asterisk (*). The proponent manual for other terms is listed in parentheses after the definition.

SECTION I – ACRONYMS AND ABBREVIATIONS

1SG	first sergeant
ACO	airspace control order
ACOS	assistant chief of staff
AG	adjutant general
AHS	Army health system
AO	area of operations
AR	Army regulation
ARFOR	*See* ARFOR under terms.
ATO	air tasking order
ATTP	Army tactics, techniques, and procedures
BCT	brigade combat team
CBRN	chemical, biological, radiological, and nuclear
CCIR	commander's critical information requirement
CJCSI	Chairman of the Joint Chiefs of Staff instruction
CJCSM	Chairman of the Joint Chiefs of Staff manual
COA	course of action
COS	chief of staff
CP	command post
CRM	composite risk management
DA	Department of the Army
DOD	Department of Defense
DS	direct support
EEFI	essential element of friendly information
FM	field manual
FRAGO	fragmentary order
G-1	assistant chief of staff, personnel
G-2	assistant chief of staff, intelligence
G-3	assistant chief of staff, operations
G-4	assistant chief of staff, logistics
G-5	assistant chief of staff, plans
G-6	assistant chief of staff, signal
G-7	assistant chief of staff, inform and influence activities
G-8	assistant chief of staff, resource management

G-9	assistant chief of staff, civil affairs operations
HRC	human resource command
IP	internet protocol
IPB	intelligence preparation of the battlefield
IR	information requirements
JFACC	joint force air component commander
JOPP	joint operation planning process
JP	joint publication
LNO	liaison officer
LOGCAP	logistics civil augmentation program
MCWP	Marine Corps Warfighting Publication
MDMP	military decisionmaking process
METL	mission-essential task list
MISO	military information support operations
MOE	measure of effectiveness
MOP	measure of performance
MWR	morale, welfare, and recreation
NCO	noncommissioned officer
OPLAN	operation plan
OPORD	operation order
S-1	personnel staff officer
S-2	intelligence staff officer
S-3	operations staff officer
S-4	logistics staff officer
S-5	plans staff officer
S-6	signal staff officer
S-7	inform and influence activities staff officer
S-9	civil affairs operations staff officer
SATCOM	satellite communications
SGS	secretary of the general staff
SOP	standard operating procedure
TDA	table of distribution and allowances
TLP	troop leading procedures
TOE	table of organization and equipment
TTP	tactics, techniques, and procedures
U.S.	United States
VTC	video teleconference
WARNO	warning order
XO	executive officer

SECTION II – TERMS

ARFOR

The Army Service component headquarters for a joint task force or a joint and multinational force. (FM 3-0)

assumption

A supposition on the current situation or a presupposition on the future course of events, either or both assumed to be true in the absence of positive proof, necessary to enable the commander in the process of planning to complete an estimate of the situation and make a decision on the course of action. (JP 1-02)

avenue of approach

An air or ground route of an attacking force of a given size leading to its objective or to key terrain in its path. (JP 2-01.3)

*backbrief

A briefing by subordinates to the commander to review how subordinates intend to accomplish their mission.

battle rhythm

A deliberate daily cycle of command, staff, and unit activities intended to synchronize current and future operations. (JP 3-33)

*be-prepared mission

A mission assigned to a unit that might be executed.

*board

(Army) A grouping of predetermined staff representatives with delegated decision authority for a particular purpose or function.

campaign plan

A joint operation plan for a series of related major operations aimed at achieving strategic or operational objectives within a given time and space. (JP 5-0)

civil considerations

The influence of manmade infrastructure, civilian institutions, and activities of the civilian leaders, populations, and organizations within an area of operations on the conduct of military operations. (FM 6-0)

combat power

(Army) The total means of destructive, constructive, and information capabilities that a military unit/formation can apply at a given time. Army forces generate combat power by converting potential into effective action. (FM 3-0)

command

The authority that a commander in the armed forces lawfully exercises over subordinates by virtue of rank or assignment. Command includes the authority and responsibility for effectively using available resources and for planning the employment of, organizing, directing, coordinating, and controlling military forces for the accomplishment of assigned missions. It also includes responsibility for health, welfare, morale, and discipline of assigned personnel. (JP 1)

*command group

The commander and selected staff members who assist the commander in controlling operations away from a command post.

*command post

(Army) A unit headquarters where the commander and staff perform their activities.

*command post cell

A grouping of personnel and equipment organized by warfighting function or by planning horizon to facilitate the exercise of mission command.

concept plan

In the context of joint operation planning level 3 planning detail, an operation plan in an abbreviated format that may require considerable expansion or alteration to convert it into a complete operation plan or operation order. (JP 5-0)

*constraint

(Army) A restriction placed on the command by a higher command. A constraint dictates an action or inaction, thus restricting the freedom of action of a subordinate commander.

control

(Army) The regulation of forces and warfighting functions to accomplish the mission in accordance with the commander's intent. (FM 6-0)

*critical event

An event that directly influences mission accomplishment.

design

A methodology for applying critical and creative thinking to understand, visualize, and describe complex, ill-structured problems and develop approaches to solve them. (FM 5-0)

decision point

A point in space and time when the commander or staff anticipates making a key decision concerning a specific course of action. (JP 5-0)

*early-entry command post

A lead element of a headquarters designed to control operations until the remaining portions of the headquarters are deployed and operational.

*essential task

(Army) A specified or implied task that must be executed to accomplish the mission.

fragmentary order

An abbreviated form of an operation order issued as needed after an operation order to change or modify that order or to execute a branch or sequel to that order. (JP 5-0)

*implied task

(Army) A task that must be performed to accomplish a specified task or mission but is not stated in the higher headquarters' order.

information requirements

(Army) All information elements the commander and staff require to successfully conduct operations. (FM 6-0)

key terrain

Any locality, or area, the seizure or retention of which affords a marked advantage to either combatant. (JP 2-01.3)

liaison

That contact or intercommunication maintained between elements of military forces or other agencies to ensure mutual understanding and unity of purpose and action. (JP 3-08)

*main command post

A facility containing the majority of the staff designed to control current operations, conduct detailed analysis, and plan future operations.

military decisionmaking process

An iterative planning methodology that integrates the activities of the commander, staff, subordinate headquarters, and other partners to understand the situation and mission; develop and compare courses of action; decide on a course of action that best accomplishes the mission; and produce an operation plan or order for execution. (FM 5-0)

mission command

(Army) The exercise of authority and direction by the commander using mission orders to enable disciplined initiative within the commander's intent to empower agile and adaptive leaders in the conduct of full spectrum operations. It is commander-led and blends the art of command and the science of control to integrate the warfighting functions to accomplish the mission. (FM 6-0)

mission command system

The arrangement of personnel; networks; information systems; processes and procedures; and facilities and equipment that enable commanders to conduct operations. (FM 6-0)

mission orders

Directives that emphasize to subordinates the results to be attained, not how they are to achieve them. (FM 6-0)

mission statement

A short sentence or paragraph that describes the organization's essential task (or tasks) and purpose—a clear statement of the action to be taken and the reason for doing so. The mission statement contains the elements of who, what, when, where, and why, but seldom specifies how. (JP 5-0)

obstacle

Any obstruction designed or employed to disrupt, fix, turn, or block the movement of an opposing force, and to impose additional losses in personnel, time, and equipment on the opposing force. Obstacles can exist naturally or can be man-made, or can be a combination of both. (JP 3-15)

*on-order mission

A mission to be executed at an unspecified time.

operation order

A directive issued by a commander to subordinate commanders for the purpose of effecting the coordinated execution of an operation. (JP 5-0)

operation plan

Any plan for the conduct of military operations prepared in response to actual and potential contingencies. (JP 5-0)

operational approach

A broad conceptualization of the general actions that will produce the conditions that define the desired end state. (FM 5-0)

operations process

The major mission command activities performed during operations: planning, preparing, executing, and continuously assessing the operation. The commander drives the operations process through leadership. (FM 3-0)

*P-hour (airborne operations)

In airborne assault operations, the specific hour on D-day at which a parachute assault commences with the exit of the first Soldier from an aircraft over a designated drop zone. P-hour may or may not coincide with H-hour.

planning horizon

A point in time commanders use to focus the organization's planning efforts to shape future events. (FM 5-0)

running estimate

The continuous assessment of the current situation used to determine if the current operation is proceeding according to the commander's intent and if planned future operations are supportable. (FM 5-0)

*specified task

(Army) A task specifically assigned to a unit by its higher headquarters.

*staff section

A grouping of staff members by area of expertise under a coordinating, special, or personal staff officer.

supporting plan

An operation plan prepared by a supporting commander, a subordinate commander, or an agency to satisfy the requests or requirements of the supported commander's plan. (JP 5-0)

*synchronization matrix

A tool the staff uses to record the results of war-gaming and helps them synchronize a course of action across time, space, and purpose in relationship to potential enemy and civil actions.

*tactical command post

A facility containing a tailored portion of a unit headquarters designed to control portions of an operation for a limited time.

tactical mission task

A specific activity performed by a unit while executing a form of tactical operation or form of maneuver. It may be expressed as either an action by a friendly force or effects on an enemy force. (FM 7-15)

task organization

(Army) A temporary grouping of forces designed to accomplish a particular mission. (FM 3-0)

task-organizing

Act of designing an operating force, support staff, or logistic package of specific size and composition to meet a unique task or mission. Characteristics to examine when task-organizing the force include, but are not limited to: training, experience, equipage, sustainability, operating environment, enemy threat, and mobility. For Army forces, it includes allocating available assets to subordinate commanders and establishing their command and support relationships. (FM 3-0)

troop leading procedures

A dynamic process used by small-unit leaders to analyze a mission, develop a plan, and prepare for an operation. (FM 5-0)

warning order

A preliminary notice of an order or action that is to follow. (JP 3-33)

*working group

(Army) A grouping of predetermined staff representatives who meet to provide analysis, coordinate, and provide recommendations for a particular purpose or function.

References

Field manuals and selected joint publications are listed by new number followed by old number.

REQUIRED PUBLICATIONS

These documents must be available to intended users of this publication.

FM 1-02 (101-5-1). *Operational Terms and Graphics*. 21 September 2004.

JP 1-02. *Department of Defense Dictionary of Military and Associated Terms*. 8 November 2010.

RELATED PUBLICATIONS

These documents contain relevant supplemental information.

JOINT AND DEPARTMENT OF DEFENSE PUBLICATIONS

Most joint publications are available online: <http://www.dtic.mil/doctrine/new_pubs/jointpub.htm.>

CJCSM 3122.03C. *Joint Operation Planning And Execution System (JOPES) Volume II Planning Formats*. 17 August 2007.

JP 1. *Doctrine for the Armed Forces of the United States*. 14 May 2007.

JP 2-01.3. *Joint Intelligence Preparation of the Operational Environment*. 16 June 2009.

JP 3-02. *Amphibious Operations*. 10 August 2009.

JP 3-02.1. *Amphibious Embarkation and Debarkation*. 30 November 2010.

JP 3-08. *Interorganizational Coordination During Joint Operations*, 24 June 2011

JP 3-14. *Space Operations*. 6 January 2009.

JP 3-15. *Barriers, Obstacles, and Mine Warfare for Joint Operations*. 17 June 2011.

JP 3-33. *Joint Task Force Headquarters*. 16 February 2007.

JP 3-57. *Civil-Military Operations*. 8 July 2008.

JP 3-61. *Public Affairs*. 25 August 2010.

JP 5-0. *Joint Operation Planning*. 11 August 2011.

ARMY PUBLICATIONS

Most Army doctrinal publications are available online: <https://armypubs.us.army.mil/doctrine/Active_FM.html>. Army regulations are produced only in electronic media. Most are available online: < http://www.army.mil/usapa/index.html>.

AR 1-201. *Army Inspection Policy*. 4 April 2008.

AR 11-7. *Army Internal Review Program*. 22 July 2011.

AR 20-1. *Inspector General Activities and Procedures*. 29 December 2010.

AR 25-50. *Preparing and Managing Correspondence*. 15 June 2002.

AR 25-55. *The Department of the Army Freedom of Information Act Program*. 1 December 1997.

AR 27-1. *Legal Services Judge Advocate Legal Services*. 30 September 1996.

AR 75-15. *Policy for Explosive Ordnance Disposal*. 22 February 2005.

AR 115-10. *Weather Support for the US Army,* 6 January 2010.

AR 165-1. *Army Chaplain Corps Activities*. 3 January 2009.

AR 360-1. *The Army Public Affairs Program*. 25 May 2011.

AR 380-5. *Department of the Army Information Security Program*. 31 September 2000.

AR 380-10. *Foreign Disclosure and Contacts with Foreign Representatives*. 22 July 2005.

AR 385-10. *The Army Safety Program*. 23 August 2007.

AR 525-13. *Antiterrorism*. 11 September 2008.

AR 530-1. *Operations Security (OPSEC)*. 19 April 2007.

AR 600-20. *Army Command Policy*. 18 April 2008.

AR 870-5. *Military History: Responsibilities, Policies, and Procedures*. 21 September 2007.

ATTP 3-11.36. *Multi-Service Tactics, Techniques, and Procedures for Chemical, Biological, Radiological, and Nuclear Aspects of Command and Control*. 12 July 2010.

ATTP 3-34.23 (FM 5-71-100, 5-100-15, 5-116). *Engineer Operations–Echelons Above Brigade Combat Team*. 8 July 2010.

ATTP 3-34.80 (FM 3-34.230, FM 5-33, and TC 5-230). *Geospatial Engineering*. 29 July 2010.

DA Pamphlet 385-10. *Army Safety Program*. 23 May 2008.

FM 1-0. *Human Resources Support*. 6 April 2010.

FM 1-04. *Legal Support to the Operational Army*. 15 April 2009.

FM 1-05 (FM 16-1). *Religious Support*. 18 April 2003.

FM 1-06. *Financial Management Operations*. 4 April 2011.

FM 2-0. *Intelligence*. 23 March 2010.

FM 2-01.3. *Intelligence Preparation of the Battlefield/Battlespace*. 15 October 2009.

FM 3-0. *Operations*. 27 February 2008.

FM 3-01 (FM 44-100). *U.S. Army Air and Missile Defense Operations*. 25 November 2009.

FM 3-05.40 (FM 41-10). *Civil Affairs Operations*. 29 September 2006.

FM 3-05.301. *Psychological Operations Process Tactics, Techniques, and Procedures*. 30 August 2007.

FM 3-05.401. *Civil Affairs Tactics, Techniques, and Procedures*. 5 July 2007.

FM 3-07. *Stability Operations*. 6 October 2008.

FM 3-11 (FM 3-100). *Multiservice Doctrine for Chemical, Biological, Radiological, and Nuclear Operations*. 1 July 2011

FM 3-11.21. *Multiservice Tactics, Techniques, and Procedures for Chemical, Biological, Radiological, and Nuclear Consequence Management Operations*. 1 April 2008.

FM 3-13 (FM 100-6). *Information Operations: Doctrine, Tactics, Techniques, and Procedures*. 28 November 2003.

FM 3-14 (FM 3-14.10). *Space Support to Army Operations*. 6 January 2010.

FM 3-16 (FM 100-8). *The Army in Multinational Operations*. 20 May 2010.

FM 3-24. *Counterinsurgency*. 15 December 2006.

FM 3-27 (FM 3-27.10). *Army Global Ballistic Missile Defense (GBMD) Operations*. 3 January 2011.

FM 3-34. *Engineer Operations*. 4 August 2011.

FM 3-34.5 (FM 3-100.4). *Environmental Considerations*. 16 February 2010.

FM 3-34.170 (FM 5-170). *Engineer Reconnaissance*. 25 March 2008.

FM 3-34.400 (FM 5-104). *General Engineering*. 9 December 2008.

FM 3-36. *Electronic Warfare in Operations*. 25 February 2009.

FM 3-37. *Protection*. 30 September 2009.

FM 3-39 (FM 3-19.1). *Military Police Operations*. 16 February 2010.

FM 3-50.1. *Army Personnel Recovery*. 10 August 2005.

FM 3-52 (FM 100-103). *Army Airspace Command and Control in a Combat Zone*. 1 August 2002.

FM 3-60 (FM 6-20-10). *The Targeting Process*. 26 November 2010.

FM 3-61.1. *Public Affairs Tactics, Techniques and Procedures*. 1 October 2000.

FM 3-90. *Tactics*. 4 July 2001.

FM 4-0. *Sustainment*. 30 April 2009.

FM 4-02.7. *Multiservice Tactics, Techniques, and Procedures for Health Service Support in a Chemical, Biological, Radiological, and Nuclear Environment*. 15 July 2009.

FM 4-02.17. *Preventive Medicine Services*. 28 August 2000.

FM 4-02.18 (FM 8-10-18). *Veterinary Service: Tactics, Techniques, and Procedures*. 30 December 2004.

FM 4-02.19. *Dental Service Support Operations*. 31 July 2009.

FM 4-30.51 (FM 21-16). *Unexploded Ordnance (UXO) Procedures*. 13 July 2006.

FM 5-0. *The Operations Process*. 26 March 2010.

FM 5-19. *Composite Risk Management*. 21 August 2006.

FM 5-34. *Engineer Field Data*. 19 July 2005.

FM 5-102. *Countermobility*. 14 March 1985.

FM 5-103. *Survivability*. 10 June 1985.

FM 6-0. *Mission Command: Command and Control of Army Forces*. 11 August 2003.

FM 6-01.1. *Knowledge Management Section*. 29 August 2008.

FM 6-02.40. *Visual Information Operations*. 10 March 2009.

FM 6-02.43. *Signal Soldier's Guide*. 17 March 2009.

FM 6-02.53. *Tactical Radio Operations*. 5 August 2009.

FM 6-02.70 (FMI 6-02.70). *Army Electromagnetic Spectrum Operations*. 20 May 2010.

FM 6-02.71. *Network Operations*. 14 July 2009.

FM 6-20-40. *Tactics, Techniques, and Procedures for Fire Support for Brigade Operations (Heavy)*. 5 January 1990.

FM 6-20-50. *Tactics, Techniques, and Procedures for Fire Support for Brigade Operations (Light)*. 5 January 1990.

FM 6-22 (FM 22-100). *Army Leadership*. 12 October 2006.

FM 6-99.2 (FM 101-5-2). *US Army Report and Message Formats*. 30 April 2007.

FM 7-15. *The Army Universal Task List*. 27 February 2009.

FM 34-81. *Weather Support for Army Tactical Operations*. 31 August 1989.

FM 46-1. Public Affairs Operations. 30 May 1997.

FM 55-1. *Transportation Operations*. 3 October 1995.

FM 71-100. *Division Operations*. 28 August 1996.

OTHER PUBLICATIONS

Professional Reference Guide. February 2010. (https://www.us.army_mil/suite/doc/22950192)

U.S. National Space Policy. 31 August 2006. (http://www.nss.org/resources/library/spacepolicy/2006NationalSpacePolicy_htm)

REFERENCED FORMS

DA Form 2028. *Recommended Changes to Publications and Blank Forms.*.

This page intentionally left blank.

Index

Entries are by paragraph number unless specified otherwise.

A–B

ACOS, civil affairs operations, 2-72
  inform and influence activities, 2-69
  intelligence, 2-40–2-46
  logistics, 2-55–2-63
  operations, 2-47–2-54
  personnel, 2-35–2-39
  plans, 2-63–2-65
  resource management, 2-70–2-71
  signal, 2-66–2-68
agenda, rehearsal, 8-78–8-80
aide-de-camp, 2-106
air and missile defense, officer, 277–2-78
air liaison, officer, 2-79
analysis, conduct, 4-172
annex, examples and procedures, 12-75–12-81
Army command, relationships, A-12
Army support, relationships, A-13–A-14
art of command, 1-7–1-9
assessment, briefing and operation update, 3-56–3-57
  building framework, 7-25–7-32
  formal plan, 7-1–7-35
  initial, 4-20–4-22
  plan, 7-1–7-2
  rehearsal responsibilities, 8-69–8-70
  running estimate and, 6-11
  steps, 7-3–7-35
assets, review, 4-36
assign responsibilities for conducting analysis and generating recommendations, 7-34
assistant chief of staff. See ACOS.
assumptions, develop, 4-41–4-43
  information and, 11-14–11-15
  list, 4-142
avenue of approach, defined, 5-30
avenue-in-depth method, 4-149–4-150
aviation, officer, 2-80

backbrief, 8-7–8-8
  defined, 8-7
battle drill, 8-11–8-12
  command post, 3-51
battle rhythm, 3-62–3-64
  defined, 3-62
belt method, 4-146–4-148
be-prepared mission, defined, 4-34
board, defined, 3-71
box method, 4-151–4-152
briefing(s), assessment, 3-56–3-57
  construct, 10-19
  course of action, 4-111
  decision, 4-179
  deliver, 10-20–10-21
  follow up, 10-22
  military, 10-1–10-22
  mission analysis, 4-69–4-71
  outline, 10-15–10-18
  shift-change, 3-52–3-54
  steps, 10-14–10-22
  types, 10-1–10-13
  war-gaming, 4-170
broad concept, 4-101–4-106

C

campaign plan, defined, 12-13
CBRN, officer, 2-81
CCIR, develop, 4-46–4-49
cell(s), current operations integration, 3-43–3-45
  fires, 3-33
  functional, 3-30–3-36
  future operations, 3-41–3-42
  integrating, 3-37–3-46
  intelligence, 3-31
  mission command, 3-36
  movement and maneuver, 3-32
  plans, 3-39–3-40
  protection, 3-34
  sustainment, 3-35
chaplain, 2-017
chemical, biological, radiological, and nuclear. See CBRN.
chief of fires, 2-73
chief of protection, 2-74
chief of staff, execution, 8-63
  planning, 8-55

preparation, 8-58
staff structure and, 2-28
war-gaming responsibilities, 4-120
chief of sustainment, 2-75
civil affairs operations, 2-72
civil considerations, analysis, 5-37
  defined, 5-37
civilian personnel, officer, 2-82
combat power, analyze, 5-39
  assess, 4-83–4-87
  defined, 4-83
combined arms rehearsal, 8-9
command, defined, 1-7
  efforts, 3-16–3-17
command group, 3-9–3-11
  defined, 3-9
command liaison, officer, 2-83
command post, battle drills, 3-51
  capacity of, 3-22
  considerations, 3-14–3-27
  continuity, 3-19–3-20
  defined, 3-2
  deployability, 3-21
  design, 3-16–3-17
  dispersion, 3-24
  early entry, 3-12–3-13
  effectiveness, 3-15–3-22
  main, 3-4
  mobility, 3-27
  operations, 3-47–3-71
  organization, 3-1–3-13
  range of, 3-22
  redundancy, 3-26
  size, 3-25
  standard operating procedures, 3-48–3-61
  standardization, 3-18
  survivability, 3-23–3-27
  transfer control, 3-60–3-61
  types, 3-2–3-13
command post cell, defined, 3-28
  staff sections and, 3-28–3-46
command sergeant major, 2-108
commander, execution, 8-62
  initial guidance, 4-23
  involvement, 4-196
  MDMP, 4-8–4-11
  planning, 8-54
  preparation, 8-57

Entries are by paragraph number unless specified otherwise.

commander *(continued)*
  staff structure and, 2-27
  support to, 2-2–2-4
  time constraints and, 4-190–4-193
commander's critical information requirement. *See* CCIR.
commander's intent, develop and issue, 4-72
  initial, 4-72
complete the plan, TLP, 5-52
composite risk management, 4-44–4-45
concept, broad, 4-101–4-106
concept of operations, 5-43
concept plan, defined, 12-16
conduct reconnaissance, TLP, 5-50–5-51
considerations, staff organization, 2-22–2-25
constraint(s), defined, 4-37
  determine, 4-37–4-40
  time, 4-186–4-200
contingency operations, 9-18–9-19
continuity, 3-19–3-20
control, defined, 1-10
  transferring, 3-60–3-61
coordinating, staff officers, 2-31–2-75
core competencies, staff and, 2-8–2-16
counterintelligence, 2-45
course of action, analysis, 5-47
  briefing, 4-111
  compare, 4-173–4-178, 5-48
  decision briefing, 4-179
  evaluation criteria, 4-77
  limit, 4-197
  process actions, 4-139–4-170
  select for analysis, 4-112, 5-48
  statement and sketch, 4-108–4-110, 5-45–5-46
course of action analysis and war-gaming, 4-113–4-170
course of action approval, 4-180–4-183
course of action comparison, 4-171–4-179
course of action development, 4-79–4-112
  TLP, 5-38–5-46
criteria, developing, 11-19–11-24
  evaluation, 11-21–11-24
  screening, 11-20

critical event, defined, 4-143
  list, 4-143–4-144
current operations integration cell, 3-43–3-45

D
decision, make and implement, 11-36–11-39
decision briefing, 10-4–10-8
  course of action, 4-179
decision paper, 11-74–11-884
decision point, defined, 4-144
  list, 4-143–4-144
dental, surgeon, 2-84
deployability, command post, 3-21
design, defined, 1-15
develop assessment measures and potential indicators, 7-9–7-32
develop the collection plan, 7-33
digital terrain-model rehearsal, 8-32–8-36
dispersion, 3-24

E
early-entry command post, 3-12–3-13
  defined, 3-12
electronic warfare officer, 2-85
enemy, analysis, 5-27
engineer, officer, 2-86
environment, time constrained, 4-186–4-200
equal opportunity, advisor, 2-88
essential element of information, 4-46–4-49
essential task, defined, 4-35
execution, rehearsal responsibilities, 8-61–8-68
  running estimate and, 6-10
executive officer, staff structure, 2-28
  war-gaming responsibilities, 4-120
explosive ordnance disposal officer, 2-87

F
facts, identify, 4-41–4-43
  information and, 11-13
fire support officer, 2-73
fires, cell, 3-33
  war-gaming responsibilities, 4-123

force, array, 4-95–4-100
  friendly, 4-141
  manning, 2-36
force management officer, 2-89
foreign disclosure officer, 2-90
fragmentary order, defined, 12-19
full-dress rehearsal, 8-15–8-20
functional cells, types, 3-30–3-36
future operations cell, 3-41–3-42

G
G-1, ACOS, 2-35–2-39
G-2, execution, 8-65
  intelligence, 2-40–2-46
G-3, execution, 8-64
  operations, 2-47–2-54
  plans and operations, 2-50–2-54
  training, 2-49
G-4, logistics, 2-55–2-63
G-5, plans, 2-63–2-65
G-6, signal, 2-66–2-68
G-7, inform and influence activities, 2-69
G-8, resource management, 2-70–2-71
G-9, civil affairs operations, 2-72
gather tools and assessment data, 7-4
guidance, planning, 4-73–4-76

H
headquarters, assignment, 4-107
  management, 2-39
higher headquarters order, 4-27–4-28
historian, 2-91
human resources, services of, 2-37

I–J–K
identify feedback mechanisms, assessment, 7-35
implied task, defined, 4-33
indicators, MOE, 7-21–7-24
inform and influence activities, 2-69
information, briefing, 10-2–10-3
  collect, 10-19
  gather, 11-9–11-18
  management, 2-68
  organizing, 11-17–11-18
information requirements, defined, 4-46

Entries are by paragraph number unless specified otherwise.

initial guidance, issue, 4-23

initiate movement, TLP, 5-49

inspector general, 2-109

integrating cells, types, 3-37–3-46

intelligence, ACOS, 2-40–2-46
  cell, 3-31
    war-gaming responsibilities, 4-121

interagency operations, liaison, 9-21–9-22

internal review officer, 2-110

introduction, rehearsal, 8-75

intelligence preparation of the battlefield, 4-29–4-30

issue a warning order, 5-16–5-18

issue the order, TLP, 5-53–5-54

joint operations, liaison, 9-20

key terrain, defined, 5-31

knowledge management officer, 2-92

L

leaders, subordinate, 8-59
  subordinate, 8-66

liaison, 9-1–9-23
  air, 2-79
  command, 2-83
  defined, 9-1
  elements, 9-7
  officer, 4-200, 9-1–9-6
  practices, 9-8
  responsibilities, 9-9–9-16
  unified action, 9-17–9-23

logistics, ACOS, 2-55–2-63

M

main command post, defined, 3-4

maintenance, 2-58

make a tentative plan, 5-19–5-48

map rehearsal, 8-42–8-46

MDMP. See also individual steps.
  characteristics of, 4-1–4-13
  commander in, 4-8–4-11
  defined, 4-1
  modifying, 4-12–4-13
  staff, 4-8–4-11
  steps, 4-6–4-7
  steps, 4-14–4-185
  TLP and, 5-1–5-9

measure of effectiveness. See MOE.

meeting, 3-65–3-71
  operations synchronization, 3-58–3-59

method, avenue-in-depth, 4-149–4-150
  belt, 4-146–4-148
  box, 4-151–4-152

military deception officer, 2-93

military decisionmaking process. See MDMP.

military information support officer, 2-94

mission analysis, 4-25–4-78, 5-21–5-26
  briefing, 4-69–4-71
  TLP, 5-20–5-37

mission briefing, 10-9–10-11

mission command, 1-1–1-17
  cell, 3-36
  defined, 1-1
  war-gaming responsibilities, 4-130–4-137

mission command system, 1-12

mission orders, 12-8–12-10
  defined, 12-8

mission statement, defined, 4-65

mobility, command post, 3-27

MOE, indicators, 7-21–7-24
  select and write, 7-12–7-20

movement and maneuver, cell, 3-32
  war-gaming responsibilities, 4-122

multinational operations, liaison, 9-23

N–O

network, operations, 2-67
  rehearsal, 8-47–8-51

obstacle, defined, 5-32

officer, liaison, 9-1–9-6

on-order mission, 4-34

operation order, defined, 12-18

operation plan, defined, 12-14

operation update, assessment briefing and, 3-56–3-57

operational approach, defined, 4-73

operations, ACOS, 2-47–2-54
  command post, 3-47–3-71
  war-game, 4-156–4-169

operations process, 1-13–1-17
  defined, 1-13
  running estimate, 6-7–6-11

operations research and system analysis officer, 2-98

operations security officer, 2-95

operations synchronization meeting, 3-58–3-59

opinions, information and, 11-16

options, generate, 4-88–4-94
  generate, 5-40–5-42
  generate, 11-27–11-28

order(s), administrative instructions, 12-43–12-74
  approval of, 12-42
  characteristics of, 12-25–12-36
  crosswalk, 12-41
  examples and procedures, 12-75–12-81
  high headquarters, 4-27–4-28
  plans and, 12-11–12-24
  preparation of, 12-37–12-42
  reconciliation, 12-40
  types, 12-17–12-21
  verbal, 12-21
  written, 12-22–12-24

orders production, 4-184–4-185

organizations, civilian, 2-6–2-7
  staff and, 2-6–2-7

organizing, command post, 3-1–3-13
  considerations, 2-22–2-25
  structure, 2-26–2-29

orientation, rehearsal, 8-76

P–Q

personal, staff officers, 2-105–2-114

personnel, ACOS, 2-35–2-39
  services of, 2-37
  support, 2-38

personnel recovery officer, 2-96

plan(s), 12-1–12-81
  ACOS, 2-63–2-65
  administrative instructions, 12-43–12-74
  approval of, 12-42
  building, 12-3–12-7
  characteristics of, 12-25–12-36
  crosswalk, 12-41
  examples and procedures, 12-75–12-81
  guidance for, 12-1–12-10
  high headquarters, 4-27–4-28
  orders and, 12-11–12-24
  preparation of, 12-37–12-42
  reconciliation, 12-40
  time constrained, 4-186–4-200
  types, 12-12–12-16
  update, 4-56–4-57

planning, collaborative, 4-199
  parallel, 4-198
  rehearsal responsibilities, 8-53–8-55

Entries are by paragraph number unless specified otherwise.

planning *(continued)*
    running estimate and, 6-8
    staff responsibilities, 2-61–2-62
planning guidance, develop and
    issue, 4-73–4-76
    initial, 4-73–4-76
planning horizon, defined, 3-37
plans and operations, 2-50–2-54
plans cell, 3-39–3-40
preparation, rehearsal
    responsibilities, 8-56–8-60
preparation, running estimate and,
    6-9
problem, identify, 11-2–11-8
problem solving, 11-1–11-39
problem statement, 4-61–4-64
protection, cell, 3-34
    chief, 2-74
    war-gaming responsibilities,
    4-124
provost marshal, 2-97
public affairs officer, 2-111

R

receipt of mission, 4-15–4-24
receive the mission, 5-11–5-15
reconnaissance and surveillance,
    plan, 4-54–4-55
    tools, 4-50–4-53
recorder, execution, 8-67
    war-gaming responsibilities,
    4-138
red team officer, 2-99
reduced-force rehearsal, 8-21–
    8-26
redundancy, command post, 3-26
rehearsal, 8-1–8-104
    after, 8-102–8-104
    basics, 8-1–8-5
    before, 8-73–8-85
    details, 8-71–8-104
    during, 8-86–8-101
    ground rules of, 8-85
    introduction, 8-75
    orientation, 8-76
    responsibilities, 8-52–8-70
    script, 8-77–8-84
    techniques, 8-13–8-51
    types, 8-6–8-12
relationships, Army command and
    support, A-11–A-14
    staff and, 2-17–2-20
reports, command post, 3-55
resource, shortfalls, 4-36

resource management, ACOS,
    2-70–2-71
response sequence, rehearsal,
    8-81–8-84
responsibilities, assign, 5-44
    rehearsal, 8-52–8-70
    staff, 2-1–2-7, 2-30
results, assess, 4-156–4-169
    record and display, 4-153–
    4-155
returns, command post, 3-55
risk management, defined, 4-44
running estimate, 6-1–6-11
    defined, 6-1
    operations process and, 6-7–
    6-11
    qualities of, 6-5–6-6
    update, 4-19

S

S-2, intelligence, 2-40–2-46
S-3, operations, 2-47–2-54
S-4, logistics, 2-55–2-63
S-5, plans, 2-63–2-65
S-6, signal, 2-66–2-68
S-7, inform and influence
    activities, 2-69
safety officer, 2-112
science of control, 1-10–1-11
secretary of the general staff,
    2-100
shift-change briefing, 3-52–3-54
signal, ACOS, 2-66–2-68
situation, analyze, 10-15–10-18
size, command post, 3-25
sketch, course of action, 4-108–
    4-110, 5-45–5-46
sketch-map rehearsal, 8-37–8-41
solution(s), analyze, 11-30–11-33
    compare, 11-34–11-35
    generate, 11-25–11-29
    summarize, 11-29
space operations officer, 2-102
special, staff officers, 2-76–2-104
specified task, defined, 4-32
staff, 2-1–2-114
    characteristics of, 2-8–2-16
    duties and responsibilities,
    2-30
    efforts, 3-16–3-17
    execution, 8-68
    MDMP, 4-8–4-11, 4-16
    officers, 2-29
    organization, 2-21–2-29

planning, 2-61–2-62
    preparation, 8-60
    relationships, 2-17–2-20
    responsibilities of, 2-1–2-7
    supervision, 2-61–2-62
    time constraints and, 4-194
staff briefing, 10-12–10-13
Staff Judge Advocate, 2-113
staff officers, coordinating, 2-31–
    2-75
    personal, 2-105–2-114
    special, 2-76–2-104
staff section, command post cell
    and, 3-28–3-46
    defined, 2-26
    integrating cells and, 3-46
staff structure, chief of staff and,
    2-28
    commander and, 2-27
    executive officer, 2-28
staff study, 11-40–11-73
    assembly, 11-85
    coordinating, 11-69–11-73
    format, 11-43–11-68
staff weather, officer, 2-101
standard operating procedure,
    command post, 3-48–3-61
    rehearsal, 8-11–8-12
standardization, command post,
    3-18
statement, course of action,
    4-108–4-110, 5-45–5-46
structure, staff organization, 2-26–
    2-29
supervise and refine, TLP, 5-55–
    5-57
supply, 2-57
support rehearsal, 8-10
supporting plan, defined, 12-15
surgeon, 2-114
survivability, command post,
    3-23–3-27
sustainment, cell, 3-35
    chief, 2-75
    plans and operations, 2-56
    war-gaming responsibilities,
    4-125–4-129
synchronization matrix, defined,
    4-154

T

tactical command post, 3-5–3-8
    defined, 3-5
tactical mission, defined, 4-68

Entries are by paragraph number unless specified otherwise.

task organization, considerations, A-1–A-10
  defined, A-1
  format and instructions, A-15–A-26
task-organizing, defined, A-1
tasks, determine, 4-31-4-35
terrain and weather, analysis, 5-28–5-34
terrain-model rehearsal, 8-27-8-31
themes and messages, develop, 4-58–4-50
  initial, 4-58–4-50
time, plan and, 4-56–4-57
time available, analysis, 5-36
time constraints, commander, 4-190–4-193
  environment and, 4-186–4-200

planning techniques, 4-195–4-200
plans, 4-186–4-200
TLP, 5-1–5-57
  background, 5-1–5-9
  defined, 5-2
  MDMP and, 5-1–5-9
  steps of, 5-10–5-57
tools, gather, 4-17–4-18, 4-140
training, G-3, 2-49
transportation, 2-59
  officer, 2-103
troop leading procedures. *See* TLP.
troops and support available, 5-35

U–V–W

understand current and desired conditions, 7-5–7-8

unified action, liaison, 9-17–9-23
units, assistance for, 2-5
  staff, 2-5
  subordinate, 2-5
verbal order, 12-21
veterinary officer, 2-104
war game, analysis, 5-47
war-gaming, briefing, 4-170
  method selection, 4-145–4-152
  responsibilities of, 4-119–4-138
  rules, 4-118
warning order, defined, 12-20
  initial, 4-24
  issue, 4-78
weather, aspects, 5-34
working group, defined, 3-69
written order, 12-22–12-2

This page intentionally left blank.

By Order of the Secretary of the Army:

RAYMOND T. ODIERNO
General, United States Army
Chief of Staff

Official:

JOYCE E. MORROW
Administrative Assistant to the
Secretary of the Army
1120309

DISTRIBUTION:
Active Army, Army National Guard, and *United States Army Reserve*: Not to be distributed.
Electronic media only.